TEACHER'S EDITION

Vocabulary
for Achievement

FIFTH COURSE

Margaret Ann Richek

Arlin T. McRae

Susan K. Weiler

GREAT SOURCE
WILMINGTON, MA

AUTHORS

Margaret Ann Richek
Professor of Education, Northeastern Illinois University; consultant in reading and vocabulary study; author of The World of Words *(Houghton Mifflin)*

Arlin T. McRae
Supervisor of English, Evansville-Vanderburgh School Corporation, Evansville, Indiana; Adjunct Instructor in English, University of Evansville

Susan K. Weiler
Instructor of Art History at John Carroll University in Cleveland, Ohio; former teacher of Latin, Beaumont School for Girls, Cleveland Heights, Ohio

CONSULTANT

Larry S. Krieger
Social Studies Supervisor, Montgomery Township Public Schools, New Jersey; author of World History *and* U.S. History *(D.C. Heath), co-author of* Mastering the Verbal SAT 1/PSAT *(Great Source)*

CLASSROOM CONSULTANTS

Jack Pelletier
Teacher of English, Mira Loma High School, Sacramento, California

Valerie M. Webster
Teacher of English, Walnut Hill School, Natick, Massachusetts

ACKNOWLEDGMENTS

Definitions for the three hundred words taught in this textbook are based on Houghton Mifflin dictionaries—in particular, the *Houghton Mifflin College Dictionary,* copyright © 1986, and *The American Heritage Dictionary of the English Language, Third Edition,* copyright © 1992. The pronunciation key on the inside front cover is adapted from the latter. Reproduced on pages 19–20 are passages from *Roget's International Thesaurus,* 4th edition revised by Robert L. Chapman (Thomas Y. Crowell), as follows: entries 14.1 (p. 7), 509.8 (p. 384), and 896.9 (pp. 700–701), as well as index entry for *sameness* (p. 1189). Copyright © 1977 by Harper & Row, Publishers, Inc. Reprinted by permission of Harper & Row, Publishers, Inc. The reading passage on page 100 is from John B. Jenkins, *Genetics,* Second Edition, copyright © 1979 by Houghton Mifflin Company. Reprinted by permission of Houghton Mifflin Company.

(Acknowledgments are continued on the bottom of page iv.)

CREDITS

Production: PC&F, Inc.

Illustrations: Nanette Biers: pages 51, 91, 177; Julie Downing: pages 71, 85, 131, 191; Sylvia Giblin: pages 17, 25, 145, 185, 197; Norman Nicholson: pages 31, 105, 125, 151

CONTENTS

(Acknowledgments, continued)

The reading passage on pages 119–120 is from *The Annals of America*, Vol. 2, Encyclopaedia Britannica, Inc. Copyright © 1968. Reprinted by permission from Encyclopaedia Britannica, Inc. The reading passage on page T11 is abridged from *Marketing Management* by William Lazer and James D. Culley. Copyright © 1983 by Houghton Mifflin Company. Reprinted by permission of Houghton Mifflin Company. The passage on page T12 is abridged from *Meteorology: The Earth and Its Weather*, Second Edition, by Joseph S. Weisberg. Copyright © 1981 by Houghton Mifflin Company. Reprinted by permission of Houghton Mifflin Company. The passage on page T25 is abridged from *Japan: Tradition and Transformation* by Edwin O. Reischauer and Albert M. Craig. Copyright © 1978 by Houghton Mifflin Company. Reprinted by permission of Houghton Mifflin Company. The passage on page T26 is abridged from *Journey Through the Universe* by Thomas L. Swihart. Copyright © 1978 by Houghton Mifflin Company. Reprinted by permission of Houghton Mifflin Company. The sample SAT questions were written by the authors and are not actual SAT questions. The directions and boxed examples were reprinted by permission of Educational Testing Service, the copyright owner. SAT and Scholastic Assessment Test are registered trademarks of the College Entrance Examination Board.

Why Study Vocabulary Systematically?

Teachers generally agree on the importance of vocabulary development in the refining of language skills. The greater the store of words we have at our disposal, the better equipped we are to comprehend what we read and to express what we think.

A systematic approach to vocabulary building helps students

- understand and use words effectively
- recognize, retain, and apply new words
- unlock meanings of new words
- learn independently for lifelong vocabulary acquisition
- improve reading comprehension across the curriculum
- improve performance on standardized tests
- select and use words forcefully in speaking and writing
- continually assimilate new words into their vocabularies

A systematic program ensures the development of the large storehouse of words that is important to achievement, both in and out of the classroom.

How Were the Vocabulary Words Selected?

The criteria for vocabulary word selection for *Vocabulary for Achievement* were three.

- The principle source for the word lists was recent Scholastic Assessment Tests (SATs), published by the College Entrance Examination Board.
- The authors and editors also consulted numerous scholarly works, including the American Heritage *Word Frequency Book*, *The Living Word Vocabulary*, and many standard thesauruses.
- Most importantly, the words were chosen for their usefulness, appropriateness to grade level, and applicability to the lesson themes or topics.

Over 80% of the *Vocabulary for Achievement* words are on a so-called "hit parade" of SAT words. The "hit parade" is a group of words representative of the difficulty level of words frequently used in analogy and sentence-completion test items in the verbal section of the SAT. Further, almost one quarter of these "hit parade" words is taught in *Vocabulary for Achievement's* Fourth Course or earlier, providing students with ample time to incorporate them into their vocabularies before encountering them on the SAT.

Vocabulary for Achievement ensures success, not only on the SAT but in lifelong vocabulary acquisition, by offering students early help with challenging new vocabulary.

A Tour of the Program

Vocabulary for Achievement is a systematic program of vocabulary development that provides comprehensive instruction and practice. In devising the seven-book program for grades 6 through 12, the authors have followed four major principles:

— Structured lessons teach best.
— Application aids retention.
— Special vocabulary-acquisition skills promote independent learning.
— Vocabulary materials must be readily accessible and easily adaptable to classroom needs.

These four principles are reflected throughout the program, which provides the structure necessary for students to learn new words; apply them in a variety of practice formats to ensure ownership; and to use dictionary, test-taking, and reading strategies to build and incorporate their growing pool of words independently. The authors' guiding principles also make the structure of the program teacher- and student-friendly.

Teacher-Friendly Elements

The consistent structure of *Vocabulary for Achievement* makes it ideal for classroom instruction or for independent use, allowing you to direct a sound and successful vocabulary program.

- **Lessons**: provide complete presentation, abundant practice (with answers), numerous examples of context, and opportunities for application.
- **Skill Features**: furnish practical strategies for ongoing vocabulary acquisition.
- **Flash Cards (in student book only)**: include all vocabulary words, with the word on one side, phonetic spelling and definition on the other. An effective tool for learning and review.

- **Tests**: 10 reproducible multiple-choice tests (with answers), each covering 3 consecutive lessons.
- **Bonuses**: 7–15 reproducible bonus activities (with answers), each covering 2–5 consecutive lessons, offer students "lighter" opportunities for reinforcement and enrichment in the forms of crossword puzzles, word searches, scrambled words, etc.
- **Teaching Suggestions**: provide concrete ideas to help you adapt the materials for special classroom needs and to extend their range and usefulness.

The Lessons

- 30 six-page lessons per level
- 10 words per lesson, theme- or root-centered
- pronunciations, part-of-speech labels, multiple definitions, etymologies, related words, usage notes, and example sentences provided dictionary-style from Houghton Mifflin dictionaries

- 4 follow-up exercises for practice in identifying definitions, using words correctly, choosing the best word, and using different forms of a word
- a reading comprehension passage, incorporating the 10 words in context, followed by a comprehension exercise. The reading passages cover all areas of the curriculum, from history, science and nature, and the arts, to myths and legends, technology, and careers.
- a writing assignment related to the theme or topic, in which students apply their newly acquired words in an effective piece of writing
- analogy exercises for practice in identifying vocabulary words in the context of word relationships
- vocabulary enrichment and activity for interesting and unusual word histories, helpful in unlocking meanings of unfamiliar words

The Anatomy of a Lesson

Lessons are **theme-centered** or **root-centered** to provide a context in which students can learn new words.

Introductions are motivational.

Pronunciations, definitions, and **etymologies** are from Houghton Mifflin dictionaries.

Word entries are presented **dictionary-style.**

Related words were chosen for their usefulness and appropriateness to grade level.

The **Word List** is a convenient reference for both students and teachers.

Writing new words on word blanks reinforces correct **spelling.**

Example sentences illustrate the primary definition of each word.

Usage notes or **memory cues** provide tips for using the words correctly or for remembering them.

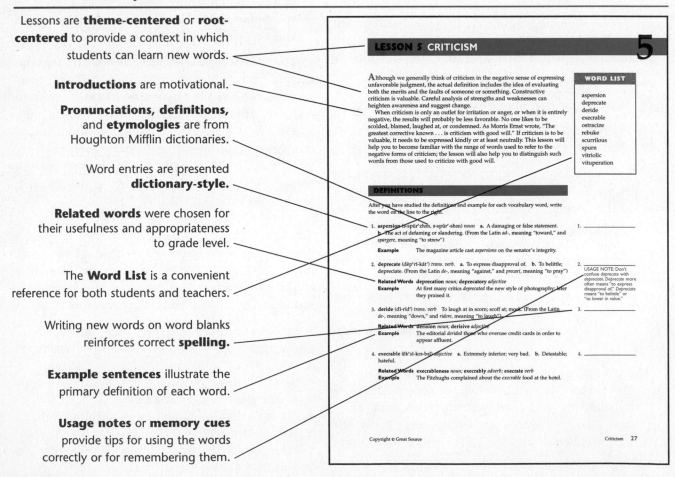

vi

A variety of **exercise formats** provides practice and aids in **recognition, recall,** and **application** of the words.

Reading passages incorporating the vocabulary words reinforce the important link between vocabulary and reading comprehension.

A **follow-up exercise** on the passage tests student understanding of the vocabulary words in context.

A **Writing Assignment,** related to the lesson theme or passage topic, lets students apply new words. Assignments are designed to stimulate interest, enthusiasm, and creativity.

Vocabulary Enrichment provides interesting and unusual word histories.

The **Activity** encourages students to investigate the origins of several related words.

A **Practice with Analogies** exercise helps students use the vocabulary words in a different context. Students learn various ways to complete analogies, to identify the different types of analogies, and to understand relationships between words.

READING COMPREHENSION EXERCISE

Each of the following statements corresponds to a numbered sentence in the passage. Each statement contains a blank and is followed by four answer choices. Decide which choice fits best in the blank. The word or phrase that you choose must express roughly the same meaning as the italicized word in the passage. Write the letter of your choice on the answer line.

1. Toulouse-Lautrec was _____ by the conservatives of his era.
   a. well loved   b. disdainfully rejected   c. criticized   d. often ignored

2. His family _____ his talent at first.
   a. welcomed   b. were astonished by   c. honestly disliked   d. expressed disapproval of

3. Henri was the object of _____ because of his handicap.
   a. general concern   b. aid   c. scornful laughter   d. compassion

4. Toulouse-Lautrec's drawing received _____ from his teacher.
   a. damaging comments   b. poor reviews   c. compliments   d. attention

5. Toulouse-Lautrec believed that the standard technique was _____.
   a. distinct   b. authoritative   c. fashionable   d. extremely inferior

6. He ignored the _____ of his teacher.
   a. reprimands   b. encouragement   c. example   d. suggestions

7. Toulouse-Lautrec thought he was _____ by Paris society.
   a. flattered   b. excluded   c. hindered   d. anticipated

8. Toulouse-Lautrec was said to be cynical and _____.
   a. excited   b. self-confident   c. antagonistic   d. foul-mouthed

9. The artist was unhappy over the art critics' _____.
   a. support   b. reviews   c. condemnation   d. assessment

10. He was disheartened by the _____ nature of the criticism.
    a. annoying   b. bitterly harsh   c. daring   d. intensely childish

1. _b_
2. _d_
3. _c_
4. _a_
5. _d_
6. _a_
7. _b_
8. _d_
9. _c_
10. _b_

WRITING ASSIGNMENT

Many times in the past, ingenious individuals have devised inventions, created artistic works, or originated ideas that were unacceptable to their contemporaries. Choose one such person, such as Galileo or Robert Fulton, and do some library research about his or her life. Write a report about this person's career and the criticism that he or she received. Use at least five of the words from this lesson and underline them.

VOCABULARY ENRICHMENT

Ostracize comes from the Greek word *ostrakon*, meaning "a piece of broken pottery." In ancient Athens any citizen who was considered by the public to be dangerous or disreputable could be banished for five to ten years through popular vote. Citizens voted for banishment by writing the person's name on a piece of broken pottery. Six thousand of these makeshift ballots were necessary to banish an individual. Although our modern usage of *ostracize* no longer includes the piece of broken pottery, we have retained the ancient idea of exclusion.

Activity Look up the following words in your dictionary, and write their meanings and Latin or Greek roots. Then write an explanation of the connection between each root and its definition.

1. veto   2. precinct   3. politics   4. campaign   5. senate

---

READING COMPREHENSION EXERCISE

Each of the following statements corresponds to a numbered sentence in the passage. Each statement contains a blank and is followed by four answer choices. Decide which choice fits best in the blank. The word or phrase that you choose must express roughly the same meaning as the italicized word in the passage. Write the letter of your choice on the answer line.

1. Machu Picchu is located in a place where the sky and earth seem to _____.
   a. separate   b. meet   c. be compressed   d. fade away

2. Twenty thousand miles of _____ stone roads once connected the Incan empire.
   a. uninterrupted   b. well-constructed   c. broken   d. primitive

3. Machu Picchu is perhaps the _____ testimony to the genius of the Incas.
   a. newest   b. sophisticated   c. most mysterious   d. greatest possible

4. Hiram Bingham knew that he had found a(n) _____ piece in the puzzle.
   a. crucial   b. minor   c. exceptional   d. missing

5. The research did not _____ with the excavation of Machu Picchu.
   a. begin   b. succeed   c. conclude   d. waver

6. The _____ the mystery lies in the purpose of Machu Picchu.
   a. interest in   b. research into   c. interpretation of   d. essence of

7. Research _____ during recent years has led archaeologists to believe that Machu Picchu had numerous purposes.
   a. accomplished   b. begun   c. proposed   d. admired

8. The expedition in 1982 was _____ the first discovery.
   a. a follow-up of   b. better than   c. complicated in comparison with   d. a replica of

9. At first, the discovery of buildings, an agricultural site, and a burial plot was thought to be _____ to the discovery of Machu Picchu.
   a. unrelated   b. equivalent   c. superficially related   d. monumentally important

10. Families of the ruling class and _____ are believed to have lived in Machu Picchu.
    a. those of lower rank   b. those of important ancestry   c. their livestock   d. their offspring

1. _b_
2. _a_
3. _d_
4. _a_
5. _c_
6. _d_
7. _b_
8. _a_
9. _c_
10. _a_

PRACTICE WITH ANALOGIES

A verbal analogy shows how two pairs of words are related. The second two words are related to each other in the same way as the first two. An analogy can be written as a sentence or with colons.

Wool is to fabric as oil is to fuel.
WOOL : FABRIC :: oil : fuel

Directions On the answer line, write the vocabulary word or a form of it that completes each analogy.

See page 79 for some strategies to use with analogies.

1. ETHICS : MORALITY :: _____ : speech (*Lesson 1*)
2. TALISMAN : OBJECT :: _____ : words (*Lesson 2*)
3. PRECIOUS : VALUABLE :: _____ : favorable (*Lesson 2*)
4. JUNCTION : ROADS :: _____ : ideas (*Lesson 3*)
5. COMMENCE : ACTIVITY :: _____ : project (*Lesson 3*)

The Test for Lessons 1, 2, and 3 is on page T1.

1. _linguistics_
2. _incantation_
3. _propitious_
4. _convergence_
5. _initiate_

Skill Features

A skill feature on dictionary use, on test taking, or on reading appears after each group of three vocabulary lessons.

- 10 special features provide students with techniques for building and using their pool of words independently.
- Clear explanation includes examples, tables of information, strategies and procedures for learning and using new words effectively.
- Accompanying exercises allow students to practice each skill.

Dictionary Skills

- Emphasis in lessons is grade-level appropriate.
- Skills range from finding the right definition, understanding parts of speech, and utilizing etymological information, to reading usage notes, differentiating among synonyms, and using a thesaurus.
- Follow-up exercises give students an opportunity to practice their new skills by using dictionary extracts and writing original sentences.

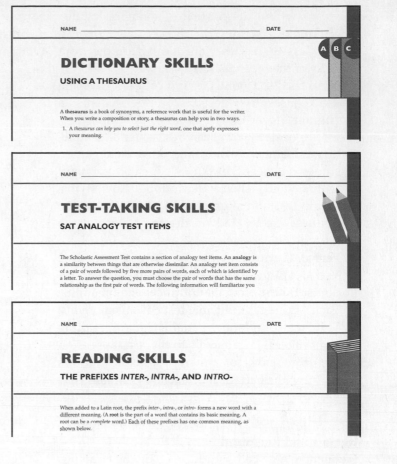

NAME _____ DATE _____

DICTIONARY SKILLS
USING A THESAURUS

A **thesaurus** is a book of synonyms, a reference work that is useful for the writer. When you write a composition or story, a thesaurus can help you in two ways.

1. A *thesaurus* can help you to select just the right word, one that aptly expresses your meaning.

NAME _____ DATE _____

TEST-TAKING SKILLS
SAT ANALOGY TEST ITEMS

The Scholastic Assessment Test contains a section of analogy test items. An **analogy** is a similarity between things that are otherwise dissimilar. An analogy test item consists of a pair of words followed by five more pairs of words, each of which is identified by a letter. To answer the question, you must choose the pair of words that has the same relationship as the first pair of words. The following information will familiarize you

NAME _____ DATE _____

READING SKILLS
THE PREFIXES *INTER-*, *INTRA-*, AND *INTRO-*

When added to a Latin root, the prefix *inter-*, *intra-*, or *intro-* forms a new word with a different meaning. (A **root** is the part of a word that contains its basic meaning. A root can be a complete word.) Each of these prefixes has one common meaning, as shown below.

Test-Taking Skills

- Students are given pointers for successfully completing different types of tests—sentence-completion, analogy, antonym, and reading comprehension—often found on standardized tests such as the SAT and ACT English Test.
- Examples are provided so students can understand the thought processes required to eliminate inappropriate answer choices and to select the correct answer.
- Accompanying exercises give students the opportunity to put the strategies into practice by becoming alert to misleading choices, sentence clues, and shades of meaning.

Reading Skills

These features address two separate areas of vocabulary proficiency: using context clues and analyzing word parts.

- Students learn to use context clues to determine the meanings of unfamiliar words.
- Methods of reasoning are illustrated so students can see how information in a sentence can be utilized.

- Students check their understanding by comparing their "working" definitions against those in a dictionary.
- Students are acquainted with a method of determining the meanings of unfamiliar words by analyzing word parts.
- Word-attack strategies focus on learning prefixes, suffixes, and roots.

Teacher's Edition

- **Teaching Suggestions:** The activities on pages x–xiii will help you to incorporate vocabulary study into every area of the English curriculum. Ideas for exercises, assignments, and discussion topics have been provided for vocabulary review, spelling, reading, word histories, grammar and usage, literature, composition, and college-entrance examination preparation.
- **Tests:** 10 reproducible multiple-choice tests, each covering 3 consecutive lessons, are found at the back of the Teacher's Edition. Each test is divided into 2 parts. Part A tests recognition and recall of definitions; Part B emphasizes placing

words within the context of sentences or discriminating among a choice of antonyms. Answers to the tests are located on the front sides of the reproducible masters.

- **Bonuses:** 7–15 Bonus activities, each covering 2–5 consecutive lessons, give students a "lighter" form of vocabulary study. In crossword puzzles, word searches, sentence completions, scrambled words, and other word games, students review their knowledge of vocabulary words and their definitions, synonyms, antonyms, and etymologies. Answers to the Bonuses are located on the front sides of the reproducible masters.

- **Verbal Aptitude Tests (4th–6th Courses):** 2 Verbal Aptitude Tests provide practice for students taking college-entrance examinations. Each 4-page reproducible test covers antonyms, sentence completions, analogies, and reading comprehension. Answers to the tests appear on the front sides of the reproducible masters found at the back of the Teacher's Edition.

Teaching Suggestions

Review and Retention

Frequent review helps students retain the meanings of new words. Use any or all of the following practices to help students learn and apply new words.

1. Have students use the **Flash Cards,** located on pages 201–220 of the student books, for individual drill or game-style classroom practice.

2. Assign the **Bonuses** (see page 201) as follow-up activities for the vocabulary lessons.

3. Have students conduct a weekly search of newspapers and magazines to locate instances of the vocabulary words. Award a set amount of extra-credit points for each word found and for the student finding the most instances of the same word, the most instances of all the words, and so forth.

Vocabulary and Spelling

Vocabulary study and spelling are complementary. Students cannot completely understand a word until they can say and write it as well as cite its definition. Make use of the numerous opportunities provided in *Vocabulary for Achievement* in order to reinforce spelling skills.

1. Once students have studied the definitions and examples for each vocabulary word, have them write the word in the blank provided for this purpose. Writing the word reinforces the visual-graphic patterns of letters, aids in sight recognition, and helps students to apply the word.

2. Encourage students to pay close attention to the listing of related forms and the use of these, along with the inflected forms of words, throughout the exercises. Point out to them how different endings can change the spelling of a root word.

3. Have students pay special heed to lessons based on word roots, since these show how similar word elements contribute to the similarity of meaning and spelling. In the same way, have them study the **Skill Features** treating prefixes and suffixes.

Vocabulary and Reading

1. To help students master the literal level of comprehension, give them a series of quotations. Ask students first to underline the key words in each quotation. Then, based on their choices, have them write in their own words the main idea of each statement.
   EXAMPLES "In life courtesy and self-possession, and in the arts style, are the sensible impressions of the free mind, for both arise out of a deliberate shaping of all things and from never being swept away, whatever the emotion, into confusion or dullness." (William Butler Yeats) "The scientist takes off from the manifold observations of predecessors, and shows his intelligence, if any, by his ability to discriminate between the important and the negligible, by selecting here and there the significant stepping-stones that will lead across the difficulties to new understanding." (Hans Zinsser)

2. Another way to reinforce reading comprehension skills at the literal level is to provide students with a paragraph like the following.
   EXAMPLE "As early as the 1830s, growing urbanization in the Northeast had made a substantial impression upon the nature of agriculture in that region. In the immediate vicinity of burgeoning factory towns and commercial centers, farmers were concentrating their energy upon supplying local markets with fresh vegetables, fruits, and dairy products. In outlying districts, farmers had begun to specialize in the raising of beef or pork, or in the production of wool for the region's new textile industry. Farmers who participated in this commercial economy soon abandoned the old practice of home manufacture which, in the past, had been an inseparable part of farm life. Store-bought

cloth replaced homespun, and factory-made furniture and farm tools were substituted for home-made ones."

Ask students questions like the following.
EXAMPLES What are the key words in the passage?
What is the main idea of the passage?
Where is it located?
What are the significant details that support the main idea?

As an alternative to answering questions about the passage, have students outline the main idea and its development.

Vocabulary and Word Analogies

1. To give students practice identifying word relationships, provide them with the first half of several analogies and have them work together to determine the types of analogy. You may want to draw from the following types of analogy:

degree	characteristic of
type of	antonym
part/whole	definition
relative size	part of
is used to	expression of
place where	

2. Challenge students to write visual analogies. Their analogies should be written entirely with pictures or symbols instead of words. Invite pairs of students to solve their partners' analogies.

3. To help students practice their analogy-solving strategies, give them several word pairs and ask them to restate the relationship between the words in a simple sentence. For example, in the word pair "scrap/paper," a restated simple sentence could be "A scrap is a small piece of paper."

Vocabulary and Word Histories

To help students appreciate language as dynamic, use the following as discussion or assignment topics.

Words that have undergone changes in meaning: *enthusiasm* (to be inspired by a god), *martyr* (witness), *naughty* (nothing), *jewel* (joke), *sinister* (on the left), *medicine* (physician), *brave* (to boast), and so forth.

Shortened forms of words: *ad/advertisement, curio/curiosity, extra/extraordinary, gym/gymnasium, wig/periwig, lab/laboratory, dorm/dormitory,* and so forth.

Doublets, or two or more words derived by different routes of transmission from the same source: *antic/antique, grammar/glamor, courtesy/curtsy, dignity/dainty, through/thorough, frail/fragile, legal/loyal, taint/tint,* and so forth. Have students use the dictionary to compare the present meanings and the common origins of the words.

Compound words: *self-control, law-abiding, cat-o'-nine-tails, coast-to-coast, hand-to-mouth, happy-go-lucky, heart-to-heart, shoplift, applesauce, grapevine, windbag,* and so forth.

Special interest words, such as those from medicine, that have been adopted for more general use: *acute, anodyne, benign, cathartic, chronic, diagnosis, emollient, malignant, congenital, incipient, prognosis,* and so forth.

Portmanteau words, in which the sounds and meanings of two or more words are merged to form a new word: *beefalo* (beef + buffalo), *technocracy* (technology + democracy), *simulcast* (simultaneous + broadcast), *telethon* (television + marathon), *transistor* (transfer + resistor), and so forth.

Acronyms, or words formed from the initial letters of words or phrases: *snafu* (situation normal all fouled up), *PAC* (political action committee), *AWOL* (absent without leave), *news* (north east west south), *tips* (to insure prompt service), *DEW* (Defense Early Warning), *SCORE* (Service Core of Retired Executives), and so forth.

Words borrowed directly from other languages, such as Italian: *piano, sonnet, trio, aria, stanza, alto, finale, violin, cameo, studio, influenza, malaria, volcano,* and so forth.

Vocabulary, Grammar, and Usage

1. Remind students that a word may be used as several different parts of speech. Then have them examine the multiple meanings of such words as *conduct, rebel, insult, digest, trim, subject, escort, compound, progress,* and so forth. Have students write groups of sentences like the following that illustrate the different meanings.
EXAMPLE Lucia will *conduct* a tour of the museum for visiting Argentinean dignitaries. *(verb)*
EXAMPLE Both speakers commented on the deplorable *conduct* of some members of the audience. *(noun)*

2. Have students write original sentences that both illustrate particular elements of grammar or rules of usage and incorporate vocabulary words. For example, when covering agreement problems, ask students to write sentences like the following.

EXAMPLE   Many a *vagary* has led to an important discovery or invention. (Rule: Use a singular verb with a single or compound subject modified by *every, many a,* or *many an.*)

EXAMPLE   Neither his *willfulness* nor his *blandishments* affect my decision. (Rule: When a compound subject consists of a singular subject and a plural subject connected by *or* or *nor,* use a verb that agrees in number with the subject that is closer to the verb in the sentence.)

3. When discussing usage problems, have the students examine the likelihood of confusion between groups of homophones like the following: *callous/callus, bale/bail, pour/pore, faze/phase, heel/heal, palette/palate/pallet, discreet/discrete, site/cite/sight,* and so forth. Then have them look up the definitions of each word and write a sentence for each illustrating its use.

As an alternative, have students examine the likelihood of confusion between groups of homographs (words spelled the same but which differ in meaning and pronunciation): *bow, compact, converse, invalid, lead, minute,* and so forth.

Vocabulary and Literature

1. To help students understand the rich nature of idioms, ask them to explain the difference between "at sea" and "confused." Help students to locate and explain the literal and figurative meanings of other expressions like the following that may appear in short stories and novels.
   EXAMPLE   *by the skin of one's teeth, miss the mark, head over heels, the rent is due, sow one's wild oats, strike while the iron is hot, through the grapevine, tooth and nail, take with a grain of salt,* and so forth.

2. When reading works of American literature, such as the fiction of John Steinbeck, Ring Lardner, Sinclair Lewis, Mark Twain, Willa Cather, and William Faulkner, point out to students how these authors use dialect in their works. Help students to analyze how these authors use the varieties of English as a literary device. Ask students questions like the following.
   EXAMPLE   What difference can you detect in the education, social status, regional background, and culture of the characters by their speech?

3. Have students study the literary effects of such rhetorical devices as *oxymoron* (two contradic-

tory terms used together for emphasis) and *hyperbole* (exaggeration).
EXAMPLE   *strenuous idleness, cruel kindness, broadly ignorant, wise folly, cheerful pessimist, sad joy, jumbo shrimp, old news, working vacation, justifiably paranoid, legal brief, weather forecaster,* and so forth.
EXAMPLES   *rivers of blood, millions of ships, all the sands of the sea, the waves were mountains high, sleep for a year,* and so forth.

Preparing for College-Entrance Examinations

While experts agree that studying does not influence college-entrance examination scores, there is some indication that preparation in test-taking strategies does have a positive effect. Use the following suggestions to help students become cognizant of helpful approaches to completing the four different types of test items on the verbal portions of these tests.

The Test as a Whole   Because each section of most college-entrance exams generally moves from the less difficult items to the more difficult items, suggest to students that they complete the first third of the items in the sentence-completion and analogy sections before continuing with the items that involve more complex reasoning.

Sentence Completions

1. Suggest to students that an effective way of approaching these items is to read every sentence carefully, looking for context clues within the sentence. They should look for punctuation and signal words, such as coordinating or correlative conjunctions, that provide signposts showing how the ideas are developed. Before considering the five answer choices, students should attempt to insert words of their own that make sense in the blanks.
   EXAMPLE   One quality that is a definite handicap is the author's style, which vacillates between a rather - - - - style and a penchant for excessively - - - - passages.
   (A) ordinary .. mundane
   (B) petulant .. irritating
   (C) earthy .. effusive
   (D) prosaic .. florid
   (E) emphatic .. ambiguous

   A student reading this sentence should see that the dependent clause that begins with *which* modifies the independent clause and explains something about the author's style. Furthermore, the dependent clause sets up a contrast between two different aspects of that style. The student might insert the words *simple* and *ornate* in the blanks. Looking at the answer choices, the student would then eliminate (A), (B), (C), and (E) since none of these establishes the necessary contrast. Thus, (D), which contains the needed contrast, is the correct choice and most closely approximates the student's own sentence insertions.

2. Help students to become aware of patterns that appear in sentence-completion items. For example, in a cause-and-effect sentence, the words selected for the blanks must make both parts of the sentence consistent in the sense of cause and effect. Tell students that words like *if, since, for, because, therefore, why, when,* and *then* signal this type of pattern.
   EXAMPLE   If we proceed - - - - and decisively, we can maintain science and technology in the - - - - state required by our national welfare and security.
   (A) assiduously .. minimal
   (B) diligently .. flourishing
   (C) capriciously .. sovereign
   (D) overtly .. judicious
   (E) radically .. congenial
   The correct answer is (B).

3. Tell students that contrast is another typical pattern used in sentence-completion items. A sentence that indicates contrast explains what something is not and helps readers to infer what it really is. Tell students to look for words and phrases like *although, even though, even if, never . . . but always, rather than,* and so forth. Remind them that a sentence of contrast is often broken into two sections by a comma or a semicolon.
   EXAMPLE   These sporadic raids seem to indicate that the enemy is waging a war of - - - - rather than attacking us directly.
   (A) insurgency   (B) attrition   (C) intensity
   (D) barbarism   (E) hypocrisy
   The correct answer is (B).

Analogies

1. Remind students that parts of speech are always consistent within individual analogies. If the capitalized words are NOUN : ADJECTIVE, then all the choices will be noun : adjective.

2. Because analogy items test logic as well as vocabulary, have students practice the reasoning

process aloud.
EXAMPLE
TRANSIENT : ETERNAL ::
(A) pensive : contemplative
(B) acute : chronic
(C) element : lenient
(D) replete : hollow
(E) former : latter

A student might analyze the analogy in the following way. The two capitalized words are antonyms expressing the relationship of duration. Choices (A) and (C) can be eliminated since *pensive* and *contemplative* and *clement* and *lenient* are synonyms. Choice (D) can be eliminated because the words, while antonyms, refer to capacity. Choice (E), referring to time, establishes a relationship of sequence. Choice (B), *acute* and *chronic*, establish a relationship of duration equivalent to the given pair and therefore is the correct answer.

Reading Comprehension

1. Suggest to students that one way of approaching the reading-comprehension section is to skim the questions following the passage in order to determine generally what they should read for. Next, the students can read the passage slowly and carefully to determine the main ideas. Finally, when answering the questions, they can return to the passage in order to locate specific details. In this way, students can make the best use of their time.

2. Explain to students that the questions on reading-comprehension passages fall into three major categories. Questions about central ideas may focus on the title that best expresses the author's point, the main idea or theme of the selection, and the author's purpose in writing the passage. Words that signal main ideas and conclusions are *therefore, consequently,* and *hence.*

   Questions about specific details may include identifying correct statements or selecting the one incorrect statement. Remind the students that details are signaled by such phrases as *for example, for instance,* and *in particular.*

   Finally, questions about logical relationships entail drawing conclusions and making assumptions about what is read. These questions will ask what the author implies or what the reader can infer.

A Reading Comprehension passage appears in each of the 30 vocabulary lessons in each level. The passage is an article, essay, or story that contains all ten vocabulary words of the lesson, thereby giving students an opportunity to understand the new words in a larger context. These passages also lend an entertaining variety to the abundant practice and provide students with enriching information drawn from a wide variety of subject matter. *Vocabulary for Achievement* truly offers students a chance to read across the curriculum while they incorporate newly learned words into their vocabularies. For your convenience, the following is a level-specific list of topics and passages.

Grade 11: Fifth Course

Lesson	Topic	Title of Passage
1	Language	American Language
2	Science and Nature	Alchemy: Science or Deception?
3	History	Machu Picchu
4	Science and Nature	Imprinting and Motherly Attachment
5	The Arts	Toulouse-Lautrec: Unconventional Artist
6	Science and Nature	Maria Mitchell: America's First Woman Scientist
7	Literature and Communication	The Language of Gesture and Pose
8	Sports and Recreation	Horse Show Jumping
9	Myths and Legends	Odysseus' Homecoming
10	Technology	Gold Rushes—New and Old
11	The Arts	The Well-Tempered Clavier: Bach's Gift to Students
12	History	The Magna Carta
13	The Arts	Ray Charles: Musical Pioneer
14	Education	Anna Leonowens: East-West Ambassador
15	History	The Evolution of the Diplomatic System
16	Myths and Legends	Pyramus and Thisbe
17	Language	Azerbaijan Changes Alphabets
18	The Arts	Leonardo da Vinci: Renaissance Genius (1452–1519)
19	History	Cortés and Moctezuma
20	Service to Humanity	Mother Teresa
21	Myths and Legends	Echo and Narcissus
22	Science and Nature	The Teeming Life of the Tropical Rain Forest
23	The Arts	Aida: Verdi's Masterpiece
24	Economics and Business	The Risky Business of Lloyd's of London
25	Economics and Business	The Commodities Exchange
26	Science and Nature	Dr. Albert Einstein
27	History	Eleanor of Aquitaine
28	Technology	Noise, Noise Everywhere
29	Science and Nature	The Lost Continent of Atlantis
30	Science and Nature	The Great Barrier Reef

COMPLETE WORD LIST FOR FIFTH COURSE

Words from this grade level used on the Verbal Aptitude Tests are marked with a colored asterisk.

abdicate, 73
abeyance, 127
abnegate, 73*
abound, 67
abrogate, 121
absolve, 73
abstemious, 127*
abstruse, 167
a cappella, 147
accommodating, 33
accord, 33*
accountable, 153
accrue, 161
acquiesce, 33
acquisition, 121
acuity, 47
acumen, 167
adamant, 33*
adhere, 81
adjure, 101
adulterate, 181
affect, 107*
affidavit, 101
affront, 87
aggregate, 81*
altercation, 87
ambivalence, 61
amplitude, 67*
amulet, 7
antagonist, 87
apocryphal, 173*
appellation, 1
arbitration, 93*
arboreal, 141*
aria, 147
ascertain, 167
aspersion, 27
attaché, 93
audit, 161
augment, 67
auspices, 41
auspicious, 41
avail, 61
avenge, 107*

banal, 133
bane, 181*
bellicose, 87
beseech, 53
blandishment, 53
bona fide, 173
boon, 181
breach, 87
brevity, 67
burgeon, 141

cadence, 147
cajole, 53
camaraderie, 33
candor, 173
cant, 173
capricious, 7*
cartel, 161
catharsis, 73*
cerebral, 167

charlatan, 173
chicanery, 173
circuitous, 127*
circumspect, 41
circumvent, 127
collateral, 161
commensurate, 67
commitment, 153
commodity, 161
compliance, 33
complicity, 21*
confidant, 101
conglomerate, 161*
conjure, 101
conquistador, 121
consulate, 93
consummate, 47
contentious, 87
contingent, 187
continuity, 13
converge, 13*
countermand, 73*
covenant, 93*
crescendo, 147
crux, 13
culminate, 113
cunning, 47*

deciduous, 141
default, 153
deft, 47
deploy, 21
deprecate, 27*
deride, 27
despicable, 41
diminish, 67*
diphthong, 1
discretion, 93
disinterested, 107*
dissension, 87
dissimulate, 81
dissonance, 147

eclipse, 113
effect, 107
egregious, 81*
elicit, 53*
elude, 127
emissary, 93
emulate, 133*
endowment, 47
enjoin, 53*
ensemble, 81
entente, 93
epitome, 113
eponym, 1
equivalent, 61*
eschew, 127*
evaluation, 61*
evasion, 127
eventuality, 187*
evince, 61
evolve, 193
execrable, 27*

exigent, 53
exorcise, 181
explicate, 21

facile, 47
facsimile, 81
faculty, 167
fatalism, 7
fauna, 141
fealty, 101*
feasible, 187*
feckless, 153
feign, 173
fiancé, 101
fidelity, 101
flora, 141

germination, 141
gregarious, 81*

horticultural, 141

immutable, 193*
impeccable, 113
imperious, 53*
implausible, 187
implicate, 21*
implicit, 21
imply, 107
incantation, 7
incompetent, 47
inconceivable, 187
incumbent, 153
inept, 47
inexplicable, 21
infer, 107*
infidel, 101
infinitesimal, 67*
inherent, 81
inimical, 181
inimitable, 113
initiate, 13*
injunction, 53
inquisitive, 121*
insidious, 173
introspective, 41*
invalid, 61*
invaluable, 61
inveterate, 193

jurisdiction, 101

liability, 153
libretto, 147
lichen, 141
linguistics, 1
liquidate, 161
lucrative, 161

Machiavellian, 93*
malinger, 127
malleable, 193
mandatory, 153
mendicant, 53
metamorphosis, 193

mimicry, 133
modicum, 67*
modulate, 193
motif, 147

negligence, 153*
neologism, 1

oblique, 127*
octave, 147
onerous, 153
optimum, 113
ostracize, 27

panacea, 181
parlance, 1
patois, 1
peerless, 113
perchance, 187
perjure, 101
pernicious, 181
perquisite, 121
perspicuity, 41
pivotal, 13*
platitude, 133
plight, 21
polyglot, 1
precede, 107
preposterous, 187
presage, 121
presumably, 187*
prevail, 61*
proceed, 107
proclivity, 187
prodigious, 67*
proficient, 47
prone, 187*
propensity, 47*
propitiate, 33*
propitious, 7
prospective, 41*
protean, 193
protocol, 93
prototype, 133*
providential, 7

query, 53
quest, 121
quintessence, 113*
quirk, 7
quota, 67

rancor, 87
rebuke, 27*
recant, 73*
recapitulate, 133
recompense, 161
recoup, 73
rectitude, 173
redundant, 133
relative, 167
remiss, 153
rendition, 133
renunciation, 73*
replica, 21

replicate, 21*
requisite, 121
rescind, 73
retribution, 87
revenge, 107
ruminate, 167

sagacity, 121*
salutary, 181*
schism, 87
scurrilous, 27
security, 161*
segregate, 81*
semblance, 81
sequel, 13
serendipity, 7*
sham, 133
shirk, 127
simulation, 133
solecism, 1*
sonata, 147
specious, 41
specter, 41
spectrum, 41
sporadic, 193*
spurn, 27*
staccato, 147
status quo, 93
sublime, 113
subordinate, 13
supple, 21
surmise, 167
surrogate, 121
sylvan, 141

tangential, 13
tenet, 167
terminate, 13
theoretical, 167
toxic, 181*
tractable, 33*
transmute, 193

ultimate, 13*
uninterested, 107

vagary, 7*
valedictory, 61*
vanquish, 61*
verdant, 141
veritable, 173
vicissitude, 7
vitiate, 181
vitriolic, 27
vituperation, 27
volatile, 193
volition, 33*
vulgar, 1

waive, 73
willfulness, 33*

zenith, 113

Level	Dictionary Skills	Test-Taking Skills	Reading Skills
Sixth	Using a Dictionary and a Thesaurus to Find Synonyms (pp. 19–20)	ACT Reading-Comprehension Tests (pp. 39–40); Tests of Standard Written English (pp. 59–60)	Context Clues and the Reading of Primary Sources (pp. 79–80); Context Clues and the Reading of British Literature (pp. 99–100); The Prefixes *bi-*, *semi-* (pp. 119–120); Prefixes Indicating Number (pp. 139–140); The Prefixes *conter-*, *contra-*, *anti-* (pp. 159–160); The Prefixes *circum-*, *peri-* (pp. 179–180); The Prefixes *extra-*, *super-*, *ultra-* (pp. 199–200)
Fifth	Using a Thesaurus (pp. 19–20)	Antonym Test Items (pp. 39–40); SAT Sentence-Completion Test Items (pp. 59–60); SAT Analogy Test Items (pp. 79–80); SAT Reading Comprehension Test Items (pp. 99–100)	Context Clues and the Reading of American History (pp. 119–120); Context Clues and the Reading of American Literature (pp. 139–140); The Prefixes *bene-*, *mal-* (pp. 159–160); The Prefixes *inter-*, *intra-*, *intro-* (pp. 179–180); The Prefixes *ante-*, *post-* (pp. 199–200)
Fourth	Synonym Paragraphs (pp. 19–20)	Antonym Test Items (pp. 39–40); Sentence-Completion Test Items (pp. 59–60); Analogy Test Items (pp. 79–80); Reading Comprehension Test Items (pp. 99–100)	Context Clues: Examples and Appositives (pp. 119–120); Context Clues: Contrast (pp. 139–140); The Prefix *ad-* (pp. 159–160); *Com-* and Related Prefixes (pp. 179–180); Five Adjective Suffixes (pp. 199–200)
Third	Finding the Appropriate Definition (pp. 19–20); Usage Notes (pp. 39–40)	Antonym Tests (pp. 59–60); Analogy Tests (pp. 79–80); Reading Comprehension Tests (pp. 99–100)	Context Clues: Substitution (pp. 119–120); The Prefixes *ex-*, *e-* (pp. 139–140); The Prefixes *ab-*, *a-*, *abs-* (pp. 159–160); The Suffixes *-ful*, *-ous* (pp. 179–180); Four Verb Suffixes (pp. 199–200)
Second	Finding the Appropriate Definition (pp. 19–20); Inflected Forms of Words (pp. 39–40); Biographical and Geographical Entries (pp. 59–60)	Sentence-Completion Tests (pp. 79–80); Synonym Tests (pp. 99–100); Analogy Tests (pp. 119–120)	Context Clues: Synonyms (pp. 139–140); The Prefix *pre-* (pp. 159–160); The Prefix *in-* (pp. 179–180); The Suffixes *-ion*, *-ness* (pp. 199–200)
First	Finding the Appropriate Definition (pp. 19–20); Part-of-Speech Labels (pp. 39–40); Understanding Etymologies (pp. 59–60)	Sentence-Completion Tests (pp. 79–80)	Context Clues: Definition in the Sentence (pp. 99–100); The Prefix *dis-* (pp. 119–120); The Prefix *re-* (pp. 139–140); The Prefix *sub-* (pp. 159–160); The Suffixes *-ance*, *-ence*, *-ancy* (pp. 179–180); The Suffix *-able* (pp. 199–200)
Introductory	Parts of a Dictionary Entry (pp. 19–20); Finding the Right Definition (pp. 39–40)	Synonym Tests (pp. 59–60); Antonym Tests (pp. 79–80)	Context Clues (pp. 99–100); Dividing Words into Parts (pp. 119–120); The Prefixes *non-*, *un-* (pp. 139–140); The Prefix *trans-* (pp. 159–160); The Prefix *de-* (pp. 179–180); The Suffixes *-ity*, *-hood* (pp. 199–200)

Vocabulary
for Achievement

FIFTH COURSE

Margaret Ann Richek

Arlin T. McRae

Susan K. Weiler

GREAT SOURCE
WILMINGTON, MA

AUTHORS

Margaret Ann Richek
Professor of Education, Northeastern Illinois University; consultant in reading and vocabulary study; author of The World of Words *(Houghton Mifflin)*

Arlin T. McRae
Supervisor of English, Evansville-Vanderburgh School Corporation, Evansville, Indiana; Adjunct Instructor in English, University of Evansville

Susan K. Weiler
Instructor of Art History at John Carroll University in Cleveland, Ohio; former teacher of Latin, Beaumont School for Girls, Cleveland Heights, Ohio

CONSULTANT

Larry S. Krieger
Social Studies Supervisor, Montgomery Township Public Schools, New Jersey; author of World History *and* U.S. History *(D.C. Heath), co-author of* Mastering the Verbal SAT 1/PSAT *(Great Source)*

CLASSROOM CONSULTANTS

Jack Pelletier
Teacher of English, Mira Loma High School, Sacramento, California

Valerie M. Webster
Teacher of English, Walnut Hill School, Natick, Massachusetts

ACKNOWLEDGMENTS

Definitions for the three hundred words taught in this textbook are based on Houghton Mifflin dictionaries—in particular, the *Houghton Mifflin College Dictionary*, copyright © 1986, and *The American Heritage Dictionary of the English Language, Third Edition*, copyright © 1992. The pronunciation key on the inside front cover is adapted from the latter. Reproduced on pages 19–20 are passages from *Roget's International Thesaurus*, 4th edition revised by Robert L. Chapman (Thomas Y. Cromwell), as follows: entries 14.1 (p. 7), 509.8 (p. 384), and 896.9 (pp. 700–701), as well as index entry for *sameness* (p. 1189). Copyright © 1977 by Harper & Row, Publishers, Inc. Reprinted by permission of Harper & Row, Publishers, Inc. The reading passage on page 100 is from John B. Jenkins, *Genetics*, Second Edition, copyright © 1979 by Houghton Mifflin Company. Reprinted by permission of Houghton Mifflin Company. The reading passaage on pages 119–120 is from *The Annals of America*, Vol. 2, Encyclopaedia Britannica, Inc. Copyright © 1968. Reprinted by permission from Encyclopaedia Britannica, Inc. SAT and Scholastic Assessment Test are registered trademarks of the College Entrance Examination Board.

CREDITS

Production: PC&F, Inc.

Illustrations: Nanette Biers: pages 51, 91, 177; Julie Downing: pages 71, 85, 131, 191; Sylvia Giblin: pages 17, 25, 145, 185, 197; Norman Nicholson: pages 31, 105, 125, 151

Printed in the United States of America

ISBN: 0-669-46481-3

1 2 3 4 5 6 7 8 9 10 HS 04 03 02 01 00 99 98

CONTENTS

COMPLETE WORD LIST

LESSON 1 WORDS ABOUT LANGUAGE

1

The language known as "English" is spoken by over a billion individuals in dozens of countries around the world. Although there is a generally accepted standard form of written English, the language as it is actually spoken is quite varied. The words in this lesson will help you to think about important elements of a language and how a language can vary from country to country and from speaker to speaker.

DEFINITIONS

After you have studied the definitions and example for each vocabulary word, write the word on the line to the right.

1. **appellation** (ăp′ə-lā′shən) *noun*   A name or title that distinguishes or identifies. (From the Latin word *appellare*, meaning "to call upon" or "to address")

   Example   That playwright was once given the *appellation* "the Shakespeare of the twentieth century."

   1. _____

2. **diphthong** (dĭf′thông′, dĭp′-thông′) *noun*   A speech sound that consists of either two vowels or a vowel and a semivowel (such as *y*) contained in a single syllable. (From the Greek *di-*, meaning "two," and *phthongos*, meaning "sound")

   Example   In spite of their spellings, in standard English the so-called long vowels, like the *i* in *hi*, are really *diphthongs*.

   2. _____

3. **eponym** (ĕp′ə-nĭm′) *noun*   A person for whom something is or is thought to be named. (From the Greek *epi-*, meaning "upon," and *ōnyma*, meaning "name")

   Related Word   eponymous *adjective*
   Example   Romulus is the legendary *eponym* of Rome.

   3. _____

4. **linguistics** (lĭng-gwĭs′tĭks) *noun*   The study of human speech, especially its components, structure, and nature, and how it changes. (From the Latin word *lingua*, meaning "language" or "tongue")

   Related Words linguist *noun*; linguistic *adjective*
   Example   Modern *linguistics* has shed light on the history and culture of ancient peoples.

   4. _____
   USAGE NOTE: Although plural in form, *linguistics* is always used with a singular verb.

5. **neologism** (nē-ŏl′ə-jĭz′ əm) *noun*   A newly made-up word, phrase, or expression. (From the Greek words *neos*, meaning "new," and *logos*, meaning "word")

    Related Word   **neologistic** *adjective*
    Example   Computer science has been responsible for the creation of many *neologisms*, some of which have become part of the standard vocabulary of English.

6. **parlance** (pär′ləns) *noun*   A particular manner or kind of speech: *legal parlance*. (From the French word *parler*, meaning "to speak")

    Example   In the *parlance* of refined Victorians, legs were often referred to as "limbs."

7. **patois** (păt′wä′, pă-twä′) *noun*   **a.** A dialect other than the standard dialect of a language, especially a regional or uneducated form of speech.   **b.** The distinctive language of a special group; jargon.

    Example   Although he lived in the area for many years, he never completely mastered the local *patois*.

8. **polyglot** (pŏl′ē-glŏt′) *adjective*   **a.** Consisting of many groups speaking different languages.   **b.** Speaking or writing several languages.   **c.** Containing elements or material from different languages: *a polyglot Bible*.   *noun*   **a.** A person who knows several languages.   **b.** A mixture of languages. (From the Greek words *polus*, meaning "many," and *glōtta*, meaning "tongue")

    Example   The need of the people to defend themselves against a common enemy was all that kept the *polyglot* nation unified.

9. **solecism** (sŏl′ĭ-sĭz′ əm, sō′lĭ-sĭz′ əm) *noun*   **a.** The ungrammatical usage of a word or construction of a sentence.   **b.** A violation of good manners or good taste.   **c.** Something out of the normal or proper order. (From Greek *Soloi*, a city where a provincial and substandard dialect of Greek was spoken)

    Example   My English teacher winces whenever he hears the common *solecism* "between you and I."

10. **vulgar** (vŭl′gər) *adjective*   **a.** Spoken by or using the language spoken by the common people rather than literary, cultured, or learned people; vernacular.   **b.** Of or associated with the common people.   **c.** Lacking taste or delicacy; coarse.   **d.** Conspicuous and excessive; pretentious: *a vulgar display of wealth*. (From the Latin word *vulgus*, meaning "the common people")

    Related Words   **vulgarity** *noun*; **vulgarly** *adverb*
    Example   French was the official language of medieval England, but it never succeeded in supplanting the *vulgar* tongue.

5. _____

6. _____

7. _____

8. _____

9. _____

10. _____

Word History: linguistics

Latin: lingua=tongue

   Linguistics involves the study of human speech and how it changes. The word *linguistics* comes from the Latin *lingua*, meaning "tongue," and contains the idea that human speech depends upon the correct functioning of the tongue. Try to speak without using your tongue. Impossible!

EXERCISE 1 MATCHING WORDS AND DEFINITIONS

Match the definition in Column B with the word in Column A. Write the letter of the correct definition on the answer line.

Column A	Column B	
1. solecism	**a.** a newly made-up word or phrase	1. _____ **i**
2. appellation	**b.** a nonstandard dialect of a language	2. _____ **f**
3. neologism	**c.** spoken by the common people; vernacular	3. _____ **a**
4. parlance	**d.** two vowels or a vowel and a semivowel in a single syllable	4. _____ **j**
5. patois		5. _____ **b**
6. diphthong	**e.** a person for whom something is named	6. _____ **d**
7. vulgar	**f.** a name or title that identifies	7. _____ **c**
8. polyglot	**g.** consisting of many groups speaking different languages	8. _____ **g**
9. linguistics	**h.** the study of human speech	9. _____ **h**
10. eponym	**i.** the ungrammatical usage of a word	10. _____ **e**
	j. a particular manner of speech	

EXERCISE 2 USING WORDS CORRECTLY

Each of the following statements contains an italicized vocabulary word. Decide whether the sentence is true or false, and write *True* or *False* on the answer line.

1. *Vulgar* Latin was the language spoken by the common people of Rome.   1. _____ True
2. "Old Ironsides" is an *appellation* of the frigate officially named the *Constitution*.   2. _____ True
3. The words *fast* and *slow* are *eponyms*.   3. _____ False
4. *Neologism* is a system for simplifying the spelling of English words.   4. _____ False
5. The word *hay* contains a *diphthong*.   5. _____ True
6. A person who studies *linguistics* learns how insects communicate.   6. _____ False
7. Doctors often use medical *parlance* when speaking among themselves.   7. _____ True
8. A *solecism* is an exception to a spelling rule.   8. _____ False
9. A *patois* can be difficult for outsiders to understand.   9. _____ True
10. A *polyglot* is a word with many different meanings.   10. _____ False

EXERCISE 3 CHOOSING THE BEST WORD

Decide which vocabulary word or related form best completes the sentence, and write the letter of your choice on the answer line.

1. Alexander the Great is the _____ of the city of Alexandria of Egypt.   1. _____ **b**
   a. appellation   **b.** eponym   **c.** patois   **d.** solecism

2. Because the children spoke only the _____ of their village, they had difficulty adjusting to living in the capital city.   2. _____ **a**
   a. patois   **b.** linguistics   **c .** neologism   **d.** solecism

3. The former Yugoslavia is a(n) _____ country much divided by ethnic and sectional discord.
   a. linguistic   **b.** neologistic   **c.** eponymous   **d.** polyglot

3. _____d_____

4. Florence Nightingale's work as a nurse during the Crimean War earned her the _____ of "the Lady with the Lamp."
   a. eponym   **b.** solecism   **c.** appellation   **d.** diphthong

4. _____c_____

5. Some people disapprove of _____ because they dislike words that are not familiar to them.
   a. neologisms   **b.** linguistics   **c.** appellations   **d.** solecisms

5. _____a_____

6. Over a long period of time, the short vowels of a language are less likely to alter in pronunciation than either long vowels or _____.
   a. neologisms   **b.** diphthongs   **c.** solecisms   **d.** appellations

6. _____b_____

7. Many languages have developed a literary form distinct from the _____ language.
   a. eponymous   **b.** polyglot   **c.** vulgar   **d.** linguistic

7. _____c_____

8. Mr. Culpepper inquired as to the whereabouts of my domicile or, in ordinary _____, asked where I lived.
   a. patois   **b.** linguistics   **c.** solecism   **d.** parlance

8. _____d_____

9. In the eighteenth century, the construction "you was" was accepted as grammatical and not considered a(n) _____, as it is today.
   a. solecism   **b.** neologism   **c.** eponym   **d.** patois

9. _____a_____

10. A(n) _____ atlas shows the geographical boundaries between dialects as well as items of vocabulary and grammar that distinguish them.
    a. polyglot   **b.** linguistic   **c.** vulgar   **d.** eponymous

10. _____b_____

EXERCISE 4 USING DIFFERENT FORMS OF WORDS

Decide which form of the vocabulary word in parentheses best completes the sentence. The form given may be correct. Write your answer on the answer line.

1. At the end of the eighteenth century, some poets praised the simplicity and directness of the _____ language over the formality and complexity of the prevailing literary style. *(vulgar)*

1. _____vulgar_____

2. Jacob Grimm was both a folklorist and a pioneer of modern _____. *(linguistics)*

2. _____linguistics_____

3. The Norsemen were the _____ conquerors of Normandy. *(eponym)*

3. _____eponymous_____

4. The President's house is probably better known by its _____, "the White House," than by its address, 1600 Pennsylvania Avenue. *(appellation)*

4. _____appellation_____

5. The traders from all nations spoke a _____ in order to communicate. *(polyglot)*

5. _____polyglot_____

6. My favorite newspaper columnist delights in _____ and puns. *(neologism)*

6. _____neologisms_____

7. Several regional varieties of American speech are characterized by their pronunciation of _____. *(diphthong)*

7. _____diphthongs_____

8. Aunt Ida considers the construction "It's me" to be a _____. *(solecism)*

8. _____solecism_____

9. The islanders had lived in isolation for so many generations that their _____ had become a separate language. *(patois)*

9. _____patois_____

10. The public insisted on calling a "war" what, in diplomatic _____, was referred to as a "police action." *(parlance)*

10. _____parlance_____

READING COMPREHENSION

Each numbered sentence in the following passage contains an italicized vocabulary word or related form. After you read the passage, you will complete an exercise.

AMERICAN LANGUAGE

To many people "American language" means "English." It is true that English is the predominant language of the United States. (1) But the United States is, and has been since the earliest days of settlement, a *polyglot* land in a polyglot hemisphere.

Over twenty thousand years ago the first migrants from Eurasia arrived in the Western Hemisphere by way of a land bridge in the North Pacific. (2) The various groups of these prehistoric settlers spoke many languages that, according to *linguists*, differed widely from one another and from any known European or Asian tongue.

The Spanish, Portuguese, and Italians were the first modern Europeans to set foot in the Western Hemisphere. (3) Amerigo Vespucci, an Italian, was the *eponym* for North and South America. Vespucci was one of the first European explorers to conclude that the newly discovered lands were separate continents and not islands or the eastern part of Asia.

(4) Explorers of other nations, especially the English, Dutch, and French, soon followed, giving distinctive *appellations* to their own territorial claims. Some names, like New England, still survive. Since 1492, people from virtually every nation in the world have made their contributions to the American linguistic melting pot.

The languages of America were the result of the shifting balance of power among the people who spoke them. The Dutch colonies, for example, were taken over by the English, and the Dutch language consequently died out. The fortunes of war left some communities surrounded by foreigners. (5) If their language did not disappear, it developed into a local *patois*. Because of the political and military success of Spain and England, Spanish and English became the most important languages in the Americas.

The linguistic diversity and relative isolation of the Americas have had a transforming effect on the development of English in the United States. (6) From very early times, people have commented on how American *parlance* differs from the British idiom. (7) Some differences are obvious, such as the *neologisms* that have always characterized American speech. Because these continents presented the settlers and explorers many animals, plants, and situations that they had never encountered before, they had to find new words for them. Many of these words were borrowed from the native inhabitants, but others came from European and African languages. Examples of the former are "hickory" and "squash"; examples of the latter are "prairie" and "banjo."

As time went on, more subtle differences developed between American and British English, and even between American dialects. (8) The pronunciation of vowels and *diphthongs*, for instance, varies widely from dialect to dialect; the southern pronunciation of the pronoun "I" is distinctive. Differences in usage and grammar have also developed. (9) In the absence of a strong and widespread literary standard, *vulgar* speech became the foundation of American English. (10) Occasionally usages that sound grammatical to one group are rejected by others as odd, or even as *solecisms*. Americans, for example, say "in the hospital," whereas the English say "in hospital." The English have completely dropped the past participle form *gotten* in favor of *got*; Americans use both and preserve a distinction of meaning between them.

The English language in America will continue to change. New ideas and new inventions will require the language to adapt. New immigrants will add their contributions. The mass media will continue to bring remote areas into communication with one another. The future may see more change than all the centuries of the past.

Each of the following statements corresponds to a numbered sentence in the passage. Each statement contains a blank and is followed by four answer choices. Decide which choice fits best in the blank. The word or phrase that you choose must express roughly the same meaning as the italicized word in the passage. Write the letter of your choice on the answer line.

1. The United States is a land of _____ .
   a. many different languages   c. unfamiliar plants and animals
   b. immigrants   d. change

   1. _____a_____

2. According to _____ , the earliest migrants spoke widely differing languages.
   a. those who study human speech   c. students of human society
   b. people who know many languages   d. Native Americans

   2. _____a_____

3. Amerigo Vespucci, an Italian, was the _____ for North and South America.
   a. person assigning the name   c. person remembering the name
   b. person giving his name to   d. person changing his name

   3. _____b_____

4. Other explorers gave distinctive _____ to their claims.
   a. histories   b. descriptions   c. names   d. governments

   4. _____c_____

5. Sometimes an isolated language developed into a local _____ .
   a. habit   b. standard   c. mother tongue   d. dialect

   5. _____d_____

6. People have commented on how American _____ differs from British.
   a. slang   b. literature   c. speech   d. history

   6. _____c_____

7. _____ have always characterized American speech.
   a. New words   c. Dialects
   b. Coarse expressions   d. Grammatical mistakes

   7. _____a_____

8. Dialects vary in the way vowels and _____ are pronounced.
   a. consonants   c. pronouns
   b. foreign words   d. combinations of vowels

   8. _____d_____

9. _____ speech became the foundation of American English.
   a. Formal   c. Literary
   b. The common people's   d. British

   9. _____b_____

10. Some groups regard the usages of other groups as _____ .
    a. odd   c. mistakes in grammar
    b. dialects   d. foreign words

   10. _____c_____

As an English project, you and several other students are compiling a report on the contributions of other languages to American English and culture. For your part of the report, you have chosen the foreign language about which you know the most, and you will do library research as needed. In your report you will discuss the kind and degree of influence that the language has had on American culture, and you will also give examples of English words (including place names, if you wish) derived from this language. Use at least four words from this lesson in the report, and underline each one.

Not everything that we do in life is the result of rational action or conscious decision. When acting spontaneously, we are said to act on whim, moved, perhaps, by some passing fancy. When good or bad things happen to us regardless of any deliberate action of our own, we tend to attribute such occurrences to luck or chance, which may simply be our terms for the causes of events that we cannot reasonably explain. In this lesson you will learn ten words about luck and whim.

WORD LIST

amulet
capricious
fatalism
incantation
propitious
providential
quirk
serendipity
vagary
vicissitude

DEFINITIONS

After you have studied the definitions and example for each vocabulary word, write the word on the line to the right.

1. **amulet** (ăm′yə-lĭt) *noun*   An object worn to bring luck or to protect against evil or injury; charm.

   Example   The ancient Egyptians often wore *amulets* in the shape of scarab beetles.

   1. _____

2. **capricious** (kə-prĭsh′əs, kə-prē′shəs) *adjective*   Characterized by or subject to sudden, unpredictable changes; fickle. (From the Italian word *capriccio*, meaning "curly head")

   Related Words   **capriciously** *adverb;* **capriciousness** *noun*
   Example   Young children at play often exhibit *capricious* behavior.

   2. _____

3. **fatalism** (fāt′l-ĭz′əm) *noun*   The belief that all events are determined in advance by fate and cannot be changed by human means.

   Related Words   **fatalist** *noun;* **fatalistic** *adjective*
   Example   The *fatalism* of the group accounted for its members' failures to take precautions against theft.

   3. _____

4. **incantation** (ĭn′kăn-tā′shən) *noun*   A set of words spoken as a magic charm or to cast a magic spell. (From the Latin word *incantare*, meaning "to enchant")

   Example   In one version of the folk tale, the witch's *incantation* turns the prince into a frog.

   4. _____

5. **propitious** (prə-pĭsh′əs) *adjective*   Presenting favorable circumstances; auspicious; advantageous. (From the Latin word *propitius*, meaning "favorable")

   Related Words   **propitiously** *adverb;* **propitiousness** *noun*
   Example   Since he had just been praised for his work, he felt that it was a *propitious* moment to ask for a raise.

   5. _____

6. **providential** (prŏv′ ĭ-dĕn′shəl) *adjective*   Resulting from or seeming to result from divine will; fortunate; opportune. (From the Latin *pro-*, meaning "before," and *videre*, meaning "to see")

Related Words   **providence** *noun;* **providentially** *adverb*
Example   The Puritans believed that *providential* forces had assured them a safe journey to North America.

6. _____

7. **quirk** (kwûrk) *noun*   **a.** A peculiarity of behavior; mannerism; idiosyncrasy. **b.** An unpredictable or unaccountable shift in action: *a quirk of fate*.

Related Words   **quirkiness** *noun;* **quirky** *adjective*
Example   Dennis has several *quirks,* such as combing his hair every time he passes a mirror.

7. _____

8. **serendipity** (sĕr′ ən-dĭp′ĭ-tē) *noun*   The ability to make valuable discoveries by chance; luck. (From Serendip, the ancient name of Sri Lanka; used in the title of a Persian fairy tale)

Related Word   **serendipitous** *adjective*
Example   Paulette's *serendipity* astounds me; she just bought a beautiful new winter coat for thirty dollars because the store where she asked for directions happened to be having a sale.

8. _____

9. **vagary** (vā′gə-rē, və-gâr′ē) *noun*   A wild or unpredictable notion or action; odd fancy. (From the Latin word *vagari*, meaning "to wander")

Example   What we saw on the sightseeing tour depended on the *vagaries* of our eccentric guide.

9. _____
See *vicissitude.*

10. **vicissitude** (vĭ-sĭs′ĭ-tood′, vĭ-sĭs′ĭ-tyood′) *noun*   **a.** One of the sudden or unexpected changes or shifts often encountered in one's life, activities, or surroundings.   **b.** A change or variation. (From the Latin word *vicissitudo*, meaning "alternation")

Example   The senator decided not to run for reelection because he was tired of the *vicissitudes* of public and political life.

10. _____
USAGE NOTE: Both *vagary* and *vicissitude* are most often used in the plural form.

EXERCISE 1 MATCHING WORDS AND DEFINITIONS

Match the definition in Column B with the word in Column A. Write the letter of the correct definition on the answer line.

Column A

1. fatalism
2. quirk
3. vicissitude
4. capricious
5. providential
6. amulet
7. vagary
8. serendipity
9. incantation
10. propitious

Column B

a. the ability to make valuable discoveries by chance
b. characterized by unpredictable changes; fickle
c. the view that all events are determined by fate
d. presenting favorable circumstances; advantageous
e. a change, usually sudden or unexpected
f. an object worn to bring luck or protection; charm
g. an unpredictable idea or action; odd fancy
h. a peculiarity of behavior
i. seeming to result from divine will; opportune
j. words spoken as a magic charm or to cast a spell

1. ___c___
2. ___h___
3. ___e___
4. ___b___
5. ___i___
6. ___f___
7. ___g___
8. ___a___
9. ___j___
10. ___d___

EXERCISE 2 USING WORDS CORRECTLY

Each of the following statements contains an italicized vocabulary word. Decide whether the sentence is true or false, and write *True* or *False* on the answer line.

1. *Quirks* are subatomic particles that physicists have identified.
2. The success of new products is subject to the *vagaries* of consumer tastes.
3. If interest rates drop, it is a *propitious* time to take out a mortgage.
4. A rabbit's foot is an *amulet* used by some superstitious people.
5. Television commercials are characterized by lively *incantations*.
6. Receiving a college scholarship is typically the result of *serendipity*.
7. The Lewis and Clark expedition was a *vicissitude* that opened the way for settlement of the West.
8. The behavior of a *capricious* person is unpredictable.
9. The development of sulfa drugs was *providential* because they saved many lives during World War II.
10. Booker T. Washington's *fatalism* spurred him on to obtain an education and then to establish Tuskegee Institute.

1. ___False___
2. ___True___
3. ___True___
4. ___True___
5. ___False___
6. ___False___
7. ___False___
8. ___True___
9. ___True___
10. ___False___

EXERCISE 3 CHOOSING THE BEST DEFINITION

For each italicized vocabulary word in the following sentences, write the letter of the best definition on the answer line.

1. The *incantation* "Double, double, toil and trouble" was uttered by three witches in the play *Macbeth*.
   a. rhyme   **b.** spell   **c.** song   **d.** poem

1. ___b___

2. Some Native Americans once wore a bear claw as an *amulet*.
   a. ornament   **b.** charm   **c.** symbol   **d.** indication of age

2. ___b___

3. The *fatalism* of Greek tragedy is evident in the story of Oedipus, who inadvertently fulfilled a prophecy of an oracle.
   a. belief that events are predetermined
   b. basic philosophy
   c. belief in the power of oracles
   d. attitude toward family life

3. _____a_____

4. Tom's discovery of sunken treasure while scuba-diving in the Bahamas could only be attributed to *serendipity*.
   a. superior technology
   b. luck
   c. dedicated research
   d. good planning

4. _____b_____

5. Literary critics attempt to understand the *vagaries* of an author's imagination by reading and comparing all of his or her writings.
   a. contradictions
   b. products
   c. unknown feelings
   d. unpredictable ideas

5. _____d_____

6. One laboratory rat had the *quirk* of going into the maze only through the left opening.
   a. habit   b. experience   c. behavioral oddity   d. routine

6. _____c_____

7. A *capricious* friend often cannot be relied upon.
   a. suspicious   b. wicked   c. fickle   d. dishonest

7. _____c_____

8. The climate of the southern states is *propitious* for cultivating cotton.
   a. mild   b. acceptable   c. favorable   d. intended

8. _____c_____

9. The *vicissitudes* of Ada's life have taken her to remote parts of the world.
   a. sudden changes
   b. adventures
   c. numerous mistakes
   d. restrictions

9. _____a_____

10. To the desperate farmers, the heavy rains seemed *providential*.
   a. unexpected   b. heaven-sent   c. timely   d. promising

10. _____b_____

EXERCISE 4 USING DIFFERENT FORMS OF WORDS

Decide which form of the vocabulary word in parentheses best completes the sentence. The form given may be correct. Write your answer on the answer line.

1. Because of her _____ approach to life, Linda believed that she would pass or fail her exams regardless of her efforts. *(fatalism)*

1. _____fatalistic_____

2. Having left all their belongings behind, the refugees looked to _____ for sustenance. *(providential)*

2. _____providence_____

3. The magician waved his wand, pronounced the customary _____, "Abracadabra," and disappeared in a puff of smoke. *(incantation)*

3. _____incantation_____

4. Garlic _____ were once believed to offer protection. *(amulet)*

4. _____amulets_____

5. The belief that intelligent life exists in this solar system may be a mere _____. *(vagary)*

5. _____vagary_____

6. People who are alert are more likely to have _____ experiences than those who are oblivious to what goes on around them. *(serendipity)*

6. _____serendipitous_____

7. Sailors must keep a sharp eye on the _____ of marine weather. *(vicissitude)*

7. _____vicissitudes_____

8. Kitty's _____ often leads her to buy things that she does not need. *(capricious)*

8. _____capriciousness_____

9. A _____ turn of events propelled Lornabeth into the forefront of her party's politics. *(quirk)*

9. _____quirky_____

10. All major economic indicators forecast a _____ start of the fiscal year. *(propitious)*

10. _____propitious_____

READING COMPREHENSION

Each numbered sentence in the following passage contains an italicized vocabulary word or related form. After you read the passage, you will complete an exercise.

ALCHEMY: SCIENCE OR DECEPTION?

Alchemy, an ancient philosophy that sought to determine the composition of matter, is the reflection of concepts about nature that prevailed before the beginning of modern science. (1) Often dismissed today as a fraud or as merely a *vagary,* alchemy actually served as the basis of modern chemistry.

Alchemy probably originated in A.D. 100 among the Greeks living in Alexandria, Egypt. The first alchemists were metalworkers who fashioned ornate gold and silver objects for the wealthy and cheaper substitutes for poorer citizens. As they made lead or copper look like gold or silver, these artisans theorized that they could produce valuable metals as good as those furnished by nature.

These early alchemists were guided by the accepted theory of the nature of matter. Based on Aristotle's teachings from the fourth century B.C., people believed that all matter was composed of different ratios of four elements—water, earth, fire, and air. With the application of hot, cold, wet, or dry agents, people thought that they could change one substance into another by changing the balance of the elements. (2) It is little wonder, then, that alchemists presumed that if they could create *propitious* conditions, an ordinary metal could be converted into gold.

Astrology played an important role in alchemy. (3) Astrologers believed that the *vicissitudes* of life on Earth were reflected in the heavens, and vice versa. Each heavenly body represented and controlled a certain metal: the sun represented gold; the moon, silver; and Venus, copper. (4) Thus, under the influence of astrology, a *providential* transformation of lead into gold might occur. (5) Not being *fatalistic,* the artisans believed that they could hasten such a process.

Eastern philosophy also had a strong influence on alchemy. (6) The lasting quality of gold led Chinese practitioners to believe that they would find the secret of immortality if only they could discover the *serendipitous* blend of ingredients. Their investigations, which strongly affected those of the Greeks, were directed at finding a philosopher's stone, a magical substance that could transform lead into gold, cure disease, and prolong life.

Under the influence of astrology and Eastern philosophy, the development of alchemy by Alexandrian metalworkers continued. Because they did not want to reveal their trade secrets, the artisans devised a system of secret symbols to conceal their materials. Before long, the secret symbols attracted the attention of philosophers who practiced religious and occult rites. Not interested in practical metallurgy, these philosophers added new elements to alchemy and changed its character. (7) Some used *incantations* to appeal to supernatural forces. (8) Others wore *amulets* to ensure successful transformations. By A.D. 476, when the Roman Empire collapsed, alchemy had degenerated into an occult practice.

Interest in alchemy was revived briefly during the eleventh and twelfth centuries in Europe when interest in classical learning was rekindled. Once again, alchemists promised kings immortality and incredible wealth. (9) But, as always, since their experiments were not based on scientific principles, the results were *capricious.* (10) Fortunately, within a short time, the *quirks* of alchemy gave way to the theories of systematic science.

None of the alchemists' goals were ever attained. However, their experiments with such processes as combustion and with such substances as sulphur and mercury did have a practical value. In trying to turn ordinary metals into gold, practitioners of alchemy discovered many important facts from which the science of chemistry gradually developed.

READING COMPREHENSION EXERCISE

Each of the following statements corresponds to a numbered sentence in the passage. Each statement contains a blank and is followed by four answer choices. Decide which choice fits best in the blank. The word or phrase that you choose must express roughly the same meaning as the italicized word in the passage. Write the letter of your choice on the answer line.

1. Alchemy is often dismissed as merely a _____.
    a. hoax   **b.** wild notion   **c.** serious theory   **d.** primitive notion

1. _____**b**_____

2. Alchemists presumed that if they could create _____ conditions, they could convert an ordinary metal into gold.
   a. trustworthy   **b.** vague   **c.** subordinate   **d.** favorable

2. _____d_____

3. Astrologers believed that _____ of life on Earth were reflected in the heavens.
   a. variations   **b.** oversights   **c.** spectacles   **d.** themes

3. _____a_____

4. Under the influence of astrology, a(n) _____ transformation of lead into gold might occur.
   a. untroubled   **b.** opportune   **c.** convenient   **d.** relentless

4. _____b_____

5. The artisans were not _____.
   a. believers in predetermined events   **c.** true scientists
   b. believers in objective science   **d.** interested in astrology

5. _____a_____

6. The Chinese wanted to discover the _____ blend of ingredients that would produce immortality.
   a. verified   **b.** precise   **c.** lucky   **d.** equal

6. _____c_____

7. Some philosophers used _____ to appeal to supernatural forces.
   a. magic potions   **c.** magic spells
   b. strange objects   **d.** reasonable arguments

7. _____c_____

8. Others wore _____ to ensure success.
   a. lucky clothing   **b.** charms   **c.** special hats   **d.** long robes

8. _____b_____

9. But, as always, since their experiments were not based on scientific principles, the results were _____.
   a. disillusioning   **b.** magical   **c.** unpredictable   **d.** unproven

9. _____c_____

10. The _____ of alchemy gave way to the theories of systematic science.
    a. habits   **b.** superstitions   **c.** practice   **d.** idiosyncrasies

10. _____d_____

WRITING ASSIGNMENT

Think back on the one event in your life in which luck played the most important role. Using this experience as the basis of your reflections on luck, write a brief speech for a panel discussion on the topic "Is luck just a name for that which we do not understand?" Use five words from this lesson in your speech and underline each one.

VOCABULARY ENRICHMENT

Horace Walpole coined the word *serendipity* in a letter that he wrote in 1754. Walpole had read a French version of the fairy tale "The Three Princes of Serendip," in which the lucky princes are always discovering unexpected things. Serendip is an ancient name for Ceylon, now Sri Lanka, where the tale is believed to have originated.

The King of Serendip sends his three sons out to find a magic scroll that will destroy the dragons that surround their island. In their travels the princes solve almost everyone's problems but their own. They return home dejected because they have been able to discover only six lines of the scroll. All ends happily, however, when the princes' characteristic serendipity has them come upon the secret unexpectedly, and the dragons are destroyed.

Activity Many English words derive from place names. Using a dictionary, identify the place name from which the word is derived, write a definition of the word, and then use the word in a sentence.

1. bedlam   2. bikini   3. fez   4. parchment   5. waterloo

The concepts of order and relationship are integral to our daily lives. Without some comprehensible organization, we would be unable to give or follow directions or to locate items in a store. The systematic design or arrangement of parts allows us to drive a car, operate a washing machine, or change a light bulb. Without customary or prescribed procedures, we might find it difficult to prepare a new dish or to address an envelope. The words in this lesson will make you aware of the extent to which organization and connectedness ensure the appropriate functioning of the things that are part of everyday experience.

WORD LIST

continuity
converge
crux
initiate
pivotal
sequel
subordinate
tangential
terminate
ultimate

DEFINITIONS

After you have studied the definitions and example for each vocabulary word, write the word on the line to the right.

1. **continuity** (kŏn´tə-nōō´ĭ-tē, kŏn´tə-nyōō´ĭ-tē) *noun*   **a.** The condition of being without a stop or interruption.   **b.** An uninterrupted succession or flow. (From the Latin *com-*, meaning "together," and *tenere*, meaning "to hold")

   Related Words   **continue** *verb;* **continuous** *adjective*
   Example   To ensure the *continuity* of the Mayfield Beautification Project, we shall hold elections today for a new director to replace the retiring director, Darlene Parks.

   1. _____

2. **converge** (kən-vûrj´) *intrans. verb*   **a.** To approach the same point from different directions; meet.   **b.** To move toward a common conclusion or result. (From the Latin *com-*, meaning "together," and *vergere*, meaning "to incline")

   Related Word   **convergence** *noun*
   Example   The three highways *converged* at Millport, which is the seat of Farr County.

   2. _____

3. **crux** (krŭks, krŏoks) *noun*   **a.** The basic or essential feature of something.   **b.** A baffling or puzzling point that is difficult to explain. (From the Latin word *crux*, meaning "cross")

   Related Word   **crucial** *adjective*
   Example   The *crux* of the physics problem is the unusual amount of gravitational force influencing the swing of the pendulum.

   3. _____

4. **initiate** (ĭ-nĭsh´ē-āt´) *trans. verb*   **a.** To begin; originate; cause to begin.   **b.** To admit into membership.   *noun* (ĭ-nĭsh´ē-ĭt) A beginner; novice. (From the Latin word *initiare*, meaning "to begin")

   Related Words   **initial** *adjective;* **initiation** *noun*
   Example   Darryl Johnson *initiated* the urban-development legislation.

   4. _____

5. **pivotal** (pĭv′ə-təl) *adjective*   **a.** Central or crucial to something; very important.   **b.** Pertaining to a pivot, the shaft about which a related part rotates or swings.

5. _____

Related Word   **pivot** *noun*
Example   Many scientists consider Albert Einstein's general and special theories of relativity to be the *pivotal* achievements of post-Newtonian physics.

6. **sequel** (sē′kwəl, sē′kwĕl′) *noun*   **a.** Something that follows; continuation.   **b.** A result or consequence.   **c.** A literary work that, while complete in itself, continues an already existing narrative. (From the Latin word *sequi*, meaning "to follow")

6. _____

Example   I told you about taking my father's car without permission; the *sequel* is that I may not use it for six months!

7. **subordinate** (sə-bôr′də-nĭt) *noun*   One subject to the authority of another. *adjective*   Of a lower class or rank; inferior.   *trans. verb*   (sə-bôr′də-nāt′) To put in a lower class or rank; make inferior. (From the Latin *sub-*, meaning "under," and *ordinare*, meaning "to put in order")

7. _____

Related Word   **subordination** *noun*
Example   Patty's uncle is Mrs. Quesada's *subordinate* at the Coachella Savings Bank.

8. **tangential** (tăn-jĕn′shəl) *adjective*   Only superficially relevant or related. (From the Latin word *tangens*, meaning "touching")

8. _____

Related Words   **tangent** *noun;* **tangentially** *adverb*
Example   The description of desert sunsets is somewhat *tangential* to your story about your year in Arizona.

9. **terminate** (tûr′mə-nāt′) *trans. verb*   To bring to an end; conclude.   *intrans. verb* To come to an end. (From the Latin word *terminus*, meaning "end")

9. _____

Related Words   **terminal** *adjective;* **termination** *noun*
Example   I shall *terminate* my subscription if your editorial policy does not change.

10. **ultimate** (ŭl′tə-mĭt) *adjective*   **a.** Last; coming at the end.   **b.** Farthest; extreme.   **c.** Greatest possible. (From the Latin word *ultimus*, meaning "farthest" or "last")

10. _____

Related Word   **ultimately** *adverb*
Example   We spent several weeks visiting places in Montana and Idaho, but our *ultimate* destination was Spokane, Washington.

EXERCISE 1 WRITING CORRECT WORDS

On the answer line, write the word from the vocabulary list that fits each definition.

1. To begin; admit into membership

2. One subject to the authority of another; of a lower class or rank

3. Last; farthest; greatest possible

4. The basic or essential feature of something

5. The condition of being without a stop or interruption; an uninterrupted succession or flow

6. Central or crucial to something

7. Something that follows; a result or consequence

8. To bring to an end; conclude

9. To approach the same point from different directions; move toward a common conclusion

10. Only superficially relevant or related

1. _____ initiate _____

2. _____ subordinate _____

3. _____ ultimate _____

4. _____ crux _____

5. _____ continuity _____

6. _____ pivotal _____

7. _____ sequel _____

8. _____ terminate _____

9. _____ converge _____

10. _____ tangential _____

EXERCISE 2 USING WORDS CORRECTLY

Decide whether the italicized vocabulary word has been used correctly in the sentence. On the answer line, write *Correct* for correct use and *Incorrect* for incorrect use.

1. The *crux* of the paper was its second, and minor, point.

2. In the army, lieutenants are *subordinate* to majors.

3. The Wright brothers believed that powered flight was a natural *sequel* to gliding.

4. To ensure *continuity* of management during the company's takeover, all of the managers were fired.

5. The school board plans to *terminate* its contract with the bus drivers at midnight.

6. After the game the crowd *converged* on the home team's locker room.

7. This year designers have *initiated* a radical change in men's fashions.

8. A *tangential* issue is one that is closely related to the matter under discussion.

9. A *pivotal* committee in Congress has little say in determining national policy.

10. Some people fail to consider the *ultimate* results of their actions.

1. _____ Incorrect _____

2. _____ Correct _____

3. _____ Correct _____

4. _____ Incorrect _____

5. _____ Correct _____

6. _____ Correct _____

7. _____ Correct _____

8. _____ Incorrect _____

9. _____ Incorrect _____

10. _____ Correct _____

EXERCISE 3 CHOOSING THE BEST DEFINITION

For each italicized vocabulary word in the following sentences, write the letter of the best definition on the answer line.

1. Mr. Devane *terminated* the interview with an abrupt nod of his head.
   a. agreed to   **b.** reflected on   **c.** observed   **d.** concluded

1. _____ d _____

2. Alexandra enjoyed studying the social, economic, and political forces that *converged* to bring about the Renaissance.
   a. occurred separately   **c.** were unnecessary
   b. came together   **d.** were believed

2. _____ b _____

3. Movie *sequels* are often more popular than the originals.
   a. continuations   **c.** adaptations
   b. fictionalizations   **d.** scenarios

3. _____ a _____

4. Brad exhibited *ultimate* courage when he crawled across the smoke-filled room to rescue the frightened children.
   a. the least possible   **c.** welcome
   b. the greatest possible   **d.** surprising

4. _____ b _____

5. The magazine article was puzzling because it lacked *continuity*.
   a. proper documentation   **c.** flow
   b. specific examples   **d.** conciseness

5. _____ c _____

6. The panelist had been interrupted so many times by the *tangential* comments of her colleague that she brought her presentation to a rapid close.
   a. varied   **c.** surprisingly humorous
   b. absurd   **d.** superficially related

6. _____ d _____

7. The land-reclamation projects have been *pivotal* to our improvement of the desert ecosystem.
   a. crucial   **c.** alarming
   b. absolutely unnecessary **d.** desirable

7. _____ a _____

8. Aaron is a superb host; he always considers his own plans as *subordinate* to those of his guests.
   a. equal in importance to **c.** less important than
   b. more important than   **d.** without reference to

8. _____ c _____

9. The *crux* of Imperial Russian painting during the early nineteenth century was opulence.
   a. ideal   **b.** essential feature   **c.** preferred style   **d.** fame

9. _____ b _____

10. Ashley *initiated* a campaign in her community to make cat owners aware of immunization for feline leukemia.
    a. began   **b.** observed   **c.** investigated   **d.** appealed for

10. _____ a _____

EXERCISE 4 USING DIFFERENT FORMS OF WORDS

Decide which form of the vocabulary word in parentheses best completes the sentence. The form given may be correct. Write your answer on the answer line.

1. The property outside of town has been in _____ use for over sixty years. *(continuity)*

1. _____ continuous _____

2. Fraternity _____ have been banned on many college campuses. *(initiate)*

2. _____ initiations _____

3. Frank has a difficult time sticking to one topic; he can be talking about insects and suddenly go off on a _____ about sailing. *(tangential)*

3. _____ tangent _____

4. The intricate design was composed of _____ and intersecting lines. *(converge)*

4. _____ converging _____

5. While I immensely enjoyed *The Clan of the Cave Bear,* I did not like either of the _____. *(sequel)*

5. _____ sequels _____

6. An unexpected railway strike brought about the _____ of their journey. *(terminate)*

6. _____ termination _____

7. Larry spent the afternoon on the basketball court practicing _____. *(pivotal)*

7. _____ pivots _____

8. The _____ of Ben's argument was totally illogical. *(crux)*

8. _____ crux _____

9. The president of the company is pleasant and courteous to her _____. *(subordinate)*

9. _____ subordinates _____

10. _____ Carl hopes to become an elementary school teacher. *(ultimate)*

10. _____ Ultimately _____

READING COMPREHENSION

Each numbered sentence in the following passage contains an italicized vocabulary word or related form. After you read the passage, you will complete an exercise.

MACHU PICCHU: PLACE OF MYSTERY

(1) Nestled between craggy peaks high in the Andes Mountains in Peru, in a place where the sky and earth seem to *converge*, is Machu Picchu. This ancient complex of ruins and landscaped terraces was not known to the outside world until 1911. Once it was a part of the great Incan empire, which flourished from A.D. 1200 through the 1500s. (2) At its height the Incan empire extended from Chile to Colombia and was connected by twenty thousand miles of *continuous* stone roads.

The Incas must have been an extraordinary people. They built an enormous, highly organized empire in a rugged place without either the horse or the wheel. (3) Both spectacular and complex, Machu Picchu is perhaps the *ultimate* testimony to their genius.

Machu Picchu is also mysterious. (4) Its first discoverer, Hiram Bingham of Yale University, knew immediately that he had found a *pivotal* piece in the puzzle of Incan civilization. Carefully excavating the site, Bingham and his colleagues learned significant information about the Incas. (5) Although the research did not *terminate* with the excavation of Machu Picchu, many questions remained.

(6) The *crux* of the mystery of Machu Picchu lies in its purpose. Hiram Bingham believed that Machu Picchu was the famous lost city in which an Incan prince and his followers hid from Spanish invaders. Other scholars proposed that the city was a military outpost or a religious center. (7) Research *initiated* during recent years, however, has led archaeologists to believe that Machu Picchu had numerous purposes.

(8) A *sequel* to the first discovery took place in 1982, when another expedition, led by Wilfredo Yépez Valdez of Peru, was mounted. Walking along the Inca Trail, just three miles away from Machu Picchu, a member of the expedition suddenly fell through a tangled mat of jungle roots. The startled explorer had literally fallen on top of an archaeological treasure. (9) This seemingly *tangential* discovery of a small group of buildings, a large agricultural site, and a nearby burial plot proved to be crucial in penetrating some of the mystery of Machu Picchu.

Archaeologists were now able to theorize that the area constituted a highly complex, self-sufficient community for which agriculture formed the economic base. Although located in a remote place, Machu Picchu was an administrative center of the entire Incan empire. It may have controlled the empire's trade; it probably did support the estimated ten thousand people who lived there and may even have supplied food to other parts of the empire. (10) Families of the ruling class, as well as their many *subordinates,* are believed to have lived in Machu Picchu. Religious ceremonies took place there, and even the emperor probably visited Machu Picchu. Clearly, it was an important, beautiful, and powerful center of one of the world's greatest empires.

Each of the following statements corresponds to a numbered sentence in the passage. Each statement contains a blank and is followed by four answer choices. Decide which choice fits best in the blank. The word or phrase that you choose must express roughly the same meaning as the italicized word in the passage. Write the letter of your choice on the answer line.

1. Machu Picchu is located in a place where the sky and earth seem to _____ .
   a. separate **b.** meet **c.** be compressed **d.** fade away

   1. _____ **b**

2. Twenty thousand miles of _____ stone roads once connected the Incan empire.
   a. uninterrupted **b.** well-constructed **c.** broken **d.** primitive

   2. _____ **a**

3. Machu Picchu is perhaps the _____ testimony to the genius of the Incas.
   a. newest **b.** sophisticated **c.** most mysterious **d.** greatest possible

   3. _____ **d**

4. Hiram Bingham knew that he had found a(n) _____ piece in the puzzle.
   a. crucial **b.** minor **c.** exceptional **d.** missing

   4. _____ **a**

5. The research did not _____ with the excavation of Machu Picchu.
   a. begin **b.** succeed **c.** conclude **d.** waver

   5. _____ **c**

6. The _____ the mystery lies in the purpose of Machu Picchu.
   a. interest in **c.** research into **b.** interpretation of **d.** essence of

   6. _____ **d**

7. Research _____ during recent years has led archaeologists to believe that Machu Picchu had numerous purposes.
   a. accomplished **b.** begun **c.** proposed **d.** admired

   7. _____ **b**

8. The expedition in 1982 was _____ the first discovery.
   a. a follow-up of **c.** complicated in comparison with **b.** better than **d.** a replica of

   8. _____ **a**

9. At first, the discovery of buildings, an agricultural site, and a burial plot was thought to be _____ to the discovery of Machu Picchu.
   a. unrelated **c.** superficially related **b.** equivalent **d.** monumentally important

   9. _____ **c**

10. Families of the ruling class and _____ are believed to have lived in Machu Picchu.
    a. those of lower rank **c.** their livestock **b.** those of important ancestry **d.** their offspring

    10. _____ **a**

PRACTICE WITH ANALOGIES

A verbal analogy shows how two pairs of words are related. The second two words are related to each other in the same way as the first two. An analogy can be written as a sentence or with colons.

See page 79 for some strategies to use with analogies.

   Wool is to fabric as oil is to fuel.
   WOOL : FABRIC :: oil : fuel

Directions On the answer line, write the vocabulary word or a form of it that completes each analogy.

1. ETHICS : MORALITY :: _____ : speech (*Lesson 1*)

   1. _____ linguistics

2. TALISMAN : OBJECT :: _____ : words (*Lesson 2*)

   2. _____ incantation

3. PRECIOUS : VALUABLE :: _____ : favorable (*Lesson 2*)

   3. _____ propitious

4. JUNCTION : ROADS :: _____ : ideas (*Lesson 3*)

   4. _____ convergence

5. COMMENCE : ACTIVITY :: _____ : project (*Lesson 3*)

   5. _____ initiate

The **Test** for Lessons 1, 2, and 3 is on page T1.

A B C

DICTIONARY SKILLS
USING A THESAURUS

A **thesaurus** is a book of synonyms, a reference work that is useful for the writer. When you write a composition or story, a thesaurus can help you in two ways.

1. *A thesaurus can help you to select just the right word,* one that aptly expresses your meaning.

2. *A thesaurus can help you to find a synonym for a word* that you have already used once or twice and do not want to repeat. Synonyms give your writing variety.

You should learn how to use the thesaurus that is available to you. In a dictionary-style thesaurus, words, followed by their synonyms, appear in a single alphabetical list. Most thesauruses, however, are divided into two parts: (1) the *text,* containing numbered idea categories and associated words, and (2) an *index of idea categories* and subentries. The following procedure will help you when you use this kind of thesaurus.

PROCEDURE

1. *Look up the word in the index and read the subentries.* Suppose, for example, that you want a synonym for *sameness.* You look up the word in the index and find four subentries, each with a different number.

2. *Choose the subentry word that is closest in meaning to the word that you want.* Each of the four subentries denotes one meaning of *sameness.* You decide that you need a synonym for *sameness* in the sense of "identity" rather than "regularity," "similarity," or "tedium."

Index Entry	Portion of Text

sameness, identity 14.1
  regularity 17.2
  similarity 20.1
  tedium 884.1
	14. IDENTITY
	.1 NOUN **identity,** identicalness; **sameness,** self-sameness; indistinguishability, no difference, not a bit of difference; **coincidence,** correspondence, agreement, congruence; **equivalence, equality** 30, coequality; **synonymousness,** synonymity, synonymy; **oneness, unity,** homogeneity; selfness, selfhood, self-identity

3. *Turn to the text and read the appropriate numbered paragraph for the subentry word.* When you turn to section 14.1 of the text, you find that it is the first part of section 14, which develops the idea category of "identity." Sections 14.1, 14.2, and 14.3 contain "identity" (or "identicalness") synonyms for nouns; they are followed by three sections on verbs (such as *identify*), two on adjectives (such as *identical*), and one on adverbs (*identically*).
   Within the 14.1 paragraph, you notice that each group of related words appears in a separate cluster set off by semicolons. You also notice that the most common words appear in boldface type and that such usage labels as "informal" are supplied with some words. Finally, you notice that references to other numbered paragraphs are occasionally given.

4. *Select the synonym that best suits the context and the degree of formality of your sentence.* You may need to consult a dictionary in order to make or confirm your choice. After reading section 14.1, you decide that *equality* fits best in the sentence that you are writing as part of a persuasive composition about the availability of scholarship aid to all students who need it.

EXERCISE USING A THESAURUS

Study the thesaurus entries at the end of this exercise. *Step 1:* Using a dictionary as needed, decide which of the italicized synonyms in each of the following sentences best fits the meaning of the sentence. All of the synonyms are taken from the thesaurus entries. *Step 2:* On the line labeled "Best Synonym," write your choice. *Step 3:* Write a sentence of your own in which you use the word correctly.

1. Is the auditorium (*accessible, approachable, available*) to the handicapped?

   Best Synonym accessible

   Sentence The librarian is always accessible to members of the public.

2. Often he wondered whether his goals were (*accessible, penetrable, attainable*).

   Best Synonym attainable

   Sentence On that test 165 is the highest score attainable.

3. Is Jonesport (*penetrable, reachable, attainable*) by ferry?

   Best Synonym reachable

   Sentence The wilderness area is reachable by a well-maintained trail.

4. This type of opal is (*attainable, obtainable, accessible*) only in Australia.

   Best Synonym obtainable

   Sentence These T-shirts are obtainable only at Sal's Sportswear.

5. Suzanne has a (*scrupulous, particular, sensitive*) ear for music.

   Best Synonym sensitive

   Sentence Many people are sensitive to criticism, no matter how well-intended it is.

6. Tino is known for his (*discriminating, punctilious, exacting*) taste in food.

   Best Synonym discriminating

   Sentence Our family is discriminating in choosing television programs to watch.

7. Our club treasurer is (*meticulous, particular, strict*) in keeping records.

   Best Synonym meticulous

   Sentence Computer programming requires meticulous attention to detail.

8. Marine drill sergeants are (*conscientious, exacting, selective*) taskmasters.

   Best Synonym exacting

   Sentence The director was exacting in his demands on the cast.

.8 **accessible, approachable,** come-at-able *or* getatable [both informal]; **reachable,** within reach; **open, open to; penetrable,** getinable [informal], **pervious; obtainable, attainable, available,** procurable, securable, findable, gettable, to be had.

.9 ADJS **fastidious, particular, scrupulous, meticulous, conscientious,** exacting, precise, punctilious; sensitive, **discriminating** 492.7, discriminative; **selective,** picky [slang], choosy, choicy [slang]; critical 969.24 "nothing if not critical" [Shakespeare]; **strict** 533.12, perfectionistic, precisianistic, puristic, puritanic(al), priggish, prudish, censorious.

The root -*pli*-, as well as its variant forms -*ploy*- and -*plic*-, comes from the Latin verb *plicare*, meaning "to fold." This root is found in over sixty English words, including *complexion, employer, multiply, triplicate,* and *reply*. The root has often been used to form words in imaginative ways. For example, *employ* means "to fold in," which suggests the way in which a new worker becomes part of a company. *Multiply* means "to fold many times," which is more or less what happens to the number being multiplied, although we perform the operation only once. In this lesson you will learn other words that incorporate the idea of folding.

WORD LIST

complicity
deploy
explicate
implicate
implicit
inexplicable
plight
replica
replicate
supple

DEFINITIONS

After you have studied the definitions and example for each vocabulary word, write the word on the line to the right.

1. **complicity** (kəm-plĭs'ĭ-tē) *noun*   Involvement as an accomplice in a crime or wrongdoing. (From the Latin *com*-, meaning "together," and *plicare*, meaning "to fold")

   Example   The judge decided that the woman was guilty of *complicity* because she had helped to destroy some of the evidence of the crime.

   1. _____

2. **deploy** (dĭ-ploi') *trans. verb*   **a.** To station (persons or forces) systematically over an area.   **b.** To spread out (troops) to form an extended front. (From the Latin *dis*-, indicating reversal, and *plicare*.)

   Related Word   **deployment** *noun*
   Example   On the day that the President visited, security personnel were *deployed* throughout the neighborhood.

   2. _____

3. **explicate** (ĕks'plĭ-kāt') *trans. verb*   To explain; make meaning clear. (From the Latin *ex*-, meaning "out," and *plicare*)

   Related Words   **explicable** *adjective;* **explication** *noun*
   Example   The calculus teacher *explicated* the concept of integrals.

   3. _____

4. **implicate** (ĭm'plĭ-kāt') *trans. verb*   **a.** To involve or connect incriminatingly. **b.** To involve or suggest by logical necessity. (From the Latin *in*-, meaning "in," and *plicare*)

   Related Word   **implication** *noun*
   Example   Checks that were made out to the businesswoman *implicated* her in the bribery scandal.

   4. _____

5. **implicit** (ĭm-plĭs'ĭt) *adjective*   **a.** Implied or understood although not expressed. **b.** Contained in the nature of something, although not readily apparent. **c.** Having no doubts; unquestioning. (From the Latin *in-*, meaning "in," and *plicare*)

Related Words   **implicitly** *adverb*; **implicitness** *noun*
Example   No legal action could be taken against the person who violated the *implicit* agreement.

5. _____
USAGE NOTE: *Implicit* means "implied," whereas *explicit* means "clearly stated."

6. **inexplicable** (ĭn-ĕk'splĭ-kə-bəl, ĭn'ĭk-splĭk'ə-bəl) *adjective*   Incapable of being explained or interpreted. (From the Latin *in-*, meaning "not," *ex-*, meaning "out," and *plicare*)

Related Word   **inexplicably** *adverb*
Example   Because we didn't know that she had recently experienced a tragedy, we found the change in her behavior *inexplicable*.

6. _____

7. **plight** (plīt) *noun*   A condition or situation of difficulty or adversity. (From the Middle English word *plit*, meaning "fold" or "condition," which comes from the Latin word *plicare*)

Example   We witnessed the hopeless *plight* of the baby birds whose mother had died.

7. _____

8. **replica** (rĕp'lĭ-kə) *noun*   **a.** A copy or reproduction of a work of art, especially one made by the original artist.   **b.** A copy or reproduction. (From the Latin *re-*, meaning "back," and *plicare*)

Example   The artist agreed to produce a small *replica* of the well-known statue for our city hall.

8. _____

9. **replicate** (rĕp'lĭ-kāt') *trans. verb*   To duplicate, copy, or repeat. (From the Latin *re-*, meaning "back," and *plicare*)

Related Word   **replication** *noun*
Example   Researchers often *replicate* experiments in order to verify results.

9. _____

10. **supple** (sŭp'əl) *adjective*   **a.** Readily bent; pliant.   **b.** Moving and bending with agility; limber.   **c.** Yielding or changing readily; compliant or adaptable. (From the Latin *sub-*, meaning "under," and *plicare*)

Related Words   **supplely** *adverb*; **suppleness** *noun*
Example   The *supple* limbs of the young tree bent easily under the weight of the ice.

10. _____

EXERCISE 1 WRITING CORRECT WORDS

On the answer line, write the word from the vocabulary list that fits each definition.

1. A condition or situation of difficulty or adversity
2. A copy or reproduction of a work of art
3. To involve or connect incriminatingly
4. Readily bent; pliant
5. Involvement as an accomplice in a crime or wrongdoing
6. To explain; make meaning clear
7. To duplicate, copy, or repeat
8. To station (persons or forces) systematically over an area
9. Incapable of being explained or interpreted
10. Implied or understood although not directly expressed

1. _____plight_____
2. _____replica_____
3. _____implicate_____
4. _____supple_____
5. _____complicity_____
6. _____explicate_____
7. _____replicate_____
8. _____deploy_____
9. _____inexplicable_____
10. _____implicit_____

EXERCISE 2 USING WORDS CORRECTLY

Each of the following statements contains an italicized vocabulary word. Decide whether the sentence is true or false, and write *True* or *False* on the answer line.

1. If all the instruments in an orchestra are in tune, they are said to be in perfect *complicity*.
2. A defendant would be *implicated* if a witness supported his plea of innocence.
3. When people are sent out of a country against their will, they are *deployed*.
4. If torrential rains flooded streets and houses, the townspeople would be in a sad *plight*.
5. An *implicit* agreement would be clearly stated in a contract.
6. A *replica* usually displays qualities of imagination, originality, and individuality.
7. Steel is more *supple* than fiberglass.
8. Certain aspects of science are *inexplicable* to the average person.
9. Teachers of literature sometimes *explicate* a complex poem for their students.
10. A decorator might *replicate* a design in a magazine by creating one exactly like it for a client's living room.

1. _____False_____
2. _____False_____
3. _____False_____
4. _____True_____
5. _____False_____
6. _____False_____
7. _____False_____
8. _____True_____
9. _____True_____
10. _____True_____

EXERCISE 3 CHOOSING THE BEST DEFINITION

For each italicized vocabulary word in the following sentences, write the letter of the best definition on the answer line.

1. Our biology teacher *explicated* the photosynthesis process that occurs in plants.
   a. failed to mention
   b. explained
   c. repeated
   d. tested

2. An investigating committee *implicated* the novelist in a crime because of her radical views.
   a. incriminatingly connected
   b. contradicted
   c. supported
   d. absolved of blame

1. _____b_____

2. _____a_____

3. "Black holes and various other cosmic phenomena are *inexplicable* at the present time," said the astronomer.
   a. capable of being explained
   b. complex
   c. not explainable
   d. under investigation

   3. _____ c

4. *Replicas* of the sculptured horses of San Marco were made in order to preserve the originals.
   a. Reproductions
   b. Photographs
   c. Supplements
   d. Preliminary sketches

   4. _____ a

5. For years the world has witnessed the *plight* of the people of Northern Ireland, who are caught in an unceasing struggle.
   a. legal status
   b. difficult situation
   c. migration
   d. oppression

   5. _____ b

6. For Peter's *complicity* in the theft, he was sentenced to six months in prison.
   a. key role   b. failure   c. involvement   d. importance

   6. _____ c

7. The sergeant *deployed* the troops along the frontier.
   a. spread out   b. commanded   c. reprimanded   d. organized

   7. _____ a

8. Alan Paton's deep concern for blacks in South Africa is *implicit* in his novel *Cry, the Beloved Country.*
   a. clearly stated   b. surprising   c. understood   d. exaggerated

   8. _____ c

9. She *replicated* sounds of other instruments by turning various switches on the computerized organ.
   a. evaluated   b. imagined   c. collected   d. duplicated

   9. _____ d

10. The *supple* ballerina moved with striking grace and beauty.
    a. experienced   b. limber   c. young   d. beautiful

    10. _____ b

EXERCISE 4 USING DIFFERENT FORMS OF WORDS

Decide which form of the vocabulary word in parentheses best completes the sentence. The form given may be correct. Write your answer on the answer line.

1. The _____ of the original work of art was so masterfully done that many thought it was the original. *(replicate)*

   1. _____ replication

2. Everyone thought that Bill was irresponsible when he _____ left on a trip to Brazil without notice. *(inexplicable)*

   2. _____ inexplicably

3. *The Grapes of Wrath* is about the _____ of the Joad family, who migrate to California during the Depression. *(plight)*

   3. _____ plight

4. The witness's _____ was that the student started the fight. *(implicate)*

   4. _____ implication

5. Although the theory is complex, it is _____. *(explicate)*

   5. _____ explicable

6. The carpenter created a beautiful _____ of the Louis XIV cabinet. *(replica)*

   6. _____ replica

7. Their _____ agreement to give each other business was reinforced with a handshake. *(implicit)*

   7. _____ implicit

8. Joe was accused of _____ in the car theft. *(complicity)*

   8. _____ complicity

9. The athlete moved _____ from hurdle to hurdle. *(supple)*

   9. _____ supplely

10. The rapid _____ of troops intimidated the enemy and delayed the battle. *(deploy)*

    10. _____ deployment

READING COMPREHENSION

Each numbered sentence in the following passage contains an italicized vocabulary word or related form. After you read the passage, you will complete an exercise.

IMPRINTING AND MOTHERLY ATTACHMENT

We know that attachment to a mother is common in birds and mammals, but we do not fully understand why. Why do baby animals do what their mothers do? Why do baby birds imitate the actions of their mothers rather than the actions of some other bird? (1) One of the most interesting and *explicable* behaviors related to motherly attachment is imprinting, which is exhibited immediately after birth. Imprinting is the process by which the young of a species learn to recognize, follow, and copy the behavior of a member of their own species, typically the mother.

For example, ducklings, which leave the nest soon after they are hatched, usually follow their mothers. However, ducklings can be imprinted to almost any conspicuous object or even to a human being. (2) In order to study this behavior, scientists have imprinted ducklings to decoys, or wooden *replicas* of ducks. The babies have acted as if these copies were their mothers.

(3) Other scientists have *replicated* these experiments to verify the original findings. They have also studied the basic imprinting process in more detail in order to explore different aspects of it. They have found that imprinting can take place in as little as ten minutes. They have also learned that the imprinting object must be presented within the first two days of the duckling's life, and that the imprinting response is especially strong during the first thirteen to sixteen hours after hatching. (4) After that time, an *inexplicable* fear of strangers and unfamiliar things develops.

Researchers have further explored imprinting in monkeys. They have asked whether young animals will become imprinted to any object, or whether they will prefer some objects to others. In one study a wire "mother" was equipped to provide food for a baby monkey while a terrycloth "mother" provided no food. (5) Experimenters found that monkeys preferred the terrycloth "mother," often clinging to it for comfort and placing their *implicit* faith in it. (6) The *implication* of this behavior is that softness is more important to motherly attachment than the ability to provide food. (7) *Suppleness,* warmth, and a rocking motion were also found to be factors in motherly attachment.

Many further inferences can be drawn from such studies. The research may explain why some animals, such as sheep, separate themselves from the herd to give birth: isolation ensures that the baby will imprint to its mother. Another implication is that what is familiar to a baby is comforting. (8) Therefore, if some baby animals see even the strangest objects—such as a bowling ball, an automobile, or a *deployment* of tanks—during the critical period, these things will seem more familiar and agreeable to them than many other objects that we more commonly and logically associate with that animal's world.

Furthermore, researchers now know that imprinting can be the basis of a long-lasting dependence. If an infant becomes attached to some other object at this time, it may later reject its mother. (9) Therefore, people should never enter lightly into such experiments, or they will be guilty at least of *complicity* in distorting the world of a baby bird or animal. In time, however, most imprinting is reversible. (10) Researchers sighed with relief when the *plight* of some ducklings imprinted to an automobile altered quite naturally as soon as the ducklings became mature animals.

Each of the following statements corresponds to a numbered sentence in the passage. Each statement contains a blank and is followed by four answer choices. Decide which choice fits best in the blank. The word or phrase that you choose must express roughly the same meaning as the italicized word in the passage. Write the letter of your choice on the answer line.

1. One of the most _____ behaviors related to motherly attachment is imprinting.
   a. mysterious   b. troublesome   c. explainable   d. extraordinary

2. Scientists have imprinted ducklings to _____ of ducks.
   a. reproductions   b. flocks   c. paintings   d. mothers

3. Other scientists have _____ these experiments.
   a. varied
   b. duplicated
   c. published
   d. debated the results of

4. A(n) _____ fear of strangers and strange things develops.
   a. extreme   b. slight   c. irreversible   d. unexplainable

5. Baby monkeys placed their _____ faith in the terrycloth "mothers."
   a. faltering   b. unquestioning   c. limited   d. comfortable

6. The _____ is that softness is more important to motherly attachment than the ability to provide food.
   a. result
   b. implied meaning
   c. crucial factor
   d. most important finding

7. _____ is also a factor in motherly attachment.
   a. Providing food
   b. Providing the nest
   c. Pliancy
   d. Time

8. If a baby animal were to see a(n) _____ of tanks, it would regard the vehicles as more agreeable and familiar than other things likely to be a part of its experience.
   a. group
   b. photograph
   c. invasion
   d. collection in a museum

9. People who enter lightly into imprinting experiments will be guilty at least of _____.
   a. a felony
   b. a misdemeanor
   c. cruelty in the name of science
   d. involvement in a crime as an accomplice

10. The _____ of ducklings imprinted to an automobile altered when the ducklings became adults.
    a. lives
    b. difficult situation
    c. motherly attachment
    d. confusion

1. _____ c
2. _____ a
3. _____ b
4. _____ d
5. _____ b
6. _____ b
7. _____ c
8. _____ a
9. _____ d
10. _____ b

Whether it was the task of molding a piece of clay into a dish or cup or the complicated construction of a model airplane, most of us have made copies or models of something. Write a short expository composition in which you explain to members of your class the process of making a copy or reproduction of something. Use at least four of the words from this lesson and underline each one.

The **Bonus activity** for Lessons 1–4 is on page T3.

Although we generally think of criticism in the negative sense of expressing unfavorable judgment, the actual definition includes the idea of evaluating both the merits and the faults of someone or something. Constructive criticism is valuable. Careful analysis of strengths and weaknesses can heighten awareness and suggest change.

When criticism is only an outlet for irritation or anger, or when it is entirely negative, the results will probably be less favorable. No one likes to be scolded, blamed, laughed at, or condemned. As Morris Ernst wrote, "The greatest corrective known . . . is criticism with good will." If criticism is to be valuable, it needs to be expressed kindly or at least neutrally. This lesson will help you to become familiar with the range of words used to refer to the negative forms of criticism; the lesson will also help you to distinguish such words from those used to criticize with good will.

WORD LIST

aspersion
deprecate
deride
execrable
ostracize
rebuke
scurrilous
spurn
vitriolic
vituperation

DEFINITIONS

After you have studied the definitions and example for each vocabulary word, write the word on the line to the right.

1. **aspersion** (ə-spûr′zhən, ə-spûr′-shən) *noun* **a.** A damaging or false statement. **b.** The act of defaming or slandering. (From the Latin *ad-*, meaning "toward," and *spargere*, meaning "to strew")

   Example The magazine article cast *aspersions* on the senator's integrity.

   1. _____

2. **deprecate** (dĕp′rĭ-kāt′) *trans. verb.* **a.** To express disapproval of. **b.** To belittle; depreciate. (From the Latin *de-*, meaning "against," and *precari*, meaning "to pray")

   Related Words **deprecation** *noun;* **deprecatory** *adjective*
   Example At first many critics *deprecated* the new style of photography; later they praised it.

   2. _____
   USAGE NOTE: Don't confuse *deprecate* with *depreciate*. *Deprecate* more often means "to express disapproval of." *Depreciate* means "to belittle" or "to lower in value."

3. **deride** (dĭ-rīd′) *trans. verb* To laugh at in scorn; scoff at; mock. (From the Latin *de-*, meaning "down," and *ridere*, meaning "to laugh")

   Related Words **derision** *noun;* **derisive** *adjective*
   Example The editorial *derided* those who overuse credit cards in order to appear affluent.

   3. _____

4. **execrable** (ĕk′sĭ-krə-bəl) *adjective* **a.** Extremely inferior; very bad. **b.** Detestable; hateful.

   Related Words **execrableness** *noun;* **execrably** *adverb;* **execrate** *verb*
   Example The Fitzhughs complained about the *execrable* food at the hotel.

   4. _____

5. **ostracize** (ŏs′trə-sīz′) *trans. verb*   To banish or exclude from a group; shun. (From the Greek word *ostrakon*, meaning "a pottery fragment")

   Related Word   **ostracism** *noun*
   Example   When English society *ostracized* them, the Puritans left their homeland and established a colony in New England.

5. _____

6. **rebuke** (rĭ-byōōk′) *trans. verb*   To criticize or reprimand sharply and sternly. *noun*   Words or actions expressing strong disapproval; a scolding.

   Example   The lifeguard *rebuked* the swimmers for going beyond the safety markers.

6. _____

7. **scurrilous** (skûr′ə-ləs) *adjective*   Using or expressed in vulgar and abusive language; foul-mouthed. (From the Latin *scurrilis*, meaning "jeering")

   Related Words   **scurrilously** *adverb*; **scurrilousness** *noun*
   Example   The magazine's political writer was known for his *scurrilous* attacks on local party leaders.

7. _____

8. **spurn** (spûrn) *trans. verb*   To reject or refuse disdainfully. (From the Old English word *spurnan*, meaning "to kick")

   Example   Insistent on proving her strength, Gretchen *spurned* all offers of help and carried the heavy box herself.

8. _____

9. **vitriolic** (vĭt′rē-ŏl′ĭk) *adjective*   Bitterly severe; harsh; sharp.

   Related Word   **vitriol** *noun*
   Example   Hal was unprepared for the *vitriolic* criticism he received from his classmates for his failure to attend the rehearsal.

9. _____

ETYMOLOGY NOTE: *Vitriol* can mean "sulfuric acid," which is highly corrosive; hence, *vitriolic* criticism is scathing.

10. **vituperation** (vī-tōō′pə-rā′shən, vĭ-tōō′pə-rā′shən) *noun*   Sustained and bitter attack or condemnation; blame. (From the Latin word *vitium*, meaning "fault" or "vice")

   Related Word   **vituperative** *adjective*
   Example   The argument eventually deteriorated into angry *vituperation*.

10. _____

EXERCISE 1 WRITING CORRECT WORDS

On the answer line, write the word from the vocabulary list that fits each definition.

1. To laugh at in scorn; mock
2. Using or expressed in vulgar and abusive language
3. To criticize or reprimand sharply; a scolding
4. Bitterly severe; harsh; sharp
5. Extremely inferior; hateful
6. A damaging or false statement; the act of slandering
7. To banish or exclude from a group; shun
8. To reject or refuse disdainfully
9. To express disapproval of; belittle
10. Sustained and bitter attack or condemnation

1. deride
2. scurrilous
3. rebuke
4. vitriolic
5. execrable
6. aspersion
7. ostracize
8. spurn
9. deprecate
10. vituperation

EXERCISE 2 USING WORDS CORRECTLY

Decide whether the italicized vocabulary word has been used correctly in the sentence. On the answer line, write *Correct* for correct use and *Incorrect* for incorrect use.

1. The critic cast *aspersions* on the pianist's ability by praising her performance.
2. Mother *rebuked* Ann for cleaning her own room.
3. The judge *spurned* the bribe offered by the defendant.
4. Wanting to *ostracize* Dana, his club asked him to take the presidency for the next year.
5. When she was younger, Sybil had an *execrable* temper.
6. As a result of *vitriolic* reviews, the play closed after opening night.
7. The other campers *derided* Zack's fear of the dark.
8. People often *deprecate* that which they do not understand.
9. She was pleased by the *vituperation* of her colleagues.
10. A *scurrilous* remark is highly complimentary.

1. Incorrect
2. Incorrect
3. Correct
4. Incorrect
5. Correct
6. Correct
7. Correct
8. Correct
9. Incorrect
10. Incorrect

EXERCISE 3 CHOOSING THE BEST WORD

Decide which vocabulary word or related form best expresses the meaning of the italicized word or phrase in the sentence. On the answer line, write the letter of the correct choice.

1. In Paul Gallico's novel *The Snow Goose,* the artist who lives in an abandoned lighthouse is *shunned* by the townspeople.
   a. rebuked   b. execrated   c. derided   d. ostracized

   1. d

2. Mara's attempts to discredit her coworker were nothing more than *vulgar and abusive* lies.
   a. derisive   b. execrable   c. scurrilous   d. deprecatory

   2. c

3. Although the play was *extremely inferior*, the musical score was captivating.
   a. execrable   b. scurrilous   c. derisive   d. vitriolic

   3. _____ a

4. She is the sort of person who *belittles* her own accomplishments.
   a. deprecates   b. ostracizes   c. rebukes   d. execrates

   4. _____ a

5. The basketball player's *bitterly severe* remarks to the official caused him to be thrown out of the game.
   a. derisive   b. vitriolic   c. execrable   d. spurning

   5. _____ b

6. Robert Fulton's steamboat was so *mocked* that it was called "Fulton's Folly."
   a. derided   b. ostracized   c. spurned   d. rebuked

   6. _____ a

7. "I deserved criticism for my error, but I never expected *bitter condemnation*," said Liam.
   a. derision   b. vituperation   c. execrableness   d. aspersion

   7. _____ b

8. Mrs. Knowlton *sharply reprimanded* Pumpkin for placing muddy paws on the guests' clothing.
   a. ostracized   b. spurned   c. rebuked   d. derided

   8. _____ c

9. Mr. Grehan learned the hard way that it was not wise to cast *damaging or false statements* on a business rival.
   a. ostracisms   b. derisions   c. asperions   d. deprecations

   9. _____ c

10. When their plans were *rejected disdainfully* by the government, the political prisoners began a hunger strike.
    a. spurned   b. rebuked   c. ostracized   d. deprecated

    10. _____ a

EXERCISE 4 USING DIFFERENT FORMS OF WORDS

Decide which form of the vocabulary word in parentheses best completes the sentence. The form given may be correct. Write your answer on the answer line.

1. Marvin's _____ of the lack of school spirit influenced a number of students. (*deprecate*)

   1. _____ deprecation

2. In ancient Greece certain citizens were _____ from society by public vote. (*ostracize*)

   2. _____ ostracized

3. Your _____ remarks deeply hurt my feelings. (*vituperation*)

   3. _____ vituperative

4. _____ laughter greeted Lynn's attempt to imitate a snake. (*deride*)

   4. _____ Derisive

5. The cartoonist cast _____ on this year's fashions. (*aspersion*)

   5. _____ aspersions

6. Mrs. Newhall _____ her son for his continuing lack of good table manners. (*rebuke*)

   6. _____ rebuked

7. The audience behaved _____ at the last lecture. (*execrable*)

   7. _____ execrably

8. The new student _____ all attempts at friendship or kindness. (*spurn*)

   8. _____ spurned

9. "You are a _____ clown," Captain Kidd told his first mate. (*scurrilous*)

   9. _____ scurrilous

10. During the argument Lyle made _____ remarks that he later regretted. (*vitriolic*)

    10. _____ vitriolic

READING COMPREHENSION

Each numbered sentence in the following passage contains an italicized vocabulary word or related form. After you read the passage, you will complete an exercise.

TOULOUSE-LAUTREC: UNCONVENTIONAL ARTIST

Toulouse-Lautrec was one of an important group of French artists who changed the world's way of looking at things. (1)Although *spurned* by the conservatives of his era, his work serves as one of the principal bridges between experimental painting of the nineteenth century and modern art of the twentieth.

Born in 1864 in southern France, Henri Marie Raymond de Toulouse-Lautrec Monfa was the eldest son of an aristocratic family. Henri was expected to enjoy the easy, carefree life of a country squire's son until two accidents put an end to his horseback riding and hunting.

At the ages of thirteen and fourteen, he suffered two major falls that left him an invalid. Confined to bed for months, he soon began to fill sketch pads with pictures of the world around him—galloping horses, seascapes, farm scenes, and portraits of relatives. (2)Although his family originally *deprecated* his talent, they soon realized the importance of art in his life. When bone disease stunted his growth and left him with a grotesque appearance, he refused to participate any longer in the familiar social life. (3)Forced to walk by dragging himself forward with the help of canes, he was often the object of *derision*. It was at this point, in 1881, that his parents agreed to allow him to go to Paris for art instruction.

Henri began his education in the studio of Leon Bonnat, a leading defender of the established traditions in art. Bonnat taught that drawing is a matter of lights and darks arranged to produce convincing depth.

Seventeen-year-old Henri Toulouse-Lautrec saw things differently; for him, art was the translation of a three-dimensional world into a pattern of line and color. Strongly influenced by the daring work of the Impressionists, his work was spontaneous and dramatic, with elaborate networks of line and large, solid areas of color. (4)Bonnat bluntly cast *aspersions* on the drawing of his new student, but Toulouse-Lautrec was not deterred. (5)He was unwilling to copy the standard technique that he considered *execrable*. (6)Ignoring the *rebukes* of his teacher, he maintained his independence and developed his own style.

Henri Toulouse-Lautrec was extremely sensitive about his appearance and handicap. (7)Believing that he was being *ostracized* by Paris society, he moved to the working-class neighborhood of Montmartre, the center of artistic life and a haven for criminals and outcasts. He frequented cafés, theaters, and nightclubs, capturing the spectacle of contemporary life. His drawings soon illustrated newspapers and magazines, and his paintings hung on the walls of local shops and restaurants. In 1891, he became famous when he produced his first poster for the Moulin Rouge, a well-known Parisian nightclub. Toulouse-Lautrec raised the poster to the level of fine art.

The only thing that Toulouse-Lautrec took seriously was art. (8)"So cynical and *scurrilous* on all other occasions," said his friend Edouard Vuillard, also a painter, "he became completely serious when art was mentioned." An extremely hard worker, he carried a sketchbook with him always. He would often do six or eight complete versions of a subject before he was satisfied with the result. Considering the brevity of his career, his output was enormous—500 paintings, more than 350 lithographs and posters, and in excess of 5000 drawings.

(9)Toulouse-Lautrec's physical disability coupled with his unhappiness over the *vituperation* of art critics caused him to lead a reckless life. (10)Disheartened by the *vitriolic* nature of the criticism, he suffered a mental and physical breakdown and died in 1901, two months before his thirty-seventh birthday. As often happens in the world of art, critical opinion changed significantly with the passage of time. Today Henri Toulouse-Lautrec is regarded as an innovator in color printmaking and a genius of original draftmanship.

Each of the following statements corresponds to a numbered sentence in the passage. Each statement contains a blank and is followed by four answer choices. Decide which choice fits best in the blank. The word or phrase that you choose must express roughly the same meaning as the italicized word in the passage. Write the letter of your choice on the answer line.

1. Toulouse-Lautrec was _____ by the conservatives of his era.
   a. well loved **b.** disdainfully rejected **c.** criticized **d.** often ignored

   1. _____ b

2. His family _____ his talent at first.
   a. welcomed **c.** honestly disliked
   b. were astonished by **d.** expressed disapproval of

   2. _____ d

3. Henri was the object of _____ because of his handicap.
   a. general concern **b.** aid **c.** scornful laughter **d.** compassion

   3. _____ c

4. Toulouse-Lautrec's drawing received _____ from his teacher.
   a. damaging comments **b.** poor reviews **c.** compliments **d.** attention

   4. _____ a

5. Toulouse-Lautrec believed that the standard technique was _____.
   a. distinct **b.** authoritative **c.** fashionable **d.** extremely inferior

   5. _____ d

6. He ignored the _____ of his teacher.
   a. reprimands **b.** encouragement **c.** example **d.** suggestions

   6. _____ a

7. Toulouse-Lautrec thought he was _____ by Paris society.
   a. flattered **b.** excluded **c.** hindered **d.** anticipated

   7. _____ b

8. Toulouse-Lautrec was said to be cynical and _____.
   a. excited **b.** self-confident **c.** antagonistic **d.** foul-mouthed

   8. _____ d

9. The artist was unhappy over the art critics' _____.
   a. support **b.** reviews **c.** condemnation **d.** assessment

   9. _____ c

10. He was disheartened by the _____ nature of the criticism.
    a. annoying **b.** bitterly harsh **c.** daring **d.** intensely childish

    10. _____ b

WRITING ASSIGNMENT

Many times in the past, ingenious individuals have devised inventions, created artistic works, or originated ideas that were unacceptable to their contemporaries. Choose one such person, such as Galileo or Robert Fulton, and do some library research about his or her life. Write a report about this person's career and the criticism that he or she received. Use at least five of the words from this lesson and underline them.

VOCABULARY ENRICHMENT

Ostracize comes from the Greek word *ostrakon*, meaning "a piece of broken pottery." In ancient Athens any citizen who was considered by the public to be dangerous or disreputable could be banished for five to ten years through popular vote. Citizens voted for banishment by writing the person's name on a piece of broken pottery. Six thousand of these makeshift ballots were necessary to banish an individual. Although our modern usage of *ostracize* no longer includes the piece of broken pottery, we have retained the ancient idea of exclusion.

Activity Look up the following words in your dictionary, and write their meanings and Latin or Greek roots. Then write an explanation of the connection between each root and its definition.

1. veto 2. precinct 3. politics 4. campaign 5. senate

LESSON 6 WILLINGNESS AND UNWILLINGNESS

6

Three helping one another will do as much as six singly. *(Spanish proverb)*

Many hands make light work. *(English proverb)*

Where there's a will, there's a way. *(English proverb)*

Whatever is borne willingly is borne easily. *(Latin proverb)*

The number of proverbs that encourage willingness seems to indicate widespread agreement about the benefit of this characteristic. As you have probably experienced, the person who offers help freely and gladly is more appreciated and respected than the one who agrees reluctantly to do something. The spirit of cooperation provides an atmosphere in which much can be accomplished. On the other hand, stubborn refusals and inflexibility are attitudes that will likely interfere with the completion of a task. The words in this lesson will help you to understand and express the full range of the willing and unwilling attitudes that you encounter.

DEFINITIONS

After you have studied the definitions and example for each vocabulary word, write the word on the line to the right.

1. **accommodating** (ə-kŏm′ə-dā′tǐng) *adjective* Willing to help; obliging. (From the Latin *ad-*, meaning "to," and *commodus*, meaning "suitable")

   Related Words **accommodate** *verb;* **accommodatingly** *adverb;* **accommodation** *noun*

   Example Mr. Nakashima, the museum curator, was very *accommodating;* he suggested several places where we might find the out-of-print book.

   1. _____
   MEMORY CUE: Remember to use two *c*'s and two *m*'s in spelling *accommodating*.

2. **accord** (ə-kôrd′) *noun* **a.** Agreement; harmony. **b.** A settlement or compromise of conflicting opinions. *trans. verb* To give wholeheartedly; grant readily: *accord praise.* *intrans. verb* To be in agreement, harmony, or unity: *His ideas accord with mine.* (From the Latin *ad-*, meaning "to," and *cor*, meaning "heart")

   Example After many hours of discussion, the members of the executive staff reached *accord* on the subject of automation.

   2. _____
   USAGE NOTE: *Of (one's) own accord* is an idiom meaning "voluntarily" or "without assistance or outside influence."

3. **acquiesce** (ăk′wē-ĕs′) *intrans. verb* To consent or comply passively or without protest; accept. (From the Latin *ad-*, meaning "to," and *quiescere*, meaning "to rest")

   Related Words **acquiescence** *noun;* **acquiescent** *adjective;* **acquiescently** *adverb*

   Example Many residents were surprised when the city manager *acquiesced* to the new zoning proposal for several neighborhoods.

   3. _____
   USAGE NOTE: The verb *acquiesce* is followed by one of two prepositions: *in* or *to*.

4. **adamant** (ăd′ə-mənt, ăd′ə-mănt′) *adjective*   Firm and unyielding in purpose or opinion; inflexible. (From the Greek word *adamas*, meaning "hard metal" or "diamond")

   Related Word   **adamantly** *adverb*
   Example   Gretchen was *adamant* on such matters of principle as arriving exactly seventeen minutes late for a party.

   4. _____

5. **camaraderie** (kä′mə-rä′də-rē, kăm′ə-răd′ə-rē) *noun*   A spirit of loyalty, mutual trust, and good will between or among friends or comrades. (From the French word *camarade*, meaning "comrade")

   Example   Breaking camp and packing up was accomplished quickly and with warm *camaraderie*.

   5. _____

6. **compliance** (kəm-plī′əns) *noun*   **a.** An act of doing as another wishes or yielding to a request or command.   **b.** A tendency to yield to others. (From the Latin word *complere*, meaning "to complete")

   Related Words   **compliant** *adjective*; **comply** *verb*
   Example   A random check of the athletes ensured that they were in *compliance* with the coach's training regulations.

   6. _____

7. **propitiate** (prō-pǐsh′ē-āt′) *trans. verb*   To prevent or reduce the anger of; soothe; appease. (From the Latin word *propitius*, meaning "favorable")

   Related Words   **propitiation** *noun*; **propitiatory** *adjective*
   Example   No amount of apologizing could *propitiate* Aaron, who was furious over having been left behind in the parking lot.

   7. _____

8. **tractable** (trăk′tə-bəl) *adjective*   Easily managed or controlled; docile. (From the Latin word *tractare*, meaning "to manage")

   Example   A small group of children at the birthday party will be more *tractable* than a large group.

   8. _____

9. **volition** (və-lǐsh′ən) *noun*   **a.** An act of willing, choosing, or deciding; power or capability of determining.   **b.** A conscious choice; decision. (From the Latin word *velle*, meaning "to wish")

   Example   Before he could be fired, Randy resigned of his own *volition*.

   9. _____

10. **willfulness** (wĭl′fəl-nĭs) *noun*   **a.** Unreasonable stubbornness.   **b.** The inclination to impose one's will on others. (From the Middle English word *willen*, meaning "to intend to")

    Related Words   **willful** *adjective*; **willfully** *adverb*
    Example   The librarian finally lost patience with the *willfulness* of the spoiled child.

    10. _____
    MEMORY CUE: *Willfulness* is spelled with two *l*'s in *will* but one *l* in *-ful*.

EXERCISE 1 WRITING CORRECT WORDS

On the answer line, write the word from the vocabulary list that fits each definition.

1. An act of doing as another wishes or commands; a tendency to yield to others

2. Agreement; to be in agreement

3. An act of willing, choosing, or deciding; a conscious choice

4. Firm and unyielding in purpose or opinion; inflexible

5. To prevent or reduce the anger of; soothe

6. Willing to help; obliging

7. Easily managed or controlled; docile

8. To consent or comply passively or without protest

9. Unreasonable stubbornness; the inclination to impose one's will on others

10. A spirit of loyalty, mutual trust, and good will between or among friends

1. _____compliance_____
2. _____accord_____
3. _____volition_____
4. _____adamant_____
5. _____propitiate_____
6. _____accommodating_____
7. _____tractable_____
8. _____acquiesce_____
9. _____willfulness_____
10. _____camaraderie_____

EXERCISE 2 USING WORDS CORRECTLY

Each of the following statements contains an italicized vocabulary word. Decide whether the sentence is true or false, and write *True* or *False* on the answer line.

1. When *camaraderie* exists among members of a group, they will not work well together.

2. An *accommodating* guest would probably be on time for meals and would keep his or her room neat.

3. If you *acquiesce* to someone's request, you argue about it loudly and fiercely.

4. A horse is generally thought to be more *tractable* than a mule.

5. If you do something of your own *volition*, you choose to do it.

6. Newspaper articles are written in *compliance* with the conventions of journalistic style.

7. Acting in *accord* with school policy means disregarding rules and regulations.

8. An *adamant* person tends to be flexible and spontaneous.

9. When people are offended, they may sometimes be *propitiated* by kind words.

10. Many people hope that their pets can be trained to exhibit *willfulness*.

1. _____False_____
2. _____True_____
3. _____False_____
4. _____True_____
5. _____True_____
6. _____True_____
7. _____False_____
8. _____False_____
9. _____True_____
10. _____False_____

EXERCISE 3 IDENTIFYING SYNONYMS AND ANTONYMS

Decide which word has the meaning that is the same as (a synonym) or opposite to (an antonym) that of the capitalized vocabulary word. Write the letter of your choice on the answer line.

1. VOLITION (synonym):
   a. extravagance   b. substance   c. choice   d. policy

2. ADAMANT (antonym):
   a. refined   b. yielding   c. enthralling   d. charmed

1. _____c_____

2. _____b_____

3. COMPLIANCE (synonym):
   a. imperfection   b. privilege   c. confidence   d. conformance

4. ACCORD (antonym):
   a. opposition   b. consent   c. torment   d. prominence

5. PROPITIATE (synonym):
   a. encourage   b. recommend   c. soothe   d. provoke

6. ACCOMMODATING (antonym):
   a. appreciative   b. hindering   c. justifying   d. warning

7. WILLFULNESS (synonym):
   a. durability   b. surrender   c. partiality   d. stubbornness

8. TRACTABLE (antonym):
   a. distracting   b. memorable   c. unruly   d. dominant

9. ACQUIESCE (synonym):
   a. consent   b. contemplate   c. differentiate   d. scorn

10. CAMARADERIE (antonym):
    a. atonement   b. evil   c. enmity   d. suspicion

3. ___d___
4. ___a___
5. ___c___
6. ___b___
7. ___d___
8. ___c___
9. ___a___
10. ___c___

EXERCISE 4 USING DIFFERENT FORMS OF WORDS

Decide which form of the vocabulary word in parentheses best completes the sentence. The form given may be correct. Write your answer on the answer line.

1. Your account of the meeting _____ with my recollections of it. (accord)

2. Colin was _____ as a one-year-old but became stubborn when he turned two. (tractable)

3. The new apartment manager tries to _____ the wishes of the tenants. (accommodating)

4. Tim did not make the decision of his own _____; for weeks he was subject to pressure from friends and relatives. (volition)

5. Maria's _____ negative opinion of fiction surprised her English teacher. (adamant)

6. The labor union negotiator practiced his _____ techniques before meeting with management. (propitiate)

7. The staff's _____ enabled its members to function as a team. (camaraderie)

8. The electric company has been charged with _____ negligence in its failure to maintain the underground lines. (willfulness)

9. Terry believed in asking his brother Dwight for a favor when Dwight was in a _____ mood. (compliance)

10. We waited patiently for their _____. (acquiesce)

1. ___accords___
2. ___tractable___
3. ___accommodate___
4. ___volition___
5. ___adamantly___
6. ___propitiatory___
7. ___camaraderie___
8. ___willful___
9. ___compliant___
10. ___acquiescence___

READING COMPREHENSION

Each numbered sentence in the following passage contains an italicized vocabulary word or related form. After you read the passage, you will complete an exercise.

MARIA MITCHELL: AMERICA'S FIRST WOMAN SCIENTIST (1818–1889)

To her contemporaries Maria Mitchell epitomized the contributions that women were able to make in science. In addition to being the only American woman to be internationally recognized and self-supporting in the field of science during the mid-nineteenth century, she was a central force in removing the mystery from science and making it a part of everyday life.

The location of Maria Mitchell's home on Nantucket Island, off the coast of Massachusetts, was an important factor in her decision to become an astronomer. Because most people there made a living in the whaling and fishing industries, nearly everyone studied the sky. Maria Mitchell's father shared the local fascination and introduced his children to his astronomical studies and instruments. (1) Maria learned quickly and, by the age of twelve, was able to *accommodate* the ship captains who brought their chronometers to her father to be regulated. (2) Independent and determined, she studied higher mathematics and navigation and learned to solve problems in trigonometry and geometry of her own *accord.*

In 1835 Maria became the assistant to the local schoolmaster. (3) Conflict soon occurred, however, because she was *adamantly* opposed to the traditional method of teaching. (4) After *willfully* resisting his methods for several months, she opened her own school. Rather than having students learn by memorizing, she taught by lecture and discussion.

Running a school proved to be extremely difficult for Maria Mitchell because she spent each night sweeping the sky with her telescope. Often she would go to class the next day without any sleep. (5) Therefore, when she was offered a job with the Nantucket Atheneum, or library, she *acquiesced.* Although she had little interest in being a librarian, the job required her presence only during the afternoons and on Saturday evenings, giving her time to pursue her observations. She also found the library to be a valuable source of technical books on astronomy and mathematics, as well as the center of the intellectual life of the island. (6) There she enjoyed the *camaraderie* of such writers as Ralph Waldo Emerson and Henry David Thoreau and the women's rights leaders Lucy Stone and Elizabeth Oakes Smith.

On October 1, 1847, Maria Mitchell made the discovery that changed her life. Noticing an unfamiliar shape in the field of her telescope, she conferred with her father, who agreed that she had found a comet. She wanted to wait and clarify her findings, but her father insisted that a report of her discovery be mailed to the director of the observatory at Harvard College immediately. (7) It was fortunate that she *complied;* the letter's postmark later verified her first claim to the discovery that was also made by several other astronomers. This discovery made Mitchell the winner of a gold medal awarded by the King of Denmark and the first woman in the

world to receive such a prize for astronomy.

In 1865 Mitchell was asked to become professor of astronomy at a newly founded women's college, Vassar. She was pleased with the honor but was hesitant about accepting the position. (8) Teaching would mean that she would have to give up, of her own *volition,* the studies of sunspots, nebulae, and satellites that had become the focus of her life. On the other hand, she was also deeply interested in higher education for women. (9) Torn by her conflicting feelings, she accepted the position when the president of the college *propitiated* her with the promise that her influence would encourage young women to compete in fields previously reserved for men.

Maria Mitchell taught at Vassar for twenty-four years, until her death in 1889. (10) She was not the most *tractable* of faculty members. She refused to teach lessons out of books and ignored the college's grading system. Yet she was a superb teacher who stimulated her students' imaginations and allowed them to discover and test ideas on their own.

The last years of Maria Mitchell's life were devoted to the crusade to involve women in science and to bring science into everyday life. The United States' first recognized woman scientist made as many contributions to education as she did to astronomy.

Each of the following statements corresponds to a numbered sentence in the passage. Each statement contains a blank and is followed by four answer choices. Decide which choice fits best in the blank. The word or phrase that you choose must express roughly the same meaning as the italicized word or phrase in the passage. Write the letter of your choice on the answer line.

1. By the age of twelve, Maria was able to _____ the ships' captains by regulating their chronometers.
   a. help   **b.** teach   **c.** ignore   **d.** report to

   1. _____ a _____

2. Maria studied navigation and higher mathematics _____.
   a. with enthusiasm   **b.** timidly   **c.** irregularly   **d.** on her own

   2. _____ d _____

3. Maria was _____ opposed to the traditional method of teaching.
   a. moderately   **b.** thoughtfully   **c.** firmly   **d.** mistakenly

   3. _____ c _____

4. After _____ resisting the schoolmaster's methods, she opened her own school.
   a. almost   **b.** stubbornly   **c.** mysteriously   **d.** simply

   4. _____ b _____

5. When Maria Mitchell was offered a job with the Nantucket Atheneum, she _____.
   a. gratefully accepted   **c.** passively consented
   b. hesitantly debated   **d.** angrily refused

   5. _____ c _____

6. She enjoyed the _____ of writers and women's rights leaders.
   a. spirit of good will   **c.** work
   b. intellectual challenge   **d.** prestige

   6. _____ a _____

7. It was fortunate that Maria Mitchell _____.
   a. did not forget   **c.** ignored the reminder
   b. responded promptly   **d.** yielded to the request

   7. _____ d _____

8. If she taught, she would have to give up her studies _____.
   a. completely   **c.** immediately
   b. of her own free will   **d.** by others' orders

   8. _____ b _____

9. The president of the college _____ her with the promise that she would have an important influence on young women.
   a. persuaded   **b.** honored   **c.** soothed   **d.** upset

   9. _____ c _____

10. Maria Mitchell was not the most _____ of the faculty members at Vassar College.
    a. docile   **b.** dedicated   **c.** stubborn   **d.** popular

    10. _____ a _____

See page 79 for some strategies to use with analogies.

Directions   On the answer line, write the vocabulary word or a form of it that completes each analogy.

1. EXCAVATE : HIDDEN :: _____ : obscure (*Lesson 4*)

   1. _____ explicate _____

2. IRRESISTIBLE : REFUSED :: _____ : explained (*Lesson 4*)

   2. _____ inexplicable _____

3. BRITTLE : BREAK :: _____ : bend (*Lesson 4*)

   3. _____ supple _____

4. DOGGED : SURRENDER :: _____ : yield (*Lesson 6*)

   4. _____ adamant _____

5. UNSTABLE : TOPPLE :: _____ : manage (*Lesson 6*)

   5. _____ tractable _____

6. SOOTHE : PAIN :: _____ : anger (*Lesson 6*)

   6. _____ propitiate _____

The **Test** for Lessons 4, 5, and 6 is on page T4.

TEST-TAKING SKILLS

ANTONYM TEST ITEMS

Many classroom vocabulary tests and some standardized tests contain sections on antonyms. **Antonyms** are words whose meanings are opposite or nearly opposite. Examples are *light* and *dark,* and *prudent* and *negligent.* Often you need to know slight differences in word meanings to answer a test item correctly. The strategies below will assist you in answering antonym test items.

STRATEGIES

1. *Read all of the answer choices and, by a process of elimination, decide which are incorrect.* In vocabulary tests the first likely answer may not be the best choice. Thus, you should read all choices.

2. *Do not be misled by synonyms.* A synonym, a word similar in meaning to the given word, is sometimes listed as an answer. Study the following test item.

   INTRIGUE: (A) detach   (B) fascinate   (C) bore   (D) disparage
   (E) deter

   Intrigue is a verb meaning "to arouse the interest or curiosity of." The second choice, *fascinate,* is a synonym of *intrigue.* If you were hasty in choosing an answer, you might select the synonym instead of an antonym of the given word.

3. *Watch for other misleading choices.* Other misleading choices that you may encounter are words that look or sound like a possible answer. In the sample item above, *detach, deter,* and perhaps even *disparage* have some resemblance. *Deter* is a possible answer, but the other two words are not: *detach* and *disparage* cannot be used in ways that are parallel to the ways in which *intrigue* can be used. A thing can *intrigue* one or *deter* one but not *detach* or *disparage* one.

4. *Choose the word most opposite in meaning to the given word.* A test item can include more than one antonym. The correct answer is the one whose meaning is most nearly opposite to the given word. The sample test item includes two possible antonym answers, *bore* and *deter. Bore* means "to make weary with dullness," while *deter* means "to prevent or discourage from acting." Of the two words, *bore* is more nearly opposite in meaning to *intrigue.*

5. *Use your knowledge of prefixes, suffixes, and roots.* Use your knowledge of word parts and related words to help you guess the meanings of words. Do not guess unless you have a good basis for eliminating one or more answer choices. There is a penalty for wrong answers.

6. *Watch the time.* Do not stop to ponder test items that stump you. Instead, go on to test items that you can answer. If any time remains, you can go back and work on the unanswered questions. Throughout the test you will want to budget your time carefully.

In each of the following items, select the word or phrase that is most nearly opposite in meaning to the word in capital letters. Write the letter of your choice on the answer line. Use your dictionary as needed.

1. ADVERSE: (A) irresponsible   (B) sarcastic   (C) absolute
   (D) favorable   (E) endless

   1. _____ D

2. REFUTE: (A) corroborate   (B) ascribe   (C) vilify
   (D) consume   (E) repudiate

   2. _____ A

3. EFFECTUALLY: (A) cautiously   (B) effortlessly   (C) gaudily
   (D) safely   (E) ineptly

   3. _____ E

4. PROLIFIC: (A) barren   (B) fertile   (C) vibrant   (D) calm
   (E) abundant

   4. _____ A

5. PERIPHERY: (A) locale   (B) nucleus   (C) paradise
   (D) circle   (E) border

   5. _____ B

6. COPIOUS: (A) inconsistent   (B) intrepid   (C) sparse
   (D) repugnant   (E) agile

   6. _____ C

7. EXHILARATE: (A) epitomize   (B) replenish   (C) depress
   (D) debase   (E) alarm

   7. _____ C

8. ETHEREAL: (A) mysterious   (B) cordial   (C) unsophisticated
   (D) concurrent   (E) mundane

   8. _____ E

9. EULOGIZE: (A) digress   (B) emancipate   (C) concoct
   (D) dilute   (E) defame

   9. _____ E

10. IMPREGNABLE: (A) easily captured   (B) not essential
    (C) very foolish   (D) widely understood
    (E) impudently confident

    10. _____ A

11. ORNATE: (A) intense   (B) ostentatious   (C) simple
    (D) elegant   (E) naive

    11. _____ C

12. INSIPID: (A) fearful   (B) stimulating   (C) irate
    (D) simultaneous   (E) dull

    12. _____ B

13. UNSAVORY: (A) wholesome   (B) stupid   (C) tasteless
    (D) handsome   (E) optimistic

    13. _____ A

14. AFFILIATED: (A) disconcerted   (B) allied   (C) innocuous
    (D) potential   (E) dissociated

    14. _____ E

15. ASSERTIVE: (A) confident   (B) bold   (C) enthusiatic
    (D) diffident   (E) lucid

    15. _____ D

16. PROFUSION: (A) paucity   (B) patience   (C) hatred
    (D) priority   (E) presumption

    16. _____ A

17. ODIOUS: (A) tangible   (B) appropriate   (C) agreeable
    (D) ordinary   (E) lyric

    17. _____ C

18. PARSIMONIOUS: (A) poignant   (B) munificent
    (C) preposterous   (D) remunerative   (E) verdant

    18. _____ B

19. OPAQUE: (A) oval   (B) devious   (C) transitional
    (D) transient   (E) transparent

    19. _____ E

20. POTENTIAL: (A) latent   (B) inherent   (C) powerful
    (D) actual   (E) reactionary

    20. _____ D

The root -*spec*-, which can also appear as -*spic*-, means "see" and occurs in many English words. The root comes from the Latin word *specere*, meaning "to see" or "to look." However, many words were borrowed after the association between this root and the idea of sight was lost. Therefore, this root is found in many diverse words in English, including *inspector, respective, spectator, spice,* and *suspect.*

WORD LIST

auspices
auspicious
circumspect
despicable
introspective
perspicuity
prospective
specious
specter
spectrum

DEFINITIONS

After you have studied the definitions and example for each vocabulary word, write the word on the line to the right.

1. **auspices** (ô′spǐ-səz′, ô′spǐ-sēz′) *plural noun*   **a.** Protection or support; patronage. **b.** A portent, omen, or augury, especially when based on the action of birds. (From the Latin words *avis,* meaning "bird," and *specere*)

   1. _____

   Example   The project to clean up the river was begun under the *auspices* of the Environmental Protection Agency.

2. **auspicious** (ô-spǐsh′əs) *adjective*   Attended by favorable circumstances. (From the Latin word *auspicium,* meaning "augury from birds")

   2. _____

   Example   The Romans often looked to the skies to determine whether it was an *auspicious* day for an important undertaking.

3. **circumspect** (sûr′kəm-spĕkt′) *adjective*   Heedful of circumstances or consequences; prudent. (From the Latin *circum-,* meaning "around," and *specere*)

   3. _____

   Related Word circumspectly *adverb*
   Example   The *circumspect* overseas representative carefully observed the customs and laws of all the countries in which he transacted business.

4. **despicable** (dĕs′pǐ-kə-bəl, dǐ-spǐk′ə-bəl) *adjective*   Deserving of scorn or contempt; vile. (From the Latin *de-,* meaning "down," and *specere*)

   4. _____

   Related Words despicably *adverb*; despise *verb*
   Example   The *despicable* woman stole money from her relatives.

5. **introspective** (ĭn′trə-spĕk′tĭv) *adjective*   Self-examining; thinking about one's own thoughts and feelings. (From the Latin words *intro,* meaning "within," and *specere*)

   Related Words   **introspection** *noun;* **introspectively** *adverb*
   Example   In her rare *introspective* moments, the busy woman considered herself to be fortunate.

   5. _____

6. **perspicuity** (pûr′spĭ-kyōō′ĭ-tē) *noun*   **a.** The quality of being clearly expressed or easily understood.   **b.** The ability to perceive or understand keenly. (From the Latin *per-,* meaning "through," and *specere*)

   Related Word   **perspicuous** *adjective*
   Example   The *perspicuity* of the text allowed students to grasp the highly technical subject.

   6. _____

7. **prospective** (prə-spĕk′tĭv) *adjective*   **a.** Likely to become or be: *a prospective client.*   **b.** Likely to happen; expected. (From the Latin *pro-,* meaning "forward," and *specere*)

   Related Word   **prospect** *noun*
   Example   The admissions officer interviewed the *prospective* college student.

   7. _____

   USAGE NOTE: Do not confuse *prospective* with *perspective.* The adjective *perspective* means "of, seen, or represented in perspective."

8. **specious** (spē′shəs) *adjective*   Having the ring of truth but actually false: *a specious statement.* (From the Latin word *species,* meaning "appearance")

   Related Words   **speciously** *adverb;* **speciousness** *noun*
   Example   The scientific paper was filled with *specious* arguments; therefore, many people were against the acceptance of its theory.

   8. _____

9. **specter** (spĕk′tər) *noun*   **a.** A phantom; apparition.   **b.** A threatening or haunting possibility: *the terrible specter of nuclear war.* (From the Latin word *specere*)

   Related Word   **spectral** *adjective*
   Example   In the stories of Edgar Allan Poe, the main characters often see *specters* and hear imagined sounds.

   9. _____

10. **spectrum** (spĕk′trəm) *noun*   **a.** A broad sequence or range of related qualities, ideas, or activities: *the whole spectrum of twentieth-century thought.*   **b.** A range of values of a quantity or set of related quantities. (From the Latin word *specere*)

    Example   The actress showed that she was capable of portraying the entire *spectrum* of human emotions.

    10. _____

EXERCISE 1 WRITING CORRECT WORDS

On the answer line, write the word from the vocabulary list that fits each definition.

1. A broad sequence or range of related qualities, ideas, or activities

2. Self-examining; thinking about one's own thoughts and feelings

3. Having the ring of truth but actually false

4. A phantom; apparition

5. Attended by favorable circumstances

6. Deserving of scorn or contempt; vile

7. Heedful of circumstances or consequences; prudent

8. Protection or support; patronage

9. The quality of being clearly expressed; the ability to perceive keenly

10. Likely to become or be

1. **spectrum**
2. **introspective**
3. **specious**
4. **specter**
5. **auspicious**
6. **despicable**
7. **circumspect**
8. **auspices**
9. **perspicuity**
10. **prospective**

EXERCISE 2 USING WORDS CORRECTLY

Each of the following statements contains an italicized vocabulary word. Decide whether the sentence is true or false, and write *True* or *False* on the answer line.

1. Losing a favorite possession is usually regarded as *auspicious*.

2. *Despicable* behavior is often imitated by people of good character and high standards.

3. A rowdy boy might be described as making a *specter* of himself.

4. Talented actors are able to portray the complete *spectrum* of emotion.

5. Journals often record one's *introspective* thoughts and feelings, as well as one's daily activities.

6. Research is often conducted under the *auspices* of the federal government.

7. If you wished to manage your money in a *circumspect* manner, you would probably make risky investments with characters who have shady reputations.

8. Consumer advocates attempt to protect the public from the *specious* claims of advertisers.

9. Instructions for assembling complicated equipment ought to be written with *perspicuity*.

10. A person who regularly browses at the same store might be regarded as a *prospective* customer.

1. **False**
2. **False**
3. **False**
4. **True**
5. **True**
6. **True**
7. **False**
8. **True**
9. **True**
10. **True**

EXERCISE 3 CHOOSING THE BEST DEFINITION

For each italicized vocabulary word in the following sentences, write the letter of the best definition on the answer line.

1. The politician was happy to make a speech on the *auspicious* occasion.
   a. famous
   b. important
   c. attended by favorable circumstances
   d. attended by unfavorable circumstances

1. **c**

2. The *specious* conclusions of Rebecca's essay on Mark Twain were not supported by the quotations that she used.
   a. unacceptable   **c.** impressive and intelligent
   b. silly   **d.** attractive but inaccurate

2. _____ d

3. Thoreau's solitary existence at Walden Pond provided him with opportunities for careful observation of nature as well as *introspective* reflection.
   a. selfish   **b.** selfless   **c.** self-examining   **d.** self-confident

3. _____ c

4. In Victorian times the *circumspect* suitor was accompanied by a chaperone when in the company of a young woman.
   a. prudent   **b.** romantic   **c.** from the privileged class   **d.** uncertain

4. _____ a

5. Shakespeare's sonnets explore the *spectrum* of human experience from romantic love to death.
   a. changes   **b.** wide range   **c.** destiny   **d.** emotions

5. _____ b

6. P. T. Barnum's business was to discover and promote the kind of spectacles that *prospective* audiences would pay to see.
   a. easily impressed   **b.** possible future   **c.** critical   **d.** enthusiastic

6. _____ b

7. The world was shocked at the *despicable* crimes perpetrated by the Third Reich during World War II.
   a. memorable   **b.** unmentionable   **c.** extraordinary   **d.** vile

7. _____ d

8. The children were not permitted to engage in many activities while they were under the *auspices* of the orphanage.
   a. complete authority   **b.** investigation   **c.** protection   **d.** roof

8. _____ c

9. The *specter* of widespread famine was publicized by the relief agency.
   a. terrible possibility   **b.** remote change   **c.** reality   **d.** continuation

9. _____ a

10. *Perspicuity* in writing is improved by the use of vivid verbs and exact modifiers.
    a. Impressiveness   **c.** A convincing style
    b. Clearness of expression   **d.** Descriptiveness

10. _____ b

EXERCISE 4 USING DIFFERENT FORMS OF WORDS

Decide which form of the vocabulary word in parentheses best completes the sentence. The form given may be correct. Write your answer on the answer line.

1. Thomas Paine boldly challenged British rule in his _____ pamphlet "Common Sense." *(perspicuity)*

1. _____ perspicuous

2. _____ analysis is a method used by chemists to identify the elements in a compound. *(spectrum)*

2. _____ Spectrum

3. Sam was delighted at the _____ of visiting his relatives for the holiday. *(prospective)*

3. _____ prospect

4. The ancient Chinese regarded eclipses as _____ events. *(auspicious)*

4. _____ auspicious

5. Horror films frequently make use of _____ to frighten audiences. *(specter)*

5. _____ specters

6. Having been advised by his doctor that his blood pressure was high and that he needed to lose thirty pounds, Mr. Cutler began to eat more _____. *(circumspect)*

6. _____ circumspectly

7. Volunteers who aided the famine victims worked under the _____ of a worldwide relief agency. *(auspices)*

7. _____ auspices

8. Anne's sea voyage gave her ample time for _____. *(introspective)*

8. _____ introspection

9. The legendary rivalry between the Hatfields and the McCoys was so strong that even the children were taught to _____ one another. *(despicable)*

9. _____ despise

10. The _____ of Renée's argument was even more difficult to detect because of the calm and rational way in which she presented it. *(specious)*

10. _____ speciousness

READING COMPREHENSION

Each numbered sentence in the following passage contains an italicized vocabulary word or related form. After you read the passage, you will complete an exercise.

THE LANGUAGE OF GESTURE AND POSE

Human beings usually communicate with one another through spoken and written language. (1)Yet, there is another form of communication that often enables us to send *perspicuous* nonverbal messages. This form of communication is achieved through gesture and pose and is often called "body language." (2)Body language communicates the entire *spectrum* of human responses and emotions, from warmth to coolness and from aggressiveness to passiveness. (3)A great deal of psychological research, conducted under the *auspices* of both profit-making and non-profit organizations, has helped us to understand this language.

Some forms of body language are extremely common and very easily understood. These include nodding our heads to answer yes, tapping our feet to signal impatience, and throwing our hands into the air to express exasperation. (4)We reserve other types of body language for more important or *auspicious* occasions. Gestures and poses that we use to communicate respect, gratitude, and sincerity include bowing our heads,

delivering a firm handshake, and standing at perfect attention.

Some types of body language serve as accompaniments to regular, verbal communication. (5)A typical response to seeing something as frightening as an apparent *specter* would be not only a scream but also a jump backward, a visible tensing of muscles, or a rapid movement of our hands to our heads.

A common interpretation of body language lies in the contrast of open and folded arm positions. Respectively, these positions signal friendliness and defensiveness. (6)If we habitually cross our arms, we may find ourselves perceived as unfriendly or threatening, or even as *despicable*. On the other hand, extending our arms in an open gesture is a way of signaling friendliness or readiness. (7)Job interviewers often note arm and other bodily movements in order to gauge a *prospective* employee's receptiveness to their ideas.

Walking styles can also communicate messages. (8)We have all seen the controlled and measured walk of a person who is trying to appear dig-

nified and *circumspect*. (9)People who are concentrating on a problem or who are feeling *introspective* tend to walk slowly, with their heads down and their hands clasped behind their backs. The more ambitious and motivated person moves rapidly, with hands swinging freely from side to side. Those who walk with their hands in their pockets tend to be critical of others.

Some forms of body language are less easily interpreted. We might hastily conclude that a person who is sitting upright with his or her head directed toward a speaker and muscles taut is paying close attention. (10)However, this interpretation would be *specious*, as this posture most commonly hides a wandering mind. True signs of attention include a slightly tilted head, a chin resting on a hand, and leaning forward in a seat.

The language of gesture and pose can be simple or complex, crude or elegant. However, no matter what its form, it helps us not only to understand one another but to put verbal messages into the perspective of the total communication process.

READING COMPREHENSION EXERCISE

Each of the following statements corresponds to a numbered sentence in the passage. Each statement contains a blank and is followed by four answer choices. Decide which choice fits best in the blank. The word or phrase that you choose must express roughly the same meaning as the italicized word in the passage. Write the letter of your choice on the answer line.

1. Body language enables us to send _____ nonverbal messages.
   a. subconscious   b. clearly expressed   c. complex   d. simple

1. _____b_____

2. Through body language we can express the entire _____ of human responses and emotions.
   a. process   b. range   c. output   d. sequence

2. _____b_____

3. Research conducted under the _____ of many organizations has helped us to understand this language.
   a. sponsorship
   b. trusteeship
   c. political agendas
   d. careful guidance

3. _____a_____

4. We reserve other types of body language for occasions that are _____.
   a. festive
   b. solemn
   c. attended by favorable circumstances
   d. attended by unfavorable circumstances

4. _____c_____

5. A typical response to a(n) _____ could include both a scream and a jump backward.
   a. accident   b. fire   c. frightening event   d. phantom

5. _____d_____

6. Habitual arm-crossers may be perceived as _____.
   a. deserving of scorn
   b. deserving of pity
   c. critical
   d. highly motivated

6. _____a_____

7. Job interviewers "read" body language in order to gauge a _____ employee's attitudes.
   a. current   b. potential   c. part-time   d. white-collar

7. _____b_____

8. A controlled and measured walk is typical of a person who is trying to appear _____.
   a. important   b. dignified   c. honest   d. prudent

8. _____d_____

9. _____ people tend to walk slowly, with their heads down and their hands clasped behind their backs.
   a. Interesting   b. Antisocial   c. Self-conscious   d. Self-examining

9. _____d_____

10. Some arguments about body language are _____.
    a. apparently false but actually true
    b. apparently true but actually false
    c. not proven
    d. not logical

10. _____b_____

WRITING ASSIGNMENT

On important occasions, such as weddings and graduations, we often both display and witness a broad range of behaviors. Think back to an important occasion, and describe it to a friend who was not present. Use at least five of the words from this lesson to describe both the event and the various ways in which people reacted to it. Underline each vocabulary word that you use.

LESSON 8 ABILITY AND INABILITY

I t is easy to be awed by the ballerina who leaps, seemingly effortlessly, across the stage, or by the quarterback who throws, with perfect accuracy, a seventy-yard touchdown pass to the only open receiver. It seems as if these performers have been graced with natural and perfect ability. Yet ability is usually a combination of talent and perseverance, just as inability may result as much from lack of effort as from lack of natural gifts. The words in this lesson will help you to understand the types and degrees of ability and inability.

WORD LIST

acuity
consummate
cunning
deft
endowment
facile
incompetent
inept
proficient
propensity

DEFINITIONS

After you have studied the definitions and example for each vocabulary word, write the word on the line to the right.

1. **acuity** (ə-kyōō′ĭ-tē) *noun*   Acuteness of perception; keenness (From the Latin word *acus*, meaning "needle")

   Related Word   **acute** *adjective*
   Example   The eagle's visual *acuity* enabled it to hunt successfully.

   1. _____

2. **consummate** (kən-sŭm′ĭt) *adjective*   **a.** Supremely accomplished or skilled: *a consummate entertainer.*   **b.** Complete or perfect in every respect: *a consummate happiness.*   **c.** Complete; utter: *a consummate bore.* (From the Latin *com-*, meaning "together," and *summa*, meaning "a sum")

   Related Word   **consummately** *adverb*
   Example   The *consummate* pianist made a world-renowned recording of the sonata.

   2. _____

3. **cunning** (kŭn′ĭng) *noun*   **a.** Skill or adeptness in performance; dexterity.   **b.** Skill in deception; guile.   *adjective*   **a.** Shrewd or crafty in manipulation or deception.   **b.** Executed with or exhibiting ingenuity. (From the Old English word *cunnan*, meaning "to know")

   Related Word   **cunningly** *adverb*
   Example   His *cunning* manipulation of the props and lights helped to make the performance spectacular.

   3. _____

4. **deft** (dĕft) *adjective*   Skillful; adroit.

   Related Words   **deftly** *adverb*; **deftness** *noun*
   Example   The *deft* weavers in Iran produce beautiful and intricate carpets.

   4. _____

5. **endowment** (ĕn-dou'mənt) *noun* **a.** A natural gift or quality. **b.** Funds or property donated to an institution, individual, or group as a source of income.

5. _____

Related Word endow *verb*
Example Climbers must have a great *endowment* of courage to conquer a mountain.

6. **facile** (făs'əl) *adjective* **a.** Done or achieved with little effort or difficulty; easy. **b.** Working, acting, or speaking effortlessly; fluent: *a facile speaker.* **c.** Arrived at without due care, effort, or examination; superficial. (From the Latin word *facilis,* meaning "easy")

6. _____

Related Words facilely *adverb;* **facileness** *noun*
Example The pole-vaulter was able to negotiate the high bar in a graceful, seemingly *facile* manner.

7. **incompetent** (ĭn-kŏm'pĭ-tənt) *adjective* **a.** Not capable; not properly or well qualified. **b.** Not adequate for the purpose; not sufficient: *an incompetent performance.* *noun* A person who is not capable or qualified for a particular task. (From the Latin *in-,* meaning "not," and *competere,* meaning "to be suitable")

7. _____

Related Words incompetence *noun;* **incompetently** *adverb*
Example The capable surgeon proved to be *incompetent* as a hospital administrator because he had no previous experience or training in management.

8. **inept** (ĭn-ĕpt') *adjective* **a.** Awkward or clumsy. **b.** Not suitable to the circumstances or occasion; inappropriate. **c.** Lacking in judgment, sense, or reason; foolish. (From the Latin *in-,* meaning "not," and *aptus,* meaning "suitable")

8. _____

Related Words ineptly *adverb;* **ineptness** *noun*
Example The *inept* cook splattered the walls of the kitchen with cake batter.

9. **proficient** (prə-fĭsh'ənt) *adjective* Performing in a given art, skill, or branch of learning with expert correctness and facility; adept. (From the Latin *pro-,* meaning "forward," and *facere,* meaning "to do")

9. _____

Related Words proficiency *noun;* **proficiently** *adverb*
Example The *proficient* programmer learned the new computer language in a very short time.

10. **propensity** (prə-pĕn'sĭ-tē) *noun* An innate inclination; tendency. (From the Latin *pro-,* meaning "forward," and *pendere,* meaning "to hang")

10. _____

Example The painter had an artistic *propensity* even as a youngster.

Word History: acuity

Latin: *acus*=needle

Visual *acuity* refers to the keenness or sharpness of your eyesight. The term *acuity* comes from the Latin word *acus,* meaning "needle," and suggests the characteristics of a needle. Think of a sleek, smooth needle whose slender body ends in a sharply pointed tip. By visualizing the needle's shape, you can *acutely* appreciate the point of this discussion.

EXERCISE 1 WRITING CORRECT WORDS

On the answer line, write the word from the vocabulary list that fits each definition.

1. An innate inclination; a tendency

2. Done with little effort or difficulty

3. Acuteness of perception; keenness

4. Skill or adeptness in performance; dexterity

5. Performing in an art, skill, or branch of learning with expert correctness

6. Skillful; adroit

7. Not capable; not properly or well qualified

8. Supremely accomplished or skilled

9. A natural gift or quality

10. Awkward or clumsy

1. propensity
2. facile
3. acuity
4. cunning
5. proficient
6. deft
7. incompetent
8. consummate
9. endowment
10. inept

EXERCISE 2 USING WORDS CORRECTLY

Each of the following statements contains an italicized vocabulary word. Decide whether the sentence is true or false, and write *True* or *False* on the answer line.

1. A director of a Broadway play would be be eager to hire as many *incompetent* stagehands as possible.

2. The post office might request that dogs having a *propensity* for biting people be restrained during mail delivery hours.

3. Through *cunning* and deviousness, a person might trick someone else into believing a false story.

4. People dread eating food prepared by a *consummate* cook.

5. *Deft* violinists usually play off-key.

6. Many people feel *inept* when first learning to knit or crochet.

7. Economists must read with *acuity* the subtle signs that indicate inflation and recovery.

8. When doctors fail to give an examination or consider all the symptoms, they are guilty of giving a *facile* diagnosis.

9. Interpreters who work at the United Nations must be *proficient* in two or more languages.

10. A generous *endowment* might enable a library to purchase a computer and to update its reference section.

1. False
2. True
3. True
4. False
5. False
6. True
7. True
8. True
9. True
10. True

EXERCISE 3 CHOOSING THE BEST WORD

Decide which vocabulary word or related form best expresses the meaning of the italicized word or phrase in the sentence. On the answer line, write the letter of the correct choice.

1. After ten years of accordion lessons, Dawn had become an *expert* player, and she could now teach beginning students.
   a. incompetent   b. inept   c. facile   d. proficient

1. d

2. A *highly skilled* writer, Ernest Hemingway is said to have spent hours perfecting short passages of his prose.
   a. facile **b.** cunning **c.** consummate **d.** acute

   2. _____c_____

3. *Keenness of perception* about events in nature helped Isaac Newton to formulate laws about physical occurrences.
   a. Endowment **b.** Acuity **c.** Ineptness **d.** Propensity

   3. _____b_____

4. The *effortless manner* with which calligraphers form graceful, beautiful letters comes after hours of tedious practice.
   a. facileness **b.** endowment **c.** propensity **d.** incompetence

   4. _____a_____

5. Melissa felt *awkward and clumsy* when it came to performing on the balance beam and parallel bars.
   a. inept **b.** deft **c.** proficient **d.** facile

   5. _____a_____

6. The robber's *skill in deception* allowed him to escape the police for months before he was finally arrested.
   a. cunning **b.** incompetence **c.** acuity **d.** ineptness

   6. _____a_____

7. Philosophers have long debated whether people have a *natural inclination* toward evil or toward good.
   a. endowment **b.** propensity **c.** proficiency **d.** acuity

   7. _____b_____

8. During the final laps, Fred wished that he had a greater *natural gift* of speed and endurance
   a. propensity **b.** acuity **c.** endowment **d.** deftness

   8. _____c_____

9. So *skillful* was Fagan's best pickpocket in the book *Oliver Twist* that he was called the "Artful Dodger."
   a. acute **b.** incompetent **c.** inept **d.** deft

   9. _____d_____

10. The *unqualified* waitress spilled soup on my dress and overcharged me for my dinner.
    a. proficient **b.** facile **c.** incompetent **d.** deft

    10. _____c_____

EXERCISE 4 USING DIFFERENT FORMS OF WORDS

Decide which form of the vocabulary word in parentheses best completes the sentence. The form given may be correct. Write your answer on the answer line.

1. Many colleges waive requirements for first-year students who demonstrate their _____ by passing an examination in the subject area. *(proficient)*

   1. _____proficiency_____

2. Switch hitters in baseball must develop a degree of _____ in order to be able to bat well on either side. *(cunning)*

   2. _____cunning_____

3. Dr. Christiaan Barnard's _____ in surgery was of prime importance in the first successful heart transplant. *(deft)*

   3. _____deftness_____

4. It was an _____ written letter, riddled with misspellings and omissions. *(incompetent)*

   4. _____incompetently_____

5. Because earthwork dams have _____ both for erosion and for instability during earthquakes, they are considered unreliable. *(propensity)*

   5. _____propensities_____

6. To succeed in professional basketball, one must be _____ with height and quick reflexes. *(endowment)*

   6. _____endowed_____

7. On their golden wedding anniversary, the couple described their marriage as _____ happy. *(consummate)*

   7. _____consummately_____

50 Ability and Inability

8. The _____ of the laboratory technician resulted in an incorrect reading of the x-rays. *(inept)*

9. _____ appendicitis was the doctor's diagnosis. *(acute)*

10. Ms. Howell moved _____ among her roles as mother, editor, and musician. *(facile)*

8. _____**ineptness**_____

9. _____**Acute**_____

10 _____**facilely**_____

READING COMPREHENSION

Each numbered sentence in the following passage contains an italicized vocabulary word or related form. After you read the passage, you will complete an exercise.

HORSE SHOW JUMPING

The idea of racing horses over hurdles probably originated in 1821 in England, when the Prince Regent and his friends decided to ride their horses in and out of sheep pens by jumping over the fences. This "sport" took a while to catch on, but today one of the fastest-growing spectator sports in the United States is horse show jumping. **(1)**Nowhere else can one see such *deft* and thrilling performances of horses and rider. **(2)**By offering large prizes and a chance for equestrian fame, show-jumping events attract the most *proficient* national and international competitors.

Demonstrating skill and power, horse and rider face sixteen or seventeen huge fences with five-foot heights and five- to six-foot widths. Their spectacular efforts to clear these nearly insurmountable obstacles always involve the elements of danger and risk. **(3)**An *inept* leap or sudden stumble can spell immediate disaster.

The scoring principle of show jumping is simple. **(4)**The horse's sole task is to clear the fences without knocking them down; whether a horse exhibits a *facile* jumping style is not important. **(5)**If a horse knocks over a rail, refuses stubbornly to jump an obstacle, or otherwise displays its *incompetence*, it incurs penalty faults. A knockdown is worth four faults and a refusal three. The horse with the lowest number of faults is the winner. Sometimes two or more horses earn the same number of faults, which results in a timed jump-off. **(6)**Because horses have a *propensity* for carelessness when they go faster, the jump-off against the clock is a true test of accuracy and talent.

(7) While thousands of equestrians strive to become successful show-jumping riders, only those with an ample *endowment* of athletic ability ever achieve their dreams. **(8)**This technical branch of horseback riding demands outstanding balance and subtle *cunning*. **(9)**Equally important is visual *acuity* combined with a perfect sense of timing, both of which enable the rider to judge precisely the distances in front of and between fences. Finally, all successful show-jumping riders must possess great courage and aggressiveness to negotiate without fear a course of towering walls, imposing triple combinations, and massive embankments. **(10)**These *consummate* riders, in partnership with their daring and responsive mounts, have the means to excite and impress a crowd. They are rapidly gaining popularity among spectators in the United States.

Each of the following statements corresponds to a numbered sentence in the passage. Each statement contains a blank and is followed by four answer choices. Decide which choice fits best in the blank. The word or phrase that you choose must express roughly the same meaning as the italicized word in the passage. Write the letter of your choice on the answer line.

1. The horse and rider put on a thrilling and _____ performance.
   a. daring   b. exciting   c. skillful   d. entertaining

1. _____ c _____

2. The most _____ riders participate in show-jumping competitions.
   a. competent   b. courageous   c. athletic   d. famous

2. _____ a _____

3. A single _____ leap or stumble can be disastrous.
   a. unexpected   b. poorly timed   c. awkward   d. misjudged

3. _____ c _____

4. A(n) _____ jumping style is not a factor in the scoring.
   a. attractive   c. effortlessly achieved
   b. competent   d. athletic

4. _____ c _____

5. A penalty is incurred every time a horse displays its _____.
   a. breeding   b. personality   c. adeptness   d. lack of ability

5. _____ d _____

6. When a horse gallops fast, it has a(n) _____ to make mistakes.
   a. tendency   b. opportunity   c. chance   d. ability

6. _____ a _____

7. Riders must possess a great _____ of athletic ability.
   a. portion   b. natural gift   c. amount   d. abundance

7. _____ b _____

8. The most successful riders exhibit extraordinary _____.
   a. balance when jumping   c. skill and adeptness
   b. communication with horses   d. response when galloping

8. _____ c _____

9. A rider needs visual _____ to judge distances accurately.
   a. assistance   c. ability
   b. awareness of the field   d. acuteness

9. _____ d _____

10. Audiences know that show-jumping riders are _____ equestrians.
    a. supremely skilled   c. expertly trained
    b. notoriously incompetent   d. aggressive

10. _____ a _____

Imagine that you are a journalist assigned to cover local rock performances for the arts section of the Sunday newspaper. For a single performance only, your favorite group is appearing in town. In your review present the highlights of the concert, and compare and contrast this concert with others that you have attended. Use at least five of the words from this lesson in your review and underline each one.

The **Bonus activity** for Lessons 5–8 is on page T6.

Requests and demands are among the commonplaces of daily life. They range from a toddler's innocent plea for a drink of water to the IRS's ultimatum to file by April 15. For those who ignore what is being asked, the polite request can quickly become an insistent demand. Also, learning to distinguish what is being asked from how and why it is being asked is an important skill. The words in this lesson will help you to understand the nature of demands and requests.

WORD LIST

beseech
blandishment
cajole
elicit
enjoin
exigent
imperious
injunction
mendicant
query

DEFINITIONS

After you have studied the definitions and example for each vocabulary word, write the word on the line to the right.

1. **beseech** (bǐ-sēch') *trans. verb* **a.** To address an earnest or urgent request to; implore. **b.** To request earnestly; beg for.

   Example I *beseech* you to see a doctor before your illness gets worse.

   1. _____

2. **blandishment** (blǎn'dǐsh-mənt) *noun* The act of coaxing by flattery or wheedling. (From the Latin word *blandus*, meaning "flattering")

   Related Word blandish *verb*
   Example Although she smiled at his *blandishments*, she didn't believe a word he said.

   2. _____

3. **cajole** (kə-jōl') *trans. verb* To coax gently and persistently; wheedle.

   Related Words cajolery *noun*; cajoling *adverb*
   Example To *cajole* her mother into buying the skates, Amanda told her mother that she was the best parent in the neighborhood.

   3. _____

4. **elicit** (ǐ-lǐs'ǐt) *trans. verb* **a.** To bring out; evoke. **b.** To call forth. (From the Latin *ex-*, meaning "out," and *lacere*, meaning "to entice")

   Example Benjamin Franklin *elicited* the assistance of France for the Colonial army during the Revolutionary War.

   4. _____
   USAGE NOTE: *Elicit* and *illicit* are often confused. *Illicit* means "illegal."

5. **enjoin** (ěn-join') *trans. verb* **a.** To direct with authority and emphasis; command. **b.** To prohibit or forbid.

   Example The director of the school *enjoined* her staff to be more aware of the needs of the gifted children.

   5. _____

6. **exigent** (ĕk′sə-jənt) *adjective*   **a.** Requiring immediate attention or remedy; urgent. **b.** Requiring or demanding a great deal. (From the Latin word *exigere*, meaning "to demand")

   Related Words   exigency *noun;* **exigently** *adverb*
   Example   His *exigent* call for help brought people to his assistance.

7. **imperious** (ĭm-pîr′ē-əs) *adjective*   Arrogantly domineering or overbearing. (From the Latin word *imperare*, meaning "to command")

   Related Words   imperiously *adverb;* **imperiousness** *noun*
   Example   Commanding and *imperious*, the president ordered his press secretary to deny all requests for information and interviews.

8. **injunction** (ĭn-jŭngk′shən) *noun*   **a.** A command, directive, or order.   **b.** A court order enjoining or prohibiting a party from a specific course of action. (From the Latin word *injungere*, meaning "to enjoin")

   Example   The serfs were forced to obey any *injunction* made by the lord of the castle.

9. **mendicant** (mĕn′dĭ-kənt) *noun*   A beggar.   *adjective*   Depending upon alms for a living; practicing begging. (From the Latin word *mendicare*, meaning "to beg")

   Related Word   mendicancy *noun*
   Example   When the *mendicant* held out her hand to ask me for money, I saw how tattered the sleeves of her blouse and jacket were.

10. **query** (kwîr′ē) *noun*   **a.** A question; inquiry.   **b.** A doubt in the mind. *trans. verb*   **a.** To express doubt or uncertainty about; question.   **b.** To put a question to. (From the Latin word *quaerere*, meaning "to ask")

    Example   In response to his *query* about tropical vegetation, the librarian gave him a reference book and told him what to look up.

6. ———————

7. ———————

8. ———————

9. ———————

10. ———————

EXERCISE 1 MATCHING WORDS AND DEFINITIONS

Match the definition in Column B with the word in Column A. Write the letter of the correct definition on the answer line.

Column A

1. mendicant
2. imperious
3. enjoin
4. elicit
5. exigent
6. injunction
7. blandishment
8. beseech
9. cajole
10. query

Column B

a. the act of coaxing by flattery
b. to direct with authority
c. to address an earnest request to; implore
d. a command, directive, or order
e. a beggar
f. to bring out; evoke
g. a question or inquiry
h. arrogantly domineering or overbearing
i. urgent; requiring prompt action
j. to coax gently and persistently

1. e
2. h
3. b
4. f
5. i
6. d
7. a
8. c
9. j
10. g

EXERCISE 2 USING WORDS CORRECTLY

Decide whether the italicized vocabulary word has been used correctly in the sentence. On the answer line, write *Correct* for correct use and *Incorrect* for incorrect use.

1. Granite is cut in large blocks from a nearby *query*.
2. The wolf frightened Little Red Riding Hood with the *blandishment* of its teeth.
3. The department store does not allow people to *enjoin* money on its premises.
4. The veterinarian could not *elicit* any kind of response from the sleeping cat.
5. Anita's *imperious* attitude alienated many people who did not like to be told what to do.
6. The cab driver tried to *cajole* the police officer out of giving him a parking ticket.
7. Lance is waiting for us at the *injunction* of Highways 93 and 128.
8. David befriended the *mendicant* by greeting him each morning.
9. Steve, this is truly an *exigent* dinner that you have fixed.
10. Aunt Helena *beseeched* her entire fortune to the heart fund.

1. Incorrect
2. Incorrect
3. Incorrect
4. Correct
5. Correct

6. Correct
7. Incorrect
8. Correct
9. Incorrect
10. Incorrect

EXERCISE 3 CHOOSING THE BEST WORD

Decide which vocabulary word or related form best expresses the meaning of the italicized word or phrase in the sentence. On the answer line, write the letter of the correct choice.

1. My father warned me not to try to *coax or wheedle* him into letting me go to the movie tonight.
   a. elicit   b. cajole   c. enjoin   d. beseech

   1. b

2. Harry has sent an *inquiry* about the job that the computer store is offering.
   a. exigency   b. query   c. blandishment   d. injunction

   2. b

3. Be gentle with my rusty old car, I *implore* you.
  a. elicit **b.** cajole **c.** blandish **d.** beseech

3. _____ d

4. Mayor Thatcher emphasized that the need for an improved waste removal system was *urgent*.
  a. exigent **b.** cajoled **c.** imperious **d.** beseeched

4. _____ a

5. The coach *commanded* Mickey to apologize to the referee.
  a. cajoled **b.** blandished **c.** queried **d.** enjoined

5. _____ d

6. The *beggar* in the fairy tale turned out to be a prince.
  a. mendicant **b.** blandishment **c.** cajolery **d.** injunction

6. _____ a

7. Now, Joan, you know you can't change my mind with such *coaxing by flattery*.
  a. blandishments **b.** queries **c.** imperiousness **d.** injunctions

7. _____ a

8. Reading Robert Frost always *calls forth* fond memories of Mrs. DeHart's ninth grade English class.
  a. enjoins **b.** elicits **c.** cajoles **d.** blandishes

8. _____ b

9. The city supervisor issued a *directive* to keep the parks open all year round.
  a. blandishment **b.** injunction **c.** query **d.** mendicants

9. _____ b

10. The supervisor shouted in an *arrogant* manner that there was to be no more tardiness.
  a. mendicant **b.** cajoling **c.** imperious **d.** beseeching

10. _____ c

EXERCISE 4 USING DIFFERENT FORMS OF WORDS

Each sentence contains an italicized vocabulary word in a form that does not fit the sentence. On the answer line, write the form of the word that does fit the sentence.

1. During the last practice, the coach *enjoin* us to continue our diets and to keep sensible hours.

1. _____ enjoined

2. *Beseech* the television audience for aid to Africa, the appeal showed scenes of suffering.

2. _____ Beseeching

3. When she was a newspaper reporter, Irene frequently *query* city officials.

3. _____ queried

4. Many Buddhist monks depend on *mendicant* to obtain food and clothing.

4. _____ mendicancy

5. *Injunction* were issued to stop the strike.

5. _____ Injunctions

6. "Will you stop sitting there and help me find my purse?" Alison asked me *imperious*.

6. _____ imperiously

7. The *exigent* of an imminent flood demanded split-second decision making.

7. _____ exigency

8. By skillfully *elicit* the students' ideas, the teacher made the class discussion lively.

8. _____ eliciting

9. Ginny asked me *cajole* if I would take her to the concert.

9. _____ cajolingly

10. Pablo's assistant, who mistakenly thinks he can manipulate Pablo into promoting him, frequently *blandishment* Pablo.

10. _____ blandishes

READING COMPREHENSION

Each numbered sentence in the following passage contains an italicized vocabulary word or related form. After you read the passage, you will complete an exercise.

ODYSSEUS' HOMECOMING

When the early Greeks went to war, they usually left their wives and children at home anxiously awaiting their return. No wife waited longer or more faithfully than Penelope, wife of Odysseus, nor was any son more eager for his father's return than Telemachus.

Odysseus fought in the Trojan War for ten years and helped destroy Troy. However, the Greeks, in their glory over victory, neglected to thank the gods, and the gods were determined to punish them for that error. (1) Furthermore, Ajax, a Greek warrior, grievously mistreated the priestess Cassandra by dragging her from Athena's temple while she was *beseeching* the goddess for protection. (2) The *imperiousness* of this action, coupled with the failure of the other Greeks to condemn it, made Athena doubly determined to seek vengeance. She asked Poseidon, god of the sea, to wreak havoc on the returning Greeks. Odysseus' punishment was to be blown off course for ten more years before returning home; therefore, Penelope had to wait twenty years for his return, and Telemachus spent his entire youth without a father.

(3) When Ithaca had been without a king for more than ten years, many suitors came to the beautiful Penelope with *blandishments*, seeking to marry her and become king, but she refused. (4) One by one they *cajoled* her, but she remained hopeful that Odysseus would return. So persistent were the suitors, however, that she knew she must resort to tactics to stall them. (5) Therefore, she issued an *injunction:* she would not remarry until she had finished weaving a shroud for Odysseus' aged father. This was a noble purpose, and even impatient suitors had to accept it.

The suitors moved into the palace to await her decision. Refusing to leave, they daily drank Odysseus' wine and killed his cattle for food. Each day Penelope worked at her weaving, and each night she unraveled what she had woven. (6) Whenever the suitors *queried* her about her progress, she told them that she needed a little more time. (7) Finally, the suitors discovered her trick and, angered, they became more insistent than ever, relentlessly *enjoining* her to choose a new king. (8) Penelope and Telemachus fully realized the *exigency* of the situation.

Luckily, during the intervening time, Athena, the goddess of wisdom, had forgiven the Greeks and had developed admiration for the clever, courageous Odysseus. (9) Therefore, Odysseus *elicited* her help to get home, and she arranged a meeting between him and Telemachus. (10) Athena then disguised Odysseus as a *mendicant* and cautioned him to approach his palace with extreme care.

When Odysseus pretended to beg for food from the palace, the suitors tried to drive him away, but the kindly Penelope told him to enter and gave him food. Then Odysseus watched her employ another stratagem to stall the persistent suitors. She said that she would marry the suitor who could string the huge bow of Odysseus and shoot an arrow through a series of rings that he had used for practice. Each of the suitors tried and failed. Then the old beggar asked to try. Although the suitors were indignant, Telemachus insisted that the beggar be permitted to make the attempt. Meanwhile, Telemachus and a trusted servant barred the exits. Odysseus quickly bent the bow and strung it, shot through the rings, and turned the bow on the arrogant suitors, whose escape was barred. After slaying them, he resumed his rightful place as king beside his faithful queen.

READING COMPREHENSION EXERCISE

Each of the following statements corresponds to a numbered sentence in the passage. Each statement contains a blank and is followed by four answer choices. Decide which choice fits best in the blank. The word or phrase that you choose must express roughly the same meaning as the italicized word in the passage. Write the letter of your choice on the answer line.

1. Cassandra was _____ Athena for protection when she was dragged from the temple.   1. _____**b**_____
   a. asking   **b.** begging   **c.** sacrificing to   **d.** praying to

2. The _____ of Ajax's action as well as others' toleration of it made Athena even more angry.
   a. arrogance   b. courageousness   c. urgency   d. persistence

2. _____ **a**

3. Wanting to marry her and become king, the suitors approached Penelope with _____.
   a. presents   b. demand   c. proposals of marriage   d. flattery

3. _____ **d**

4. The suitors _____ Penelope.
   a. begged   b. coaxed   c. commanded   d. questioned

4. _____ **b**

5. She issued a(n) _____ stating that she would not remarry until she had finished weaving a shroud for Odysseus' father.
   a. answer   b. request   c. directive   d. letter

5. _____ **c**

6. Whenever the suitors _____ her about her progress on the shroud, Penelope said that she needed a little more time.
   a. flattered   b. wheedled   c. questioned   d. threatened

6. _____ **c**

7. In the end, however, the suitors were relentlessly _____ Penelope to choose a new king.
   a. imploring   b. coaxing   c. commanding   d. urging

7. _____ **c**

8. By this time Penelope and Telemachus fully realized the _____ of the situation.
   a. urgency   b. demands   c. implications   d. horror

8. _____ **a**

9. Knowing that Athena had forgiven the Greeks, Odysseus _____ her aid to help him get home.
   a. called for   b. insisted upon   c. refused   d. pleaded for

9. _____ **a**

10. When Odysseus came to the palace, his disguise made him look like a(n) _____.
    a. weary traveler   b. old sailor   c. traveling musician   d. beggar

10. _____ **d**

PRACTICE WITH ANALOGIES

See page 79 for some strategies to use with analogies.

Directions   On the answer line, write the letter of the phrase that best completes the analogy.

1. BUNGLER : INEPT :: (A) loiterer : responsible   (B) laggard : tardy
   (C) acrobat : clumsy   (D) employee : ambitious   (E) soldier : brave

1. _____ **B**

2. EXPERT : PROFICIENCY :: (A) procrastinator : aimless
   (B) hypocrite : insincerity   (C) loser : bitterness   (D) scholar : recognition
   (E) spendthrift : frugal

2. _____ **B**

3. DESPICABLE : SCORN :: (A) predictable : imitation   (B) laughable : abuse
   (C) reprehensible : praise   (D) noteworthy : attention
   (E) exemplary : rejection

3. _____ **D**

4. EXIGENT : URGENT :: (A) watershed : important   (B) theory : original
   (C) ruse : straightforward   (D) strain : comforting   (E) upheaval : calm

4. _____ **A**

5. INJUNCTION : REQUEST :: (A) converse : chat   (B) praise : honor
   (C) demand : ask   (D) support : enlist   (E) estimate : calculate

5. _____ **C**

6. MENDICANT : BEGS :: (A) advisor : recommends   (B) prisoner : guards
   (C) patient : complains   (D) customer : sells   (E) miser : gives

6. _____ **A**

The **Test** for Lessons 7, 8, and 9 is on page T7.

TEST-TAKING SKILLS

SAT SENTENCE-COMPLETION TEST ITEMS

One section of the verbal part of the Scholastic Assessment Test (SAT) is made up of sentence-completion test items. This type of question calls upon your knowledge of vocabulary as well as your reasoning skills. The following procedure will help you to choose correct answers for sentence-completion test items.

PROCEDURE

1. *Read the entire sentence, noting where the missing word or words are.* Each test item consists of a single sentence with one or two blanks, followed by five answer choices. Each answer choice is a single word or a pair of words. You must select the word or words that make sense in the sentence. A sample test item follows.

   Invented by Evangelista Torricelli in the seventeenth century, the - - - - is a device that measures air - - - - - .
   (A) diameter .. pollution   (D) perimeter .. currents
   (B) altimeter .. temperature   (E) kilometer .. speed
   (C) barometer .. pressure

2. *Analyze the structure of the sentence, searching the context for clues to the overall meaning.* A sentence may offer reasons or examples, present a contrast, or give a definition. The sample test item is a definition of a measuring device.

3. *Eliminate the incorrect answer choices.* In the sample sentence, choices A, D, and E can be eliminated because the first word in each is not a device.

4. *Substitute the remaining answer choices in the sentence, and select the better one.* If choice B is substituted, the sentence does not make sense, since an altimeter measures height, not air pressure. Choice C, therefore, is the correct answer: a barometer measures air pressure.

EXERCISE ANSWERING SENTENCE-COMPLETION TEST ITEMS

Select the word or pair of words that best completes each of the following sentences. Write the letter of your choice on the answer line. Use your dictionary as needed.

1. Like a true - - - -, Louise believes that all events are determined in advance and cannot be changed by human means.
   (A) mendicant   (D) skeptic
   (B) miser   (E) optimist   1. _____C_____
   (C) fatalist

2. Many - - - - believe that our ability to learn language is at least in part - - - -, that it is somehow woven into our genetic makeup.
   (A) theorists .. accidental   (D) linguists .. innate
   (B) magicians .. lucky   (E) orators .. rhetorical   2. _____D_____
   (C) pessimists .. diminishing

3. Spanish America was characterized by cultural - - - -: Native Americans, Africans, and Spaniards each absorbed some customs of the other groups.
   (A) ostracism
   (B) convergence
   (C) cunning
   (D) duplication
   (E) homogeneity

3. _____ **B**

4. Although the hustler claimed that his tickets were - - - -, concert officials refused to accept them saying that they were - - - -.
   (A) authentic .. genuine
   (B) forged .. void
   (C) obsolete .. current
   (D) inferior .. defective
   (E) valid .. specious

4. _____ **E**

5. Historians now believe that the fall of the Berlin Wall was - - - - event because it marked the end of the Cold War and the beginning of a new world order.
   (A) an insignificant
   (B) a fleeting
   (C) a desperate
   (D) an imperceptible
   (E) a pivotal

5. _____ **E**

6. The committee was characterized by extreme contrasts: periods of - - - - alternated with periods of - - - -.
   (A) camaraderie .. discord
   (B) compliance .. accord
   (C) caution .. circumspection
   (D) deviousness .. cunning
   (E) acquiescence .. harmony

6. _____ **A**

7. Although - - - - dancer who had trouble remembering steps, Ted was a - - - - magician who could dazzle audiences with his skillful tricks.
   (A) a proficient .. an incompetent
   (B) a clumsy .. a cunning
   (C) an inept .. an awkward
   (D) an accomplished .. a deft
   (E) an amateurish .. an untrained

7. _____ **B**

8. Ann Marie's distinguishing trait is her - - - -: she carefully considers her thoughts and feelings before reaching a decision.
   (A) perspicuity
   (B) dexterity
   (C) introspection
   (D) ambivalence
   (E) arrogance

8. _____ **C**

9. Michelangelo is often called the - - - - Renaissance artist because he mastered painting, sculpture, and architecture.
   (A) crafty
   (B) imperious
   (C) forgotten
   (D) consummate
   (E) rigid

9. _____ **D**

10. Water is the most - - - - liquid in the world, for without it people can survive for only two or three days.
    (A) indomitable
    (B) infamous
    (C) indigenous
    (D) indispensable
    (E) indiscreet

10. _____ **D**

11. The dictator's ruthless and - - - - abuse of basic human rights deserves the scorn and - - - - of concerned citizens around the world.
    (A) callous .. esteem
    (B) despicable .. contempt
    (C) compassionate .. abhorrence
    (D) heartless .. regard
    (E) lenient .. derision

11. _____ **B**

12. Like a true martinet, the new boss gave - - - - orders which he expected his - - - - to obey.
    (A) tentative .. tractable
    (B) ambiguous .. rebellious
    (C) imperious .. subordinate
    (D) stylish .. prominent
    (E) simultaneous .. obstinate

12. _____ **C**

The root *-val-* is derived from the Latin word *valere*, meaning "to be strong" or "to be worth." The root *-vinc-* comes from the Latin word *vincere*, meaning "to conquer." Both of these roots have given us a number of English words. If you are *convalescing* from an illness, you are gradually returning to health. When you behave *valiantly*, you act boldly and courageously. On the other hand, someone who is *invincible* is incapable of being defeated or overcome. A *conviction* is a fixed or strong belief that is difficult to change. In this lesson you will learn other words that contain the idea of "to be strong" or "to conquer."

WORD LIST

ambivalence
avail
equivalent
evaluation
evince
invalid
invaluable
prevail
valedictory
vanquish

DEFINITIONS

After you have studied the definitions and example for each vocabulary word, write the word on the line to the right.

1. **ambivalence** (ăm-bĭv′ə-ləns) *noun* **a.** The simultaneous existence of conflicting feelings or thoughts, such as love and hate, about a person, an object, or an idea. **b.** Uncertainty or indecisiveness as to what course to follow; fluctuation. (From the Latin *ambi-*, meaning "on both sides," and *valere*, meaning "to be strong")

   Related Words **ambivalent** *adjective;* **ambivalently** *adverb*
   Example   The reviewer's *ambivalence* about the author's latest book was apparent in her contradictory comments about it.

   1. _____

2. **avail** (ə-vāl′) *noun* Use, benefit, or advantage.   *trans. verb* To be of use or advantage to; help.   *intrans. verb* To be of use, value, or advantage; serve: *Good intentions will not avail without effort.* (From the Latin *ad-*, meaning "to," and *valere*)

   Example   Our efforts to help the flood victims were of no *avail*.

   2. _____

   USAGE NOTE: The idiomatic expression *avail oneself of* means "to make use of" or "to profit by."

3. **equivalent** (ĭ-kwĭv′ə-lənt) *adjective* **a.** Equal in quantity, force, meaning, or value. **b.** Having similar or identical functions or effects. **c.** Practically equal: *a wish that was equivalent to a command.*   *noun* Something that is equivalent. (From the Latin words *aequus*, meaning "equal," and *valere*)

   Example   The time it took Don to prepare and bake the wedding cake was *equivalent* to the time it took him to decorate it.

   3. _____

4. **evaluation** (ĭ-văl′yōō-ā′shən) *noun* **a.** The act of judging the value or worth of. **b.** The result of evaluating; a judgment or appraisal. (From the Latin *ex-*, meaning "out," and *valere*)

   Related Words **evaluate** *verb;* **evaluative** *adjective*
   Example   The appraiser's *evaluation* of the antiques set minimum prices for the auction.

   4. _____

5. **evince** (ĭ-vĭns′) *trans. verb*   **a.** To show or exhibit, as an emotion.   **b.** To demonstrate clearly or convincingly; make evident. (From the Latin *ex-*, an intensive prefix, and *vincere*, meaning "to conquer")

   Example   The judges *evinced* surprise at the young gymnast's outstanding performance.

5. _____

6. **invalid** (ĭn-văl′ĭd) *adjective*   **a.** Being without foundation or force in fact, truth, or law; not in effect; worthless.   **b.** Falsely based or reasoned; faulty; unjustified: *invalid conclusion.*   *noun* (ĭn′və-lĭd)   A chronically ill or disabled person. (From the Latin *in-*, meaning "not," and *valere*)

   Related Words   **invalidate** *verb;* **invalidly** *adverb*
   Example   Since the contract was not signed by the deadline, the agreement is *invalid.*

6. _____

7. **invaluable** (ĭn-văl′yoo-ə-bəl) *adjective*   **a.** Of inestimable use or help; indispensable.   **b.** Having great value; priceless.

   Example   The poster that you gave Denise has been an *invaluable* source of inspiration for her.

7. _____

8. **prevail** (prĭ-vāl′) *intrans. verb*   **a.** To be greater in strength or influence; triumph.   **b.** To be or become effective.   **c.** To be most common or frequent; be predominant. (From the Latin *prae-*, meaning "before," and *valere*)

   Related Word   **prevailing** *adjective*
   Example   After ten years of battle, the Greeks *prevailed* against the Trojans.

8. _____

   USAGE NOTE: *To prevail on* or *upon* is an idiom meaning "to persuade successfully."

9. **valedictory** (văl′ĭ-dĭk′tə-rē) *adjective*   Bidding farewell.   *noun*   A farewell address. (From the Latin words *vale*, meaning "farewell," and *dicere*, meaning "to say")

   Related Word   **valedictorian** *noun*
   Example   Gwen's *valedictory* comments to the staff were particularly sad because she would not be present to witness the completion of the project.

9. _____

10. **vanquish** (văng′kwĭsh, văn′kwĭsh) *trans. verb*.   **a.** To defeat in a battle, conflict, or competition.   **b.** To overcome or subdue, as an emotion; suppress. (From the Latin word *vincere*)

    Example   Seth has *vanquished* all of his wrestling opponents this season.

10. _____

Word History: ambivalence

Latin: *ambi*=on both sides + *valere*=to be strong

   Ambivalence comes from the Latin words *ambi-*, meaning "on both sides," and *valere*, meaning "to be strong," and indicates strong feelings both for and against something. Such opposing feelings can result in uncertainty about making decisions. Whenever *ambi-* occurs in an English derivative, it causes that word to contain the idea "on both sides." For example, an *ambidextrous* person can write equally well with both the right and left hands, while an *ambiguous* situation leaves a person wondering whether to turn this way or that.

EXERCISE 1 MATCHING WORDS AND DEFINITIONS

Match the definition in Column B with the word in Column A. Write the letter of the correct definition on the answer line.

Column A

1. avail
2. equivalent
3. evince
4. prevail
5. vanquish
6. ambivalence
7. invaluable
8. evaluation
9. invalid
10. valedictory

Column B

a. to show or exhibit; demonstrate clearly
b. indispensable; priceless
c. to be greater in strength or influence; be or become effective
d. the act of judging the value or worth of; appraisal
e. bidding farewell
f. equal in quantity, meaning, or value
g. to defeat in battle or competition; overcome or subdue
h. being without foundation in fact, truth, or law
i. use, benefit, or advantage; to be of use or advantage to
j. the simultaneous existence of conflicting feelings or thoughts; uncertainty

1. __i__
2. __f__
3. __a__
4. __c__
5. __g__
6. __j__
7. __b__
8. __d__
9. __h__
10. __e__

EXERCISE 2 USING WORDS CORRECTLY

Each of the following statements contains an italicized vocabulary word. Decide whether the sentence is true or false, and write *True* or *False* on the answer line.

1. A person retiring from a job would be likely to make *valedictory* comments to his or her colleagues.
2. Weaker forces usually *prevail* over stronger forces.
3. People who are good judges of character usually make accurate *evaluations* of other people.
4. An *invaluable* lesson is one that is extremely worthwhile.
5. A diamond ring and a silver spoon are *equivalent* in value.
6. When an army surrenders, it has *vanquished* its enemy.
7. If you have strong convictions concerning something, you feel *ambivalence*.
8. If you have searched for something to no *avail*, you have not found it.
9. An *invalid* driver's license is up-to-date.
10. A volunteer usually *evinces* an unselfish spirit.

1. __True__
2. __False__
3. __True__
4. __True__
5. __False__
6. __False__
7. __False__
8. __True__
9. __False__
10. __True__

EXERCISE 3 CHOOSING THE BEST DEFINITION

For each italicized vocabulary word in the following sentences, write the letter of the best definition on the answer line.

1. Jascha Heifetz, the talented Russian-born violinist, *evinced* impressive musical ability at an early age.
   a. dreamed of   b. demonstrated   c. learned   d. built up

1. __b__

2. The conclusions were declared *invalid* because the scientists had tested only a small number of subjects.
   a. falsely based
   b. effective
   c. slightly vague
   d. somewhat excessive

3. The Peary High School team *vanquished* its two opponents during a recent academic competition.
   a. supported   b. defeated   c. surrendered to   d. met

4. Scott's *ambivalence* about accepting that new job is apparent.
   a. fear
   b. positive outlook
   c. enthusiasm
   d. conflict of emotion

5. Their resource center is *equivalent* to our library.
   a. equal   b. helpful   c. adjacent   d. inattentive

6. Several *invaluable* Renaissance paintings were stolen from a museum.
   a. authentic   b. old-fashioned   c. priceless   d. extraordinary

7. In spite of its ability to strike quickly, the cobra could not *prevail* over the mongoose.
   a. extend itself   b. escape   c. reach   d. triumph

8. Mr. Yong *availed himself of* consumer information before deciding which refrigerator he would buy.
   a. made use of   b. ignored   c. sought   d. acted upon

9. Ms. Johnson's *evaluation* of the play was scornful.
   a. judgment   b. interpretation   c. introduction   d. enjoyment

10. Max Singer will give the *valedictory* at graduation this year.
    a. award   b. diploma   c. opening speech   d. farewell address

2. _____ a
3. _____ b
4. _____ d
5. _____ a
6. _____ c
7. _____ d
8. _____ a
9. _____ a
10. _____ d

EXERCISE 4 USING DIFFERENT FORMS OF WORDS

Decide which form of the vocabulary word in parentheses best completes the sentence. The form given may be correct. Write your answer on the answer line.

1. The amount of effort expended and the results attained are not always _____. *(equivalent)*

2. The results of this week's opinion poll _____ those of last week. *(invalid)*

3. Clara _____ excitement every time she thought about her anticipated trip to Williamsburg, Virginia. *(evince)*

4. The Aztecs _____ over most of their enemies. *(prevail)*

5. Jules likes to _____ himself of the free samples at the grocery store. *(avail)*

6. Words of encouragement _____ the toddler's fears, and she took her first steps. *(vanquish)*

7. I wonder who will be the _____ of the next graduating class. *(valedictory)*

8. Matt is _____ about which college to attend. *(ambivalence)*

9. Mrs. Shawn has been assigned to _____ the effectiveness of the city's clean-up campaign. *(evaluation)*

10. We had overlooked their _____ support for the program. *(invaluable)*

1. **equivalent**
2. **invalidate**
3. **evinced**
4. **prevailed**
5. **avail**
6. **vanquished**
7. **valedictorian**
8. **ambivalent**
9. **evaluate**
10. **invaluable**

READING COMPREHENSION

Each numbered sentence in the following passage contains an italicized vocabulary word. After you read the passage, you will complete an exercise.

GOLD RUSHES—NEW AND OLD

While building a sawmill near San Francisco in 1848, James Marshall stooped down to inspect a shiny rock and discovered gold. His discovery sparked the California Gold Rush. (1) Thousands of men and women rushed to California to *avail* themselves of the opportunity to claim quick riches. But after the first blush of easily claimed gold, conditions became more challenging. To make money, many miners had to endure the long, dangerous trip to California, find a good claim and, with their gold pans in hand, try to capture the precious metal from stones in the river. As they waited for gold that often never materialized, they endured cold, hunger, and exhaustion. (2) Even if one miner found gold, another might accuse the claim of being *invalid.* (3) To *prevail* in a claim dispute might involve a bitter legal battle. (4) Although *invaluable* for populating California and building the city of San Francisco, the 1848–1849 Gold Rush brought riches to only a few of the many thousands of hopefuls.

Over a hundred and fifty years later, a new Gold Rush is taking place in Nevada. But this time, the miners are armed with high technology and advanced degrees in geology rather than gold pans. Today's treasure is called "invisible gold." Since the specks are so small that they are invisible with many microscopes, new techniques must be used to extract this gold. In one, bacteria is used to separate the gold from other minerals. (5) High tech tools are also needed to *evaluate* whether a site contains enough gold in the rocks to make it worth mining. Miners must then try to interest a company in investing the considerable resources needed to develop a site. At times this can be a difficult process. Pat Cavanaugh suspected that gold was lying beneath a bed of shallow gravel, but 21 companies turned down his proposal. Finally receiving financing, Cavanaugh went on to discover a gold reserve of more than 2.5 million ounces. (6) At today's prices, this is *equivalent* to over a billion dollars!

In the past, gold mining often stripped the land of grass and trees, leaving only a scarred, abandoned countryside. Now environmental regulations require companies to restore the land they have mined. (7) This has softened the *ambivalence* that many states and cities once felt toward mining on their territory.

What do modern miners, equipped with laptop computers and machines for measuring seismic waves, have in common with the miners of days gone by? (8) Both *evince* a common persistence and a pioneering spirit. (9) Both have had to *vanquish* many difficulties; whether the obstacle is cold, hunger, or lack of money, mining is not easy. (10) Perhaps the most fitting *valedictory* comment on the vanished way of "gold pan" mining is that the road to riches is seldom easy. Modern miners would certainly agree!

Each of the following statements corresponds to a numbered sentence in the passage. Each statement contains a blank and is followed by four answer choices. Decide which choice fits best in the blank. The word or phrase that you choose must express roughly the same meaning as the italicized word in the passage. Write the letter of your choice on the answer line.

1. Thousands of men and women rushed to California to _____ the opportunity to claim quick riches.
   a. miss   b. use   c. enjoy   d. help

   1. _____ b

2. Even if one miner found gold, another might accuse the claim of being _____ .
   a. meager   b. second   c. over   d. worthless

   2. _____ d

3. To _____ in a claim dispute might involve a bitter legal battle.
   a. escape   b. win   c. suffer   d. sue

   3. _____ b

4. Although _____ for populating California and building the city of San Francisco, the 1848–1849 Gold Rush brought riches to only a few of the many thousands of hopefuls.
   a. used   b. admired   c. indispensable   d. acknowledged

   4. _____ c

5. High tech tools are also needed to _____ whether a site contains enough gold in the rocks to make it worth mining.
   a. judge   b. describe   c. know   d. present

   5. _____ a

6. At today's prices, this is _____ to over a billion dollars!
   a. similar   b. equal   c. inferior   d. superior

   6. _____ b

7. This has softened the _____ that many states and cities once felt toward mining on their territory.
   a. negative feelings   c. mixed feelings
   b. positive feelings   d. proud feelings

   7. _____ c

8. Both _____ a common persistence and pioneering spirit.
   a. feel   b. demonstrate   c. contain   d. long for

   8. _____ b

9. Both have had to _____ many difficulties; whether the obstacle is cold, hunger, or lack of money, mining is not easy.
   a. put up with   b. conquer   c. face   d. fight

   9. _____ b

10. Perhaps the most fitting _____ comment onthe vanished way of "gold pan" mining is that the road to riches is seldom easy.
    a. complimentary   b. valuable   c. true   d. final

    10. _____ d

Suppose that you have been chosen to give a speech at your graduation. As you think about a topic for your speech, you realize how different you and your classmates are now from when you were freshmen. Concentrating on those differences, write your farewell address. Add details of specific memories that will illustrate how your high school years have contributed to the change. Use at least five of the words from this lesson and underline them.

Verbal Aptitude Test I is on page T9.

Some products are measured by volume, while others are available in small, family, or jumbo packages. However, such differentiations of amount and size are very general and limited in comparison with the range of descriptive terms available. Each day you quantify (express the number or amount of) and qualify (describe the characteristics of) mass, dimension, proportion, capacity, content, strength, and extent. To make clear the attributes of whatever you are describing or exploring, you need to choose words that are as specific as possible. The vocabulary words in this lesson will help you to express some of the distinctions of size and amount that you encounter.

WORD LIST

abound
amplitude
augment
brevity
commensurate
diminish
infinitesimal
modicum
prodigious
quota

DEFINITIONS

After you have studied the definitions and example for each vocabulary word, write the word on the line to the right.

1. **abound** (ə-bound') *intrans. verb* **a.** To be great in number of amount. **b.** To be fully supplied or filled; teem. (From the Latin *ab-*, meaning "from," and *undare*, meaning "to surge")

   Related Word **abundant** *adjective*
   Example Caribou *abound* in the arctic regions of the world.

   1. _____

2. **amplitude** (ăm'plĭ-tōōd', ăm'plĭ-tyōōd') *noun* **a.** Greatness of size; magnitude. **b.** Fullness. **c.** Breadth or range, as of intelligence. (From the Latin word *amplus*, meaning "large")

   Related Word **ample** *adjective*
   Example From the *amplitude* of his wealth, the philanthropist gave abundantly to charitable organizations.

   2. _____

3. **augment** (ôg-měnt') *trans. verb* **a.** To make greater, as in size, extent, or quantity; increase. **b.** In music, to increase (an interval) by a half tone. *intrans. verb* To become greater; enlarge.

   Related Words **augmentation** *noun;* **augmented** *adjective*
   Example Mr. Acala took a second job at night in order to *augment* his income.

   3. _____

4. **brevity** (brěv'ĭ-tē) *noun* **a.** Briefness of duration. **b.** Concise expression; terseness. (From the Latin word *brevis*, meaning "short")

   Related Word **brief** *adjective*
   Example The *brevity* of Lincoln's Gettysburg Address was responsible for his audience's failure to recognize its greatness.

   4. _____

5. **commensurate** (kə-mĕn′sər-ĭt, kə-mĕn′shər-ĭt) *adjective*   **a.** Of the same size, extent, or duration.   **b.** Corresponding in size or degree; proportionate. (From the Latin *com-*, meaning "together," and *mensura*, meaning "measure")

   Related Word   **commensurately** *adverb*
   Example   The commercial artist decided against leaving her current job for a different position in the company when she discovered that the salaries were *commensurate*.

5. _____

6. **diminish** (dĭ-mĭn′ĭsh) *trans. verb.*   **a.** To make smaller or less or cause to appear smaller or less.   **b.** To detract from the authority, rank, or prestige of.   **c.** In music, to reduce (an interval) by a half tone.   *intrans. verb*   To become smaller or less.

   Related Words   **diminished** *adjective;* **diminishment** *noun*
   Example   The passage of time did not *diminish* the vigor and enthusiasm of the elderly couple.

6. _____

7. **infinitesimal** (ĭn′fĭn-ĭ-tĕs′ə-məl) *adjective*   Immeasurably or incalculably tiny.

   Related Word   **infinitesimally** *adverb*
   Example   The *infinitesimal* flaw in the gem could be detected only under high-power magnification.

7. _____

8. **modicum** (mŏd′ĭ-kəm) *noun*   A small amount or quantity. (From the Latin word *modus*, meaning "measure")

   Example   With his *modicum* of athletic ability, Gregory could not hope for a place on the varsity team.

8. _____

9. **prodigious** (prə-dĭj′əs) *adjective*   **a.** Impressively great in size, force, or extent; enormous.   **b.** Extraordinary; marvelous.

   Related Words   **prodigiously** *adverb;* **prodigy** *noun*
   Example   By the time she entered the university, Molly had done a *prodigious* amount of reading.

9. _____

10. **quota** (kwō′tə) *noun*   **a.** A proportional share assigned to a group or a member of a group; allotment.   **b.** A maximum or fixed number or amount. (From the Latin word *quot*, meaning "how many")

    Example   In this dry country, each farm receives its *quota* of water for irrigation.

10. _____

Word History: brevity

Latin: *brevis*=short, brief

Brevity means "briefness of duration" and comes from the Latin word *brevis*, "short." Numerous derivatives, all having to do with the idea of "short" or "brief," arise from this root. An *abbreviation* is a "shortened" form of a word; a *breviary* is a "short" church prayer book; and a lawyer's *brief* is a "short" document containing all the facts concerning a specific case. To end this "brief" discussion, the word *briefs* turns up in the vocabulary of clothing as "short, tight-fitting underwear"!

EXERCISE 1 WRITING CORRECT WORDS

On the answer line, write the word from the vocabulary list that fits each definition.

1. To make smaller or less; detract from the authority or prestige of

2. A small amount or quantity

3. Briefness of duration; concise expression

4. To be great in number or amount; be fully supplied or filled

5. Immeasurably tiny

6. Greatness of size; fullness; breadth or range

7. Impressively great in size, force, or extent; extraordinary

8. A proportional share; a maximum or fixed number or amount

9. Of the same size, extent, or duration; corresponding in size or degree

10. To make greater in size, extent, or quantity; become greater

1. ____diminish____

2. ____modicum____

3. ____brevity____

4. ____abound____

5. ____infinitesimal____

6. ____amplitude____

7. ____prodigious____

8. ____quota____

9. ____commensurate____

10. ____augment____

EXERCISE 2 USING WORDS CORRECTLY

Decide whether the italicized vocabulary word has been used correctly in the sentence. On the answer line, write *Correct* for correct use and *Incorrect* for incorrect use.

1. The *amplitude* of this year's crop helped the farmer to pay her debts and realize a small profit.

2. The precocious child was placed in a grade that was *commensurate* with his social development.

3. The poll showed that the president's popularity had not *diminished*.

4. The *brevity* of the speech caused the students to squirm in their seats, daydream, and finally fall asleep.

5. A *prodigious* number of workers were needed to build the first transcontinental railroad.

6. Only a *modicum* of effort is needed for most people to lift 250 pounds.

7. The teacher *augmented* the children to stay within the confines of the playground.

8. Yoshi rarely exceeds his *quota* of one classic movie a week.

9. The lake so *abounds* in trout that most people left after several hours, having caught nothing.

10. There was such an *infinitesimal* amount of food at the party that the family ate the remainder of it for several days.

1. ____Correct____

2. ____Correct____

3. ____Correct____

4. ____Incorrect____

5. ____Correct____

6. ____Incorrect____

7. ____Incorrect____

8. ____Correct____

9. ____Incorrect____

10. ____Incorrect____

EXERCISE 3 CHOOSING THE BEST DEFINITION

For each italicized vocabulary word in the following sentences, write the letter of the best definition on the answer line.

1. The buffet selections were *augmented* by several seafood and vegetable dishes.
   a. cut in half   **b.** replaced   **c.** influenced   **d.** enlarged

1. ____d____

2. She chose a punishment *commensurate with* Eli's misbehavior.
   a. inappropriate for   **c.** in proportion to
   b. unrelated to   **d.** out of proportion to

2. _____ c

3. Darryl was astounded by what he considered a *prodigious* increase in his allowance.
   a. impressively great   **c.** acceptable
   b. extremely tiny   **d.** modest

3. _____ a

4. With a *modicum* of patience and determination, Paige will undoubtedly finish her needlepoint pillow.
   a. background   **b.** excessive portion   **c.** small amount   **d.** lack

4. _____ c

5. The Fus' kitchen *abounds with* an amazing variety of flowering plants.
   a. houses   **b.** is filled with   **c.** hides   **d.** is the setting for

5. _____ b

6. Each fifth grade student has a *quota* of recipe cards to sell.
   a. fixed number   **c.** secret number
   b. excessive number   **d.** reasonable number

6. _____ a

7. Unless you want to spend a lot of money, *brevity* is important in composing a classified ad.
   a. clarity   **c.** alphabetical arrangement
   b. lengthy explanation   **d.** concise expression

7. _____ d

8. Mack is such a selective eater that he will spend fifteen minutes picking *infinitesimal* pieces of onion out of a bowl of stew.
   a. any   **c.** impressively large
   b. immeasurably tiny   **d.** unsavory

8. _____ b

9. Neither distance nor time *diminished* Wendy and Diane's friendship.
   a. made smaller   **b.** made larger   **c.** re-created   **d.** compensated for

9. _____ a

10. We were delighted with the *amplitude* of the museum's collection of French Impressionist paintings.
   a. pleasing variety   **b.** excellence   **c.** great size   **d.** arrangement

10. _____ c

EXERCISE 4 USING DIFFERENT FORMS OF WORDS

Decide which form of the vocabulary word in parentheses best completes the sentence. The form given may be correct. Write your answer on the answer line.

1. Having accepted the hazardous assignment, Jill was paid _____. (*commensurate*)

1. **commensurately**

2. The city government started its _____ of flood-control measures this morning. (*augment*)

2. **augmentation**

3. This year Mr. Bartoni is convinced that he will exceed his sales _____ by at least 25 percent. (*quota*)

3. **quota**

4. No one could explain the _____ popularity of the trivia game. (*diminish*)

4. **diminished**

5. We were amazed at the _____ of Craig's knowledge of old movies. (*amplitude*)

5. **amplitude**

6. The witnesses' testimonies lacked even a _____ of truth. (*modicum*)

6. **modicum**

7. _____ in poetry is sometimes referred to as compression. (*brevity*)

7. **Brevity**

8. Atoms are _____ small units of matter. (*infinitesimal*)

8. **infinitesimally**

9. The Galápagos Islands have _____ species of animals and birds. (*abound*)

9. **abundant**

10. Having spent several hours gardening in the hot sun, Eliza drank orange juice slowly but _____. (*prodigious*)

10. **prodigiously**

READING COMPREHENSION

Each numbered sentence in the following passage contains an italicized vocabulary word or related form. After you read the passage, you will complete an exercise.

THE WELL-TEMPERED CLAVIER: BACH'S GIFT TO STUDENTS

(1) Every serious piano student knows that years of committed, patient practice may result in only a *modicum* of achievement. Practicing scales and studying musical effects, dedicated students spend hours learning technique. (2) As if these tasks are not tedious enough, practice exercises *augment* the burden. More than 250 years ago, however, the German composer Johann Sebastian Bach did much to infuse routine drill with creative and expressive music.

(3) Even talented young Wilhelm Friedemann Bach and Karl Philip Emanuel Bach had to play their *quota* of exercises when their celebrated father began to teach them music. Friedemann and Emanuel, like any other students of the clavier, or early piano, had to learn how to read music and what keyboard fingering to use. In the interest of his sons' musical studies, Johann Sebastian Bach wrote a number of compositions intended for the practice of specific skills. (4) One outstanding result of Bach's dedication to teaching is *The Well-Tempered Clavier*, a collection that *abounds* in challenging preludes and fugues (compositions with melodies that are repeated with variations).

(5) The practical and instructional value of the pieces in no way *diminishes* their artistic merit. Consisting of twenty-four preludes and twenty-four fugues in all keys, *The Well-Tempered Clavier* reflects Bach's skill and genius.

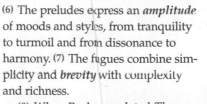

(6) The preludes express an *amplitude* of moods and styles, from tranquility to turmoil and from dissonance to harmony. (7) The fugues combine simplicity and *brevity* with complexity and richness.

(8) When Bach completed *The Well-Tempered Clavier*, he was so pleased with it that he made only *infinitesimal* changes before giving manuscript copies to his sons. (9) Friedemann and Emanuel appreciated and benefited from the more artistic practice, which was *commensurate* with the level of their ability as keyboard musicians. (10) Neither they nor their father anticipated the *prodigious* impact of the work on future students, however. The collection immediately began to fulfill the purpose stated on the title page: "For the Use and Profit of the Musical Youth Desirous of Learning as well as for the Pastime of Those Already Skilled in the Study."

Countless piano teachers have used *The Well-Tempered Clavier* with their students, college composition students have studied its artistry, and the public has been delighted by its occasional performance. What began merely as a set of keyboard exercises by Bach has become a musical classic of great distinction and beauty.

Each of the following statements corresponds to a numbered sentence in the passage. Each statement contains a blank and is followed by four answer choices. Decide which choice fits best in the blank. The word or phrase that you choose must express roughly the same meaning as the italicized word in the passage. Write the letter of your choice on the answer line.

1. Serious piano students know that years of practice may result in only a(n) _____ of achievement.
   a. false sense   **b.** small amount   **c.** average amount   **d.** lessening

   1. _____**b**_____

2. Practice exercises _____ the burden.
   a. increase   **b.** decrease   **c.** remove   **d.** rigidly establish

   2. _____**a**_____

3. Even Bach's sons had to play their _____ exercises.
   a. father's   **b.** own   **c.** average number of   **d.** allotment of

   3. _____**d**_____

4. *The Well-Tempered Clavier* _____ with challenging preludes and fugues.
   a. is filled   **b.** delights pianists   **c.** is performed   **d.** is flawless

   4. _____**a**_____

5. The practical and instructional value of the pieces does not _____ their artistic merit.
   a. emphasize   **b.** influence   **c.** detract from   **d.** contradict

   5. _____**c**_____

6. The preludes express a(n) _____ moods and styles.
   a. guide to   **b.** rule for   **c.** inconsistency of   **d.** range of

   6. _____**d**_____

7. The fugues combine simplicity and _____ with complexity and richness.
   a. sophistication
   b. showy touches
   c. light touches
   d. concise expression

   7. _____**d**_____

8. Bach made only _____ changes before giving manuscript copies to his sons.
   a. immeasurably tiny
   b. extremely general
   c. relevant
   d. reluctant

   8. _____**a**_____

9. The more artistic practice was _____ the level of Friedemann and Emanuel's ability.
   a. too simple for
   b. appropriate to
   c. too complex for
   d. a challenge to

   9. _____**b**_____

10. Bach did not anticipate the _____ impact of the work on future students.
    a. negative   **b.** rare   **c.** appealing   **d.** extraordinary

    10. _____**d**_____

WRITING ASSIGNMENT

Our impressions of size seem to change as we get older. What once seemed enormous from the viewpoint of a child very often shrinks later to an average size. Describe an object or a place, such as the skeleton of a dinosaur or an amusement park, that once seemed huge to you, and contrast the former description with your present impression. Use at least five of the words from this lesson in your description and underline each one.

LESSON 12 RELEASING AND TAKING BACK

The word *releasing* may make us think of freedom from obligation, just as the phrase *taking back* may make us think of an unjust action that robs us of what is rightfully ours. However, these words do not always have the same connotations. Parents may release their children from a particularly undesirable household chore, but they might also release a new set of rules about responsibilities at home. Similarly, a friend might take back an invitation to a party, but he or she also might take back an unkind word. In this lesson you will study words that have to do with the ways, means, and varieties of releasing and taking back.

WORD LIST

abdicate
abnegate
absolve
catharsis
countermand
recant
recoup
renunciation
rescind
waive

DEFINITIONS

After you have studied the definitions and example for each vocabulary word, write the word on the line to the right.

1. **abdicate** (ăb′dĭ-kāt′) *trans. verb*   To relinquish formally.   *intrans. verb*   To relinquish high office or responsibility. (From the Latin *ab-*, meaning "away," and *dicare*, meaning "to proclaim")

   Related Word   abdication *noun*
   Example   During a recent press conference, the representative to the town council *abdicated* his authority over the project.

1. _____
   See *abnegate*.

2. **abnegate** (ăb′nĭ-gāt′) *trans. verb*   To deny to oneself; renounce. (From the Latin *ab-*, meaning "away," and *negare*, meaning "to deny")

   Related Word   abnegation *noun*
   Example   She decided to *abnegate* the privilege for the sake of her conscience.

2. _____
   USAGE NOTE: *Abdicate* has a public, formal sense; *abnegate* is likely to refer to a private matter.

3. **absolve** (əb-zŏlv′, əb-sŏlv′) *trans. verb*   **a.** To pronounce clear of blame or guilt. **b.** To relieve from obligation.   **c.** To pardon (a sin). (From the Latin *ab-*, meaning "away," and *solvere*, meaning "to loosen")

   Example   The students were *absolved* of all responsibility for the damaged equipment.

3. _____

4. **catharsis** (kə-thär′sĭs) *noun*   A purifying or figurative cleaning or release of tension. (From the Greek word *katharos*, meaning "pure")

   Related Word   cathartic *adjective*
   Example   Watching the movie enabled me to understand the woman's problems, and I experienced a *catharsis* when I cried in sympathy for her.

4. _____

5. **countermand** (koun′tər-mănd′, koun′tər-mănd′) *trans. verb*   **a.** To cancel or reverse.   **b.** To recall by contrary order.   *noun*   An order or command reversing another. (From the Latin words *contra*, meaning "opposite," and *mandare*, meaning "to command")

   Example   When the lieutenant assessed the size of the attacking force, he quickly *countermanded* his order to advance.

5. _____

6. **recant** (rĭ-kănt′) *trans. verb*   To make a formal retraction or disavowal of (a statement or previously held belief).   *intrans. verb*   To make a formal retraction or disavowal of a previously held belief. (From the Latin *re-*, meaning "back," and *cantare*, meaning "to sing")

   Related Word   **recantation** *noun*
   Example   When the star witness *recanted* his testimony, the prosecution's case fell apart.

6. _____

7. **recoup** (rĭ-ko͞op′) *trans. verb*   To receive an equivalent for; make up for.

   Example   Before the army could *recoup* its losses, the enemy attacked again.

7. _____

8. **renunciation** (rĭ-nŭn′sē-ā′shən) *noun*   The act of giving something up, especially by formal announcement. (From the Latin *re-*, meaning "back," and *nuntiare*, meaning "to announce")

   Related Word   **renounce** *verb*
   Example   Emily Dickinson calls *renunciation* "a piercing virtue" because of the pain and difficulty involved in giving something up.

8. _____

9. **rescind** (rĭ-sĭnd′) *trans. verb*   To make void; repeal or annul. (From the Latin *re-*, an intensive prefix, and *scindere*, meaning "to cut")

   Related Word   **rescindable** *adjective*
   Example   The military regime *rescinded* almost all of the civil liberties of the populace.

9. _____

10. **waive** (wāv) *trans. verb*   **a.** To relinquish or give up voluntarily.   **b.** To refrain from insisting upon or enforcing; dispense with. (From the Anglo-Norman word *weyver*, meaning "to abandon")

    Related Word   **waiver** *noun*
    Example   By signing the treaty with England, France *waived* all of its rights to Canada and the Northwest Territory.

10. _____

EXERCISE 1 COMPLETING DEFINITIONS

On the answer line, write the word from the vocabulary list that best completes each definition.

1. A release of emotions is a(n) _____.

2. To take back a belief publicly is to _____ it.

3. _____ is the act of giving something up publicly.

4. To repeal or annul something is to _____ it.

5. A person who gives up a high office is said to _____ it.

6. If you clear someone of blame or guilt, you _____ him or her.

7. When you deny yourself an opportunity, you _____ it.

8. To reverse or cancel something is to _____ it.

9. To surrender or give up something voluntarily is to _____ it.

10. If you are able to recover a loss or make good on it, you are able to _____ that loss.

1. _____ catharsis _____
2. _____ recant _____
3. _____ Renunciation _____
4. _____ rescind _____
5. _____ abdicate _____
6. _____ absolve _____
7. _____ abnegate _____
8. _____ countermand _____
9. _____ waive _____
10. _____ recoup _____

EXERCISE 2 USING WORDS CORRECTLY

Decide whether the italicized vocabulary word has been used correctly in the sentence. On the answer line, write *Correct* for correct use and *Incorrect* for incorrect use.

1. The accused man *waived* his right to a trial by jury.

2. The queen was reluctant to *abdicate* because she had no faith in her successor's ability.

3. The carpenter's *abnegation* of the wood left it smooth and shiny.

4. At the sawmill Mike *countermanded* the trees into large, rough boards.

5. When she was discharged from the army, Kristen was *absolved* from any further military duty.

6. Farmer Oak's chickens were cramped in their chicken house, so he *recouped* them.

7. The colonel *rescinded* his order before it could be carried out.

8. In the fairy tale, only the prince's *renunciation* of his claim to the throne could enable him to marry a peasant girl.

9. When Jamell's truck came out of the *catharsis*, it sparkled like new.

10. The district attorney's office *recanted* its earlier statements to the press.

1. _____ Correct _____
2. _____ Correct _____
3. _____ Incorrect _____
4. _____ Incorrect _____
5. _____ Correct _____
6. _____ Incorrect _____
7. _____ Correct _____
8. _____ Correct _____
9. _____ Incorrect _____
10. _____ Correct _____

EXERCISE 3 IDENTIFYING SYNONYMS AND ANTONYMS

Decide which word or phrase has the meaning that is the same as (a synonym) or opposite (an antonym) that of the capitalized vocabulary word. Write the letter of your choice on the answer line.

1. RECOUP (antonym):
   a. give trouble   b. tear down   c. gain   d. lose

2. WAIVE (synonym):
   a. offer help   b. relinquish   c. show respect   d. signal

1. _____ d _____

2. _____ b _____

3. CATHARSIS (antonym):
   a. persistence of tension
   b. release of tension
   c. fear
   d. cure

3. _____ a

4. RENUNCIATION (synonym):
   a. consideration   b. self-denial   c. self-fulfillment   d. freedom

4. _____ b

5. COUNTERMAND (synonym):
   a. release   b. cancel   c. reclaim   d. command

5. _____ b

6. RECANT (synonym):
   a. recall   b. lose   c. retract   d. promise

6. _____ c

7. ABDICATE (antonym):
   a. transfer   b. separate   c. assume formally   d. deny informally

7. _____ c

8. RESCIND (synonym):
   a. annul   b. peel off   c. reinforce   d. take away

8. _____ a

9. ABSOLVE (antonym):
   a. make disappear
   b. forgive
   c. blend
   d. hold accountable

9. _____ d

10. ABNEGATE (antonym):
    a. indulge oneself
    b. deny oneself
    c. forgive oneself
    d. overrate oneself

10. _____ a

EXERCISE 4 USING DIFFERENT FORMS OF WORDS

Decide which form of the vocabulary word in parentheses best completes the sentence. The form given may be correct. Write your answer on the answer line.

1. Before going on the field trip, Lulu's parents signed a _____ that released the school from responsibility for any accidents. (*waive*)

1. _____ waiver

2. Once General D'Amato gives a command, it is usually not _____. (*rescind*)

2. _____ rescinded

3. My insurance policy allows me to _____ losses due to injury. (*recoup*)

3. _____ recoup

4. The king's _____ from the throne startled people all over the world. (*abdicate*)

4. _____ abdication

5. Only the _____ of all of his privileges will allow him to regain his integrity. (*renunciation*)

5. _____ renunciation

6. Samuel's _____ of his authority over his estate has lasted six months. (*abnegate*)

6. _____ abnegation

7. Some dramatic performances have a _____ effect on audiences. (*catharsis*)

7. _____ cathartic

8. Was Lou's _____ of his campaign platform printed in the newspaper? (*recant*)

8. _____ recantation

9. The court _____ Jim of responsibility for his actions. (*absolve*)

9. _____ absolved

10. The vice chancellor has _____ his country's trade embargo. (*countermand*)

10. _____ countermanded

READING COMPREHENSION

Each numbered sentence in the following passage contains an italicized vocabulary word or related form. After you read the passage, you will complete an exercise.

THE MAGNA CHARTA

In 1215 a document was drawn up and signed in England that has had a great impact on basic political and legal rights. This document was the Magna Charta, which means "Great Charter." It has been declared the basis for civil liberties both in England and in the United States.

Like many great political advances, the Magna Charta arose out of conflict. When Richard I died in A.D. 1199, his brother John became king. Because Richard had spent all but about six months of his ten-year reign outside of England fighting in the Crusades, his barons had had free reign in controlling England. Furthermore, they were unprepared for a tyrant like John. (1) The emotional and political *catharsis* resulting from the revered Richard's death had hardly subsided when the barons felt the heavy hand of the new king. (2) John increased old taxes and imposed new ones, *rescinded* freedoms, and showed little respect for the law. (3) The barons, angered and alienated, would have wholeheartedly welcomed John's *abdication*.

At the same time, King John had two strong adversaries. Philip II, King of France, wanted to attack England in order to gain its continental possessions. Pope Innocent III wanted his favorite bishop appointed archbishop of Canterbury, but King John refused. Therefore, with the Pope's blessing, Philip of France prepared to attack. (4) Realizing that the clergy would not help him, King John *recanted* his previous statements, accepted the Pope's choice as archbishop of Canterbury, and made peace with the Pope.

(5) Knowing that similar *countermands* affecting the nobility were unlikely, and seeing King John's power weakened, the barons rebelled. (6) By 1215 at least one third of the barons *renounced* their oaths of fealty to John and prepared for war against him. (7) John was not willing to *abnegate* any more of his authority; yet, without assistance, he could not oppose the barons. (8) Furthermore, they remained very determined to *recoup* the privileges that they had lost. Finally, John met with the rebellious nobility at Runnymede, on the River Thames, and agreed to sign the document that they had drawn up.

Today many people believe that the Magna Charta secured liberties for everyone. However, while a few of its sixty-three clauses dealt with the rights of the middle class, it primarily benefited the nobility. Nonetheless, the Magna Charta has had an extraordinary effect on the evolution of constitutional government. (9) Certain clauses, including one in which John *waived* his power to buy or sell justice, resulted in what we now know as the due process of law. (10) Another key clause, which *absolved* the barons from paying taxes that were not approved by a council of their own choosing, has come to be known as "no taxation without representation." Thus, the efforts of the barons did unintentionally help to guarantee to United States citizens "liberty and justice for all."

READING COMPREHENSION EXERCISE

Each of the following statements corresponds to a numbered sentence in the passage. Each statement contains a blank and is followed by four answer choices. Decide which choice fits best in the blank. The word or phrase that you choose must express roughly the same meaning as the italicized word in the passage. Write the letter of your choice on the answer line.

1. The barons felt the heavy hand of John soon after the _____ resulting from Richard's death was over.
   a. shock
   b. release of emotion
   c. buildup of tension
   d. investigation

   1. _____b_____

2. John imposed new taxes, _____ freedoms, and showed little respect for the law.
   a. repealed   b. restored   c. suppressed   d. ignored

   2. _____a_____

3. The barons would have welcomed John's _____.
   a. alienating the church
   b. triumphing over Philip II
   c. relinquishing high office
   d. abolishing taxation

3. _____c_____

4. John _____ his refusal to name the Pope's choice as archbishop of Canterbury.
   a. regretted   **b.** reiterated   **c.** retracted   **d.** renounced

4. _____c_____

5. Seeing the king's power weakened, the barons knew that similar _____ affecting them were unlikely.
   a. orders reversing previous orders
   b. laws annulling other laws
   c. claims
   d. proclamations

5. _____a_____

6. At least one third of the barons _____ their oaths of fealty to John and prepared to go to war against him.
   a. swore
   b. reaffirmed
   c. publicly questioned
   d. formally gave up

6. _____d_____

7. John was unwilling to _____ his authority, but without help he could not oppose the barons.
   a. relinquish   **b.** fight for   **c.** share   **d.** redefine

7. _____a_____

8. The barons remained very determined to _____ the privileges that they had lost.
   a. abandon   **b.** regain   **c.** forget   **d.** fight for

8. _____b_____

9. In a famous clause of the Magna Charta, John _____ his power to buy and sell justice.
   a. redefined   **b.** reclaimed   **c.** relished   **d.** relinquished

9. _____d_____

10. The barons were _____ paying taxes that were not approved by a council of their own choosing.
   a. tired of   **b.** angered by   **c.** freed from   **d.** pleased at

10. _____c_____

PRACTICE WITH ANALOGIES

Directions   On the answer line, write the letter of the phrase that best completes the analogy.

See page 79 for some strategies to use with analogies.

1. AMBIVALENT : CONVICTION :: (A) inept : skill   (B) formidable : awe
   (C) profound : depth   (D) obliging : thanks   (E) restrained : limit

1. _____A_____

2. DIMINISH : SMALL :: (A) discredit : better   (B) envy : defiant
   (C) disclose : known   (D) conquer : tranquil   (E) conceal : cheap

2. _____C_____

3. ABDICATE : POWER :: (A) deride : reputation   (B) relinquish : claim
   (C) suppress : evidence   (D) maintain : calm   (E) simulate : crime

3. _____B_____

4. ABSOLVE : GUILT :: (A) abstain : drink   (B) relieve : duty
   (C) enforce : decision   (D) accept : invitation   (E) pardon : penalty

4. _____E_____

5. WAIVE : RIGHTS :: (A) register : vote   (B) privileges : revoke
   (C) salute : flag   (D) demand : satisfaction   (E) surrender : army

5. _____E_____

6. RECOUP : LOSSES :: (A) gloat : victories   (B) memories : forget
   (C) redeem : mistakes   (D) pardon : forgive   (E) count : blessings

6. _____C_____

The **Bonus activity** for Lessons 9–12 is on page T14. The **Test** for Lessons 10, 11, and 12 is on page T15.

TEST-TAKING SKILLS

SAT ANALOGY TEST ITEMS

The Scholastic Assessment Test contains a section of analogy test items. An **analogy** is a similarity between things that are otherwise dissimilar. An analogy test item consists of a pair of words followed by five more pairs of words, each of which is identified by a letter. To answer the question, you must choose the pair of words that has the same relationship as the first pair of words. The following information will familiarize you with different types of analogies. It will also explain the most efficient procedure for answering analogy test items.

PROCEDURE

1. *Determine the relationship between the words in the given pair.* The first pair of words appears in capital letters and is followed by a double colon. Study the following sample test item.

   DRY : ARID :: (A) tepid : lukewarm   (B) cold : glacial   (C) humid : dry
   (D) ice : freeze   (E) torrid : warm

   The word *dry* describes a certain degree of dryness; *arid* denotes a more intense dryness. The relationship of the two words, then, is one of degree: less intense to more intense. Degree is only one of numerous kinds of relationships that appear in analogy test items. Following are examples of other common relationships.

RELATIONSHIP	EXAMPLE
is a type of	gold : metal
is a part of	tree : forest
is a place where	zoo : animals
is used to	tractor : plow
is an expression of	smile : happiness
relative size	hill : mountain
is characteristic of	braggart : boastful
definition	dawn : day
antonym	temporary : permanent
degree	happy : elated

2. *Eliminate the word pairs that have different relationships.* Knowing that you are looking for a relationship of degree, you can eliminate choices A, C, and D in the sample test item. The words in choice A are synonyms, and the words in choice C are antonyms. Choice D expresses an object/action relationship.

3. *Find the pair of words that has the correct relationship.* Choices B and E both express a relationship of degree. In choice E, however, the progression is from more intense *(torrid)* to less *(warm)*. Since you are searching for a progression of less intense to more intense, choice B, *cold : glacial*, must be the corret answer. Watch for answer choices that express the desired relationship in reverse, and be sure to choose the answer that expresses the relationship in the correct order.

EXERCISE ANSWERING ANALOGY TEST ITEMS

In each of the following items, select the lettered pair of words that best expresses a relationship similar to that expressed by the two capitalized words. Write the letter of your choice on the answer line. Use your dictionary as needed.

1. MAHOGANY : WOOD :: (A) pencil : paper   (B) bark : tree
   (C) alloy : element   (D) marble : stone   (E) flour : bread

1. _____**D**_____

2. ACTOR : CAST :: (A) entertainer : audience   (B) voter : candidate
   (C) patient : physician   (D) student : faculty   (E) singer : choir

2. _____**E**_____

3. CHAPTER : BOOK :: (A) act : play   (B) ink : paper
   (C) teacher : exam   (D) reviewer : film   (E) editor : text

3. _____**A**_____

4. STY : PIGS :: (A) corral : horses   (B) litter : dogs   (C) garden : bees
   (D) field : rabbits   (E) desert : camels

4. _____**A**_____

5. ALMANAC : FACTS :: (A) skit : jokes   (B) novel : facts
   (C) diary : quotes   (D) page : definitions   (E) atlas : maps

5. _____**E**_____

6. CHEER : APPROVAL :: (A) forget : confidence   (B) growl : delight
   (C) twitch : fury   (D) sob : grief   (E) shout : contentment

6. _____**D**_____

7. POND : LAKE :: (A) shirt : fabric   (B) hill : mountain   (C) clay : potter
   (D) mile : distance   (E) valley : river

7. _____**B**_____

8. BREEZE : GALE :: (A) surf : shore   (B) decibel : sound
   (C) trickle : flood   (D) cloudburst : rainfall   (E) flower : plant

8. _____**C**_____

9. OPTIMIST : HOPEFUL :: (A) braggart : boastful   (B) oaf : graceful
   (C) liar : truthful   (D) soldier : peaceful   (E) athlete : cheerful

9. _____**A**_____

10. ANONYMOUS : NAME :: (A) informal : style   (B) vast : area
    (C) analogous : parallel   (D) aimless : goal   (E) fleeting : fame

10. _____**D**_____

11. REQUEST : INJUNCTION :: (A) ask : reply   (B) suggest : order
    (C) praise : honor   (D) leave : departure   (E) chat : discussion

11. _____**B**_____

12. EMBARK : JOURNEY :: (A) conclude : activity   (B) interrupt : performance
    (C) launch : mission   (D) receive : gift   (E) reject : membership

12. _____**C**_____

13. PROLOGUE : PLAY :: (A) suffix : word   (B) climax : story
    (C) chapter : book (D) location : address   (E) preamble : document

13. _____**E**_____

14. SAVORY : TASTE :: (A) offensive : odor   (B) vanilla : flavor
    (C) inaudible : sound   (D) fragrant : smell   (E) discordant : voice

14. _____**D**_____

15. ENRAGED : ANGRY :: (A) ambitious : idle   (B) cunning : vague
    (C) elated : happy   (D) concerned : indifferent   (E) generous : polite

15. _____**C**_____

The root -*greg*- means "flock" or "herd"; the root -*her*- means "to stick"; and the root -*sim*- means "like." Each of these roots comes from a Latin word and has given us many English words. If you *congregate* with your friends, you stand with them in a flock or group. *Incoherent* speech and writing are difficult to understand because the words do not stick together or make sense. *Similar* outfits look alike. In this lesson you will learn other words that refer to "flock," "stick," and "like."

DEFINITIONS

After you have studied the definitions and example for each vocabulary word, write the word on the line to the right.

1. **adhere** (ăd-hîr′) *intrans. verb* **a.** To stick fast or together by or as if by grasping, suction, or being glued. **b.** To be devoted as a follower or supporter. **c.** To follow closely; carry out without deviation: *adhere to a plan.* (From the Latin *ad-*, meaning "to," and *haerere*, meaning "to stick")

   Related Words **adherence** *noun;* **adherent** *noun*
   Example It was painful to remove the bandage because it *adhered* to the wound.

   1. _____

2. **aggregate** (ăg′rĭ-gĭt) *adjective* Gathered together into a mass so as to constitute a whole; total. *noun* Any total or whole considered with reference to the parts that make it up: *The British Empire was an aggregate of many colonies under a common rule.* (From the Latin *ad-*, meaning "to," and *grex*, meaning "flock")

   Example The bracelet featured a dazzling *aggregate* of diamonds and rubies.

   2. _____

3. **dissimulate** (dĭ-sĭm′yə-lāt′) *trans. verb* To disguise under a feigned appearance. *intrans. verb* To conceal one's true feelings or intentions. (From the Latin *dis-*, meaning "reverse of," and *similis*, meaning "like")

   Related Words **dissimulation** *noun;* **dissimulator** *noun*
   Example To *dissimulate* her intention to steal the vase, she pretended to be uninterested in the item.

   3. _____
   USAGE NOTE: Do not confuse *dissimulate* with *dissimilate*. *Dissimilate* means "to make dissimilar or unlike."

4. **egregious** (ĭ-grē′jəs, ĭ-grē′-jē-əs) *adjective* Outstandingly bad; flagrant. (From the Latin *ex-*, meaning "out," and *grex*)

   Related Words **egregiously** *adverb;* **egregiousness** *noun*
   Example An *egregious* example of business correspondence, the letter was littered with errors in form and misspellings.

   4. _____

5. **ensemble** (ŏn-sŏm'bəl) *noun* **a.** Any unit or group of complementary parts that contribute to a single effect. **b.** A coordinated outfit or costume. **c.** A group of musicians, singers, dancers, or actors who perform together. **d.** Music for two or more vocalists or instruments. (From the Latin *in-*, meaning "in," and *simul*, meaning "at the same time")

   Example   When the dance *ensemble* performed, the audience was awed by the perfect coordination of movement and music.

5. _____

6. **facsimile** (făk-sĭm'ə-lē) *noun* An exact reproduction or copy. *adjective* Exactly reproduced; duplicate. (From the Latin phrase *facsimile*, meaning "make it similar")

   Example   The *facsimile* of the Declaration of Independence was passed around so that students could examine the various signatures.

6. _____

7. **gregarious** (grĭ-gâr'ē-əs) *adjective* **a.** Seeking and enjoying the company of others; sociable. **b.** Tending to move in or form a group. (From the Latin word *grex*)

   Related Words **gregariously** *adverb;* **gregariousness** *noun*
   Example   The *gregarious* family was always having company for dinner.

7. _____

8. **inherent** (ĭn-hîr'ənt, ĭn-hĕr'ənt) *adjective* Existing in someone or something as a natural, essential part, quality, or characteristic. (From the Latin *in-*, meaning "in," and *haerere*)

   Related Word **inherently** *adverb*
   Example   The photographer had an *inherent* ability to capture people's emotions.

8. _____

9. **segregate** (sĕg'rĭ-gāt') *trans. verb* To isolate or separate from others or from the main group. *adjective* Separated; isolated. (From the Latin *se-*, meaning "apart," and *grex*)

   Related Word **segregation** *noun*
   Example   The teacher *segregated* the most motivated students by placing them in the quietest corner of the room.

9. _____

10. **semblance** (sĕm'bləns) *noun* **a.** An outward or token appearance; form. **b.** The barest trace: *a semblance of truth.* (From the Latin word *similis*, meaning "like")

    Example   There was a *semblance* of order when the principal entered the classroom.

10. _____

EXERCISE 1 MATCHING WORDS AND DEFINITIONS

Match the definition in Column B with the word in Column A. Write the letter of the correct definition on the answer line.

Column A

1. segregate
2. egregious
3. dissimulate
4. semblance
5. aggregate
6. facsimile
7. gregarious
8. ensemble
9. inherent
10. adhere

Column B

a. existing as an essential, natural part or characteristic
b. to stick together
c. enjoying the company of others
d. to isolate from the main group
e. outstandingly bad
f. a group of people or parts that contribute to a single effect
g. an outward appearance
h. an exact copy
i. to disguise under a feigned appearance
j. gathered together into a mass; total

1. _____ d
2. _____ e
3. _____ i
4. _____ g
5. _____ j
6. _____ h
7. _____ c
8. _____ f
9. _____ a
10. _____ b

EXERCISE 2 USING WORDS CORRECTLY

Each of the following questions contains an italicized vocabulary word. Choose the correct answer to the question, and write *Yes* or *No* on the answer line.

1. Would you expect a *facsimile* of a document to be difficult to distinguish from the original?

2. Does oiling a hinge cause it to *adhere* to itself?

3. Is a string quartet a type of *ensemble*?

4. Is it reasonable to assume that Einstein had an *inherent* ability for mathematics?

5. Do teachers become *aggregated* when students are habitually tardy?

6. Do *gregarious* people prefer to live fifteen miles away from their nearest neighbors?

7. Would you *dissimulate* if you wished to hide your real intentions?

8. If a scientific theory were said to lack any *semblance* of proof, would you expect it to be well supported by experimental evidence?

9. Might a doctor attempt to *segregate* a patient who had a communicable disease until that disease was no longer contagious?

10. Would an *egregious* piece of writing be well organized, well supported, and carefully crafted?

1. _____ Yes
2. _____ No
3. _____ Yes
4. _____ Yes
5. _____ No
6. _____ No
7. _____ Yes
8. _____ No
9. _____ Yes
10. _____ No

EXERCISE 3 IDENTIFYING ANTONYMS

Decide which word or phrase has the meaning that is opposite to that of the capitalized vocabulary word. Write the letter of your choice on the answer line.

1. SEGREGATE:
   a. isolate   b. permeate   c. integrate   d. celebrate

1. _____ c

2. EGREGIOUS:
   a. outstandingly good
   b. outstandingly evil
   c. perfect
   d. imperfect

2. _____ a

3. ADHERE:
   a. stick together   b. pull apart   c. disagree to   d. agree to

3. _____ b

4. ENSEMBLE:
   a. outfit   b. individual   c. monopoly   d. team

4. _____ b

5. GREGARIOUS:
   a. having an insulting nature
   b. preferring to be alone
   c. outgoing
   d. selective

5. _____ b

6. FACSIMILE:
   a. original   b. counterfeit   c. duplicate   d. photocopy

6. _____ a

7. DISSIMULATE:
   a. make similar   b. make dissimilar   c. make believe   d. make obvious

7. _____ d

8. INHERENT:
   a. innate   b. unusual   c. acquired   d. talented

8. _____ c

9. AGGREGATE:
   a. cluster   b. sum   c. fragment   d. batch

9. _____ c

10. SEMBLANCE:
    a. inward reality
    b. outward appearance
    c. possibility
    d. similarity

10. _____ a

EXERCISE 4 USING DIFFERENT FORMS OF WORDS

Decide which form of the vocabulary word in parentheses best completes the sentence. The form given may be correct. Write your answer on the answer line.

1. In Guy de Maupassant's story "The Necklace," a missing piece of jewelry is replaced by a _____ made of costly gems. *(facsimile)*

   1. __facsimile__

2. Many philosophers have argued whether people are _____ good or evil. *(inherent)*

   2. __inherently__

3. Ms. King's _____ was a great advantage as she campaigned for mayor. *(gregarious)*

   3. __gregariousness__

4. _____ of American Transcendentalism included Ralph Waldo Emerson and Henry David Thoreau. *(adhere)*

   4. __Adherents__

5. In order to infiltrate the gambling ring, the undercover agent had to maintain a convincing _____ of wealth. *(semblance)*

   5. __semblance__

6. _____ examples of weaving can be found at some of the beginning students' looms. *(egregious)*

   6. __Egregious__

7. To complete her new _____, Sarita bought a paisley scarf and a new pair of shoes. *(ensemble)*

   7. __ensemble__

8. Because Phillip so often lied about his motivations, he gained a reputation as a _____. *(dissimulate)*

   8. __dissimulator__

9. Cement is an _____ made of powered lime, silica, and several other hard substances. *(aggregate)*

   9. __aggregate__

10. Initially, the Nazis _____ the Jewish people in Warsaw by restricting them to ghettos. *(segregate)*

    10. __segregated__

READING COMPREHENSION

Each numbered sentence in the following passage contains an italicized vocabulary word or related form. After you read the passage, you will complete an exercise.

RAY CHARLES: MUSICAL PIONEER

Known primarily as a blues singer, pianist, and composer, Ray Charles (b. 1930) is associated with a wide range of musical styles. His audience is a large and diverse one, which includes country and western fans, blues artists, singers of Southern gospel music, and music students.

Ray Charles's rise to fame was not an easy one. By the age of five, he had already begun to go blind. (1) Totally blind by the age of seven, he was placed in a state institution, where he began to develop some of his *inherent* talent for music. There he learned to memorize music, as well as to play the piano and clarinet.

Charles first found work touring the South with local rhythm and blues bands. (2) When he moved to Seattle in 1950, he formed his own *ensemble*, which played traditional gospel music as well as some of his own jazz arrangements. (3) After successfully molding his own vocal style into a *facsimile* of the then-popular Nat King Cole's, he realized that it was time to develop, both vocally and instrumentally, a more individual and experimental style. (4) By 1954 he had evolved his own unique sound, an *aggregate* of gospel and blues that drew nationwide critical acclaim. By 1959 he had been named the country's leading male vocalist.

(5) A few years later, when Charles expressed his desire to record country and western music, many people, including managers of his record company, thought this

would be an *egregious* error. Nevertheless, his first country and western album sold well over one million copies.

Ray Charles did not make an impact only on music, however. (6) Because he refused to play for *segregated* audiences, he made history in 1961 by playing to the first integrated audience in a municipal auditorium in Memphis, Tennessee. (7) Nevertheless, he is not known as an *adherent* of particular causes. His reputation derives from his extraordinary musical talents and his impact on modern music.

During recent years Ray Charles has become known for his elaborate stage productions, and he has maintained his reputation as a consum-

mate blues, jazz, and country music star. An expert businessman, he runs Ray Charles Enterprises, tours widely, and maintains an active life. (8) However, no one would label him *gregarious*. (9) Hidden behind his dark glasses, Ray Charles can appear to be an isolated figure, a malcontent, or a *dissimulator*. Some critics have viewed him as a tormented artist; others have seen him as acutely frustrated by his blindness. (10) Yet Charles, who maintains much more than a mere *semblance* of sighted life by engaging in a wide range of activities, explains, "Seeing people or not seeing them, life is still life. The match that burns you also burns me."

Each of the following statements corresponds to a numbered sentence in the passage.
Each statement contains a blank and is followed by four answer choices. Decide which
choice fits best in the blank. The word or phrase that you choose must express roughly
the same meaning as the italicized word in the passage. Write the letter of your choice
on the answer line.

1. While he was in a state institution, Charles began to develop some of
   his _____ talent.
   a. naturally existing   c. hidden
   b. abnormally great   d. obvious

     1. _____ a

2. In Seattle he formed his own _____.
   a. record company   c. school for blind people
   b. task force   d. group of musicians

     2. _____ d

3. Charles initially molded his vocal style into a(n) _____ of Nat King Cole's.
   a. exact copy   b. mockery   c. parody   d. approximation

     3. _____ a

4. His unique sound was a(n) _____ of gospel and blues.
   a. hodgepodge   b. mixture   c. replica   d. example

     4. _____ b

5. Many people believed his switch to country and western music would be
   a(n) _____ error.
   a. extremely minor   c. embarrassing
   b. outstandingly bad   d. financial

     5. _____ b

6. Ray Charles refused to play for _____ audiences.
   a. hostile   b. small   c. extremely large   d. racially separated

     6. _____ d

7. He is not known as a(n) _____ of particular causes.
   a. opponent   b. instigator   c. follower   d. leader

     7. _____ c

8. No one would label him _____.
   a. modest   c. extremely unsociable
   b. immodest   d. extremely sociable

     8. _____ d

9. He can appear to be _____.
   a. one who hides his intentions   c. one who makes false promises
   b. one who boasts arrogantly   d. one who lacks self-confidence.

     9. _____ a

10. Charles maintains much more than a(n) _____ of sighted life.
    a. duplication   c. approximation
    b. outward appearance   d. likeness

     10. _____ b

Imagine that you are a jeweler who deals in precious gems. A customer wants you to
design two rings, one of them made of valuable materials and the other an
inexpensive copy. Being an artist of skill and creativity, you undertake the project with
confidence. Using at least five of the words from this lesson, write a report for the
customer describing your plans to design and execute the two rings. Underline each
vocabulary word that you use.

Some of the greatest figures in history have been those who have disagreed most persistently and vocally with other people and with established conventions in order to end tyranny, to stop slavery, and to ensure liberty. Yet few of us would want to be characterized as *disagreeable* because the word suggests being unreasonable and even egocentric. The words in this lesson deal with forms of disagreement and their results, and they will help you to understand the difference between purposeful refusal and selfish defiance.

affront
altercation
antagonist
bellicose
breach
contentious
dissension
rancor
retribution
schism

DEFINITIONS

After you have studied the definitions and example for each vocabulary word, write the word on the line to the right.

1. **affront** (ə-frŭnt′) *trans. verb* To insult intentionally.   *noun* An open or intentional offense, slight, or insult. (From the Latin *ad-*, meaning "to," and *frons*, meaning "face")

   Example The woman *affronted* the waitress by announcing in a loud voice that the service was substandard.

   1. _____

2. **altercation** (ôl′tər-kā′shən) *noun* A heated and noisy quarrel. (From the Latin word *alter*, meaning "other")

   Example Frightened, we rushed next door to settle the *altercation* that had started moments before.

   2. _____

3. **antagonist** (ăn-tăg′ə-nĭst) *noun* One who opposes and actively competes with another; adversary. (From the Greek *anti-*, meaning "against," and *agōn*, meaning "contest")

   Related Words **antagonism** *noun;* **antagonist** *adjective;* **antagonistically** *adverb;* **antagonize** *verb*
   Example In World War I, the Allies regarded the Red Baron, a German flier, as a formidable *antagonist*.

   3. _____
   MEMORY CUE: An *antagonist* usually opposes a *protagonist.*

4. **bellicose** (bĕl′ĭ-kōs′) *adjective* Warlike in manner or temperament. (From the Latin word *bellum*, meaning "war")

   Related Words **bellicosely** *adverb;* **bellicoseness** *noun*
   Example The *bellicose* manner of the big man made everyone afraid.

   4. _____

5. **breach** (brēch) *noun*   **a.** A breaking up or disruption of friendly relations; estrangement.   **b.** A violation or infraction, as of a law, legal obligation, or promise.

   Example   There was a prolonged and extremely hostile *breach* between the neighbors when one accused the other of stealing some tools.

5. _____

6. **contentious** (kən-tĕn'shəs) *adjective*   Quarrelsome. (From the Latin *com-*, meaning "with," and *tendere*, meaning "to strive")

   Related Word   **contentiousness** *noun*
   Example   The *contentious* partners often argued about the management of their business.

6. _____

7. **dissension** (dĭ-sĕn'shən) *noun*   A difference of opinion, especially one that leads to contention or strife.

   Related Words   **dissent** *verb;* **dissenter** *noun*
   Example   *Dissension* among the campaign workers led indirectly to the candidate's defeat.

7. _____

8. **rancor** (răng'kər) *noun*   Bitter, long-lasting resentment; ill will. (From the Latin word *rancere*, meaning "to stink")

   Related Words   **rancorous** *adjective;* **rancorously** *adverb*
   Example   The *rancor* that resulted from their argument even affected their friends, who felt forced to take sides.

8. _____

9. **retribution** (rĕt'rə-byoo'shən) *noun*   Something given or demanded in repayment, especially punishment. (From the Latin word *retribuere*, meaning "to repay")

   Related Word   **retributive** *adjective*
   Example   The angry man wanted a thousand dollars as *retribution* for the damage done to his reputation.

9. _____

10. **schism** (sĭz'əm, skĭz'əm) *noun*   A separation or division into factions. (From the Greek word *skhizein,* meaning "to split")

    Example   Martin Luther brought about a *schism* in the church that resulted in the formation of many new sects.

10. _____

NAME _____ DATE _____

EXERCISE 1 WRITING CORRECT WORDS

On the answer line, write the word from the vocabulary list that fits each definition.

1. Warlike in manner or temperament

2. Quarrelsome

3. Something given or demanded in repayment

4. One who opposes or competes with another

5. A noisy quarrel

6. Bitter, long-lasting resentment; ill will

7. To insult intentionally

8. A breaking up or disruption of friendly relations; estrangement

9. A separation into factions

10. A difference of opinion, especially one that leads to strife

1. __bellicose__

2. __contentious__

3. __retribution__

4. __antagonist__

5. __altercation__

6. __rancor__

7. __affront__

8. __breach__

9. __schism__

10. __dissension__

EXERCISE 2 USING WORDS CORRECTLY

Decide whether the italicized vocabulary word has been used correctly in the sentence. On the answer line, write *Correct* for correct use and *Incorrect* for incorrect use.

1. Johanna took her dance instructor's suggestions as an *affront* rather than as constructive criticism.

2. In Shakespeare's *Othello*, Iago, *antagonist* to the noble hero, is an evil schemer.

3. A *bellicose* person would be reluctant to start an argument.

4. Ronda demanded *retribution* for the insult that she had received.

5. The lawyer's *contentious* questioning of the witness caused the prosecutor to object.

6. The promotion of an inexperienced assistant caused *dissension* among the other employees.

7. We were forced to throw out the food that had become *rancor* during our vacation.

8. She wore a beautiful *breach* that perfectly complemented her gown.

9. When two people get married, they are joined by a *schism* of love.

10. Jack went to the tailor to arrange for the *altercation* of a suit that was too big.

1. __Correct__

2. __Correct__

3. __Incorrect__

4. __Correct__

5. __Correct__

6. __Correct__

7. __Incorrect__

8. __Incorrect__

9. __Incorrect__

10. __Incorrect__

EXERCISE 3 IDENTIFYING SYNONYMS AND ANTONYMS

Decide which word or phrase has the meaning that is the same as (a synonym) or opposite to (an antonym) that of the capitalized vocabulary word. Write the letter of your choice on the answer line.

1. SCHISM (synonym):
   a. split   b. scheme   c. argument   d. faction

2. BELLICOSE (antonym):
   a. argumentative b. angry   c. agreeable   d. amusing

1. __a__

2. __c__

Copyright © Great Source

Disagreement **89**

3. ALTERCATION (synonym):
   a. settlement   b. harmony   c. insult   d. dispute

4. ANTAGONIST (synonym):
   a. adversary   b. mediator   c. defender   d. victim

5. DISSENSION (synonym):
   a. tension   b. irresolution   c. determination   d. disagreement

6. AFFRONT (antonym):
   a. flatter   b. offend   c. help   d. annoy

7. CONTENTIOUS (synonym):
   a. agreeable   b. quarrelsome   c. different   d. odd

8. RANCOR (antonym):
   a. difference   b. argument   c. good will   d. diligence

9. RETRIBUTION (synonym):
   a. contribution   b. punishment   c. surprise   d. anger

10. BREACH (synonym):
    a. breakup   b. burden   c. bond   d. banquet

3. _____ d
4. _____ a
5. _____ d
6. _____ a
7. _____ b
8. _____ c
9. _____ b
10. _____ a

EXERCISE 4 USING DIFFERENT FORMS OF WORDS

Decide which form of the vocabulary word in parentheses best completes the sentence. The form given may be correct. Write your answer on the answer line.

1. The coach was thrown out of the game after an _____ with the umpire over a call. (altercation)

2. The diplomat considered the request an _____. (affront)

3. _____ among the troops increased when they were under pressure. (contentious)

4. Although many of the representatives appeared to dislike the new foreign policy, Petrocelli was the only one to _____ openly. (dissension)

5. The Civil War did not create the _____ between the North and South; rather, the war resulted from it. (schism)

6. Warren's _____ sometimes made rational conversation difficult. (bellicose)

7. After the long argument, Amanda was feeling hostile and answered her friend's questions _____. (rancor)

8. The dispute involved a legal _____ of contract. (breach)

9. Scott was so _____ toward our travel plan that we gave it up. (antagonist)

10. Because the judge pronounced a _____ sentence on the men guilty of fraud, they had to pay back the money taken from their victims. (retribution)

1. _____ altercation
2. _____ affront
3. _____ Contentiousness
4. _____ dissent
5. _____ schism
6. _____ bellicoseness
7. _____ rancorously
8. _____ breach
9. _____ antagonistic
10. _____ retributive

READING COMPREHENSION

Each numbered sentence in the following passage contains an italicized vocabulary word or related form. After you read the passage, you will complete an exercise.

ANNA LEONOWENS: EAST-WEST AMBASSADOR

Adventurous, daring, and *courageous* are words that could easily be applied to Anna Leonowens, the British woman who served as governess to the royal children of Siam at a time when the differences between people living in Asia and Europe were far more pronounced and intimidating than they are today. (1) This *schism* was rooted more in ignorance and fear than in open clashes over religion, territory, or politics, although these also played their role.

When Leonowens, mother of two, lost her husband and her fortune, she needed to find a position quickly in order to support herself and her family. Because the King of Siam had requested the aid of the British government in securing a governess for his family, Leonowens went to Bangkok in 1862. (2) From the very first, she knew that she was in an extremely *alien* environment, where ignorance of the new culture could easily result in hostility, and hostility could easily result in *affronts*.

(3) It was King Mongkut himself who turned out to be Leonowens's most formidable *antagonist:* she found herself in conflict with him from the outset. He was a domineering and arrogant ruler who regarded Anna as a servant and who did not hesitate to make extravagant demands of her. (4) Their first *altercation* took place only days after her arrival, when the king insisted that she live within the confines of the palace walls, and Leonowens, realizing how constraining that would be, openly and vehemently disagreed.

This was brave and unusual behavior for anyone—male or female, Asian or European—and it both angered the king and made him respect the governess.

For five years Leonowens taught English to the many royal children and also assisted the king with his correspondence. During that time she learned much about life within the palace, about the Siamese people and their culture, and about the country. (5) Her relationship with the royal children, with whom she shared affection and kindness, was a satisfying and rewarding one, but life was always difficult under the direction of the unpredictable and *contentious* king. Furthermore, Leonowens continually witnessed things that offended her deeply, such as slave auctions and public executions.

(6) One incident in particular nearly resulted in a permanent *breach* between the king and Leonowens. When the French government, which had been extending its imperialist influence over Southeast Asia, was putting pressure on the Siamese over territory, King Mongkut asked Leonowens to write a letter to the French that shifted responsibility for his own actions to

the British consul. (7) Since this was completely untrue, Anna refused, drawing so many threats and such *rancor* from the King that she feared for her personal safety. (8) When she tried to enter the palace the next day, armed soldiers thrust her back *bellicosely,* and she retreated to her house, where she had iron bars put on the windows. (9) Next, she sought the protection of the British consul, as well as his aid in easing and erasing the extreme *dissension* that now existed between her and many of the Siamese. (10) His efforts were eventually successful, and the king demanded no further *retribution* for her disobedience to his authority.

Leonowens left Siam in 1867 because she needed to attend to her own children's education. She regretfully left behind many people with whom she had established friendships. The king, who was at first—typically—angered by her desire to depart, did eventually express his respect for her and also his good will. Leonowns spent the remainder of her life teaching, as well as writing and lecturing about her experiences in Siam.

Each of the following statements corresponds to a numbered sentence in the passage. Each statement contains a blank and is followed by four answer choices. Decide which choice fits best in the blank. The word or phrase that you choose must express roughly the same meaning as the italicized word in the passage. Write the letter of your choice on the answer line.

1. The _____ between Asia and Europe resulted from ignorance, fear, and other causes.
   a. separation **b.** alienation **c.** contention **d.** rivalry

1. _____ **a**

2. Hostility could easily result in _____.
   a. armed conflict **c.** disputes
   b. diplomatic overtures **d.** intentional insults

2. _____ **d**

3. King Mongkut was Leonowens's most formidable _____.
   a. combatant **b.** adversary **c.** role model **d.** judge

3. _____ **b**

4. Their first _____ took place only days after her arrival.
   a. animosity **c.** heated argument
   b. difference of opinion **d.** battle

4. _____ **c**

5. Life was always difficult under the direction of the unpredictable and _____ king.
   a. quarrelsome **b.** devious **c.** autocratic **d.** repugnant

5. _____ **a**

6. One incident nearly resulted in a permanent _____ between the king and Leonowens.
   a. disruption of friendly relations **c.** bitterness
   b. interruption of hostilities **d.** disagreement

6. _____ **a**

7. Anna's refusal to write the letter drew such _____ from the king that she feared for her personal safety.
   a. violence **b.** tirades **c.** ill temper **d.** ill will

7. _____ **d**

8. When she tried to enter the palace, armed guards thrust her back _____.
   a. in an aggressive way **c.** intending to kill her
   b. in a warlike manner **d.** intending to frighten her

8. _____ **b**

9. Leonowens sought the aid of the British consul in easing the extreme _____ that now existed between the king and her.
   a. hatred **c.** violence
   b. difference of opinion **d.** competition

9. _____ **b**

10. The king demanded no further _____ for her disobedience to his authority.
    a. payment **b.** arguments **c.** punishment **d.** explanations

10. _____ **c**

Directions On the answer line, write the vocabulary word or a form of it that completes each analogy.

See page 79 for some strategies to use with analogies.

1. STALWART : CAUSE :: _____ : party (Lesson 13)

1. _____ **adherent**

2. MUSICIAN : ORCHESTRA :: _____ : actor (Lesson 13)

2. _____ **ensemble**

3. VAIN : FLATTERY :: _____ : company (Lesson 13)

3. _____ **gregarious**

4. QUIBBLE : CRITICISM :: _____ : riot (Lesson 14)

4. _____ **altercation**

5. FRACTURE : BONE :: _____ : church (Lesson 14)

5. _____ **schism**

6. VIOLATION : LAW :: _____ : contract (Lesson 14)

6. _____ **breach**

Although we generally connect negotiation and diplomacy with international politics, the two terms have a personal application as well. Any time you confer with another person in order to reach an agreement, you are bargaining and making compromises. When you use tact and sensitivity in dealing with others, you exercise diplomacy. The words in this lesson will help you to understand both the practical and political sides of the ability to secure advantages without arousing hostility.

WORD LIST

arbitration
attaché
consulate
covenant
discretion
emissary
entente
Machiavellian
protocol
status quo

DEFINITIONS

After you have studied the definitions and example for each vocabulary word, write the word on the line to the right.

1. **arbitration** (är′bĭ-trā′shən) *noun*   The process by which the parties in a dispute submit their differences to the judgment of an impartial person or group appointed by mutual consent. (From the Latin word *arbitrari*, meaning "to give judgment")

   Related Words   **arbitrate** *verb*; **arbitrator** *noun*
   Example   When the trade union and company management reached an impasse during contract negotiations, they opted for *arbitration*.

   1. _____

2. **attaché** (ăt′ə-shā′, ă-tă′shā′) *noun*   A person officially assigned to the staff of a diplomatic office in a foreign country to serve in some particular capacity. (From the French word *attacher*, meaning "to attach")

   Example   The Greek *attaché* in charge of cultural affairs arranged an exhibition of sculpture at the museum in order to increase Canadian awareness of his country's rich artistic achievements.

   2. _____

3. **consulate** (kŏn′sə-lĭt) *noun*   The premises occupied by a consul, an official appointed by a government to reside in a foreign city in order to represent his or her government's commercial interests and to give assistance to its citizens there. (From the Latin word *consul*, meaning "a Roman official")

   Related Words   **consul** *noun*; **consular** *adjective*
   Example   When the tourist accidentally dropped his passport into the Mediterranean, he went to the nearest United States *consulate* for assistance in getting a replacement.

   3. _____

4. **covenant** (kŭv'ə-nənt) *noun*   **a.** A binding agreement made by two or more persons or parties; compact.   **b.** In law, a formally sealed agreement or contract. (From the Latin *com-*, meaning "together," and *venire*, meaning "to come")

   Example   The *covenant* of the League of Nations, an international organization founded after World War I, outlined guiding purposes and ideals.

4. _____

5. **discretion** (dĭ-skrĕsh'ən) *noun*   **a.** The quality of demonstrating a cautious reserve in one's speech or behavior; prudence.   **b.** Freedom to act or judge on one's own. (From the Latin *dis-*, meaning "apart," and *cernere*, meaning "to deceive")

   Related Word   discretionary *adjective*
   Example   A president must exercise *discretion* when negotiating with foreign powers in matters of trade and national defense.

5. _____
USAGE NOTE: Another related adjective is *discreet*. Do not confuse *discreet* with *discrete*, which means "constituting a separate thing; distinct."

6. **emissary** (ĕm'ĭ-sĕr'ē) *noun*   An agent sent to represent or advance the interests of a person, group, or nation. (From the Latin *ex-*, meaning "out," and *mittere*, meaning "to send")

   Example   The French ambassador's cold response to the request of the British *emissary* brought their meeting to an end.

6. _____

7. **entente** (ŏn-tŏnt') *noun*   An agreement between two or more governments or powers for cooperative action or policy. (From the French word *entendre*, meaning "to understand")

   Example   The *entente* of the two nations concerning educational exchange was viewed as a beginning attempt to establish more friendly relations.

7. _____
USAGE NOTE: *Entente*, an agreement to cooperate, may follow *détente*, an easing of tension between nations.

8. **Machiavellian** (măk'ē-ə-věl'ē-ən) *adjective*   Of or pertaining to the doctrine of the Italian diplomat Niccolò Machiavelli, a doctrine that denies the relevance of morality in political affairs and holds that craft and deceit are justified in pursuing and maintaining political power.

   Example   The *Machiavellian* party official betrayed his long-time ally when he saw a chance for his own political advancement.

8. _____

9. **protocol** (prō'tə-kôl', prō'tə-kŏl') *noun*   The forms of ceremony and etiquette observed by diplomats and heads of states. (From the Late Greek word *prōtokollon*, meaning "table of contents")

   Example   According to the rules of *protocol*, a commoner must not touch the queen of England.

9. _____

10. **status quo** (stā'təs kwō', stăt'əs kwō') *noun*   The existing condition or state of affairs. (From the Latin phrase *status quo*, meaning "the state in which")

    Example   In order to maintain the *status quo*, the rapidly growing company decided not to alter personnel policies.

10. _____

EXERCISE 1 WRITING CORRECT WORDS

On the answer line, write the word from the vocabulary list that fits each definition.

1. An agent who represents the interests of a person, group, or nation

2. The existing condition or state of affairs

3. The process by which parties in a dispute submit their differences to the judgment of an impartial person or group

4. The premises occupied by a government official who represents his or her government's interests in a foreign city

5. Cautious reserve in speech or behavior; freedom to act or judge on one's own

6. Ceremony and etiquette observed by diplomats and heads of state

7. A member of the staff of a diplomatic office in a foreign country

8. An agreement between two or more powers for cooperative action

9. Pertaining to the theory that craft and deceit are justified in pursuing and maintaining political power

10. A binding agreement between two or more parties; contract

1. _____ emissary _____
2. _____ status quo _____
3. _____ arbitration _____
4. _____ consulate _____
5. _____ discretion _____
6. _____ protocol _____
7. _____ attaché _____
8. _____ entente _____
9. _____ Machiavellian _____
10. _____ covenant _____

EXERCISE 2 USING WORDS CORRECTLY

Each of the following questions contains an italicized vocabulary word. Choose the correct answer to the question, and write *Yes* or *No* on the answer line.

1. Is *discretion* a desirable quality in a public official?

2. Would a *Machiavellian* leader be likely to submit easily to the demands of numerous special-interest groups?

3. When a farmer signs an agreement with a buyer to sell wheat at a certain amount per bushel, has the farmer made a *covenant* with the buyer?

4. Is a diplomat expected to follow *protocol* in dealing with foreign rulers?

5. Is an *attaché* a supplement to a book or political document?

6. Is an *entente* a resumption of conflict between nations?

7. Is a supporter of the *status quo* a person who encourages change?

8. Is *arbitration* between countries a method of resolving a dispute?

9. Is a *consulate* a branch of a political party located in a foreign city?

10. Would the president's *emissary* need to be knowledgeable and trustworthy?

1. _____ Yes _____
2. _____ No _____
3. _____ Yes _____
4. _____ Yes _____
5. _____ No _____
6. _____ No _____
7. _____ No _____
8. _____ Yes _____
9. _____ No _____
10. _____ Yes _____

EXERCISE 3 CHOOSING THE BEST WORD

Decide which vocabulary word or related form best completes the sentence, and write the letter of your choice on the answer line.

1. The Celtic chieftain used _____ tactics to control the competing clans.
   a. Machiavellian   **b.** discretionary   **c.** consular   **d.** entente

2. Because of the complexity of Asian customs, the corporate executives received a briefing on _____ before their trip to the Far East.
   a. covenants   **b.** emissaries   **c.** arbitration   **d.** protocol

1. _____ a _____
2. _____ d _____

3. The territories of Bistonia and Argovia made a(n) _____ to defend each other in the event of an attack by their warlike neighbors.
   a. consulate   b. arbitration   c. status quo   d. covenant

3. _____ d _____

4. Mercury, the Roman god of commerce, travel, and thievery, often served as Jupiter's _____ to other gods and mortals.
   a. emissary   b. consulate   c. arbitrator   d. protocol

4. _____ a _____

5. The coach had so much confidence in the abilities of the rookie quarterback that he allowed him to use his own _____ in calling plays.
   a. arbitration   b. covenant   c. discretion   d. protocol

5. _____ c _____

6. The dispute between city employees and the mayor may go to _____.
   a. entente   b. arbitration   c. discretion   d. status quo

6. _____ b _____

7. Mexico and the United States have a long-standing _____ on border disputes.
   a. consulate   b. entente   c. emissary   d. discretion

7. _____ b _____

8. The British _____ in the Seychelle Islands was once a social and cultural center.
   a. consulate   b. emissary   c. discretion   d. protocol

8. _____ a _____

9. The naval _____ from the embassy will inspect the property.
   a. consulate   b. covenant   c. discretion   d. attaché

9. _____ d _____

10. Because of her extensive investments in the stock market, Catherine Beaumont had a vested interest in seeing the economic _____ maintained.
   a. arbitration   b. protocol   c. status quo   d. discretion

10. _____ c _____

EXERCISE 4 USING DIFFERENT FORMS OF WORDS

Decide which form of the vocabulary word in parentheses best completes the sentence. The form given may be correct. Write your answer on the answer line.

1. Letitia Baldridge was Jacqueline Kennedy's social secretary and adviser on _____. (*protocol*)

1. _____ protocol _____

2. To reduce court case loads, independent attorneys may _____ between the parties in a civil suit. (*arbitration*)

2. _____ arbitrate _____

3. The Colonas sent two _____ backstage to deliver their congratulations to the stars. (*emissary*)

3. _____ emissaries _____

4. The two rulers added changes to the _____ that made it a formal alliance. (*entente*)

4. _____ entente _____

5. Whenever he leaves the country, Mr. Chung gives _____ power to his administrative aide. (*discretion*)

5. _____ discretionary _____

6. In her history class, Doris studied the _____ exploits of ancient Rome's declining government. (*Machiavellian*)

6. _____ Machiavellian _____

7. Captain Kate Moffett will be the military _____ at our embassy in Brazil. (*attaché*)

7. _____ attaché _____

8. "Does the family of a foreign _____ have diplomatic immunity in the United States?" Oliver asked the ambassador. (*consulate*)

8. _____ consul _____

9. Thirteen countries have entered into a _____ to reduce oil production. (*covenant*)

9. _____ covenant _____

10. After having moved twelve times in the last ten years, the Gluckstern family is hoping to preserve the _____. (*status quo*)

10. _____ status quo _____

READING COMPREHENSION

Each numbered sentence in the following passage contains an italicized vocabulary word or related form. After you read the passage, you will complete an exercise.

THE EVOLUTION OF THE DIPLOMATIC SYSTEM

Diplomacy, the practice of conducting negotiations between nations for the attainment of mutually satisfying terms, has existed ever since the first disagreement. (1) At first military force settled arguments more often than formal *covenants* or treaties did. (2) However, there are also indications that in ancient civilizations prominent citizens were asked to settle disputes through *arbitration.* (3) As early as 1500 B.C., the rulers of Egypt, China, India, Babylonia, and Mesopotamia sent *emissaries* to resolve conflicts with foreign heads of state. In 950 B.C. the Queen of Sheba herself visited Israel's King Solomon on a diplomatic mission.

The diplomatic system was refined in ancient Greece. Greece consisted of many small city-states, and official representatives traveled between them to deliver messages. (4) These first ambassadors, in accordance with established rules, received special immunity, followed specific *protocol,* and were forbidden to accept favors or gifts.

Diplomacy became an art in medieval Italy. Because Italy was composed of many separate states ruled by powerful groups or families, such as the Medicis, diplomacy became the key to everyday governing. For the first time, permanent representatives were placed in critical locations to preserve the interests of the Italian states. (5) From these sites diplomats interacted, using tact and *discretion* in their routine work.

While the diplomatic system flourished in Italy, it also became associated with underhanded practices. (6) Through Niccolò Machiavelli's famous book *The Prince,* which describes how to rule successfully without morality, diplomats acquired the unfortunate reputation of being unscrupulous spies with *Machiavellian* tendencies.

The diplomatic system continued to evolve throughout the centuries. (7) Today embassies in foreign capitals around the world guard their countries' interests in foreign lands, maintain the *status quo* with allies, and provide important information about foreign powers. (8) An embassy is headed by an ambassador and is staffed by *attachés,* advisers, and administrators.

(9) Another branch of the diplomatic system is the *consulate,* which is less directly involved in political affairs. Consulates in foreign cities regulate commercial concerns, protect citizens in foreign countries, regulate shipping in foreign waters, and notarize important documents.

(10) Dealing with matters as minor as a missing passport or as major as a significant *entente,* modern diplomats enjoy challenging, rewarding, and even dangerous careers. Modern diplomacy, which can be traced to the earliest human contact, still influences millions of people and hundreds of countries in a system that helps promote global understanding and cooperation.

READING COMPREHENSION EXERCISE

Each of the following statements corresponds to a numbered sentence in the passage. Each statement contains a blank and is followed by four answer choices. Decide which choice fits best in the blank. The word or phrase that you choose must express roughly the same meaning as the italicized word in the passage. Write the letter of your choice on the answer line.

1. At first military force settled arguments more often than _____ did.
   a. sensitive negotiating
   b. binding agreements
   c. assemblies
   d. promptness

   1._____b_____

2. In ancient civilizations prominent citizens were asked to settle disputes through _____.
   a. voting procedures
   b. combat
   c. impartial judgments
   d. systematic arrangements

   2._____c_____

3. The rulers of Egypt and China sent _____ to resolve conflicts with foreign heads of state.
   a. agents   b. soldiers   c. nobles   d. observers

3. _____a_____

4. The first ambassadors followed specific _____.
   a. forms of ceremony and etiquette   c. rules of debate
   b. authorizations from their rulers   d. diplomatic disclosures

4. _____a_____

5. Diplomats used _____ in their routine work.
   a. comprehensive guidelines   c. civilized methods
   b. standard rules   d. cautious reserve

5. _____d_____

6. In Italy diplomats acquired the unfortunate reputation of having _____ tendencies.
   a. powerful   b. deceitful   c. dangerous   d. popular

6. _____b_____

7. Embassies guard their countries' interests and maintain the _____ with allies.
   a. reluctant relationship   c. existing conditions
   b. positive relationship   d. appropriate observances

7. _____c_____

8. An embassy consists of an ambassador, _____, and advisers.
   a. diplomatic staff members   c. consuls
   b. lawyers   d. foreign authorities

8. _____a_____

9. The _____ is less directly involved in political affairs.
   a. eminent authority on economic affairs   c. cultural adviser
   b. premises of a government's representative   d. military adviser

9. _____b_____

10. Modern diplomats deal with issues from a missing passport to _____.
    a. funding   c. an everyday argument
    b. a commercial negotiation   d. an agreement among governments

10. _____d_____

WRITING ASSIGNMENT

For a social studies assignment, you have been asked to write an essay illustrating that diplomacy plays a significant role in solving international problems. Choose a foreign policy issue from history, such as the Monroe Doctrine, or a more recent event, such as the reduction in nuclear weapons, and do some library research about it. Then write an essay, using at least five of the vocabulary words from this lesson, to show the importance of diplomacy. Underline each vocabulary word that you use.

VOCABULARY ENRICHMENT

The word *Machiavellian* comes from Niccolò Machiavelli (1469–1527), a citizen of Florence at a time when Italy was divided into constantly warring city-states. The city-states were dominated by brutal rulers who would seize power from one another and throw the government into turmoil.

In his book *The Prince*, Machiavelli proposed that a strong ruler might be justified in using harsh or underhanded means if these guaranteed stability. Although the word *Machiavellian* is now used to mean deceitful manipulations of power, we should remember that Machiavelli's political philosophy was based upon the necessities of difficult times.

Activity Many other English words come from the names of their originators. Using a dictionary, look up the derivations and definitions for each of the following words.

1. boycott   2. chauvinism   3. gerrymander   4. quisling   5. solon

The **Test** for Lessons 13, 14, and 15 is on page T17.

TEST-TAKING SKILLS

SAT AND ACT READING COMPREHENSION TEST ITEMS

A section on reading comprehension is part of the Scholastic Assessment Test (SAT) as well as the American College Testing (ACT) Assessment Program. In a reading comprehension test, you are asked to read one or more paragraphs and then answer questions about them. Both the SAT and the ACT test contain reading passages on a variety of subjects in the humanities, the social sciences, and the natural sciences. Both contain narrative passages as well, fiction or nonfiction in the SAT and fiction only in the ACT test. Although the test items in this lesson are closer in format to the SAT than to the ACT test, the strategies that follow apply to both.

STRATEGIES

1. *Determine the main idea as you read.* Understanding the main idea of a passage will give you a better understanding of its details and of the test items that follow. The main idea may not be stated directly in the passage. Furthermore, test items calling for the main idea may do so indirectly. For example, a question may require you to select the best title or to identify the author's writing purpose.

2. *Identify sentences that support the main idea.* Such sentences contain reasons and examples. You will need to return to some of these supporting sentences in order to answer test items about detailed information.

3. *Distinguish conclusions from supporting sentences.* Conclusions are statements that summarize ideas already presented. Such words as *thus* and *therefore* may signal conclusions.

4. *Be prepared to make inferences about the reading passage.* You are already prepared to identify conclusions that are stated in the passage. You must also be ready to identify *inferences:* conclusions that are not stated in the passage but may reasonably be drawn from it.

5. *Read at a speed that is just slow enough to enable you to retain the meaning.* Read the passage; then answer the questions. Your first reading of the passage should familiarize you with the way in which the author develops his or her main idea. Then you will return to the passage as you answer each question; do not rely on your memory alone. Be sure to answer the questions in terms of the passage, not in terms of what you have read elsewhere about the subject. Always read each question all the way through before selecting an answer.

EXERCISE ANSWERING READING COMPREHENSION TEST ITEMS

Read the following passage and then answer the questions about it. For each question write the letter of your choice on the answer line.

The segregation of members of a pair of genes was demonstrated by Mendel in a cross of a tall pea plant with a dwarf pea plant. When self-fertilized, tall plants produced tall offspring only. Dwarf plants, when self-fertilized, produced only dwarf offspring. This held true no matter how many generations of peas were followed, demonstrating that these strains were *pure lines*. However, when cross-pollination occurred between a tall plant and a dwarf plant, the first-generation plants (F_1) were all tall, illustrating that tallness was *dominant* over dwarfness, which was *recessive*. When these tall hybrid F_1 plants were self-fertilized, the second (F_2) generation produced was composed of both tall and dwarf plants in a 3:1 ratio. This type of cross, involving one trait in alternative forms, is termed a *monohybrid* cross. A cross involving two traits in alternative forms is a *dihybrid* cross, and a cross involving three traits is a *trihybrid* cross.

To prove that this 3:1 ratio was indeed the result of a pair of segregating genes, with the gene for tallness being dominant over the gene for dwarfness, Mendel self-fertilized the F_2 generation. Because dwarfness was recessive, he predicted that the F_2 dwarf plants would produce only dwarf F_3 progeny. He also predicted that one-third of the F_2 tall plants would be *homozygous* for the dominant tall gene—that is, both members of the gene pair were the same, both determining tallness. Therefore, one-third of the F_2 tall plants would, when self-fertilized, produce only tall F_3 progeny. The remaining two-thirds of the F_2 tall plants, Mendel predicted, would be *heterozygous*— that is, one member of the gene pair would specify tallness and the other dwarfness. These heterozygous plants would have progeny in a tall-to-dwarf ratio of 3:1. Mendel's predictions were borne out by his experimental results.

1. Which of the following titles best fits the passage?
   (A) The Work of Mendel
   (B) Self-Fertilization and Cross-Pollination of Plants
   (C) The Principle of Segregation in Genetics
   (D) Dominant and Recessive Genes
   (E) Tallness and Dwarfness in Plants

   1. _____C_____

2. Which of the following generations of plants are discussed in the passage?
   I. F1
   II. F2
   III. F3
   (A) I only   (B) II only   (C) III only   (D) I and II only   (E) I, II, and III

   2. _____E_____

3. In the cultivation of plants, the term *self-fertilization* refers to
   (A) pollination of a plant with its own pollen
   (B) pollination of a plant with pollen from another plant
   (C) random pollination of a plant
   (D) cross-pollination
   (E) pollination of a plant by bees

   3. _____A_____

4. When a heterozygous plant is self-fertilized,
   (A) its offspring have identical traits
   (B) its offspring have traits of the dominant gene
   (C) its offspring have traits of the recessive gene
   (D) some offspring have the dominant trait; others have the recessive
   (E) it is impossible to predict the traits of the offspring

   4. _____D_____

5. The F_2 generation contained dwarf plants and tall plants in the ratio of
   (A) 3:1   (B) 1:3   (C) 2:1   (D) 1:2   (E) 1:1

   5. _____B_____

6. The F_2 generation of pea plants is an example of a
   (A) monohybrid cross   (B) dihybrid cross   (C) trihybrid cross
   (D) decahybrid cross   (E) none of these

   6. _____A_____

The Latin root *-fid-* means "faith," "to trust," or "to confide." The Latin root *-jur-* means "law," "judge," or "as sworn by oath." Both of these roots have served as the basis for many English words. If you have faith in someone, you have a *confident* belief in that person's trustworthiness. A *confidential* matter is done or communicated in secret. A *juror* swears to judge and give a verdict on a specific legal matter. In this lesson you will learn other words that refer to the concepts of faith or law and judging.

WORD LIST

adjure
affidavit
confidant
conjure
fealty
fiancé
fidelity
infidel
jurisdiction
perjure

DEFINITIONS

After you have studied the definitions and example for each vocabulary word, write the word on the line to the right.

1. **adjure** (ə-jŏŏr´) *trans. verb* **a.** To command solemnly, as under oath. **b.** To request, urge, or advise earnestly. (From the Latin *ad-*, meaning "to," and *jurare*, meaning "to swear")

   Related Word **adjuration** *noun*
   Example The probation officer *adjured* the frightened teenager to tell the truth.

   1. _____

2. **affidavit** (ăf´ĭ-dā´vĭt) *noun* A written declaration made under oath before a notary public or some other official. (From the Latin *ad* , meaning "to," and *fidus*, meaning "faithful")

   Example The witnesses signed an *affidavit* that they were present at the scene of the accident.

   2. _____

3. **confidant** (kŏn´fĭ-dănt´, kŏn´fĭ-dänt´) *noun* A person to whom secrets or private matters are confided. (From the Latin *com-*, an intensive prefix, and *fidere*, meaning "to trust")

   Related Words **confide** *verb*; **confidence** *noun*; **confidential** *adjective*
   Example A *confidant* should be a good listener and a trustworthy person.

   3. _____

4. **conjure** (kŏn´jər, kən-jŏŏr´) *trans. verb* **a.** To produce as if by magic. **b.** To call upon or request, especially by an oath. **c.** To summon (a spirit) by oath, incantation, or magic spell. *intrans. verb* To practice magic; perform magic tricks. (From the Latin *com-*, an intensive prefix, and *jurare*, meaning "to swear")

   Related Word **conjurer** *noun*
   Example Edith stared intently out the window, as if the landscape would offer her the inspiration to *conjure* a miracle.

   4. _____
   USAGE NOTE: The idiom *conjure up* means "to call to mind" or "to evoke."

5. **fealty** (fē′əl-tē) *noun* **a.** The loyalty and duty of a vassal, or tenant, to his feudal lord. **b.** Allegiance to a government, a superior, or to persons or things in general. (From the Latin word *fides*, meaning "faith")

   Example   During the Middle Ages, a pledge of *fealty* to a lord could entail serving in his private army.

   5. _____

6. **fiancé** (fē′än-sā′, fē-än′sā′) *noun* A man engaged to be married. (From the Latin word *fidere*, meaning "to trust")

   Related Word **fiancée** *noun*
   Example   It is customary for a *fiancé* to give his future bride an engagement ring.

   6. _____
   USAGE NOTE: A *fiancée* is a woman engaged to be married.

7. **fidelity** (fĭ-dĕl′ĭ-tē, fī-dĕl′ĭ-tē) *noun* **a.** Faithfulness to obligations, duties, or observances; loyalty. **b.** Exact correspondence with fact or with a given quality, condition, or event; accuracy: *the fidelity of the translation.* **c.** Degree to which an electronic system, such as a radio, reproduces sound without distortion. (From the Latin word *fides*, meaning "faith")

   Example   Mr. Garrison carried out his responsibilities to his employer with commendable *fidelity.*

   7. _____

8. **infidel** (ĭn′fĭ-dəl, ĭn′fĭ-dĕl′) *noun* **a.** A person who does not accept a particular faith. **b.** A person who does not believe in religion. (From the Latin *in-*, meaning "not," and *fides*, meaning "faith")

   Example   During the Crusades, Moslems and Christians called one another *infidels.*

   8. _____

9. **jurisdiction** (jŏŏr′ĭs-dĭk′shən) *noun* **a.** Authority, power, or control. **b.** The extent of authority: *within the county's jurisdiction.* **c.** The territory over which authority extends. **d.** The right and power to administer justice or exercise judicial functions. (From the Latin words *jus*, meaning "law," and *dicere*, meaning "to say")

   Related Word **jurisdictional** *adjective*
   Example   A principal has *jurisdiction* over students and teachers in a school.

   9. _____

10. **perjure** (pûr′jər) *trans. verb* To render (oneself) guilty of a crime by giving deliberately false, misleading, or incomplete testimony under oath. (From the Latin *per-*, meaning "thoroughly away," and *jurare*, meaning "to swear")

    Related Word **perjury** *noun*
    Example   Mrs. Conklin *perjured* herself on the witness stand when she stated that she purchased the television set.

    10. _____

EXERCISE 1 COMPLETING DEFINITIONS

On the answer line, write the word from the vocabulary list that best completes each definition.

1. To produce as if by magic or to call upon by an oath is to _____.

2. A man engaged to be married is called a(n) _____.

3. A(n) _____ is a person who does not accept a particular faith or does not believe in religion.

4. A close friend to whom one confides secrets is a(n) _____.

5. A written and sworn declaration made before an authorized person is called a(n) _____.

6. Authority, power, or control is called _____.

7. To command solemnly is to _____.

8. The loyalty of a vassal to his feudal lord is called _____.

9. To give false, misleading, or incomplete testimony under oath is to _____ oneself.

10. Faithfulness to obligations, duties, or observances is _____.

1. __conjure__
2. __fiancé__
3. __infidel__

4. __confidant__
5. __affidavit__

6. __jurisdiction__
7. __adjure__
8. __fealty__
9. __perjure__
10. __fidelity__

EXERCISE 2 USING WORDS CORRECTLY

Decide whether the italicized vocabulary word has been used correctly in the sentence. On the answer line, write *Correct* for correct use or *Incorrect* for incorrect use.

1. Robin *perjured* herself by telling the truth in court.

2. Sharon and her *fiancé* are planning to be married in August.

3. As an *infidel* Joseph goes to a house of worship at least once a week.

4. Grandfather *adjured* me not to become an actress.

5. In Shakespeare's *Macbeth,* the three witches perform feats of *conjuring* in Macbeth's presence.

6. Mrs. Hastings was fired for *fidelity* to her employer and dedication to her job.

7. Ted wrote and signed the *affidavit* in the privacy of his room.

8. Fu Chang-so and his family were forced to pledge their *fealty* to the warlord.

9. Martha considered Gerald her *confidant* because she could tell him all of her secrets.

10. Most children have *jurisdiction* over their parents.

1. __Incorrect__
2. __Correct__
3. __Incorrect__
4. __Correct__
5. __Correct__

6. __Incorrect__
7. __Incorrect__
8. __Correct__
9. __Correct__

10. __Incorrect__

EXERCISE 3 CHOOSING THE BEST WORD

Decide which vocabulary word or related form best completes the sentence, and write the letter of your choice on the answer line.

1. Nelson never forgot his father's _____ to make a living by honest means.
   a. affidavit   **b.** infidel   **c.** jurisdiction   **d.** adjuration

2. Linda and her _____ discussed their wedding plans with both families.
   a. confidant   **b.** fiancé   **c.** infidel   **d.** fealty

1. __d__

2. __b__

3. The governor told his closest _____ that he would retire at the end of his term.
   a. confidants   b. infidels   c. conjurers   d. jurisdictions

3. _____ a

4. As an expert witness on trademark law, Mr. Davidson was required to sign a(n) _____ that contained his testimony about the similarity of the two package designs.
   a. fidelity   b. affidavit   c. perjury   d. confidant

4. _____ b

5. Because he omitted the detail about Dixon's being late to dinner on the night in question, Morgan was prosecuted for _____.
   a. adjuring   b. conjuring   c. perjury   d. fidelity

5. _____ c

6. To become a citizen of the United States, you must give up your foreign citizenship and pledge _____ to the United States.
   a. confidants   b. jurisdiction   c. perjury   d. fidelity

6. _____ d

7. Lila prepares such lavish meals from leftovers that she seems to have the powers of a(n) _____.
   a. conjurer   b. confidant   c. affidavit   d. infidel

7. _____ a

8. Even when he is away at college, Erroll operates his car under the _____ of Wisconsin, his home state.
   a. affidavit   b. jurisdiction   c. fealty   d. fidelity

8. _____ b

9. Centuries ago, the army of _____ stormed the gates of the holy place.
   a. confidants   b. affidavits   c. infidels   d. conjurers

9. _____ c

10. Joe's _____ to the company was questioned after he discussed company policy with reporters.
    a. fealty   b. jurisdiction   c. perjury   d. affidavit

10. _____ a

EXERCISE 4 USING DIFFERENT FORMS OF WORDS

Decide which form of the vocabulary word in parentheses best completes the sentence. The form given may be correct. Write your answer on the answer line.

1. The high priest considered all who did not practice his religion to be _____. (infidel)

1. _____ infidels

2. Ellen was an ideal _____ for Lucy. (confidant)

2. _____ confidant

3. _____ us to extinguish the fire before we went to sleep, our counselor zipped herself into her sleeping bag. (adjure)

3. _____ Adjuring

4. Over the weekend Bruce introduced Leslie, his _____, to the family. (fiancé)

4. _____ fiancée

5. Before leaving for the world championships, the athletes participated in a ceremony of _____ to their country. (fealty)

5. _____ fealty

6. Yesterday the aromas of roast turkey and pumpkin pie _____ up happy memories of their childhood Thanksgivings at the farm. (conjure)

6. _____ conjured

7. Ann tried to locate a notary public to witness the _____ that proved her ownership of the property. (affidavit)

7. _____ affidavit

8. Hans van Meergeren, an art forger, copied the paintings of Jan Vermeer with astounding _____. (fidelity)

8. _____ fidelity

9. In addition to being sentenced for embezzlement, Ms. Bradshaw was convicted of _____. (perjury)

9. _____ perjury

10. The _____ dispute was settled by an objective mediator. (jurisdiction)

10. _____ jurisdictional

READING COMPREHENSION

Each numbered sentence in the following passage contains an italicized vocabulary word or related form. After you read the passage, you will complete an exercise.

PYRAMUS AND THISBE

(1) According to the Roman poet Ovid (43 B.C.–A.D. 17), the heart's *jurisdiction* is often greater than the mind's in matters of love. (2) Ovid's sentimental tale of Pyramus and Thisbe depicts how *fealty* can interfere with logic and end in tragedy.

Pyramus and Thisbe, neighbors in the beautiful Asian city of Babylon, fell in love and wished to marry. Unfortunately, their families had been feuding for years over a forgotten misdeed. (3) When Pyramus sought permission to become Thisbe's *fiancé*, they were forbidden to marry or even to speak to each other. (4) Although the young couple took their parents' *adjurations* seriously, they could not remain apart and found a way to keep their love alive.

One day Pyramus and Thisbe discovered that there was a loose brick in the wall that separated their houses. With little difficulty they found that they could slip the brick out and whisper to each other when no one was around. This method of communication was not satisfactory for long, however. (5) The opening was so small that Thisbe could not even get her hand in it, and the *confidants* could only take turns putting their ears to the wall while listening anxiously for the sound of someone coming. Finally, no longer able to tolerate separation, Pyramus and Thisbe decided to run away.

Pyramus planned their escape carefully. They would wait until night to sneak out of their houses, and each would leave the city through a separate gate. He explained that he did not want the guards at the gates to remember the pair being together.

(6) He knew that the guards, if asked to testify about their escape, would never *perjure* themselves, even for the sake of love. Pyramus suggested that they meet outside the city at the monument called Ninus' Tomb, where a tall mulberry tree with silvery white berries grew.

On the appointed night, all went well until Thisbe arrived at the tomb. As she stood under the tree to await Pyramus, she was suddenly frightened by a lion returning from its kill. Leaving her cloak behind, the terrified young woman ran for her life. The lion, filled with the calf it had eaten, was not interested in Thisbe. The animal sniffed her cloak and picked it up in its blood-stained mouth but dropped it again before disappearing into the trees.

At this point Pyramus arrived at the tomb. Discovering the lion tracks and Thisbe's blood-stained cloak under the tree, Pyramus panicked. (7) In his confused state of mind, he *conjured* up a horrible picture of Thisbe's death in the lion's jaws. (8) Pyramus was so distraught that he probably would not have believed the true story even if it had been part of an eyewitness's *affidavit*. In utter despair Pyramus drew his sword and killed himself.

In the meantime Thisbe's terror had diminished. Worrying about Pyramus, she returned to the tomb only to find her beloved dying. (9) Feeling like an *infidel* without a guiding faith, Thisbe could not face the future alone. Taking Pyramus' sword, she, too, killed herself.

The young couple died, but their fate was not forgotten. Their parents, finally reconciled by the tragedy, buried Pyramus and Thisbe together in a common tomb. (10) Their blood, spilled out of tragic *fidelity*, stained the mulberry tree forever. From that time forth, the tree's fruit has been dark red rather than white as a reminder of the misfortunes of Pyramus and Thisbe.

Each of the following statements corresponds to a numbered sentence in the passage. Each statement contains a blank and is followed by four answer choices. Decide which choice fits best in the blank. The word or phrase that you choose must express roughly the same meaning as the italicized word in the passage. Write the letter of your choice on the answer line.

1. According to the poet Ovid, the heart often has greater _____ than the mind.
   a. faith   b. pain   c. authority   d. sacrifice

2. The story of Pyramus and Thisbe shows how _____ can end in tragedy.
   a. pride   b. dependence   c. punishment   d. loyalty

3. Pyramus wanted to become the _____.
   a. future husband of Thisbe   c. equal of Thisbe
   b. champion of Thisbe   d. rival of Thisbe

4. The young couple took their parents' _____ seriously, but they could not stay apart.
   a. anger   c. unkind words
   b. solemn commands   d. promises

5. The _____ took turns putting their ears to the wall.
   a. people who share secrets   c. sweethearts
   b. people who gossip   d. watchful couple

6. Pyramus knew that the guards would never _____.
   a. allow them to escape   c. give false testimony
   b. stop them   d. report them

7. Pyramus _____ a horrible picture of Thisbe's death.
   a. drew   c. vividly wrote about
   b. called to mind   d. prayed against

8. Pyramus would never have believed the _____ of a witness.
   a. lie   c. objective account
   b. sworn testimony   d. written declaration

9. Thisbe felt like a(n) _____ without a guiding faith.
   a. traitor   b. sailor   c. fool   d. unbeliever

10. Their blood was spilled out of tragic _____.
   a. faithfulness   b. stupidity   c. impulsiveness   d. speechlessness

1. _____c_____

2. _____d_____

3. _____a_____

4. _____b_____

5. _____a_____

6. _____c_____

7. _____b_____

8. _____b_____

9. _____d_____

10. _____a_____

WRITING ASSIGNMENT

William Shakespeare used the story of Pyramus and Thisbe in two of his plays. Read his humorous version in *A Midsummer Night's Dream* or his tragic portrayal of "star-crossed" lovers in *Romeo and Juliet*. Then write a composition in which you compare or contrast Ovid's story with one of the Shakesperean versions. Use at least five of the vocabulary words from this lesson in your composition and underline them.

The **Bonus activity** for Lessons 13–16 is on page T19.

The English language is rich and varied, and it provides us with thousands of choices for expressing our ideas. Yet, because there are so many words in our language, some of them are confusingly similar. Using the wrong word is a trap that everyone—including teachers, editors, and scholars—falls into from time to time. For example, a United States president once called his speech "fulsome," which means "offensive." He had meant to say it was very full or long. This lesson will help you to avoid making similar errors with commonly confused words.

WORD LIST

affect
avenge
disinterested
effect
imply
infer
precede
proceed
revenge
uninterested

DEFINITIONS

After you have studied the definitions and example for each vocabulary word, write the word on the line to the right.

1. **affect** (ə-fĕkt′) *trans. verb* **a.** To have an influence on; bring about a change in.
   b. To touch or move the emotions of. (From the Latin *ad-*, meaning "to," and *facere*, meaning "to do")

   Example   The way that a person dresses for an interview can *affect* the employer's impression of him or her.

1. _____
USAGE NOTE. Try this mnemonic: RAVEN (Remember Affect Verb Effect Noun)

2. **avenge** (ə-vĕnj′) *trans. verb* **a.** To take revenge on or get satisfaction for: *avenge a crime.* **b.** To take vengeance on behalf of: *avenge one's father.*

   Example   In the novel the knight seeks to *avenge* the murder of his brother.

2. _____
USAGE NOTE: *Avenge* is always a verb; *revenge* is both a noun and a verb.

3. **disinterested** (dĭs-ĭn′trĭ-stĭd, dĭs-ĭn′tə-rĕs′tĭd) *adjective* Free of bias or self-interest; impartial. (From the Latin *dis-*, meaning "absence of"; *inter-*, meaning "between"; and *esse*, meaning "to be")

   Related Word disinterest *noun*
   Example   Carla Zerbini was chosen to judge the case because she has a good record for being fair, knowledgeable, and *disinterested*.

3. _____
USAGE NOTE: *Disinterested* means free of bias; *uninterested* means unconcerned.

4. **effect** (ĭ-fĕkt′) *noun* **a.** Something brought about by a cause or agent; result.
   b. The way in which something acts upon or influences an object. **c.** The final or comprehensive result; outcome. *trans. verb* To produce as a result. (From the Latin *ex-*, meaning "out," and *facere*, meaning "to make")

   Related Words effective *adjective*; effectively *adverb*
   Example   The demonstrators seemed to have no *effect* on the legislators; the bill being protested was passed by a large margin.

4. _____
See *affect.*

5. **imply** (ĭm-plī′) *trans. verb* **a.** To say or express indirectly; hint; suggest. **b.** To involve or suggest by logical necessity: *His aims imply a good deal of energy.* (From the Latin *in-*, meaning "in," and *plicare*, meaning "to fold")

   Related Word   implication *noun*
   Example   Ralph's hasty dismissal of my suggestion *implied* that he did not like my idea at all.

5. _____
USAGE NOTE: To *imply* is to suggest; to *infer* is to deduce something.

6. **infer** (ĭn-fûr′) *trans. verb*   To conclude from evidence; deduce.

   Related Words   inference *noun;* inferential *adjective*
   Example   On the basis of several experiments, the doctor *inferred* that the new drug was only marginally effective.

6. _____
See *imply.*

7. **precede** (prĭ-sēd′) *trans. verb*   **a.** To come before in time; exist or occur prior to. **b.** To come before in order or rank.   **c.** To be in a position in front of. (From the Latin *prae-*, meaning "before," and *cedere*, meaning "to go")

   Related Words   precedent *noun;* preceding *adjective*
   Example   Olivia's winning the citizenship award *preceded* her being asked to speak at graduation.

7. _____
USAGE NOTE: To *precede* is to come before; to *proceed* is to continue.

8. **proceed** (prō-sēd′, prə-sēd′) *intrans. verb*   **a.** To go forward or onward, especially after an interruption; continue.   **b.** To undertake and carry on some action or process.   **c.** To move on in an orderly manner. (From the Latin *pro-*, meaning "forward," and *cedere,* meaning "to go")

   Related Word   procedure *noun*
   Example   Despite the hurricane warnings, Dana *proceeded* to give the water-skiing exhibition.

8. _____
See *precede.*

9. **revenge** (rĭ-vĕnj′) *noun*   **a.** Vengeance; retaliation.   **b.** The act of taking vengeance. (From the Latin *re-*, meaning "in response," and *vindicare,* meaning "to avenge")

   Related Word   revengeful *adjective*
   Example   When Jodie broke Matthew's doll, he got *revenge* by telling her mother.

9. _____
See *avenge.*

10. **uninterested** (ŭn-ĭn′trĭs-tĭd, ŭn-ĭn′tə-rĕs′tĭd) *adjective*   **a.** Not paying attention; indifferent; unconcerned.   **b.** Without an interest: *uninterested parties.* (From the Latin *un-*, meaning "not"; *inter-*, meaning "between"; and *esse,* meaning "to be")

    Example   During the trial the jury seemed *uninterested* in the detailed testimony of the insurance company representative.

10. _____
See *disinterested.*

EXERCISE 1 WRITING CORRECT WORDS

On the answer line, write the word from the vocabulary list that fits each definition.

1. Something brought about by a cause or agent; to produce as a result

2. To come before in time

3. To have an influence on; bring about a change in

4. To take revenge or get satisfaction for; take vengeance on behalf of

5. Not paying attention; indifferent; unconcerned; without an interest

6. Vengeance; retaliation

7. To conclude from evidence; deduce

8. To go forward or onward, especially after an interruption

9. Free of bias or self-interest; impartial

10. To say or express indirectly; hint; suggest; involve or suggest by logical necessity

1. _____ effect _____

2. _____ precede _____

3. _____ affect _____

4. _____ avenge _____

5. _____ uninterested _____

6. _____ revenge _____

7. _____ infer _____

8. _____ proceed _____

9. _____ disinterested _____

10. _____ imply _____

EXERCISE 2 USING WORDS CORRECTLY

Decide whether the italicized vocabulary word has been used correctly in the sentence. On the answer line, write *Correct* for correct use or *Incorrect* for incorrect use.

1. After dusting the furniture and washing the curtains, Emilio *preceded* to wash the floor.

2. Matt wanted desperately to take *avenge* for the insult he had received.

3. The *disinterested* town clerk granted licenses to all applicants who met the requirements.

4. Stanley thought the flowers would have a positive *affect* on his mother's state of mind.

5. Despite the dangerous drop in the patient's pulse rate, Dr. Landowski decided to *proceed* with the operation.

6. Several of the employees stated that they were *uninterested* in their company's stress-management program.

7. Sarah's *revenge* was complete when her sister sat on the gum that Sarah had placed on her chair.

8. When she spoke with the college interviewer, Marsha *inferred* that the college was her first choice.

9. From the evidence the researcher *implied* that the experiment proved her hypothesis.

10. The ending of the movie *effected* me so strongly that I cried.

1. _____ Incorrect _____

2. _____ Incorrect _____

3. _____ Correct _____

4. _____ Incorrect _____

5. _____ Correct _____

6. _____ Correct _____

7. _____ Correct _____

8. _____ Incorrect _____

9. _____ Incorrect _____

10. _____ Incorrect _____

EXERCISE 3 CHOOSING THE BEST DEFINITION

For each italicized vocabulary word in the following sentences, write the letter of the best definition on the answer line.

1. The percentage of protein in cows' feed *affects* the amount of milk produced.
   a. determines   **b.** counteracts   **c.** influences   **d.** limits

1. _____ c _____

2. When tryouts for the team were announced, Julia was *uninterested*.
   a. highly motivated **b.** indifferent **c.** ineligible **d.** regretful

2. _____ b

3. The foreign minister *implied* that insufficient airport security was responsible for the hijacking.
   a. suggested **b.** stated **c.** declared **d.** avowed

3. _____ a

4. The cold remedies had no noticeable *effects*.
   a. results **b.** benefits **c.** dangerous ingredients **d.** warning labels

4. _____ a

5. Because my father was so angry, I *inferred* that something more than my stereo was bothering him.
   a. learned **b.** suggested **c.** declared **d.** concluded

5. _____ d

6. The dinosaurs of the Mesozoic era *preceded* the mammals and birds of the Cenozoic era.
   a. came after **c.** were simultaneous with
   b. came before **d.** were unrelated to

6. _____ b

7. A *disinterested* observer, the witness reported the events with surprising accuracy and clarity.
   a. without greed **c.** without self-interest
   b. without sin **d.** without charity

7. _____ c

8. The detective story was about a man who vows to *avenge* the murder of a friend.
   a. get satisfaction for **c.** make public
   b. request payment for **d.** determine responsibility for

8. _____ a

9. Following the communications delay, plans for the satellite launch *proceeded* according to schedule.
   a. came to a halt **b.** were revised **c.** continued **d.** were changed

9. _____ c

10. *Revenge* was not the motive for the kidnapping.
    a. Getting money **b.** Getting even **c.** A wish for notoriety **d.** Hatred

10. _____ b

EXERCISE 4 USING DIFFERENT FORMS OF WORDS

Decide which form of the vocabulary word in parentheses best completes the sentence. The form given may be correct. Write your answer on the answer line.

1. When asked to invest in the new software company, my dad replied that he was completely _____. *(uninterested)*

1. _____ uninterested

2. Spiteful and _____, Lorraine was a person to be feared. *(revenge)*

2. _____ revengeful

3. The completion of the transcontinental railroad _____ the final stages of westward expansion. *(precede)*

3. _____ preceded

4. The _____ for assembling the model was not sufficiently detailed. *(proceed)*

4. _____ procedure

5. Massive waves of immigration during the late nineteenth century strongly _____ the growth of industry in the United States. *(affect)*

5. _____ affected

6. Known for his _____, Ted was chosen to referee the championship game. *(disinterested)*

6. _____ disinterest

7. Piaget based both _____ on extended case studies of children's development. *(infer)*

7. _____ inferences

8. The press secretary _____ that a full statement would be forthcoming. *(imply)*

8. _____ implied

9. Vaccines have _____ ended the threats of polio and smallpox. *(effect)*

9. _____ effectively

10. Seeking to _____ the insult, Hillary schemed to embarrass her rival in front of the entire class. *(avenge)*

10. _____ avenge

READING COMPREHENSION

Each numbered sentence in the following passage contains an italicized vocabulary word or related form. After you read the passage, you will complete an exercise.

AZERBAIJAN CHANGES ALPHABETS

"It's as easy as ABC," states a common English expression. But the alphabet is not always easy, particularly when a country is changing from one to another, as Azerbaijan is currently doing. **(1)** To complicate matters further, two other alphabet changes have *preceded* this one, and all three have occurred since 1900. **(2)** From the signs on the street, sometimes written in three alphabets, the visitor can *infer* that this is a country with some linguistic confusion. Is the country آذربايجان, Азәрбајчан, or Azərbaycan?

Formerly a part of the Soviet Union, Azerbaijan is a small country nestled among three larger states: Iran, Turkey, and Russia. For centuries the Azerbaijani language was written with Persian script, reflecting the influence of Iran. In the 1920s, when it was taken over as a Soviet state, it was decreed that Azerbaijan change to Latin letters, the ones used in English. **(3)** The 1928 alphabet reform *proceeded,* and the Latin alphabet was used for eleven years.

(4) But in 1939, Soviet dictator Joseph Stalin, perhaps seeking *revenge* on some of his more independently-minded provinces, decreed that Azeri should be written in the Cyrillic script used in the Russian alphabet. The change was abrupt and resented by many. In a famous poem, Bakhtyar Vahabzade described how the Latin and then the Cyrillic alphabets were used to separate his country from its thousand-year-old literature, written in Arabic script.

Fifty years later, as the Soviet empire crumbled and Azerbaijan became an independent state, it decided to change yet another time. In 1991, the country readopted the Latin alphabet. This time the Parliament of Azerbaijan, rather than a foreign power, made the decision. **(5)** This helped to assure that the decision was relatively *disinterested* and not motivated by the wishes of outsiders.

To assure usability in their own language, the Azerbaijans have modified the Latin alphabet by adding four letters. One, an upside-down "c" (ə), is used to represent the most common sound in Azeri, "a" as in "bat." Formerly "a" with two dots above it (ä) was used for this sound, but it slowed down writing considerably. Even the "ə" causes some problems as it is difficult to insert from most computer programs. One professor teaching the Azeri language in the United States reported that, since he didn't have the new character in his computer yet, he was writing out all of his instructional material by hand.

(6) The adoption of a script has important political, economic, and social *implications,* for communication is much easier among countries that share the same alphabet. By adopting the Latin alphabet, Azerbaijan strengthens its ties with Turkey, the rest of Europe, and the United States. **(7)** Some also suspect that the decision to drop the Cyrillic alphabet was partly based on the Azerbaijanis' wish to *avenge* themselves on their former Russian rulers.

(8) The many changes have had some confusing *effects.* Street names remain carved into old buildings in Arabic script, but appear on most signs in Cyrillic letters. Recently some new signs have appeared in the Latin alphabet. Newspapers print headlines in Latin letters, but most articles are written in Cyrillic. In fact, the decree adopting the Latin alphabet was written in Cyrillic!

The cost of the change is also enormous. To convert from Cyrillic to Latin script, new printing equipment is required and staff must be retrained. Textbooks must all be converted, and teachers need to master the Latin alphabet so that they can teach it to children. **(9)** The changes have also *affected* communication among generations, with parents and children often finding it difficult to write to each other. **(10)** At times, the burden of change becomes overwhelming, and people, *uninterested* in making the effort, simply continue to use the script they find most comfortable. As of 1997, fewer than 200 textbooks have been translated into the Latin script. But, as the years pass, Latin letters are expected to become more widely used, fostering closer ties with the European/American bloc countries whose exports have already become popular.

Each of the following statements corresponds to a numbered sentence in the passage. Each statement contains a blank and is followed by four answer choices. Decide which choice fits best in the blank. The word or phrase that you choose must express roughly the same meaning as the italicized word in the passage. Write the letter of your choice on the answer line.

1. To complicate matters further, two other alphabet changes have _____ this one, and all three have occurred since 1900.
   a. come before   **b.** come after   **c.** contradicted   **d.** resulted in

1. _____ **a**

2. From the signs on the street, sometimes written in three alphabets, the visitor can _____ that this is a country with some linguistic confusion.
   a. claim   **b.** suggest   **c.** hope   **d.** conclude

2. _____ **d**

3. The 1928 alphabet reform _____, and the Latin alphabet was used for eleven years.
   a. triumphed   **b.** went onward   **c.** was quick   **d.** was forced

3. _____ **b**

4. But in 1939, Soviet dictator Joseph Stalin, perhaps seeking _____ some of his more independently-minded provinces, decreed that Azeri should be written in the Cyrillic script used in the Russian alphabet.
   a. control of   **b.** retaliation on   **c.** affection from   **d.** power over

4. _____ **b**

5. This helped to assure that the decision was relatively _____ and not motivated by the wishes of outsiders.
   a. intelligent   **b.** painless   **c.** impartial   **d.** useful

5. _____ **c**

6. The adoption of a script has important political, economic, and social _____, for communication is much easier among countries that share the same alphabet.
   a. consequences   **b.** direct meaning   **c.** indirect meaning **d.** necessities

6. _____ **c**

7. Some also suspect that the decision to drop the Cyrillic alphabet was partly based on the Azerbaijanis' wish to _____ their former Russian rulers.
   a. take vengeance on   **c.** stay in contact with
   b. thank gratefully   **d.** separate themselves from

7. _____ **a**

8. The many changes have had some confusing _____.
   a. problems   **b.** outcomes   **c.** meanings   **d.** reports

8. _____ **b**

9. The changes have also _____ communication among generations, with parents and children often finding it difficult to write to each other.
   a. aided   **b.** hindered   **c.** slowed   **d.** influenced

9. _____ **d**

10. At times, the burden of change becomes overwhelming, and people, _____ making the effort, simply continue to use the script they find most comfortable.
    a. unconcerned about   **b.** lazy about   **c.** frustrated by   **d.** tired by

10. _____ **a**

See page 79 for some strategies to use with analogies.

Directions   On the answer line, write the vocabulary word or a form of it that completes each analogy.

1. PARTIAL : BIASED :: impartial : _____ (Lesson 17)

1. _____ **disinterested**

2. JURY : TRIAL :: _____ : dispute (Lesson 15)

2. _____ **arbitrator**

3. GUARD : PROTECTS :: _____ : represents (Lesson 15)

3. _____ **emissary**

4. LIE : STATEMENT :: _____ : testimony (Lesson 16)

4. _____ **perjury**

5. TREATY : NATIONS :: _____ : parties (Lesson 15)

5. _____ **covenant**

18

Excellence means different things to different people. For an Olympic gymnast, a perfect score of ten represents an exceptional performance. For someone in the entertainment world, winning an Oscar, Emmy, Tony, or Grammy is a sign of excellence. Journalists, authors, and composers regard the Pulitzer Prize as a reward for superior accomplishment in their fields.

Excellence does not necessarily lead to fame or reward, however. Sometimes excellence exists only to be enjoyed and regarded with respect. One can admire the precision of a well-crafted timepiece or the distinctive performance of a car. The color, shape, and delicacy of a handmade glass bowl can be appreciated. Or one can simply experience the pleasure and pride of doing the best job possible. The words in this lesson will provide you with the vocabulary to express the excellence that you encounter and achieve.

WORD LIST

culminate
eclipse
epitome
impeccable
inimitable
optimum
peerless
quintessence
sublime
zenith

DEFINITIONS

After you have studied the definitions and example for each vocabulary word, write the word on the line to the right.

1. **culminate** (kŭl′mə-nāt′) *intrans. verb* **a.** To reach the highest point or degree; climax. **b.** To achieve full effect. (From the Latin word *culmen*, meaning "summit")

   Related Word culmination *noun*
   Example During Mardi Gras in New Orleans, the festivities *culminate* in a variety of masquerade parties.

   1. _____

2. **eclipse** (ĭ klĭps′) *trans. verb* **a.** To obscure or overshadow the importance, fame, or reputation of; surpass; outshine. **b.** To cause an eclipse; darken. *noun* **a.** A decline into obscurity or disuse; downfall. **b.** A partial or complete obscuring of one celestial body by another. (From the Greek *ek-*, meaning "out," and *leipein*, meaning "to leave")

   Example Alexander the Great *eclipsed* other conquerors of his time when he defeated the forces of Greece, Persia, and Egypt.

   2. _____

3. **epitome** (ĭ-pĭt′ə-mē) *noun* Someone or something that is the typical or perfect example of an entire class or type; embodiment. (From the Greek *epi-*, meaning "upon," and *temnein*, meaning "to cut")

   Related Word epitomize *verb*
   Example Abraham Lincoln was the *epitome* of the American virtues of self-reliance, honesty, and industriousness.

   3. _____

4. **impeccable** (ĭm-pĕk′ə-bəl) *adjective* Without flaw; perfect. (From the Latin *in-*, meaning "not," and *peccare*, meaning "to sin")

   Related Words impeccability *noun;* impeccably *adverb*
   Example After ten years of foreign language training, Nathan spoke *impeccable* French and German.

   4. _____

5. **inimitable** (ĭn-ĭm′ĭ-tə-bəl) *adjective*   Impossible to imitate or copy; matchless; unique.

   Related Words   **inimitability** *noun;* **inimitably** *adverb*
   Example   The song was an excellent vehicle for the singer's *inimitable* voice.

6. **optimum** (ŏp′tə-məm) *adjective*   Most favorable or advantageous; best.   *noun* The best or most favorable condition, degree, or amount for a particular purpose or situation. (From the Latin word *optimus,* meaning "best")

   Related Word   **optimize** *verb*
   Example   Mrs. Mirez is a fine teacher who combines various teaching strategies to their *optimum* degree.

7. **peerless** (pîr′lĭs) *adjective*   Without equal; unmatched.

   Related Words   **peerlessly** *adverb;* **peerlessness** *noun*
   Example   Mohandas Gandhi was respected as a *peerless* spiritual leader.

8. **quintessence** (kwĭn-tĕs′əns) *noun*   **a.** The most complete instance; the finest or most representative example.   **b.** The essence of a thing in its purest and most concentrated form. (From the Medieval Latin phrase *quinta essentia,* meaning "fifth essence")

   Related Word   **quintessential** *adjective*
   Example   The fictional character Dracula is often viewed as the *quintessence* of evil.

9. **sublime** (sə-blīm′) *adjective*   **a.** Not to be excelled; supreme.   **b.** Tending to inspire awe usually because of an elevated quality, such as beauty, nobility, or grandeur.   **c.** Of high spiritual, moral, or intellectual worth.   *noun* Something that is sublime: *from the ridiculous to the sublime.* (From the Latin word *sublimis,* meaning "uplifted")

   Related Words   **sublimely** *adverb;* **sublimity** *noun*
   Example   The *sublime* clarinetist, Charlie "Bird" Parker, was superb at jazz improvisation.

10. **zenith** (zē′nĭth) *noun*   **a.** The highest point; peak.   **b.** The point of the celestial sphere that is directly above the observer.   **c.** The upper region of the sky. (From the Arabic phrase *samt arra's,* meaning "path over the head")

    Example   At the *zenith* of his power, the man controlled a world-wide financial empire.

5. _____

USAGE NOTE: Do not confuse *inimitable* with *inimical,* meaning "harmful" or "hostile."

6. _____

7. _____

8. _____

9. _____

10. _____

EXERCISE 1 MATCHING WORDS AND DEFINITIONS

Match the definition in Column B with the word in Column A. Write the letter of the correct definition on the answer line.

Column A

1. quintessence
2. epitome
3. zenith
4. inimitable
5. impeccable
6. peerless
7. eclipse
8. optimum
9. culminate
10. sublime

Column B

a. the highest point; peak
b. to reach the highest point or degree
c. to overshadow the importance of; surpass
d. without a flaw; perfect
e. not to be excelled; supreme
f. impossible to imitate or copy; unique
g. the most complete instance; the finest example
h. the typical or perfect example of a class or type; embodiment
i. without equal; unmatched
j. most favorable or advantageous

1. ___g___
2. ___h___
3. ___a___
4. ___f___
5. ___d___
6. ___i___
7. ___c___
8. ___j___
9. ___b___
10. ___e___

EXERCISE 2 USING WORDS CORRECTLY

Decide whether the italicized vocabulary word has been used correctly in the sentence. On the answer line, write *Correct* for correct use or *Incorrect* for incorrect use.

1. Senator Brown's distinguished career *culminated* in his resounding defeat last November.

2. The baseball team's record this year was an *impeccable* 7 and 0.

3. The speaker quoted what she considered to be the most *sublime* lines of poetry in the English language.

4. Everyone copied his *inimitable* style of dress.

5. Mike hoped to find an *epitome* he could afford.

6. Sylvia is *optimum* about her chances to win the school election.

7. Adam, a *peerless* violinist, easily won the competition.

8. Mrs. Swinburne's inability to accept offers of help was the *quintessence* of pride.

9. At the *zenith* of her acting career, Louisa Stanton gave seven performances a week.

10. Ansel Adams's photography students have not yet *eclipsed* the fame of their teacher.

1. ___Incorrect___
2. ___Correct___
3. ___Correct___
4. ___Incorrect___
5. ___Incorrect___
6. ___Incorrect___
7. ___Correct___
8. ___Correct___
9. ___Correct___
10. ___Correct___

EXERCISE 3 CHOOSING THE BEST WORD

Decide which vocabulary word or related form best expresses the meaning of the italicized word or phrase in the sentence. On the answer line, write the letter of the correct choice.

1. The Calgary Stampede *reaches its highest point* in a major rodeo.
   a. optimizes   **b.** culminates   **c.** eclipses   **d.** epitomizes

1. ___b___

2. Carla attended to the problem in her own *impossible-to-copy* fashion.
   a. impeccable   **b.** inimitable   **c.** optimum   **d.** sublime

2. _____ b

3. The spy was given a set of *flawless* credentials.
   a. optimum   **b.** impeccable   **c.** sublime   **d.** quintessential

3. _____ b

4. Until the seventeenth century, a concentration on religious theory *diminished the importance of* scientific experiment.
   a. epitomized   **b.** culminated   **c.** optimized   **d.** eclipsed

4. _____ d

5. The character of Friday, Robinson Crusoe's companion, is the *representative example* of a faithful and willing attendant.
   a. optimum   **b.** culmination   **c.** quintessence   **d.** zenith

5. _____ c

6. At the *highest point* of his fame, the magician Harry Houdini attracted huge crowds of devoted fans.
   a. quintessence   **b.** optimum   **c.** eclipse   **d.** zenith

6. _____ d

7. Sir Gawain, a member of King Arthur's round table, is idealized in a poem as the *perfect example* of a knight.
   a. epitome   **b.** sublime   **c.** impeccability   **d.** culmination

7. _____ a

8. The *supreme* view of the turquoise-blue lake with its thick glacier makes an excellent photograph.
   a. optimum   **b.** sublime   **c.** eclipsed   **d.** quintessential

8. _____ b

9. The rocket launch was postponed because the weather was not at its *most favorable condition*.
   a. eclipse   **b.** culmination   **c.** optimum   **d.** quintessence

9. _____ c

10. The Brazilian soccer player Pele was *without equal* throughout his career.
   a. impeccable   **b.** eclipsed   **c.** peerless   **d.** quintessential

10. _____ c

EXERCISE 4 USING DIFFERENT FORMS OF WORDS

Decide which form of the vocabulary word in parentheses best completes the sentence. The form given may be correct. Write your answer on the answer line.

1. The _____ of Commander Robert Peary's fourth expedition was the discovery of the North Pole in 1909. *(culminate)*

1. _____ culmination

2. Peary hoped to _____ his chances of success. *(optimum)*

2. _____ optimize

3. Even the most _____ planned expedition could not control the Arctic weather. *(impeccable)*

3. _____ impeccably

4. Peary's _____ in Arctic exploration has never been successfully challenged. *(peerless)*

4. _____ peerlessness

5. Peary was a _____ explorer—courageous, determined, and energetic. *(quintessence)*

5. _____ quintessential

6. The students made a crude pinhole camera to view the solar _____. *(eclipse)*

6. _____ eclipse

7. Mikhail has always _____ tactfulness and diplomacy. *(epitome)*

7. _____ epitomized

8. Anna Pavlova, one of the greatest ballerinas in the world, danced _____. *(inimitable)*

8. _____ inimitably

9. Darryl saw what he thought was a shooting star in the _____. *(zenith)*

9. _____ zenith

10. "Nightingales sing _____," Monica observed romantically. *(sublime)*

10. _____ sublimely

READING COMPREHENSION

Each numbered sentence in the following passage contains an italicized vocabulary word or related form. After you read the passage, you will complete an exercise.

LEONARDO DA VINCI: RENAISSANCE GENIUS (1452–1519)

During the fourteenth through the sixteenth centuries, the Renaissance in Europe marked the transition between the Middle Ages and modern times. Western civilization witnessed a rebirth of learning. (1) Leonardo da Vinci was the *epitome* of the Renaissance person endowed with many talents. (2) Considered to be one of the most versatile geniuses in history, the *inimitable* da Vinci was a scientist and inventor as well as a famous artist.

Leonardo da Vinci was born in a small town in the Tuscany region of Italy. Little is known of his childhood beyond his coming from a poor family and receiving no formal education. At the age of fourteen or fifteen, he was apprenticed to a leading Florentine painter and sculptor. (3) Da Vinci made *optimum* use of his mentor's talents, learning metalworking and figure drawing. (4) In 1472 his apprenticeship *culminated* in his acceptance into the painters' guild and his assuming responsibility for one of the leading workshops in Florence.

(5) In the late 1400s, Leonardo da Vinci decided to leave Florence because he thought his talents were being *eclipsed* by other painters. Opportunities for artists skilled in many areas seemed limited in the atmosphere of philosophical speculation that dominated Florence. In Milan he found an outlet for his artistic and practical inventiveness.

As the court artist for the Duke of Milan, da Vinci made diverse contributions. He painted portraits of the duke and his family and friends, arranged the decorations for court festivities, consulted on architecture, and designed artillery.

(6) Sometime after his arrival in Milan, da Vinci began keeping a series of notebooks in which he *impeccably* recorded quantities of drawings and ideas. It is in these manuscripts that the artist and scientist in da Vinci are said to unite. His explorations of nature were a means of gaining knowledge of the visible world that he needed for his paintings and sculpture. An acute observer, da Vinci rejected authority in favor of the evidence yielded by his senses.

(7) Studying anatomy through dissection, he revealed the presence and function of bones, tendons, and other parts of the body in *peerless* drawings. The notebooks chronicle his observations and his experiments with all aspects of nature, including water, light, energy, and motion.

Leonardo da Vinci undertook research because of his insatiable curiosity. However, many of his ideas were never carried out. Once he solved a problem for himself, he was apt to lose interest—there were so many other mysteries to be explored. (8) His paddle-wheel boat, diving bell, parachute, and helicopter may never have existed outside of the notebook pages, but they illustrate his *sublimely* creative mind.

(9) The *Mona Lisa*, his famous portrait of an unidentified young woman, is the *quintessence* of da Vinci the artist. Because of his fascination with the nature of light, he was able to leave the corners of his model's eyes and mouth in shadow, creating an air of mystery and the famous ambiguous smile. He posed his subject against a strange landscape that seems to glow from within.

(10) A landmark in the development of portraiture, the painting was completed in 1506, at the *zenith* of Leonardo da Vinci's career.

READING COMPREHENSION EXERCISE

Each of the following statements corresponds to a numbered sentence in the passage. Each statement contains a blank and is followed by four answer choices. Decide which choice fits best in the blank. The word or phrase that you choose must express roughly the same meaning as the italicized word in the passage. Write the letter of your choice on the answer line.

1. Leonardo da Vinci was the _____ of the Renaissance person.
   a. forerunner   **b.** perfect example   **c.** instigator   **d.** inappropriate model

1. _____ **b**

2. Da Vinci was _____ as a scientist, inventor, and artist.
   a. matchless   b. unhappy   c. disorganized   d. overlooked

3. Da Vinci made _____ use of his mentor's talents.
   a. full   b. poor   c. permissible   d. economic

4. His outstanding apprenticeship _____ his acceptance into the painters' guild.
   a. determined   b. hastened   c. prospered after   d. resulted in

5. Da Vinci thought his talents were being _____ by other painters.
   a. gossiped about   b. overshadowed   c. ignored   d. idealized

6. He _____ recorded drawings and ideas in a series of notebooks.
   a. nervously   b. dejectedly   c. flawlessly   d. thoughtfully

7. Leonardo da Vinci's anatomical drawings were _____.
   a. without equal   b. shocking   c. published   d. unimpressive

8. His inventions illustrate his _____ creative mind.
   a. indifferently   b. sensibly   c. supremely   d. intellectually

9. The *Mona Lisa* is the _____ of da Vinci the artist.
   a. most creative work   c. most famous painting
   b. poorest example   d. finest example

10. The painting was completed at the _____ of da Vinci's career.
    a. low point   b. peak   c. end   d. beginning

2. _____ a
3. _____ a
4. _____ d
5. _____ b
6. _____ c
7. _____ a
8. _____ c
9. _____ d
10. _____ b

WRITING ASSIGNMENT

As the public relations director of your community, you have decided to initiate yearly awards for excellence honoring the achievements of those living in the community. To make people aware of the awards and to solicit nominations, write an explanation of your idea for the newspaper. Using at least five of the words from this lesson, define excellence, give several specific examples of it, and explain the categories for which people may submit nominations. Underline each vocabulary word that you use.

VOCABULARY ENRICHMENT

The word *quintessence* comes from the Medieval Latin phrase *quinta essentia*, a translation of the Greek *pemptē ousia*, meaning "fifth essence." In ancient Greece scholars were fascinated with the concept of change. They wanted to be able to explain birth, growth, and death. According to Empedocles, a Greek philosopher, everything in the world was composed of different proportions of four elements—fire, water, air, and earth. He theorized that nothing comes into being or is destroyed; all changes are due to the way in which the elements are mixed.

Aristotle believed that the four elements themselves were responsible for change. According to his theory, everything changed except the heavens. Therefore, he added a fifth element, which he called *aithēr*, or *ether*. The most stable element and the one that held the others together, ether made up the sun, moon, planets, and stars and was therefore divine. Today we have maintained the ideas of purity and completeness associated with *quintessence*, the "fifth essence."

Activity Many other words are derived from the philosophical and scientific ideas of ancient Greece. Look up the etymology and principal present-day definition of each of the following words. Then write a brief explanation connecting the derivation with the current meaning.

1. atom   2. agnostic   3. sophomoric   4. pantheism   5. physics

The **Test** for Lessons 16, 17, and 18 is on page T20.

READING SKILLS

CONTEXT CLUES AND THE READING OF AMERICAN HISTORY

As your history courses become more advanced, you may be asked to read works that were written during the periods that you are studying. You already know some techniques for determining the meaning of unfamiliar words by using the context. The following strategies will also be helpful when you read historical works from earlier times.

STRATEGIES

1. *Consider the date of the work.* Doing so will give you a better understanding of its words and ideas. In the eighteenth century, for example, the word *enthusiasm* meant something like "fanaticism."

2. *Consider the type of writing and the subject.* A personal letter and a formal speech will have different levels of vocabulary. The subject of a work also determines its vocabulary. Keeping in mind literary form and subject will enable you to make informed guesses about the meanings of unfamiliar words.

3. *Find out what you can about the author.* Knowing who wrote a work will give you a useful background for reading it.

4. *Use a dictionary.* Use it to check meanings that you have tentatively assigned to words, working from context clues. Use it also to check meanings of words that lack a helpful context.

EXERCISE USING CONTEXT CLUES IN READING HISTORY

The following excerpt is from a work by Thomas Jefferson and John Dickinson. Addressed to the British government, it was approved by the Second Continental Congress on July 6, 1775, a full year before the Declaration of Independence. It makes many of the assertions that may be found in the more famous declaration. Begin by reading the entire passage. *Step 1:* Write your own definition of each italicized word in the passage. *Step 2:* Write the appropriate dictionary definition of the word.

But why should we (1)*enumerate* our injuries in detail? By one statute it is declared that Parliament can "of right make laws to bind us in all cases whatsoever." What is to defend us against so enormous, so unlimited a power? Not a single man of those who assume it is chosen by us, or is subject to our control or influence; but, on the contrary, they are all of them exempt from the operation of such laws. . . . We saw the misery to which such (2)*despotism* would reduce us. We for ten years (3)*incessantly* and ineffectually besieged the throne as (4)*supplicants;* we reasoned, we (5)*remonstrated* with Parliament, in the most mild and decent language.

Administration, (6)*sensible* that we should regard these (7)*oppressive* measures as freemen ought to do, sent over fleets and armies to enforce them. The indignation of the Americans was roused, it is true; but it was the indignation of a virtuous, loyal, and affectionate people. A congress of delegates from the United Colonies was assembled at Philadelphia, on the 5th day of last September. we resolved again to offer a humble and dutiful petition to the King, and also addressed our fellow subjects of

Great Britain. We have pursued every (8) *temperate*, every respectful measure; we have even proceeded to break off our [commerce] with our fellow subjects, as the last peaceable (9) *admonition*, that our attachment to no nation upon earth should (10) *supplant* our attachment to liberty. This, we flattered ourselves, was the ultimate step of the controversy. . . .

1. *enumerate*

   Your Definition number

   Dictionary Definition count off or name one by one; list

2. *despotism*

   Your Definition unfairness

   Dictionary Definition rule by, or as if by, one who wields power tyrannically

3. *incessantly*

   Your Definition without cease

   Dictionary Definition continuously

4. *supplicants*

   Your Definition pleaders

   Dictionary Definition those who ask for something humbly or earnestly

5. *remonstrated*

   Your Definition raised objections

   Dictionary Definition made objections; argued against an action

6. *sensible*

   Your Definition aware

   Dictionary Definition having a perception of something

7. *oppressive*

   Your Definition heavy; unfair

   Dictionary Definition difficult to bear; harsh

8. *temperate*

   Your Definition mild

   Dictionary Definition exercising moderation and self-restraint

9. *admonition*

   Your Definition protest

   Dictionary Definition cautionary advice or warning

10. *supplant*

    Your Definition weaken

    Dictionary Definition take the place of

The Latin roots -*quisit*-, -*rog*-, and -*sag*- serve as the basis of many English words having to do with discovery and understanding. The root -*quisit*- and its alternate form -*quir*- come from the Latin word *quaerere*, meaning "to seek." Words like *require* and *request* derive from this word. The Latin word *rogare*, meaning "to ask" or "to propose," has given us words like *arrogance* and *interrogate*. The root -*sag*- comes from the Latin *sagire*, meaning "to perceive acutely," and is the basis of words like *presage* and *sagacious*. In this lesson you will learn words from these three roots that will help you to express the lifelong process of inquiry.

WORD LIST

abrogate
acquisition
conquistador
inquisitive
perquisite
presage
quest
requisite
sagacity
surrogate

DEFINITIONS

After you have studied the definitions and example for each vocabulary word, write the word on the line to the right.

1. **abrogate** (ăb′rə-gāt′) *trans. verb*   To abolish or annul by authority; cancel. (From the Latin *ab-*, meaning "away," and *rogare*, meaning "to propose")

   Related Word abrogation *noun*
   Example   At the first opportunity, the German Third Reich *abrogated* its treaty with Russia and attacked.

   1. _____

2. **acquisition** (ăk′wĭ-zĭsh′ən) *noun*   **a.** The act or process of gaining possession. **b.** Something gained, especially an addition to an established category or group. (From the Latin *ad-*, meaning "to," and *quaerere*, meaning "to seek")

   Related Words acquire *verb*; **acquisitive** *adjective*; **acquisitiveness** *noun*
   Example   His *acquisition* of the choice property took place illegally.

   2. _____

3. **conquistador** (kŏn-kwĭs′tə-dôr′, kŏng-kē′stə-dôr′) *noun*   A conqueror, especially one of the Spanish conquerors of Mexico and Peru in the sixteenth century. (From the Medieval Latin word *conquerere*, meaning "to conquer")

   Example   Many *conquistadors* were searching for gold in the Americas.

   3. _____

4. **inquisitive** (ĭn-kwĭz′ə-tĭv) *adjective*   **a.** Eager to learn; curious.   **b.** Unduly curious; prying. (From the Latin *in-*, an intensive prefix, and *quaerere*, meaning "to seek")

   Related Words inquisitively *adverb*; **inquisitiveness** *noun*
   Example   The teacher preferred *inquisitive* students to those who sat passively and did not ask questions.

   4. _____

5. **perquisite** (pûr'kwĭ-zĭt) *noun* **a.** A payment or profit received in addition to a regular wage or salary, especially a benefit expected as one's due. **b.** A tip. **c.** Something claimed as an exclusive right. (From the Latin *per-*, an intensive prefix, and *quaerere*, meaning "to seek")

5. _____
USAGE NOTE: Do not confuse *perquisite* with *prerequisite*, meaning "something that is required beforehand."

   Example   One of the *perquisites* of Mrs. Salt's job is traveling first class on her business trips.

6. **presage** (prĭ-sāj', prĕs'ĭj) *trans. verb* **a.** To indicate or warn of in advance. **b.** To foretell or predict. *intrans. verb* To make or utter a prediction. *noun* (prĕs'ĭj) **a.** An indication or warning of a future occurrence; omen. **b.** A feeling or intuition of what is going to occur. (From the Latin *prae-*, meaning "before," and *sagire*, meaning "to perceive acutely")

6. _____

   Example   To Bill, the backfiring engine *presaged* doom.

7. **quest** (kwĕst) *noun* The act or instance of seeking or pursuing something; search. (From the Latin word *quaerere*, meaning "to seek")

7. _____

   Example   During the 1840s many people moved to California to join the *quest* for gold.

8. **requisite** (rĕk'wĭ-zĭt) *adjective* Required; essential. *noun* Something that is required or essential. (From the Latin word *requirere*, meaning "to require")

8. _____

   Related Word   **requisition** *noun*
   Example   Climbing in the Tetons without the *requisite* supplies and equipment can be disastrous.

9. **sagacity** (sə-găs'ĭ-tē) *noun* Keenness of perception; soundness of judgment; wisdom. (From the Latin word *sagax*, meaning "of keen perception")

9. _____

   Related Word   **sagacious** *adjective*
   Example   The professor was known for his *sagacity*, which he most frequently displayed in his judgments of people and their abilities.

10. **surrogate** (sûr'ə-gĭt, sûr'ə-gāt') *noun* Someone or something that takes the place of another; substitute. *adjective* Substitute. (From the Latin word *surrogare*, meaning "to substitute")

10. _____

   Example   Because the kitchen was being remodeled and the family needed a place to eat, the local diner had to serve as a *surrogate* for the day.

EXERCISE I COMPLETING DEFINITIONS

On the answer line, write the word from the vocabulary list that best completes each definition.

1. A person who is eager to learn or is unduly curious is _____.

2. To act as a substitute for someone or something is to be a(n) _____.

3. The act of seeking or pursuing something is a(n) _____.

4. To abolish by authority is to _____.

5. A conqueror is also called a(n) _____.

6. The act or process of gaining possession is _____.

7. To indicate or warn of in advance is to _____.

8. A benefit or payment received in addition to a regular salary is a(n) _____.

9. Something that is required or essential is _____.

10. Keenness of perception, soundness of judgment, and wisdom are known as _____.

1. _____ inquisitive
2. _____ surrogate
3. _____ quest
4. _____ abrogate
5. _____ conquistador
6. _____ acquisition
7. _____ presage
8. _____ perquisite
9. _____ requisite
10. _____ sagacity

EXERCISE 2 USING WORDS CORRECTLY

Decide whether the italicized vocabulary word has been used correctly in the sentence. On the answer line, write *Correct* for correct use and *Incorrect* for incorrect use.

1. A desire to increase the national wealth of Spain as well as a personal greed for gold motivated many of the *conquistadors*.

2. In addition to their salaries, all of the employees received *requisites* such as health club memberships and travel allowances.

3. Without exercise most people's muscles will show signs of *sagacity*.

4. The four-year-old boy was so *inquisitive* that we soon became impatient with his constant questions.

5. Many college courses may not be taken until certain *perquisites* are taken.

6. The *acquisition* of much of the American Southwest was accomplished through a treaty with Mexico in 1848.

7. The cable company *abrogated* responsibility for its poor service to customers.

8. Because Hope's mother is out of town, her aunt will attend the school program as Mrs. Simons's *surrogate*.

9. The hot, humid day of departure was a *presage* of what Maxine and Marc would encounter in the Amazon.

10. The newspaper columnist announced his annual *quest* for the best original recipe.

1. _____ Correct
2. _____ Incorrect
3. _____ Incorrect
4. _____ Correct
5. _____ Incorrect
6. _____ Correct
7. _____ Correct
8. _____ Correct
9. _____ Correct
10. _____ Correct

EXERCISE 3 CHOOSING THE BEST WORD

Decide which vocabulary word or related form best expresses the meaning of the italicized word or phrase in the sentence. On the answer line, write the letter of the correct choice.

1. Jana is in charge of art *additions* at the museum.
   a. requisitions   **b.** perquisites   **c.** acquisitions   **d.** presages

1. _____ c

2. The reporter became known for her aggressive style and her *keenness of perception* in political matters.
   a. abrogation   b. sagacity   c. requisition   d. inquisitiveness

2. _____ **b**

3. The Twenty-First Amendment *annulled* the Eighteenth Amendment, which had prohibited the sale of alcoholic beverages.
   a. quested   b. presaged   c. acquired   d. abrogated

3. _____ **d**

4. Some baby monkeys that have been separated from their mothers and placed with *substitutes* made of wire or cloth later exhibit behavioral disorders.
   a. requisites   b. surrogates   c. quests   d. perquisites

4. _____ **b**

5. The *Spanish conquerors* of the sixteenth century destroyed some priceless artifacts of the civilizations in the New World.
   a. requisites   b. presages   c. conquistadors   d. surrogates

5. _____ **c**

6. Jason's *search* for the golden fleece is the subject of a long poem by Apollonius of Rhodes, an ancient Greek poet.
   a. quest   b. requisition   c. perquisite   d. acquisition

6. _____ **a**

7. Gary's new employer promised him a *payment other than wages* in the form of a generous Christmas bonus.
   a. acquisition   b. abrogation   c. conquistador   d. perquisite

7. _____ **d**

8. The Robertsons were warned that they could not buy the house without the *required* credit checks.
   a. inquisitive   b. acquisitive   c. sagacious   d. requisite

8. _____ **d**

9. Some people say that a hard winter is an *indication* of an early spring.
   a. acquisition   b. presage   c. abrogation   d. perquisite

9. _____ **b**

10. Curious George, a monkey who is too *eager to learn* for his own good, has long been a favorite character in young children's literature.
    a. requisite   b. sagacious   c. acquisitive   d. inquisitive

10. _____ **d**

EXERCISE 4 USING DIFFERENT FORMS OF WORDS

Decide which form of the vocabulary word in parentheses best completes the sentence. The form given may be correct. Write your answer on the answer line.

1. The _____ doctor was admired for his quick and invariably correct diagnoses. *(sagacity)*

1. _____ **sagacious**

2. Isabella Stewart Gardner was one of the most _____ art lovers of her time in the United States. *(acquisition)*

2. _____ **acquisitive**

3. Some people fear that the use of robots as _____ laborers will lead to increased unemployment. *(surrogate)*

3. _____ **surrogate**

4. The _____ of the export contract dismayed the owners of the seafood company. *(abrogate)*

4. _____ **abrogation**

5. Ponce de León led a group of _____ who were searching for the fountain of youth. *(conquistador)*

5. _____ **conquistadors**

6. A _____ commonly received by reviewers is a free copy of the book that they review. *(perquisite)*

6. _____ **perquisite**

7. Natural _____ helps most children learn about their world. *(inquisitive)*

7. _____ **inquisitiveness**

8. Don Quixote's life was a _____ for lost gallantry. *(quest)*

8. _____ **quest**

9. The secretary submitted a _____ for several reams of paper. *(requisite)*

9. _____ **requisition**

10. The ancient seer said that the unusual configuration of the planets _____ a famine. *(presage)*

10. _____ **presaged**

READING COMPREHENSION

Each numbered sentence in the following passage contains an italicized vocabulary word or related form. After you read the passage, you will complete an exercise.

CORTÉS AND MOCTEZUMA

(1) The most successful of the Spanish *conquistadors* was Hernando Cortés. (2) His efforts enabled Spain to *acquire* Mexico as part of its empire. However, his conquest of the great Aztec civilization and its emperor, Moctezuma, was ruthless.

Like many Spaniards during the sixteenth century, Cortés was intrigued by rumors of the fabulous wealth to be found in the Americas. In particular the fabled wealth of the Aztec emperor, Moctezuma, lured Cortés and motivated him to undertake a long march into the interior of Mexico with more than six hundred soldiers. (3) Along the way other battles interrupted his progress but never diminished the intensity of his *quest* for riches. Luckily for Cortés, some of the Indians whom he defeated were traditional enemies of the Aztecs, and they joined Cortés and his army.

Cortés's triumph over the Aztecs was relatively easy. (4) On the way to the Aztec capital, Tenochtitlán, he learned of Moctezuma's belief that the coming of the white, bearded god Quetzalcoatl *presaged* fearful events for the Aztecs. (5) Not surprisingly, Cortés quickly decided to become a *surrogate* god.

When Moctezuma learned of the arrival of Cortés, the Aztec emperor immediately believed that the conquistador was Quetzalcoatl. (6) Moctezuma had been *inquisitive* enough to learn that Cortés had terrible weapons that killed the enemy by the thousands. (7) Convinced that only a god would have such powers,

Moctezuma went to meet Cortés with rich gifts of embellished gold, the *perquisites* of a deity. (8) Cortés received Moctezuma with all the *requisite* dignity and authority that a god would accord an emperor.

After Moctezuma returned to his palace, Cortés acted more ruthlessly. Although he and the Aztec leader had entered into an understanding, Cortés feared treachery. (9) Quickly, he *abrogated* the agreement and imprisoned Moctezuma. Cortés then governed Tenochtitlán, using Moctezuma as a puppet.

Not long after, when Cortés learned that another conquistador had landed on the coast of Mexico, he journeyed to meet him. Although

Cortés had left Tenochtitlán under the control of one of his officers, the Aztecs took advantage of Cortés's absence to rebel. (10) Moctezuma, who may have questioned the *sagacity* of this action, pleaded with the rebels to end the uprising. He died mysteriously soon after, and the Aztecs drove the Spaniards out of the city.

The Aztecs' victory was shortlived. Cortés amassed a large army of Indians and Spaniards, destroyed the city of Tenochtitlán, and claimed all of Mexico for Spain. Tenochtitlán later became the colonial capital of the Spanish empire, and the great Aztec empire fell into complete submission.

Each of the following statements corresponds to a numbered sentence in the passage. Each statement contains a blank and is followed by four answer choices. Decide which choice fits best in the blank. The word or phrase that you choose must express roughly the same meaning as the italicized word in the passage. Write the letter of your choice on the answer line.

1. The most successful of the Spanish _____ was Hernando Cortés.
   a. soldiers **b.** explorers **c.** speakers **d.** conquerors

   1. _____d_____

2. His efforts enabled Spain to _____ Mexico.
   a. defeat **b.** conquer **c.** gain possession of **d.** triumph over

   2. _____c_____

3. Other battles never diminished the intensity of Cortés's _____ for riches.
   a. thirst **b.** greed **c.** search **d.** hunger

   3. _____c_____

4. Cortés learned of Moctezuma's belief that the coming of a white, bearded god _____ fearful events.
   a. warned of
   b. was unrelated to
   c. would increase
   d. had no bearing on

   4. _____a_____

5. He quickly decided to become a(n) _____ god.
   a. Aztec **b.** bearded **c.** substitute **d.** false

   5. _____c_____

6. Moctezuma had been _____ enough to learn about Cortés's weapons and their great power.
   a. smart **b.** curious **c.** well-informed **d.** frightened

   6. _____b_____

7. Moctezuma brought Cortés rich gifts that were the _____ of a god.
   a. exclusive rights **b.** offerings **c.** requirements **d.** specific promises

   7. _____a_____

8. Cortés received Moctezuma with all the _____ dignity and authority that a god would accord an emperor.
   a. solemn **b.** condescending **c.** essential **d.** unquestionable

   8. _____c_____

9. He _____ the agreement and imprisoned Moctezuma.
   a. made **b.** changed **c.** ignored **d.** annulled

   9. _____d_____

10. Moctezuma may have questioned the _____ of the rebellion.
    a. leaders **b.** wisdom **c.** motives **d.** outcome

    10. _____b_____

Think of something practical that you would very much like to own. Describe it in detail for your parents or for someone else who might be willing to obtain it for you. Explain why you need this object, being sure to emphasize its usefulness. Use at least five of the words from this lesson and underline them.

WORD LIST

abeyance
abstemious
circuitous
circumvent
elude
eschew
evasion
malinger
oblique
shirk

Situations that people generally try to avoid are those which cause discomfort. For example, you may avoid an argument with a friend by agreeing with him or her instead of expressing your own opinion. You may escape some illnesses by eating a proper diet and practicing good hygiene and preventive medicine, such as immunization. Some things, on the other hand, are unavoidable. You may try to postpone cleaning your room, doing an assignment, or planning your future, but you know that such tasks must inevitably be done. The words in this lesson will help you to express the different types of avoidance that people indulge in.

DEFINITIONS

After you have studied the definitions and example for each vocabulary word, write the word on the line to the right.

1. **abeyance** (ə-bā′əns) *noun*   The condition of being temporarily set aside; suspension. (From the Latin word *abaer*, meaning "to yearn for")

    Example   During the parade the police officers kept the automobile traffic on Main Street in *abeyance*.

1. _____

USAGE NOTE: *Abeyance* is used most often as the object of the preposition *in* or *into*.

2. **abstemious** (ăb-stē′mē-əs, əb-stē′mē-əs) *adjective*   **a.** Sparing, especially in the use of food and drink; moderate; temperate.   **b.** Restricted to bare necessities; very plain.

    Related Words **abstemiously** *adverb*; **abstemiousness** *noun*
    Example   So that he would be at his best, the discus thrower was always *abstemious* before a competition.

2. _____

3. **circuitous** (sər-kyōō′ĭ-təs) *adjective*   **a.** Being or taking a roundabout, lengthy course; indirect.   **b.** Not being forthright in language or action. (From the Latin words *circum*, meaning "around," and *ire*, meaning "to go")

    Related Words **circuitously** *adverb*; **circuitousness** *noun*
    Example   Hoping to stay outdoors as long as possible, Josh chose a *circuitous* route home.

3. _____

4. **circumvent** (sûr′kəm-vĕnt′) *trans. verb*   **a.** To avoid by or as if passing around. **b.** To overcome or get the better of by artful maneuvering; outwit. (From the Latin words *circum*, meaning "around," and *venire*, meaning "to come")

    Related Word   **circumvention** *noun*
    Example   Mr. Hull always *circumvents* rush-hour traffic by using secondary roads.

4. _____

5. **elude** (ĭ-lōōd′) *trans. verb* **a.** To escape from, as by artfulness, cunning, or daring. **b.** To escape the understanding of; baffle. (From the Latin *ex-*, meaning "away," and *ludere*, meaning "to play")

Related Words **elusive** *adjective;* **elusively** *adverb;* **elusiveness** *noun*
Example For three days the battalion managed to *elude* capture by the enemy.

5. _____
USAGE NOTE: Do not confuse *elude* with *allude*, meaning "to make an indirect reference to."

6. **eschew** (ĭs-chōō′) *trans. verb* To avoid habitually, especially on moral or practical grounds; shun; abstain from.

Example A truly devout person, he *eschewed* pretentious displays of piety.

6. _____

7. **evasion** (ĭ-vā′zhən) *noun* **a.** The act of escaping or avoiding by cleverness or deceit; dodging. **b.** A means of evading; a trick or excuse used to avoid something. (From the Latin *ex-*, meaning "out," and *vadere*, meaning "to go")

Related Words **evade** *verb;* **evasive** *adjective;* **evasively** *adverb*
Example Mariel had no excuse for her *evasion* of her numerous responsibilities.

7. _____

8. **malinger** (mə-lĭng′gər) *intrans. verb* To pretend to be ill or injured in order to avoid duty or work. (From the French word *malingre*, meaning "sickly")

Related Word **malingerer** *noun*
Example We suspected that Reggie was *malingering* when his absences from work coincided with the days he was scheduled for the stockroom.

8. _____

9. **oblique** (ō-blēk′, ə-blēk′) *adjective* **a.** Indirect; not straightforward. **b.** Devious, misleading, or dishonest. **c.** Having a slanting or sloping direction, course, or position; inclined: *oblique angle.* (From the Latin word *obliquus*, meaning "slanting")

Related Words **obliquely** *adverb;* **obliqueness** *noun*
Example The newspaper reporter questioned the *oblique* statements of the politician.

9. _____

10. **shirk** (shûrk) *trans. verb* To neglect, put off, or avoid discharging (a duty, obligation, or responsibility).

Example The firefighters would be *shirking* their duty if they did not respond quickly to fire alarms.

10. _____

EXERCISE I   COMPLETING DEFINITIONS

On the answer line, write the word from the vocabulary list that best completes
each definition.

1. The act of escaping or avoiding by cleverness or deceit is _____.

2. To neglect, put off, or avoid a duty or obligation is to _____ it.

3. Someone who is sparing or moderate, especially in the use of food and drink,
is _____.

4. If you avoid something by passing around it, you _____ it.

5. To escape by the use of daring or cunning is to _____.

6. A course that is roundabout or indirect is _____.

7. Something that is indirect, misleading, or devious is _____.

8. To be temporarily set aside or suspended is to be held in _____.

9. To avoid habitually or to shun is to _____.

10. To pretend to be sick or injured in order to avoid work is to _____.

1. _____evasion_____
2. _____shirk_____
3. _____abstemious_____
4. _____circumvent_____
5. _____elude_____
6. _____circuitous_____
7. _____oblique_____
8. _____abeyance_____
9. _____eschew_____
10. _____malinger_____

EXERCISE 2   USING WORDS CORRECTLY

Decide whether the italicized vocabulary word has been used correctly in the sentence.
On the answer line, write *Correct* for correct use and *Incorrect* for incorrect use.

1. Juan gets home before his sister Serena does because he takes a *circuitous* route.

2. People who fail to pay taxes on their earnings can be prosecuted for income
tax *evasion*.

3. Because the Coast Guard regularly *shirks* its duties, many lives are saved.

4. Scientists held the decision in *abeyance* until all tests could be performed.

5. The prosecutor's *oblique* line of questioning confused the witness.

6. Glenn *circumvented* the crowd by pushing his way through it to the front row.

7. Vegetarians *eschew* meat, chicken, and fish.

8. Resolving to stick to an *abstemious* diet, Heather ate a huge lunch.

9. Tim often *malingers* so that he can get more work accomplished.

10. For two weeks the escaped convicts managed to *elude* capture.

1. _____Incorrect_____
2. _____Correct_____
3. _____Incorrect_____
4. _____Correct_____
5. _____Correct_____
6. _____Incorrect_____
7. _____Correct_____
8. _____Incorrect_____
9. _____Incorrect_____
10. _____Correct_____

EXERCISE 3   CHOOSING THE BEST WORD

Decide which vocabulary word or related form best expresses the meaning of the
italicized word or phrase in the sentence. On the answer line, write the letter of the
correct choice.

1. Because of Mrs. Ayala's *indirect* glances at the closet, the children were convinced
that she had hidden their presents there.
   a. abstemious   **b.** circuitous   **c.** shirking   **d.** oblique

1. _____d_____

2. The causes and cures of many diseases continue to *escape the understanding of medical researchers.*
   a. circumvent **b.** elude **c.** eschew **d.** shirk

2. _____**b**_____

3. After the holiday feast, the whole family decided to be *sparing.*
   a. abstemious **b.** circuitous **c.** oblique **d.** evasive

3. _____**a**_____

4. Mrs. Leibowitz reminded her daughter that if she *neglected* her chores, she would have twice as many to do tomorrow.
   a. shirked **b.** circumvented **c.** malingered **d.** eluded

4. _____**a**_____

5. Although the path was *roundabout,* it led to a waterfall that we would have missed had we taken the main trail.
   a. abstemious **b.** elusive **c.** circuitous **d.** evasive

5. _____**c**_____

6. Work was held in *suspension* during the power loss.
   a. circumvention **b.** obliqueness **c.** abstemiousness **d.** abeyance

6. _____**d**_____

7. The Puritans *habitually avoided* dancing and reading novels because they believed those activities were sinful.
   a. shirked **b.** eschewed **c.** circumvented **d.** eluded

7. _____**b**_____

8. The boat barely *skirted* the shallow coral reef.
   a. eschewed **b.** malingered **c.** shirked **d.** circumvented

8. _____**d**_____

9. Last night's political debate was pointless due to the candidates' *clever act of avoidance* of the issues.
   a. evasion **b.** abstemiousness **c.** abeyance **d.** malingering

9. _____**a**_____

10. Greta had *pretended to be sick in order to avoid work* so often that when she really was ill, no one believed her.
    a. circumvented **b.** shirked **c.** malingered **d.** eluded

10. _____**c**_____

EXERCISE 4 USING DIFFERENT FORMS OF WORDS

Decide which form of the vocabulary word in parentheses best completes the sentence. The form given may be correct. Write your answer on the answer line.

1. _____ all human company since her husband died, Mrs. Smythe has become a recluse. *(eschew)*

1. _____**Eschewing**_____

2. Although Karen and Hugh adored fresh raspberries, they ate the fruit _____. *(abstemious)*

2. _____**abstemiously**_____

3. The _____ of the question caught me off guard. *(oblique)*

3. _____**obliqueness**_____

4. The narrow road wound _____ down through Sausalito and seemed to end abruptly in San Francisco Bay. *(circuitous)*

4. _____**circuitously**_____

5. The town council voted to hold the matter of a new public swimming pool in _____ until next month's meeting. *(abeyance)*

5. _____**abeyance**_____

6. The local television station somehow achieved the _____ of technical problems during the hurricane. *(circumvent)*

6. _____**circumvention**_____

7. Victory seems to be an _____ goal for this year's gymnastics team. *(elude)*

7. _____**elusive**_____

8. No one could believe that Marybeth had left school early and had _____ her responsibility to the club. *(shirk)*

8. _____**shirked**_____

9. Larry's _____ response to my question convinced me he did not want to attend the concert. *(evasion)*

9. _____**evasive**_____

10. Although Alice has a reputation as a _____, she truly is accident-prone. *(malinger)*

10. _____**malingerer**_____

READING COMPREHENSION

Each numbered sentence in the following passage contains an italicized vocabulary word or related form. After you read the passage, you will complete an exercise.

MOTHER TERESA: A LIFETIME OF SERVICE

Mother Teresa (1910–1997) was a Roman Catholic nun who dedicated her life to the care of poor, abandoned, and dying people all over the world. She was the 1979 winner of the Nobel Peace Prize for her efforts in setting up hospitals, shelters, orphanages, schools, and youth centers. (1) Although her reasons for devoting herself to the unwanted of the world may *elude* some people, few would deny the power she had to communicate compassion and to transmit hope.

Mother Teresa was born Agnes Gonxha Bojaxhiu in the former Yugoslavia. From the time she was twelve years old, Agnes wanted to be a missionary in India. Her interest had been sparked by letters read in her church from Jesuits working in India. At eighteen she left home to join the Sisters of Loreto, a community of Irish nuns with a mission in Calcutta. She taught and served as principal of the Loreto convent school there.

During the years that Sister Teresa spent in the Loreto convent, she was struck by the suffering she glimpsed in the teeming streets outside the cloister walls. Gradually she came to know that her real mission was to leave the convent and to devote herself to the poor. Before she could leave, however, she had to get a series of permissions. (2) At the first level was the Archbishop of Calcutta who, thinking that the idea of a lone nun working in the slums was foolhardy, asked her to put her dream in *abeyance* for a year. (3) When an acquaintance suggested that she *circumvent* the archbishop and write directly to the Vatican, she refused, knowing that her patience and dedi-

cation were being tested. (4) Finally, the archbishop relented and allowed her to complete the remainder of the steps in the *circuitous* process.

In 1948 she left the convent and began the order of the Missionaries of Charity. Within a short time, donors offered facilities, and volunteers, many of whom were her former students, came to devote their lives to the poor. The sisters in Mother Teresa's order take the traditional vows, but the vow of poverty is stricter than usual. As Mother Teresa said, "To be able to love the poor and know the poor, we must be poor ourselves." (5) This means *abstemiousness* and the adoption of Indian clothing rather than the usual nun's habit. (6) Mother Teresa did not *eschew* the rich, however, if they could help her work. When someone gave her a limousine, for example, she promptly raffled it off for $100,000 without ever riding in it. She used the $25,000 she received from the Pope John XXIII Peace Prize to build a new leper colony.

(7) Whether in the streets of Calcutta, the rural areas of Australia, the leper colonies of Asia and Africa,

or the slums of Mexico and the United States, Mother Teresa was a vigorous worker who never *shirked* her numerous responsibilities, regardless of her own illness or exhaustion. (8) She expected the same from her coworkers and was intolerant only of *malingerers*. She asked people to give of themselves as well as their resources. "No matter how tired [you are], no matter how physically exhausting this work may be," said Mother Teresa, "it's beautiful to bring a smile into someone's life, to care for someone in need. What greater joy can you have?"

Age, authority, and renown did not change Mother Teresa. (9) Shy and modest, she *evaded* reporters' attempts to glorify her work, allowing interviews and photographs only when publicity might have helped her people. (10) She answered most questions *obliquely*, insisting, in spite of a large number of international honors, that she was not important. She saw her fame only as "recognition that the poor are our brothers and sisters, that there are people in the world who need love, who need care, who have to be wanted."

Each of the following statements corresponds to a numbered sentence in the passage. Each statement contains a blank and is followed by four answer choices. Decide which answer choice fits best in the blank. The word or phrase that you choose must express roughly the same meaning as the italicized word in the passage. Write the letter of your choice on the answer line.

1. Mother Teresa's reasons for devoting herself to the unwanted of the world may _____ some people.
   a. flatter   **b.** baffle   **c.** offend   **d.** reach

   1. _____ b

2. The Archbishop of Calcutta asked her to _____ her dream.
   a. rephrase   **c.** temporarily set aside
   b. write about   **d.** think deeply about

   2. _____ c

3. An acquaintance suggested that she _____ the archbishop.
   a. bypass   **b.** beg   **c.** argue with   **d.** should impress

   3. _____ a

4. The archbishop allowed her to complete the _____ process.
   a. burdensome   **b.** accepted   **c.** roundabout   **d.** unnecessary

   4. _____ c

5. The sisters in Mother Teresa's order adhere to _____.
   a. a code of ethics   **c.** strict rules of dress
   b. specific laws   **d.** moderation in food and drink

   5. _____ d

6. Mother Teresa did not _____ the rich.
   a. endorse   **b.** shun   **c.** encourage   **d.** beg from

   6. _____ b

7. Mother Teresa was a vigorous worker who never _____ her responsibilities.
   a. neglected   **b.** fulfilled   **c.** organized   **d.** yielded to

   7. _____ a

8. She was intolerant only of _____.
   a. the wealthy   **c.** those who pretend illness to avoid duty
   b. the poor   **d.** those who visit out of curiosity

   8. _____ c

9. She _____ reporters' attempts to glorify her work.
   a. respected   **b.** avoided   **c.** followed   **d.** enjoyed

   9. _____ b

10. She answered most questions _____.
    a. indirectly   **b.** completely   **c.** humorously   **d.** sarcastically

    10. _____ a

PRACTICE WITH ANALOGIES

Directions   On the answer line, write the vocabulary word or a form of it that completes each analogy.

See page 79 for some strategies to use with analogies.

1. CLIMAX : STORY :: _____ : project (*Lesson 18*)

   1. _____ culmination

2. AIMLESS : PURPOSE :: _____ : flaw (*Lesson 18*)

   2. _____ impeccable

3. BOUNDLESS : LIMIT :: _____ : equal (*Lesson 18*)

   3. _____ peerless

4. IMPLAUSIBLE : BELIEVE :: _____ : copy (*Lesson 18*)

   4. _____ inimitable

5. PEAK : MOUNTAIN :: _____ : career (*Lesson 18*)

   5. _____ zenith

6. CANCEL : CONTRACT :: _____ : treaty (*Lesson 19*)

   6. _____ abrogate

7. ELATED : HAPPY :: _____ : curious (*Lesson 19*)

   7. _____ inquisitive

8. DENSE : PENETRATE :: _____ : catch (*Lesson 20*)

   8. _____ elusive

9. PACIFIST : FIGHT :: _____ : work (*Lesson 20*)

   9. _____ malingerer

10. NEGLECT : RESPONSIBILITY :: _____ : duty (*Lesson 20*)

    10. _____ shirk

The **Bonus activity** for Lessons 17–20 is on page T22.
Verbal Aptitude Test 2 is on page T23.

21

LESSON 21   COPYING AND REPEATING

All of us copy and repeat every day. A child first learns to write by copying letters and to speak by imitating sounds. Some forms of copying, such as imitating a style of dress or using someone else's recipes, are considered to be compliments. Yet other forms of copying, such as using someone else's homework or repeating words in the same sentence, are not regarded as positive behavior. This lesson includes words about both the desirable and the undesirable varieties of repetition and copying.

WORD LIST

banal
emulate
mimicry
platitude
prototype
recapitulate
redundant
rendition
sham
simulation

DEFINITIONS

After you have studied the definitions and example for each vocabulary word, write the word on the line to the right.

1. **banal** (bə-năl′, bā′nəl, bə-näl′) *adjective*   Lacking freshness or originality; trite.

   Related Word   **banality** *noun*
   Example   The employees easily lost interest in the *banal* speech of their supervisor.

   1. _____

2. **emulate** (ĕm′yə-lāt′) *trans. verb*   To strive to equal or excel, especially through imitation. (From the Latin word *aemulari*, meaning "to try to equal")

   Related Word   **emulation** *noun*
   Example   The young writers tried to *emulate* the styles of their favorite authors.

   2. _____

3. **mimicry** (mĭm′ĭ-krē) *noun*   A close copying or imitation of the speech, expression, or gesture of another; close resemblance. (From the Greek word *mimos*, meaning "imitator")

   Related Word   **mimic** *verb*
   Example   The impersonator's *mimicry* of the famous singer delighted the crowd.

   3. _____

4. **platitude** (plăt′ĭ-tōōd′, plăt′ĭ-tyōōd′) *noun*   A trite remark or statement. (From the French word *plat*, meaning "flat")

   Related Word   **platitudinous** *adjective*
   Example   The crowd became bored listening to the politician's *platitudes*.

   4. _____

5. **prototype** (prō'tə-tīp') *noun*   **a.** An original type, form, or instance that serves as a model on which later stages are based or judged.   **b.** An early and typical example. (From the Greek words *prōtos*, meaning "first," and *typos*, meaning "model")

Related Word   **prototypical** *adjective*
Example   The author wrote a *prototype* of a chapter for the publisher's approval.

5. _____

6. **recapitulate** (rē'kə-pĭch'ə-lāt') *trans. verb*   To repeat in concise form. (From the Latin *re-*, meaning "again," and *capitulare*, meaning "to put under headings")

Related Word   **recapitulation** *noun*
Example   First Simon explained the incident to his mother; then he *recapitulated* the story for his father.

6. _____

7. **redundant** (rĭ-dŭn'dənt) *adjective*   **a.** Exceeding what is necessary or natural; superfluous.   **b.** Repeating the same idea, usually in different words; wordy. (From the Latin word *redundare*, meaning "to overflow")

Related Words   **redundancy** *noun;* **redundantly** *adverb*
Example   The chef agreed that a second dessert would be *redundant*.

7. _____

8. **rendition** (rĕn-dĭsh'ən) *noun*   **a.** An interpretation of a musical score or dramatic piece.   **b.** A performance of a musical or dramatic work. (From the Old French word *rendre*, meaning "to give back")

Related Word   **render** *verb*
Example   The company's *rendition* of *Romeo and Juliet* was modern and innovative, but most people would have preferred a more traditional interpretation.

8. _____

9. **sham** (shăm) *noun*   **a.** Something false or empty that is supposed to be genuine.   **b.** The quality of deceitfulness; empty pretense.   **c.** A person who assumes a false character; impostor.   *adjective*   Not genuine; fake.

Example   The contestants were angry when they learned that the competition was a *sham* that had been created for advertising purposes.

9. _____

10. **simulation** (sĭm'yə-lā'shən) *noun*   The taking on of the appearance, form, or sound of something else; an imitation. (From the Latin word *similis*, meaning "like")

Related Word   **simulate** *verb*
Example   The museum had an attraction that *simulated* a ride through space.

10. _____

EXERCISE I WRITING CORRECT WORDS

On the answer line, write the word from the vocabulary list that fits each definition.

1. A trite remark or statement

2. Lacking freshness or originality

3. An interpretation of a musical score or dramatic piece

4. The taking on of the appearance, form, or sound of something else; an imitation

5. A close copying or imitation of the speech, expression, or gesture of another; close resemblance

6. Something false that is supposed to be genuine; fake

7. To try to equal or excel, especially through imitation

8. An original type, form, or instance that serves as a model for later stages; an early or typical example

9. To repeat in concise form

10. Exceeding what is necessary; repeating the same idea

1. _____platitude_____

2. _____banal_____

3. _____rendition_____

4. _____simulation_____

5. _____mimicry_____

6. _____sham_____

7. _____emulate_____

8. _____prototype_____

9. _____recapitulate_____

10. _____redundant_____

EXERCISE 2 USING WORDS CORRECTLY

Each of the following statements contains an italicized vocabulary word. Decide whether the sentence is true or false, and write *True* or *False* on the answer line.

1. "Have a nice day" could be called a *banal* expression.

2. One can find a *rendition* in most elevators.

3. The mockingbird got its name from its *mimicry* of other birds' calls.

4. A person who uses *platitudes* exclusively makes an excellent speaker.

5. Describing something as "outstanding and excellent" is *redundant*.

6. Consumers are sometimes asked to test *prototypes* of new products.

7. It is a good idea to *emulate* someone whose qualities and achievements you do not respect.

8. To *recapitulate* a story is to give it a slightly different ending.

9. Television commercials sometimes use *simulations* of person-on-the-street interviews rather than actual interviews in order to sell products.

10. If your every reaction is a *sham*, people will learn to distrust you.

1. _____True_____

2. _____False_____

3. _____True_____

4. _____False_____

5. _____True_____

6. _____True_____

7. _____False_____

8. _____False_____

9. _____True_____

10. _____True_____

EXERCISE 3 CHOOSING THE BEST WORD

Decide which vocabulary word or related form best expresses the meaning of the italicized word or phrase in the sentence. On the answer line, write the letter of the correct choice.

1. The fire department used an *imitation* of a fire emergency to train its recruits in rescue operations.
   a. sham   **b.** simulation   **c.** emulation   **d.** mimicry

1. _____b_____

2. Because he was able to *repeat in concise form* the story, I gave him credit for understanding the situation.

   a. mimic   b. simulate   c. emulate   d. recapitulate

   2. _____d_____

3. The viceroy butterfly is protected from birds by its *imitation of the appearance* of the monarch butterfly, which is unpalatable to birds.

   a. sham   b. mimicry   c. recapitulation   d. redundancy

   3. _____b_____

4. Joseph *tried to equal or excel* his older sister in school, hoping to make the honor roll.

   a. emulated   b. simulated   c. recapitulated   d. mimicked

   4. _____a_____

5. The conversation at the dinner party was so *trite* that several of the guests left early.

   a. sham   b. redundant   c. prototypical   d. banal

   5. _____d_____

6. The *performance of a musical work* was both original and perfectly executed.

   a. emulation   b. simulation   c. rendition   d. sham

   6. _____c_____

7. Carrying coal to Newcastle, England, a coal-mining center, would be *going beyond what is necessary.*

   a. prototypical   b. banal   c. redundant   d. simulated

   7. _____c_____

8. D. H. Lawrence called Benjamin Franklin "the real practical *typical example* of the American."

   a. sham   b. prototype   c. simulation   d. platitude

   8. _____b_____

9. Not wanting to offend the artist, Gracie uttered a few polite *trite statements* about the painting and then changed the subject.

   a. redundancies   b. prototypes   c. recapitulations   d. platitudes

   9. _____d_____

10. The detective's story was an elaborate *fake* designed to gain entry into the ring of car thieves.

   a. sham   b. mimicry   c. emulation   d. banality

   10. _____a_____

EXERCISE 4 USING DIFFERENT FORMS OF WORDS

Decide which form of the vocabulary word in parentheses best completes the sentence. The form given may be correct. Write your answer on the answer line.

1. The _____ of "Let It Be" was off-key and too slow. *(rendition)*

   1. _____rendition_____

2. "I myself prefer observing with my eyes the natural wonders of nature," said Marvin _____. *(redundant)*

   2. _____redundantly_____

3. As part of his comedy routine for the senior show, Alan will _____ the principal and several teachers. *(mimicry)*

   3. _____mimic_____

4. Willa's _____ of a great athlete helped her to make the Olympic track team. *(emulate)*

   4. _____emulation_____

5. "Little Boxes" is a 1960s song about conformity and the _____ of modern life. *(banal)*

   5. _____banality_____

6. Shakespeare's poem "Shall I compare thee to a summer's day?" is _____ of the English sonnet form. *(prototype)*

   6. _____prototypical_____

7. Sheila's first novel was rejected by the publisher because it was _____. *(platitude)*

   7. _____platitudinous_____

8. Ronnie's _____ story that his dog ate his homework did not impress the teacher. *(sham)*

   8. _____sham_____

9. The _____ of the news story at the end of the hour served as a good summary. *(recapitulate)*

   9. _____recapitulation_____

10. NASA has a machine that _____ zero gravity so that astronauts can practice being weightless. *(simulation)*

   10. _____simulates_____

READING COMPREHENSION

Each numbered sentence in the following passage contains an italicized vocabulary word or related form. After you read the passage, you will complete an exercise.

ECHO AND NARCISSUS

The story of Echo and Narcissus is frequently retold. In classical mythology, however, the two figures did not always appear together. (1) The *prototype* of the Narcissus story dates from the seventh or eighth century B.C. Echo did not appear in the Narcissus tale until the first century A.D., when the Roman poet Ovid wove her into his *Metamorphoses*. (2) Because of its appealing treatment, Ovid's version is the one that later writers have *emulated*. (3) *Renditions* of the myth have even been enacted on the stage and incorporated into film.

The commonest modern version of the story begins with Echo, a woodland nymph, who was gifted with extraordinary wit and cunning. One day, however, Echo made a grievous error at the request of Zeus, who had slipped away from his palace on Olympus to visit the mortals on Earth, as he often did. (4) Echo detained Hera, Zeus' jealous wife, who had followed him, by *recapitulating* curious stories, one after the other, so entertaining that Zeus had time to return to Olympus. (5) When Hera found that she had been deceived, she punished Echo by depriving her of normal speech and allowing her only to *mimic* the words of others. (6) Thus Echo was banished to a life of senseless repetition: the reiteration of the wise words, *platitudes,* and nonsense of others.

Echo felt the full weight of this horrible punishment when she fell in love with the handsome but conceited Narcissus, a youth who did not return her affection. During their first and only meeting, she was capable of nothing more than mindlessly echoing Narcissus' every question and comment. (7) Frustrated, miserable, and destined to repeat his *banalities,* Echo succeeded only in making Narcissus angry. He ran from her, and Echo grieved until her flesh melted away. Before she died, however, she offered a prayer to Aphrodite that one day Narcissus might suffer as she had.

Her prayer was answered. One day Narcissus happened to gaze into a pool of water and noticed an extremely handsome face staring back at him. Never having seen his own reflection, he tried repeatedly to seize the lovely image, but reaching into the water caused the image to shatter and disappear. (8) Nevertheless, every day he looked at the intriguing *simulation* and grew to love it more and more. (9) Never realizing it was a *sham,* and filled with love just as Echo had been, he pined away next to the pool until he died.

Both Echo and Narcissus left behind earthly reminders of their fate. Where Narcissus died, a lovely white flower sprouted, which was named after him. (10) When Echo's flesh melted away, nothing was left of her but a voice *redundantly* uttering the words of others. Myth tells us that this is the voice that echoes back to us from caves, cliffs, and canyons.

READING COMPREHENSION EXERCISE

Each of the following statements corresponds to a numbered sentence in the passage. Each statement contains a blank and is followed by four answer choices. Decide which choice fits best in the blank. The word or phrase that you choose must express roughly the same meaning as the italicized word in the passage. Write the letter of your choice on the answer line.

1. The _____ of the Narcissus story dates from the seventh or eighth century B.C.
   a. history   b. beginning   c. original form   d. best version

1. _____c_____

2. Ovid's version of the story is the one that later writers have _____.
   a. tried to rewrite
   b. wanted to adapt
   c. wanted to improve
   d. followed

2. _____d_____

3. _____ of the story of Echo and Narcissus have been staged.
   a. Interpretations   c. Exact duplicates
   b. Repetitions   d. Inaccurate versions

3. _____a_____

4. Echo _____ many strange tales in order to delay Hera.
   a. listened to   c. embroidered on
   b. repeated concisely   d. thought of

4. _____b_____

5. Hera allowed Echo only to _____ the words of others.
   a. use   b. utter   c. distort   d. imitate

5. _____d_____

6. Thus Echo repeated the wisdom, _____, and nonsense of others.
   a. advice   c. indiscreet remarks
   b. prayers   d. trite statements

6. _____d_____

7. Echo was destined to repeat _____.
   a. expressions lacking originality   c. expressions filled with wit
   b. expressions of frustration   d. expressions of love

7. _____a_____

8. Every day Narcissus looked at the intriguing _____ in the water.
   a. imitation   b. face   c. sight   d. scene

8. _____a_____

9. Narcissus never realized that the face in the water was only a _____.
   a. reflection   b. duplicate   c. fake   d. game

9. _____c_____

10. Nothing remained of Echo except a voice _____ uttering the words of others.
    a. hauntingly   b. continually   c. loudly   d. repetitively

10. _____d_____

WRITING ASSIGNMENT

Because your public speaking skills are excellent, you have been asked to write a short expository composition on how to make an effective speech. Your readers will be students who have never addressed groups of more than ten people. Using at least five of the words in this lesson, explain how effective speakers get their points across, hold their audiences' attention, and avoid the common pitfalls of public speaking. Underline each vocabulary word that you use.

VOCABULARY ENRICHMENT

The word *mimicry* derives from the Greek word *mimos,* meaning "imitator." Theatrical entertainments began in Greece, where actors, or mimes, presented myths and scenes of daily life by means of gestures rather than speech. This dramatic form developed fully in Rome, where comic entertainments played a role in festivals. Roman mimes performed by means of dance steps, gestures, and postures and by using masks, which enabled them to assume the parts of different characters.

Activity   Many other English words relating to acting and the stage have Greek origins. Look up the following words in a dictionary. Write a short account of the Greek origins of each one, supplying the Greek word or words from which each is derived, along with its meaning.

1. chorus   2. comedy   3. drama   4. theater   5. tragedy

The **Test** for Lessons 19, 20, and 21 is on page T28.

READING SKILLS

CONTEXT CLUES AND THE READING OF AMERICAN LITERATURE

As you continue to study the literature of the United States, you will read an increasing number of works from earlier periods as your courses become more advanced. The following strategies suggest ways of using the context to determine the meanings of unfamiliar words.

STRATEGIES

1. *Consider the period in which the work was written.* In an older work, some words may not be in use today or may have different meanings. For example, when the character in "Yankee Doodle" put a feather in his cap "and called it *macaroni*," he was using a word that meant "fashionable" in the eighteenth century.

2. *Consider the author and his or her style.* Be on the alert for the frequent use of metaphors or literary allusions that you will need to understand. Emily Dickinson wrote of a train that used to "lap the Miles" and neighed "like Boanerges" (a biblical reference).

3. *Consider the genre (type of literature) and the subject of the work.* If the work is fiction, in what period is it set? If it is nonfiction, what is the author's main idea? The setting and the subject of a work help to determine its vocabulary.

4. *Use a dictionary for checking the meanings of unfamiliar words.* Be sure to do so if a word is crucial to the meaning of a passage. In some cases you may need to consult an unabridged dictionary.

EXERCISE USING CONTEXT CLUES IN READING LITERATURE

The following passage is the beginning of Edgar Allan Poe's famous short story "The Masque of the Red Death." Begin by reading the entire passage. *Step 1:* Write your own definition of each italicized word. *Step 2:* Write the appropriate dictionary definition of the word.

The "Red Death" had long devastated the country. No (1) *pestilence* had ever been so fatal or so hideous. Blood was its (2) *Avatar* and its seal—the redness and the horror of blood. There were sharp pains, and sudden dizziness, and then profuse bleeding at the pores, with (3) *dissolution.* The scarlet stains upon the body, and especially upon the face of the victim, were the (4) *pest ban* which shut him out from the aid and from the sympathy of his fellow-men; and the whole seizure, progress, and termination of the disease, were the incidents of half-an-hour.

But the Prince Prospero was happy and dauntless and (5) *sagacious.* When his dominions were half-depopulated, he summoned to his presence a thousand hale and light-hearted friends from among the knights and dames of his court, and with these retired to the deep seclusion of one of his (6) *castellated* abbeys. This was an extensive and magnificent structure, the creation of the prince's own eccentric yet (7) *august* taste. A strong and lofty wall girdled it in. This wall had gates of iron. The courtiers, having entered, brought furnaces and massy hammers and welded the bolts. They resolved to leave means neither of ingress or (8) *egress* to the sudden impulses of despair from without or of frenzy from within. The abbey was amply provisioned.

With such precautions the courtiers might (9) *bid* defiance to contagion. The external world could take care of itself. In the meantime it was folly to grieve or to think. . . . (10) *Without* was the "Red Death."

1. *pestilence*

   Your Definition severe disease

   Dictionary Definition usually fatal epidemic disease

2. *Avatar*

   Your Definition telltale sign

   Dictionary Definition manifestation or aspect

3. *dissolution*

   Your Definition state of getting much worse

   Dictionary Definition disintegration; death

4. *pest ban*

   Your Definition mark of the pestilence

   Dictionary Definition curse of an epidemic disease

5. *sagacious*

   Your Definition like a sage

   Dictionary Definition wise

6. *castellated*

   Your Definition made like a castle

   Dictionary Definition furnished with turrets and battlements in the style of a castle

7. *august*

   Your Definition splendid

   Dictionary Definition inspiring awe or admiration; majestic

8. *egress*

   Your Definition exit

   Dictionary Definition the act of going out; exit

9. *bid*

   Your Definition offer

   Dictionary Definition order; command

10. *Without*

    Your Definition Outside

    Dictionary Definition On the outside

22

LESSON 22 NATURE

No living thing—plant or animal—lives in isolation. Every organism depends in some way on other living and nonliving things in its environment, and no organism lives without affecting its environment in turn.

This interdependence of living organisms and their environments is perhaps best illustrated by the food chain. Green plants utilize the energy of sunlight for the manufacture of food. A mouse that eats grasses may be eaten, in turn, by a weasel. A hawk may then eat the weasel. When the last animal in the food chain dies, bacteria and fungi break its body down into simple nutrients that go back into the soil. Without the organic matter provided by living organisms, there would be fewer nutrients in the soil. The soil that develops is therefore important in determining what types of plants will grow in it and what types of animals will eat the plants, thereby renewing the cycle of life.

The words in this lesson are about nature's rich endowment of plants and animals. These words will help you to understand the interdependence that is vital to the survival of all living things.

WORD LIST

arboreal
burgeon
deciduous
fauna
flora
germination
horticultural
lichen
sylvan
verdant

DEFINITIONS

After you have studied the definitions and example for each vocabulary word, write the word on the line to the right.

1. **arboreal** (är-bôr′ē-əl) *adjective*   **a.** Pertaining to or resembling a tree.   **b.** Living in trees. (From the Latin word *arbor*, meaning "tree")

   Related Word arbor *noun*
   Example Monkeys and squirrels are regarded as *arboreal* creatures.

   1. _____

2. **burgeon** (bûr′jən) *intrans. verb*   **a.** To put forth new buds, leaves, or branches; sprout.   **b.** To begin to grow or blossom.   **c.** To develop rapidly; flourish. (From the Old French word *burjon*, meaning "a bud")

   Example Within four days the lettuce seeds had *burgeoned* into tiny seedlings.

   2. _____

3. **deciduous** (dĭ-sĭj′o͞o-əs) *adjective*   **a.** Shedding or losing foliage at the end of the growing season.   **b.** Falling off or shed at a specific season or stage of growth: *deciduous antlers of deer*. (From the Latin *de-*, meaning "off," and *cadere*, meaning "to fall")

   Example Maples, elms, birches, and oaks are *deciduous* trees.

   3. _____

4. **fauna** (fô′nə) *noun*   Animals collectively, especially the animals of a particular region, period, or special environment. (From the name of the Roman goddess *Fauna*, the protector of nature and fertility)

   Example Alexa looked forward to studying the *fauna* of Australia, especially the koala bear and the kangaroo.

   4. _____

5. **flora** (flôr′ə) *noun*   Plants collectively, especially the plants of a particular region, period, or special environment. (From the name of the Roman goddess *Flora*, the protector of flowers)

> **Related Word**   floral *adjective*
> **Example**   The *flora* of the southwestern United States is sparse because it seldom rains there.

5. _____

6. **germination** (jûr′mə-nā′shən) *noun*   The process of beginning to grow or develop. (From the Latin word *germen*, meaning "seed")

> **Related Words**   germinate *verb;* **germination** *adjective*
> **Example**   *Germination* takes place when warmth and moisture cause the shell of a seed to break.

6. _____

7. **horticultural** (hôr′tə-kŭl′chər-əl) *adjective*   **a.** Relating to the science or art of cultivating fruits, vegetables, flowers, and plants.   **b.** Having to do with tending a garden. (A blend of the Latin word *hortus*, meaning "garden," and the English word *agriculture*)

> **Related Words**   horticulture *noun;* **horticulturist** *noun*
> **Example**   Leonard hoped that his *horticultural* experience would help him to get a job as a landscape designer.

7. _____

8. **lichen** (lī′kən) *noun*   Any of the numerous plants consisting of a fungus in close combination with certain blue-green or green algae that form a crustlike, scaly, or branching growth on rocks or tree trunks.

> **Example**   Because they look so much alike, moss and *lichen* are often difficult to distinguish.

8. _____

9. **sylvan** (sĭl′vən) *adjective*   **a.** Abounding in trees; wooded.   **b.** Pertaining to or characteristic of woods or forest regions.   **c.** Located in or inhabiting a wood or forest. (From the Latin word *silva*, meaning "forest")

> **Example**   The Black Hills of South Dakota are a *sylvan* delight after the barren stretches of the Badlands.

9. _____

10. **verdant** (vûr′dnt) *adjective*   **a.** Green with vegetation.   **b.** Green in color. (From the Latin word *veridis*, meaning "green")

> **Related Words**   verdancy *noun;* **verdantly** *adverb*
> **Example**   We drove through the fertile, *verdant* countryside.

10. _____

Word History: sylvan

Latin: *silva*=woods

If you were asked to picture a *sylvan* area, trees and woods should immediately come to mind. *Sylvan* comes from the Latin word *silva*, meaning "woods," and is often used to describe places abounding in trees. *Pennsylvania* is a state whose name derives from the word *sylvan*. In 1681, King Charles II of England granted some land in the New World to William Penn. Although Penn wanted to call the area Sylvania, meaning "woodland," King Charles insisted that it include the name of William's illustrious father, Admiral William Penn. Thus, Sylvania became *Pennsylvania* which translates to "Penn's Woodland" or "Penn's Woods."

EXERCISE I WRITING CORRECT WORDS

On the answer line, write the word from the vocabulary list that fits each definition.

1. The animals of a particular region, period, or environment

2. Pertaining to or resembling a tree; living in trees

3. The process of beginning to grow or develop

4. Shedding foliage at the end of the growing season

5. To put forth new buds, leaves, or branches

6. Abounding in trees; pertaining to or characteristic of woods or forest regions

7. Green with vegetation

8. Relating to the science or art of cultivating plants, flowers, fruits, and vegetables

9. Plants that form a crustlike or scaly growth on rocks or tree trunks

10. The plants of a particular region, period, or environment

1. _____ fauna _____
2. _____ arboreal _____
3. _____ germination _____
4. _____ deciduous _____
5. _____ burgeon _____
6. _____ sylvan _____
7. _____ verdant _____
8. _____ horticultural _____
9. _____ lichen _____
10. _____ flora _____

EXERCISE 2 USING WORDS CORRECTLY

Decide whether the italicized vocabulary word has been used correctly in the sentence. On the answer line, write *Correct* for correct use and *Incorrect* for incorrect use.

1. Glenda described the desert as a setting of *arboreal* splendor.

2. The *flora* in the forest outside of town includes deer, raccoons, squirrels, and chipmunks.

3. My uncle's *horticultural* skill shows in his beautiful garden.

4. The texture of the *lichen*-covered tree trunk resulted in an interesting close-up photograph.

5. As we walked through the *sylvan* preserve, we could see the setting sun through the trees.

6. The pioneers traveled for days through the arid, *verdant* desert.

7. During our camping trip in the Grand Teton mountains, we saw bears and other *fauna*.

8. Already the crocuses are *burgeoning* in our garden.

9. We like to have a few *deciduous* trees in the yard to produce greenery during the winter.

10. The best time for *germination* is in the dead of winter when nothing grows.

1. _____ Incorrect _____
2. _____ Incorrect _____
3. _____ Correct _____
4. _____ Correct _____
5. _____ Correct _____
6. _____ Incorrect _____
7. _____ Correct _____
8. _____ Correct _____
9. _____ Incorrect _____
10. _____ Incorrect _____

EXERCISE 3 CHOOSING THE BEST DEFINITION

For each italicized vocabulary word in the following sentences, write the letter of the best definition on the answer line.

1. Noah uses *lichen* as a natural dye for his woven baskets.
   a. roots   **b.** flower petals   **c.** algae and fungi   **d.** seeds and fruits

1. _____ c _____

2. Robin Hood is said to have lived in a *sylvan* area of Nottinghamshire in England.
   a. wooded   **b.** marshy   **c.** undeveloped   **d.** farming

2. _____ a _____

3. Carrie did an experiment on seed *germination,* contrasting seedlings produced under artificial light with those produced under natural light.
     a. diversion   **b.** growth   **c.** transformation   **d.** typing

3. _____**b**_____

4. Mozart's musical talent *burgeoned* when he was very young.
     a. developed rapidly   **c.** became evident
     b. was discovered   **d.** persisted

4. _____**a**_____

5. The Huntington Botanical Garden in San Marino, California, contains *flora* from all over the world.
     a. plants   **b.** orchids   **c.** animals   **d.** birds

5. _____**a**_____

6. A *horticultural* expert gave a demonstration on how to prune trees.
     a. scientific   **c.** pertaining to the science of insecticides
     b. farming   **d.** pertaining to the science of cultivating

6. _____**d**_____

7. *Deciduous* trees shade our house during the summer but let the sun in during the winter.
     a. evergreen   **c.** shedding foliage at the end of the growing season
     b. fruit-bearing   **d.** shedding leaves throughout the year

7. _____**c**_____

8. The sculpture was *arboreal* in height and shape.
     a. authentic   **b.** treelike   **c.** agreeable   **d.** ordinary

8. _____**b**_____

9. Marlene was fascinated by bats and other cave *fauna.*
     a. plants of a particular region   **c.** dwellers
     b. animals of a special environment   **d.** geological features

9. _____**b**_____

10. After the spring rains, the whole countryside was *verdant.*
     a. flooded   **c.** in flower
     b. marshy   **d.** green with vegetation

10. _____**d**_____

EXERCISE 4   USING DIFFERENT FORMS OF WORDS

Decide which form of the vocabulary word in parentheses best completes the sentence. The form given may be correct. Write your answer on the answer line.

1. The two-year-old's _____ use of language delighted his parents. *(burgeon)*

   1. _____**burgeoning**_____

2. "You should watch young plants carefully for signs of disease," warned the _____. *(horticultural)*

   2. _____**horticulturist**_____

3. _____ are an important food source for many birds and animals. *(lichen)*

   3. _____**Lichens**_____

4. The hoya, or honey plant, will _____ from stem cuttings. *(germination)*

   4. _____**germinate**_____

5. The _____ of the Arctic includes moose, caribou, reindeer, polar bears, walrus, seals, and whales. *(fauna)*

   5. _____**fauna**_____

6. Arctic _____ is limited to dwarf trees, grasses, mosses, lichens, sedges, and a few flowering plants. *(flora)*

   6. _____**flora**_____

7. The stage had been masterfully transformed into a _____ glen. *(sylvan)*

   7. _____**sylvan**_____

8. Dad did not know whether the tree was _____ until autumn, when all the leaves fell. *(deciduous)*

   8. _____**deciduous**_____

9. Puffins, which build nests in rock crevices, are not _____ birds. *(arboreal)*

   9. _____**arboreal**_____

10. The _____ of the oasis welcomed the weary desert travelers. *(verdant)*

   10. _____**verdancy**_____

READING COMPREHENSION

Each numbered sentence in the following passage contains an italicized vocabulary word or related form. After you read the passage, you will complete an exercise.

THE TEEMING LIFE OF THE TROPICAL RAIN FOREST

Tropical rain forests are biologically the richest and most diverse areas of the world. Although they cover less than 2 percent of the earth, they contain between 40 and 50 percent of the planet's animal, bird, insect, and plant species. (1) Located along the equator in Central and South America, Africa, and islands off the coast of southeast Asia, these complex *sylvan* areas have long been a source of fascination for scientists in many different fields.

(2) The typical image one has of the rain forest is that of a storybook jungle of dense *verdant* foliage. In fact, the dense appearance of a rain forest is misleading. It actually has an underlying order of three levels, or layers, each having its own characteristics and each providing a distinct environment.

The main canopy of the rain forest is formed by evergreen trees 100 to 130 feet high. Below the canopy are the shorter trees, 50 to 80 feet high, which struggle upward toward the sunlight that is blocked by the branches of the taller trees.

(3) These two levels furnish the support for several kinds of unusual *flora*. Climbing vines attach themselves to trees in order to grow toward the light. (4) Epiphytes, or air plants, *burgeon* in small amounts of debris that lodge in the crannies of the trees. Their waxy leaves and bulging stems are environmental adaptations that allow them to absorb water quickly when it is available and thus protect them from dehydration. (5) *Horticulturists* are astounded by the exotic varieties of staghorn ferns, orchids, and bromeliads that literally "grow on trees."

(6) The two top levels of the rain forest also support an assortment of *fauna*. Because of the pools of water stored by epiphytes, the typically terrestrial cockroach, earthworm, and snake, as well as the aquatic salamander and frog, can live in the forest canopy. (7) Many of these *arboreal* creatures never descend to the rain forest floor. (8) They obtain their food from the trees in the form of fruits, nuts, *lichens*, and insects. Like the plants, the animals that live in the trees have adapted to their environment. Some frogs and squirrels have winglike membranes that allow them to glide through the trees. Other animals, such as monkeys, sloths, and marsupials, have strong claws, adhesive pads, or tails that allow them to swing from branch to branch.

The rain forest floor, in comparison to the canopy, is relatively bare. (9) Receiving little sunlight, this third level consists of shrubs, nonwoody plants, and a thin layer of *deciduous* leaves. Occasionally a fallen tree will take others with it, clearing the canopy and allowing light to reach the floor. (10) As the thin soil heats up, seeds *germinate.* The strongest of the seedlings will survive to replenish the canopy. Like the animals in the

canopy, those on the rain forest floor are well adapted to their environments. Elephants, buffalo, wild hogs, and leopards all possess characteristics for moving through hanging vines and closely spaced trees—strength and weight, short limbs, and a wedge-shaped head. Wild pigs and anteaters have long snouts, allowing them to root out insects and fungi easily. Since most of the animals on the forest floor are not good climbers, speed and camouflage are necessary for evading predators or surprising prey. Striped cats and spotted deer move quickly and blend in well with the shadows and ground vegetation.

In spite of their adaptations to their environmental conditions, the plants and animals of the tropical rain forest are being threatened. Today the rapid growth of the world's population and the increasing demands for natural resources are disrupting the balance of nature. Scientists fear that unless this disruption is halted, countless species of plants and animals will become extinct, and Earth's most complex natural habitat will be devastated.

Each of the following statements corresponds to a numbered sentence in the passage. Each statement contains a blank and is followed by four answer choices. Decide which choice fits best in the blank. The word or phrase that you choose must express roughly the same meaning as the italicized word in the passage. Write the letter of your choice on the answer line.

1. These complex _____ areas fascinate scientists from many different fields.
   a. garden   b. physical   c. wooded   d. aquatic

   1. _____c_____

2. The typical image of the rain forest is that of a jungle with dense _____ foliage.
   a. green   b. twisted   c. dried   d. colorful

   2. _____a_____

3. The two levels of trees support several kinds of unusual _____.
   a. animal life   b. insects   c. plant life   d. birds

   3. _____c_____

4. Air plants _____ in small amounts of debris caught in the crannies of trees.
   a. die   b. sprout   c. nestle   d. hang

   4. _____b_____

5. _____ are astounded by exotic varieties of plants and flowers.
   a. Those interested in flower arranging
   b. Those interested in landscape design
   c. Those interested in photographing nature
   d. Those interested in the science of cultivating plants

   5. _____d_____

6. The top two levels of the rain forest also support an assortment of _____.
   a. insects   b. plant life   c. animal life   d. birds

   6. _____c_____

7. Many of these _____ creatures never descend to the forest floor.
   a. tree-dwelling b. climbing   c. nest-sitting d. lazy

   7. _____a_____

8. They eat fruits, nuts, and _____ provided by the trees.
   a. various types of leaves   c. bacteria
   b. algae and fungi   d. bark

   8. _____b_____

9. The floor is covered with a thin of layer of _____ leaves.
   a. growing   b. tiny   c. poisonous   d. fallen

   9. _____d_____

10. Seeds _____ when the soil heats up.
    a. wither and die b. are lost   c. grow   d. are planted

    10. _____c_____

Imagine that you are a writer for a magazine for junior high school students. You have been asked to write about the coexistence of living organisms within an environment, such as a national park, nature preserve, or zoo. Do some library research, and write a brief article about the interaction of plants and animals in the setting you have chosen. Use at least five of the words from this lesson and underline them.

The universality of music is demonstrated by the fact that every culture contains sounds arranged into pleasing or interesting patterns of one form or another. Though the shapes and styles may differ considerably, music has fascinated, entertained, and influenced its performers and listeners since time began. Whether used to accompany religious ceremony, to advertise a product, or to establish a strong, steady beat that makes work or marching easier, music has played an important role in the activities of all people. The words in this lesson will help you to understand some of the specialized terminology used in this appealing art form.

WORD LIST

a cappella
aria
cadence
crescendo
dissonance
libretto
motif
octave
sonata
staccato

DEFINITIONS

After you have studied the definitions and example for each vocabulary word, write the word on the line to the right.

1. **a cappella** (ä´kə pĕl´ə) *adjective* Without musical accompaniment. *adverb* In a style marked by the absence of instrumental accompaniment. (From the Italian phrase *a cappella*, meaning "as in the chapel")

   Example The traveling expenses of the *a cappella* choir were low, since the cost of an orchestra could be omitted from its budget.

   1. _____

2. **aria** (är´ē-ə) *noun* **a.** An elaborate vocal piece sung by a single voice, as in an opera. **b.** A tune or melody. (From the Latin word *aer*, meaning "air")

   Example The famous opera *Aïda* provides beautiful *arias* for the tenor lead.

   2. _____

3. **cadence** (kād´ns) *noun* The balanced, rhythmic flow or beat of poetry, oratory, dancing, or music. (From the Latin word *cadere*, meaning "to fall")

   Example The slow *cadence* of the drums intensified the somberness of the funeral procession.

   3. _____

4. **crescendo** (krə-shĕn´dō) *noun* A gradual increase, especially in the volume or intensity of sound in a musical passage. (From the Latin word *crescere*, meaning "to increase")

   Example Cynthia ended her violin solo with a screeching *crescendo* that sent the family cat scampering for cover.

   4. _____

5. **dissonance** (dĭs'ə-nəns) *noun* **a.** A harsh or disagreeable combination of sounds; discord. **b.** Lack of agreement, consistency, or harmony; conflict. (From the Latin *dis-*, meaning "apart," and *sonare*, meaning "to sound")

> **Related Word** **dissonant** *adjective*
> **Example** The *dissonance* created by my three-year-old brother's pounding on the piano keys gave me a headache.

6. **libretto** (lĭ-brĕt'ō) *noun* **a.** The text of an opera or other dramatic musical work. **b.** A book containing a libretto. (From the Latin word *liber*, meaning "book")

> **Related Word** **librettist** *noun*
> **Example** Richard Rodgers composed the music, and Oscar Hammerstein wrote the *librettos* for *The Sound of Music*, *The King and I*, and many other musical plays.

7. **motif** (mō-tēf') *noun* **a.** In a musical composition, a repeated significant phrase that identifies an idea or character. **b.** A recurring theme. (From the Latin word *movere*, meaning "to move")

> **Example** A particular musical *motif* in the movie prepared the audience for the appearance of the villain.

8. **octave** (ŏk'tĭv, ŏk'tāv') *noun* **a.** The musical interval of eight full tones. **b.** Two notes, eight full tones apart, in which the frequency of vibration of the higher is double that of the lower. **c.** A tone that is eight full tones above or below another given tone. (From the Latin word *octo*, meaning "eight")

> **Example** The keys of a piano span more than seven *octaves*.

9. **sonata** (sə-nä'tə) *noun* An instrumental musical composition, as for the piano, usually consisting of three or four movements, or parts, varying in key, mood, and tempo. (From the Latin word *sonare*, meaning "to sound")

> **Example** Beethoven's "Moonlight *Sonata*" for piano starts with a beautifully slow first movement and ends with a third movement of breathtaking ferocity.

10. **staccato** (stə-kä'tō) *adjective* **a.** In music, cut short crisply; disconnected. **b.** Composed of short, sharp sounds or parts. (From the Italian word *staccare*, meaning "to detach")

> **Example** The band ceased playing as the lead guitarist plucked his guitar in *staccato* fashion.

EXERCISE 1   WRITING CORRECT WORDS

On the answer line, write the word from the vocabulary list that fits each definition.

1. A harsh or disagreeable combination of sounds; lack of agreement, consistency, or harmony

2. The musical interval of eight full tones

3. Without musical accompaniment

4. Cut short crisply; composed of short, sharp sounds

5. The text of an opera or other dramatic musical work

6. The balanced, rhythmic flow or beat of poetry, oratory, dancing, or music

7. An instrumental musical composition usually consisting of three or four movements that vary in key, mood, and tempo

8. An elaborate vocal piece sung by a single voice

9. A gradual increase in the volume or intensity of sound

10. A repeated significant phrase that identifies a character or idea; a recurring theme

1. _____dissonance_____

2. _____octave_____

3. _____a cappella_____

4. _____staccato_____

5. _____libretto_____

6. _____cadence_____

7. _____sonata_____

8. _____aria_____

9. _____crescendo_____

10. _____motif_____

EXERCISE 2   USING WORDS CORRECTLY

Each of the following questions contains an italicized vocabulary word. Choose the correct answer to the question, and write *Yes* or *No* on the answer line.

1. Would a symphony orchestra give an *a cappella* concert?

2. As an overture reaches a *crescendo*, does the music become softer?

3. Are *staccato* notes disconnected and sharp?

4. Were Roman *arias* places where dance music was played?

5. Does an *octave* consist of eight full tones?

6. Does a *libretto* familiarize the audience with the plot of an opera?

7. Might a flute *motif* be repeated throughout a concerto?

8. Is *dissonance* pleasant to the ear?

9. Is a *sonata* a long musical composition for two or more voices?

10. Is *cadence* the rhythm of a piece of music?

1. _____No_____

2. _____No_____

3. _____Yes_____

4. _____No_____

5. _____Yes_____

6. _____Yes_____

7. _____Yes_____

8. _____No_____

9. _____No_____

10. _____Yes_____

EXERCISE 3   CHOOSING THE BEST WORD

Decide which vocabulary word or related form best completes the sentence, and write the letter of your choice on the answer line.

1. Many church and synagogue choirs sing _____.
   a. motifs   **b.** a cappella   **c.** librettos   **d.** staccato

2. In preparation for attending our first opera, we read the _____ of Debussy's *Pelléas et Mélisande* and listened to the album.
   a. motif   **b.** sonata   **c.** crescendo   **d.** libretto

1. _____b_____

2. _____d_____

3. Since Thelma could not reach high C, her teacher suggested that she sing the piece one _____ lower.
   a. octave   **b.** crescendo   **c.** dissonance   **d.** aria

3. _____a_____

4. The _____ of Viennese composer Arnold Schoenberg's "Book of the Hanging Gardens" challenged traditional concepts of harmony.
   a. libretto   **b.** cadence   **c.** dissonance   **d.** crescendo

4. _____c_____

5. The musician played the _____ notes of the song by crisply plucking the strings of his violin.
   a. crescendo   **b.** staccato   **c.** octave   **d.** dissonant

5. _____b_____

6. The dramatic _____ in Beethoven's Fifth Symphony moves the piece smoothly from serenity to electrifying intensity.
   a. crescendo   **b.** libretto   **c.** sonata   **d.** staccato

6. _____a_____

7. The Asian _____ in Puccini's *Madame Butterfly* contributes to the exotic character of the opera.
   a. octave   **b.** a cappella   **c.** sonata   **d.** motif

7. _____d_____

8. In choosing his concert program, Leon Nadler rejected the Schubert _____ in favor of one by Mozart.
   a. sonata   **b.** motif   **c.** crescendo   **d.** a cappella

8. _____a_____

9. In Beethoven's only opera, *Fidelio,* one of the loveliest _____ is sung by Leonore, who rescues her husband from unjust punishment.
   a. librettos   **b.** octaves   **c.** arias   **d.** cadences

9. _____c_____

10. People always tap their fingers and toes to the _____ of John Philip Sousa's marches.
    a. motifs   **b.** cadences   **c.** sonatas   **d.** arias

10. _____b_____

EXERCISE 4 USING DIFFERENT FORMS OF WORDS

Decide which form of the vocabulary word in parentheses best completes the sentence. The form given may be correct. Write your answer on the answer line.

1. During music appreciation the class listened to a Gregorian chant sung _____ by a group of monks. *(a cappella)*

   1. _____a cappella_____

2. Da Ponte was the _____ for Mozart's operas *Don Giovanni* and *The Marriage of Figaro*. *(libretto)*

   2. _____librettist_____

3. Mrs. Xavier will not accept children as piano students until their hands are large enough to span an _____ on the keyboard. *(octave)*

   3. _____octave_____

4. The _____ were written for the lute but are played today on the guitar or mandolin. *(sonata)*

   4. _____sonatas_____

5. Eating at her desk, Shirley soon found herself chewing in time to the _____ taps of her neighbor's typewriter. *(staccato)*

   5. _____staccato_____

6. The flower _____ of the bedspread was repeated in a wallpaper border and in the curtain tiebacks. *(motif)*

   6. _____motif_____

7. The badly tuned piano made only ugly, _____ noises. *(dissonance)*

   7. _____dissonant_____

8. The measured _____ of Walt Whitman's poetry are perfect for reading aloud. *(cadence)*

   8. _____cadences_____

9. Opera singers are judged chiefly on their renditions of _____. *(aria)*

   9. _____arias_____

10. The rain and wind of the hurricane reached a _____ at midnight. *(crescendo)*

    10. _____crescendo_____

READING COMPREHENSION

Each numbered sentence in the following passage contains an italicized vocabulary word or related form. After you read the passage, you will complete an exercise.

AÏDA: VERDI'S MASTERPIECE

Many music critics believe that Guiseppe Verdi, the foremost composer of Italian romantic opera, reached the height of his career with *Aïda.* In this opera, perhaps more than in any of his twenty-five other musical-dramatic works, Verdi shows a mastery of theatrical effect, musical characterization, and richly expressive orchestration.

When the ruler of Egypt asked Verdi to compose a piece to celebrate the opening of the Suez Canal, Verdi decided to base the new opera on a true story uncovered in the archaeological explorations of a French Egyptologist. **(1)** Although he employed Antonio Ghislanzoni to write the Italian *libretto*, Verdi himself created the characterizations and composed the music in less than a year. Performed for the first time on December 24, 1871, at the new Cairo Opera House, *Aïda* was an immediate critical and popular success.

(2) Unlike a symphony or a *sonata*, an opera consists of a dramatic story that is set to music and presented through song. The story of *Aïda,* set in Egypt at the time of the pharaohs, concerns Aïda, an Ethiopian princess enslaved by the Egyptians, the hero Radames, and the jealous Princess Amneris.

When Aïda's father invades Egypt to rescue his daughter, his army is defeated by Radames. Radames is named to the Egyptian throne and receives permission to marry Princess Amneris, but he loves Aïda. Aïda betrays Radames by obtaining military secrets from him and escaping to help her father defeat the Egyptians. Radames is convicted as a traitor and is sentenced to be sealed up in a cave. In the final scene of the opera, Aïda returns to be entombed with Radames.

Despite the obvious dramatic appeal of the story, *Aïda* is most often admired for the beauty and variety of Verdi's music. **(3)** The opera challenges its singers with lyrical solos, stirring duets, vigorous ensemble pieces, and one song that forces the soprano to shift her voice abruptly from one *octave* to another. **(4)** Verdi's musical contrasts, ranging from soft, delicate *a cappella* pieces to blaring military marches, captivate listeners.

(5) Musical contrast is also heard in the way in which Verdi effectively introduces each character with a musical *motif.* Aïda's theme is the first melody heard in the overture; as the story unfolds it becomes more complicated. **(6)** Radames is represented by the *staccato* fanfare of trumpets and trombones. **(7)** The priestesses of Isis, who both crown and entomb Radames, are introduced with *dissonant* semitones that have an archaic, mysterious, exotic flavor. Throughout the opera these themes are juxtaposed and blended to mirror the events and to unify action and emotion.

Building his scenes around a few emotionally charged confrontations, Verdi used music to reflect and intensify feelings. **(8)** For example, following Radames' trial, the music builds to a stirring *crescendo* as he is sentenced. **(9)** In the final scene, Aïda sings a famous *aria* just before she enters the cave to join Radames. **(10)** Here the music has the same *cadence* as a sob or cry of sorrow, underscoring her conflicting emotions and the pathos of the situation.

Audiences love *Aïda* because of its tragic story and its passionate music. The result of Guiseppe Verdi's subtle, artistic blending of music and drama is one of his most enduring operatic masterpieces.

READING COMPREHENSION EXERCISE

Each of the following statements corresponds to a numbered sentence in the passage. Each statement contains a blank and is followed by four answer choices. Decide which choice fits best in the blank. The word or phrase that you choose must express roughly the same meaning as the italicized word in the passage. Write the letter of your choice on the answer line.

1. Verdi employed Antonio Ghislanzoni to write the Italian _____.
   a. background   b. translation   c. setting   d. text

   1. _____d_____

2. An opera is not like a symphony or a(n) _____.
   a. instrumental musical piece   c. piece for solo voice
   b. choral composition   d. single musical theme

   2. _____a_____

3. One song forces the soprano to shift her voice abruptly from one _____ to another.
   a. span of eight full tones   c. tune
   b. descending series of notes   d. chord

   3. _____a_____

4. Verdi's contrasts range from delicate _____ to blaring military marches.
   a. pieces without accompaniment   c. choral pieces
   b. ballads   d. duets

   4. _____a_____

5. Verdi introduces each character with a musical _____.
   a. alteration of a single theme   c. repetition of chords
   b. repeated significant phrase   d. connection of melodies

   5. _____b_____

6. Radames is represented by a _____ fanfare of trombones and trumpets.
   a. short, crisp   c. slow, smooth
   b. prolonged, repetitive   d. fast, spirited

   6. _____a_____

7. The priestesses are introduced with _____ semitones.
   a. liquid   c. harsh-sounding
   b. strange-sounding   d. colorful

   7. _____c_____

8. The music builds to a stirring _____ as Radames is sentenced.
   a. abrupt decrease of sound   c. conclusion
   b. gradual increase of sound   d. interruption

   8. _____b_____

9. Aïda sings a famous _____ as she enters the cave.
   a. love song   b. prayer   c. elaborate solo   d. finale

   9. _____c_____

10. The music has the same _____ as a cry of sorrow.
   a. words   b. series of tones   c. forcefulness   d. rhythm

   10. _____d_____

PRACTICE WITH ANALOGIES

Directions   On the answer line, write the vocabulary word or a form of it that completes each analogy.

See page 79 for some strategies to use with analogies.

1. PLATITUDINOUS : DEPTH :: _____ : originality (*Lesson 21*)

   1. ___banal___

2. MIMIC : MODEL :: _____ : hero (*Lesson 21*)

   2. ___emulate___

3. ZOOLOGIST : ANIMALS :: _____ : plants (*Lesson 22*)

   3. ___horticulturist___

4. NOVEL : LITERARY :: _____ : musical (*Lesson 23*)

   4. ___sonata___

5. REFRAIN : SONG :: _____ : painting (*Lesson 23*)

   5. ___motif___

6. IMPROMPTU : REHEARSAL :: _____ : accompaniment (*Lesson 23*)

   6. ___a cappella___

As you grow older, you have an increasing number of obligations and duties that you are expected to carry out. Whether you are responsible for helping with the care of a younger brother or sister or you are in charge of training new employees at your job, you are expected to accomplish these tasks in a dependable fashion. Acting responsibly means that you have learned to function with a minimum of guidance. When you accept responsibility to do something, you are answerable for your own behavior. The words in this lesson will help you to describe responsible and irresponsible actions, promises, decisions, and plans.

WORD LIST

accountable
commitment
default
feckless
incumbent
liability
mandatory
negligence
onerous
remiss

DEFINITIONS

After you have studied the definitions and example for each vocabulary word, write the word on the line to the right.

1. **accountable** (ə-koun′tə-bəl) *adjective*   Required to answer for one's actions; responsible. (From the Latin *ad-*, meaning "to," and *computare*, meaning "to sum up")

   Related Word   accountability *noun*
   Example   In his job Josh was *accountable* to Ms. Ortiz for the accuracy of the forms that he handled.

   1. _____

2. **commitment** (kə-mĭt′mənt) *noun*   **a.** The state of being bound emotionally or intellectually to a person, group, cause, or course of action.   **b.** A pledge or obligation to do something: *a treaty commitment.*   **c.** The act of placing in confinement or custody: *commitment of a child to a foster home.*

   Related Word   commit *verb*
   Example   Jill felt a strong *commitment* to the tutoring program in which she took part.

   2. _____

3. **default** (dĭ-fôlt′) *noun*   **a.** The failure to perform a task or fulfill an obligation, particularly a financial obligation.   **b.** The failure of a competitor or team to participate in a contest.   *intrans. verb*   **a.** To fail to do what is required; fail to pay money when it is due.   **b.** In sports, to fail to compete in a scheduled contest. (From the Latin *de-*, an intensive prefix, and *fallere*, meaning "to fail")

   Example   The farm family's *default* on the loan was caused by the tornado's devastation of their crops.

   3. _____

4. **feckless** (fĕk′lĭs) *adjective*   **a.** Careless; irresponsible.   **b.** Lacking purpose or vitality; ineffectual.

   Related Words   fecklessly *adverb;* fecklessness *noun*
   Example   A lifelong series of failures and disappointments had made Reginald *feckless.*

   4. _____

5. **incumbent** (ĭn-kŭm′bənt) *adjective* **a.** Imposed as an obligation or duty; obligatory. **b.** Currently holding office: *an incumbent mayor.* *noun* A person who holds an office. (From the Latin word *incumbens,* meaning "leaning upon")

   Example Tak felt it *incumbent* upon him to help his parents learn English.

   5. _____

6. **liability** (lī′ə-bĭl′ĭ-tē) *noun* **a.** The condition of being legally responsible. **b.** Something owed; an obligation or debt. **c.** Something that holds one back; a handicap. (From the Latin word *ligare,* meaning "to bind")

   Related Word liable *adjective*
   Example The driver's insurance policy covered *liability* for damage to other cars and injury to their occupants.

   6. _____

7. **mandatory** (măn′də-tôr′ē) *adjective* **a.** Required; compulsory. **b.** Having to do with a mandate, or authoritative command. (From the Latin word *mandare,* meaning "to order")

   Related Word mandate *noun*
   Example Three years of foreign language study are *mandatory* at Tall Mesa High School.

   7. _____

8. **negligence** (nĕg′lĭ-jəns) *noun* **a.** Lack of proper care or attention; neglect. **b.** A careless or indifferent act or failure to act. **c.** In law, the failure to take reasonable precaution or care.

   Related Words negligent *adjective;* **negligently** *adverb*
   Example Pat admitted that his *negligence* in paying bills had led to his being judged a poor credit risk.

   8. _____

9. **onerous** (ŏn′ər-əs, ō′nər-əs) *adjective* Troublesome; oppressive; burdensome. (From the Latin word *onus,* meaning "burden")

   Related Word onerousness *noun*
   Example Some people enjoy taking care of a yard, while others find it an *onerous* task.

   9. _____

10. **remiss** (rĭ-mĭs′) *adjective* **a.** Lax in attending to duty. **b.** Exhibiting carelessness or slackness. (From the Latin word *remissus,* meaning "slack")

    Example The custodian was *remiss* in complying with fire-safety regulations.

    10. _____

EXERCISE I COMPLETING DEFINITIONS

On the answer line, write the word from the vocabulary list that best completes each definition.

1. A person who is lax in attending to duty can be described as being _____.

2. If you are required to answer for your actions, you are held _____ for them.

3. Lack of proper attention or a careless or indifferent act is _____.

4. The condition of being legally responsible is _____.

5. Something that is oppressive, troublesome, or burdensome is _____.

6. The failure to perform a task or fulfill an obligation is _____.

7. One who is careless or irresponsible is _____.

8. If something is imposed as an obligation or duty, it is _____ upon you to fulfill it.

9. If you are emotionally or intellectually bound to a cause or a course of action, then you have a(n) _____ to it.

10. Something that is required or compulsory is _____.

1. _____remiss_____
2. _____accountable_____
3. _____negligence_____
4. _____liability_____
5. _____onerous_____
6. _____default_____
7. _____feckless_____
8. _____incumbent_____
9. _____commitment_____
10. _____mandatory_____

EXERCISE 2 USING WORDS CORRECTLY

Decide whether the italicized vocabulary word has been used correctly in the sentence. On the answer line, write *Correct* for correct use and *Incorrect* for incorrect use.

1. Astrid hopes to *default* on her car loan by paying it off early.

2. To forget to lock the front door was a *feckless* thing to do.

3. Conrad's failure to insure his new car before driving it is an example of his *negligence*.

4. Each time Mrs. Melia leaves on a business trip, her family feels *remiss* for her.

5. Although some businesses establish a retirement age for their employees, *mandatory* retirement at age sixty-five is no longer practiced.

6. Parents are usually held *accountable* for the actions of their children.

7. Melva's unwavering *commitment* to helping her family is laudable.

8. In an election an *incumbent* politician may have an edge over his or her opponent.

9. Vacations are *onerous* experiences for most people.

10. Jana's collection of antique perfume bottles is so extensive that she has run out of room to display even one more *liability*.

1. _____Incorrect_____
2. _____Correct_____
3. _____Correct_____
4. _____Incorrect_____
5. _____Correct_____
6. _____Correct_____
7. _____Correct_____
8. _____Correct_____
9. _____Incorrect_____
10. _____Incorrect_____

EXERCISE 3 IDENTIFYING SYNONYMS AND ANTONYMS

Decide which word has the meaning that is the same as (a synonym) or opposite to (an antonym) that of the capitalized vocabulary word. Write the letter of your choice on the answer line.

1. MANDATORY (antonym):
   a. complex   **b.** required   **c.** voluntary   **d.** partial

1. _____c_____

2. LIABILITY (synonym):
   a. pain   b. caution   c. asset   d. debt

3. ONEROUS (antonym):
   a. advantageous   b. hateful   c. believable   d. porous

4. INCUMBENT (synonym):
   a. exempt   b. vegetative   c. politician   d. obligatory

5. FECKLESS (antonym):
   a. careful   b. spotted   c. momentary   d. posh

6. ACCOUNTABLE (synonym):
   a. rejuvenated   b. balanced   c. suitable   d. responsible

7. NEGLIGENCE (antonym):
   a. equality   b. carefulness   c. burden   d. unhappiness

8. REMISS (synonym):
   a. sad   b. lax   c. dependable   d. uncontrollable

9. DEFAULT (antonym):
   a. fulfill   b. crack   c. misrepresent   d. forego

10. COMMITMENT (synonym):
    a. obligation   b. irresolution   c. operation   d. resolve

#	Answer
2.	d
3.	a
4.	d
5.	a
6.	d
7.	b
8.	b
9.	a
10.	a

EXERCISE 4   USING DIFFERENT FORMS OF WORDS

Decide which form of the vocabulary word in parentheses best completes the sentence. The form given may be correct. Write your answer on the answer line.

1. Damita felt it _____ on her to complete all of the interviews before she went on vacation. *(incumbent)*   **1. incumbent**

2. Garth apologized for being _____ in responding to the wedding invitation. *(remiss)*   **2. remiss**

3. When the visiting team's bus broke down, Benjamin Banneker High School was declared the winner by _____. *(default)*   **3. default**

4. We were astonished at Audra's _____ in leaving on a vacation without taking enough money. *(feckless)*   **4. fecklessness**

5. The official _____ of the court cannot be ignored. *(mandatory)*   **5. mandate**

6. Performance reviews and salary increases were based on each staff member's _____ for some aspect of the project. *(accountable)*   **6. accountability**

7. The security guard was charged with _____ for leaving his post without authorization. *(negligence)*   **7. negligence**

8. I refuse to _____ myself to any plan that I feel will not work. *(commitment)*   **8. commit**

9. The courts held Mr. Tremain _____ for the injury done by his dog. *(liability)*   **9. liable**

10. "Don't you think that you have overstated the _____ of your share of the household chores?" Liza asked her husband. *(onerous)*   **10. onerousness**

READING COMPREHENSION

Each numbered sentence in the following passage contains an italicized vocabulary word or related form. After you read the passage, you will complete an exercise.

THE RISKY BUSINESS OF LLOYD'S OF LONDON

Insurance, the business of guaranteeing to cover specified potential losses in return for premiums paid, is a common and necessary practice. Nearly everyone has some involvement with typical forms of insurance, such as automobile, health, life, fire, and theft. However, there are also some fairly unusual items of value not covered by ordinary policies. A surgeon's hands, a dancer's legs, an opera star's vocal chords, and a movie star's beard are only a few of the specialties of Lloyd's of London, a world-famous insurance association that has earned a reputation for unconventional insurance risks.

Lloyd's of London was founded in 1688. The insurance association actually began as a coffee house where ship owners, bankers, and merchants gathered to discuss trade and shipping. (1) Wealthy businessmen and bankers *committed* themselves to financial responsibility for ships or their cargoes, which might be lost or damaged at sea. Each risk taker wrote his name under the total amount of risk he was willing to accept at a specified price, thus becoming an insurance underwriter. (2) If the ship or cargo were lost, it was *incumbent* upon the underwriter to pay the amount he had specified;

if the ship or cargo reached port safely, the underwriter profited from the premium paid by the owner. As the shipping industry in England grew, Lloyd's of London became a leader in marine insurance.

By 1911 Lloyd's had extended its business interests to include every form of insurance except long-term life insurance. (3) Although considered *feckless* by other insurance associations, Lloyd's was a pioneer in offering theft, earthquake, hurricane, and profit-loss insurance. (4) Lloyd's underwriters were *accountable* for insurance on property lost in the 1906 San Francisco earthquake and fire, the ill-fated sinkings of the ocean liners *Titanic* and *Andrea Doria*, and the 1937 explosion of the German airship *Hindenburg*.

Unlike a regular insurance agency that transacts business as a unit, Lloyd's of London consists of over seven thousand individual underwriters grouped into syndicates. Agents for each syndicate bid competitively for contracts in much the same manner as stockbrokers working at the stock exchange do. (5) The underwriters accept *liability* on their own accounts and bear the full risk individually.

(6) The Corporation of Lloyd's of London sets the rules for underwriters to follow and takes disciplinary action if members are *remiss* in complying with these rules. (7) However, while the Corporation governs the way in which the underwriters operate, it does not assume responsibility for any *negligence* on their part.

(8) Although underwriters have the *onerous* responsibility for their own transactions, many seek to become a part of this elite institution. (9) In order to qualify for membership, underwriters must follow several *mandatory* policies. (10) First, they deposit at least $45,000 with Lloyd's as security against their possible *default* on risks that they accept. Second, they must maintain detailed records, and third, they contribute a percentage of their profits to Lloyd's central fund, from which policyholders are paid.

Housed in a fifteen-million-dollar palace in the heart of London, Lloyd's has grown from its humble start in a local meeting place. Whether insuring ship travel or space travel, the possibility of having twins, or the capture of the Loch Ness monster, Lloyd's of London maintains its famous and impressive place in insurance history.

READING COMPREHENSION EXERCISE

Each of the following statements corresponds to a numbered sentence in the passage. Each statement contains a blank and is followed by four answer choices. Decide which choice fits best in the blank. The word or phrase that you choose must express roughly the same meaning as the italicized word in the passage. Write the letter of your choice on the answer line.

1. Wealthy businsessmen and bankers _____ themselves to take financial responsibility for ships or their cargoes.

   a. pledged   **b.** reminded   **c.** challenged   **d.** alerted

1. _____ a _____

2. It was _____ for the underwriter to pay the amount he had specified.
   a. unnecessary   **b.** a motivation   **c.** obligatory   **d.** confusing

2. _____ **c**

3. Other insurance associations regarded Lloyd's as _____.
   a. irresponsible   **b.** inadequate   **c.** indulgent   **d.** competitive

3. _____ **a**

4. Lloyd's underwriters were _____ insurance on property lost in the San Francisco earthquake and fire.
   a. inadequately covered for   **c.** prudent about
   b. answerable for   **d.** dependent upon

4. _____ **b**

5. The underwriters accept _____ on their own accounts.
   a. new contracts   **c.** legal responsibility
   b. competitive bidding   **d.** negative consequences

5. _____ **c**

6. The Corporation of Lloyd's takes disciplinary action if members are _____ in complying with the rules.
   a. slow   **b.** marginal   **c.** unparalleled   **d.** lax

6. _____ **d**

7. The Corporation does not assume responsibility for any _____ on the part of the underwriters.
   a. lack of formality   **c.** shortsightedness
   b. lack of proper care   **d.** isolated errors

7. _____ **b**

8. Underwriters have the _____ responsibility for their own transactions.
   a. burdensome   **b.** impartial   **c.** agreeable   **d.** clear

8. _____ **a**

9. Underwriters must follow several _____ policies to qualify for membership.
   a. optional   **b.** simple   **c.** inconsistent   **d.** required

9. _____ **d**

10. They must deposit money with Lloyd's as security against their possible _____ on risks.
    a. chances of benefiting   **c.** losing transactions
    b. failure to fulfill obligations   **d.** immense profits

10. _____ **b**

WRITING ASSIGNMENT

Suppose that your local civic association is sponsoring an essay contest, and you have decided to enter. The topic of the essay, responsibility, is very general, and part of the challenge of the contest will be to narrow the topic. You might consider (1) defining the term and illustrating it with examples, (2) narrating the incident that taught you the meaning of the term, or (3) explaining what you think will be your greatest future responsibility. Use at least five vocabulary words from this lesson in your essay and underline each one.

VOCABULARY ENRICHMENT

The word *feckless* is of Scottish origin. It is a shortened form of the pairing of the word *effect* with the suffix *-less*, which can mean "without." Some other English words have entered the language by a similar process of shortening.

Activity   Each of the following words comes from a longer word or phrase. Consulting a dictionary, write the present meaning of each word and list the word or words from which it is derived.

1. bus   **2.** fan   **3.** good-by   **4.** van   **5.** tawdry

The **Test** for Lessons 22, 23, and 24 is on page T30.

READING SKILLS

THE PREFIXES *BENE-* AND *MAL-*

A **prefix** is a letter or group of letters that is added to the beginning of a root to change its meaning. (A **root** is the part of a word that contains its basic meaning. A root can be a complete word.) The prefix *bene-* and the prefix *mal-* or its variant form *male-* help to form such words as *benefactor, malfunction,* and *malediction. Bene-* and *mal-* or *male-* have opposite meanings, as shown below.

Prefix Meaning	Root Word	Word	Word Definition
bene-: well; good	*facere,* "to do"	benefactor	one who gives aid
mal-/male-: bad; badly	*functio,* "performance"	malfunction	to fail to function
	dicere, "to speak"	malediction	a curse or slander

A knowledge of prefixes and roots can help you analyze the meaning of unfamiliar words in your reading and on tests. Use the following procedure to determine the meaning of words that begin with *bene-* or *mal-* or with some other prefix.

PROCEDURE

1. *Substitute the prefix and root definitions for the prefix and root.* For example, the noun *beneficiary* is formed from the prefix *bene-* and the Latin root *-fic-*, from the common root word *facere.* The prefix means "well" or "good," and the root means "to do."

2. *Think of a possible definition of the entire word.* Combining the prefix and root meanings given above results in "to do well" or "to do good toward."

3. *If the word appears in a sentence, use the context to help you develop the possible definition.* Suppose that someone announced, "Grandmother's insurance policy names you as a beneficiary." The context makes it clear that you must be the recipient, not the donor, of a good act.

4. *Check your definition of the word in the dictionary.* A dictionary definition of *beneficiary* is "the recipient of funds, property, or other benefits, as from an insurance policy or will."

EXERCISE USING THE PREFIXES *BENE-* AND *MAL-*

Each sentence in the following exercise contains an italicized word beginning with the prefix *bene-* or *mal-/male-*. When appropriate, the root word and its meaning are given in parentheses after the sentence. *Step 1:* Taking the context into consideration, write your own definition of the word. *Step 2:* Write the dictionary definition of the word. *Step 3:* Write a sentence of your own in which you use the word correctly.

1. People who are *malnourished* are subject to other diseases.

    Your Definition ___Badly fed_____

    Dictionary Definition ___Suffering from improper nutrition or insufficient food___

    Sentence ___Some people who could afford to eat properly do not do so and thus become malnourished.___

2. The graduation speaker gave a *benediction* at the end of the ceremony. (Root word: *dicere*, "to say")

Your Definition Good saying

Dictionary Definition A blessing

Sentence After the benediction the family began to eat Thanksgiving dinner.

3. During the first days of his convalescence, the patient suffered from *malaise*. (French root word: *aise*, "ease")

Your Definition The feeling of being ill at ease

Dictionary Definition A vague feeling of illness or depression

Sentence While she awaited her test results, Fujiko experienced symptoms of malaise.

4. The chemistry students created a *malodorous* compound that hung in the air for hours.

Your Definition Bad-smelling

Dictionary Definition Having a bad odor; ill-smelling

Sentence Although malodorous, the stew tasted delicious.

5. Although we usually think of bacteria as harmful, some are actually *beneficent*. (Root word: *facere*, "to do")

Your Definition Doing good

Dictionary Definition Producing benefit; beneficial

Sentence In French history one beneficent king was known as "the well liked."

6. After the umpire called the third strike, the batter gave him a *malevolent* glance. (Root word: *velle*, "to wish)

Your Definition Wishing ill (toward someone)

Dictionary Definition Having or exhibiting ill will; malicious

Sentence In the painting the miser is depicted as having a malevolent expression.

7. No one wanted to work next to the *maladroit* riveter.

Your Definition Badly skilled

Dictionary Definition Characterized by a lack of dexterity; clumsy

Sentence All thumbs, I felt like the most maladroit carpenter in the world.

8. The nurse's *benevolence* was perfectly suited to her job. (Root word: *velle*, "to wish")

Your Definition Kindly wishing

Dictionary Definition An inclination or tendency to do kind or charitable acts

Sentence The elderly woman was known for her quiet benevolence to young musicians.

LESSON 25 BUSINESS AND FINANCE

The business and financial worlds of today are increasingly sophisticated and technical. Because business involves the production and sales of goods and services, and finance involves the management of money, banking, investments, and credit, these two areas influence many parts of your life. You hear or read daily about complex forms of ownership, changes in the stock market, multinational corporations, and fluctuations in interest rates. The words in this lesson will help to expand your understanding of business and financial concepts that affect everyone.

WORD LIST

accrue
audit
cartel
collateral
commodity
conglomerate
liquidate
lucrative
recompense
security

DEFINITIONS

After you have studied the definitions and example for each vocabulary word, write the word on the line to the right.

1. **accrue** (ə-krōō′) *intrans. verb* **a.** To increase or grow; accumulate. **b.** To come to someone or something as a gain or benefit. (From the Latin *ad-*, meaning "to," and *crescere*, meaning "to arise")

   Related Word accrual *noun*
   Example If you keep your money in this bank account for a year, interest will *accrue* at the rate of 5.25 percent.

   1. _____

2. **audit** (ô′dĭt) *trans. verb* **a.** To examine, verify, or correct, as financial accounts. **b.** To attend a course without receiving a grade or academic credit for it. *noun* An examination of financial records and accounts.

   Related Word auditor *noun*
   Example The Internal Revenue Service reserves the right to *audit* the financial records of any person or business that should pay taxes.

   2. _____

3. **cartel** (kär-tĕl′) *noun* A combination of independent or government-owned businesses formed to control the production and distribution of its members' goods.

   Example The Organization of Petroleum Exporting Countries, or OPEC, is a *cartel* that was founded in 1960 to control the production and distribution of petroleum.

   3. _____

4. **collateral** (kə-lăt′ər-əl) *noun* Property pledged by a borrower to secure a loan and to protect the interests of the lender. *adjective* **a.** Serving to support or confirm: *collateral evidence.* **b.** Coinciding in tendency or effect; accompanying: *collateral purpose.* (From the Latin *com-*, meaning "together," and *latus*, meaning "side")

   Example Edwin used his valuable coin collection as *collateral* for the loan that he needed to buy a motorcycle.

   4. _____

5. **commodity** (kə-mŏd′ĭ-tē) *noun*   **a.** An article of trade, such as an agricultural or mining product, that can be transported.   **b.** Something that is useful or can be turned to advantage. (From the Latin word *commodus*, meaning "convenient")

   Example   Cocoa is one *commodity* that the United States must import.

5. _____

6. **conglomerate** (kən-glŏm′ər-ĭt) *noun*   **a.** A corporation made up of a large number of separate companies operating in different industries.   **b.** A collected heterogeneous mass; cluster.   *adjective*   Massed; gathered together.   *intrans. verb* (kən-glŏm′ə-rāt′)   To form into a heterogeneous mass. (From the Latin *com-*, meaning "together," and *glomere*, meaning "to wind into a ball")

   Example   Torstead Enterprises is a large *conglomerate* that has important mining, publishing, and entertainment divisions.

6. _____

7. **liquidate** (lĭk′wĭ-dāt′) *trans. verb*   **a.** To settle the affairs of (a business, for example) by determining the liabilities and using the assets to discharge them. **b.** To pay off or settle (a debt or obligation).   **c.** To convert (assets) into cash. **d.** To put an end to. (From the Late Latin word *liquidare*, meaning "to melt")

   Related Word   **liquidation** *noun*
   Example   The officers of the Duulakkey Company saw no option other than to *liquidate* the firm.

7. _____

8. **lucrative** (lōō′krə-tĭv) *adjective*   Profitable; producing wealth. (From the Latin word *lucrum*, meaning "profit")

   Related Word   **lucre** *noun*
   Example   Mercedes's money-making schemes sound bizarre to me, but I have to admit that they are always *lucrative*.

8. _____

9. **recompense** (rĕk′əm-pĕns′) *noun*   **a.** Payment made in return for something given or done.   **b.** Amends made for damage or loss.   *trans. verb*   **a.** To pay as a reward.   **b.** To pay as compensation.

   Example   When Stanley's lost wallet was returned, he gave the finder ten dollars as *recompense* for her trouble.

9. _____

10. **security** (sĭ-kyŏŏr′ĭ-tē) *noun*   **a.** Written evidence of ownership or creditorship, such as a stock or bond certificate.   **b.** A guarantee of fulfilling an obligation. **c.** Freedom from fear, anxiety, or danger.   **d.** Safety.

    Related Words   **secure** *adjective;* **secure** *verb*
    Example   Marta enjoys buying *securities* with the money she earns each summer.

10. _____

USAGE NOTE: When referring to evidence of ownership, the word *security* is usually used in its plural form, *securities*.

EXERCISE 1 MATCHING WORDS AND DEFINITIONS

Match the definition in Column B with the word in Column A. Write the letter of the correct definition on the answer line.

Column A

1. commodity
2. liquidate
3. recompense
4. lucrative
5. accrue
6. cartel
7. conglomerate
8. audit
9. collateral
10. security

Column B

a. payment made in return for something given or done

b. written evidence of ownership or creditorship; a guarantee of fulfilling an obligation

c. a combination of independent or government-owned businesses formed to control production and distribution of its members' goods

d. to settle the affairs of; pay off (a debt)

e. to examine, verify, or correct financial accounts

f. an article of trade that can be transported

g. to increase or grow; accumulate

h. profitable; producing wealth

i. a corporation made up of separate companies operating in different industries

j. property pledged by a borrower to secure a loan and to protect the interests of the lender

1. ____f____
2. ____d____
3. ____a____
4. ____h____
5. ____g____
6. ____c____
7. ____i____
8. ____e____
9. ____j____
10. ____b____

EXERCISE 2 USING WORDS CORRECTLY

Each of the following questions contains an italicized vocabulary word. Choose the correct answer to the question, and write *Yes* or *No* on the answer line.

1. Will money *accrue* in a savings account if you withdraw and spend it?
2. Can a quarterback *collateral* the football to a fullback?
3. Might an oil *cartel* try to regulate the price of the oil that it produces?
4. If you make a lot of money selling your car, has the sale been *lucrative* for you?
5. Does a *conglomerate* specialize in one specific industry?
6. Would it be possible to use the deed to a house as *security* for a loan?
7. Would someone *audit* a VCR tape of a television program in order to remove the commercials?
8. Can you *liquidate* your assets in a food processor?
9. When it is traded, bought, or sold, is gold a *commodity*?
10. Would an individual receive *recompense* for a promise to complete work?

1. ____No____
2. ____No____
3. ____Yes____
4. ____Yes____
5. ____No____
6. ____Yes____
7. ____No____
8. ____No____
9. ____Yes____
10. ____No____

EXERCISE 3 CHOOSING THE BEST WORD

Decide which vocabulary word or related form best completes the sentence, and write the letter of your choice on the answer line.

1. In the Middle Ages, _____ called *guilds* controlled the manufacture of goods and set prices.
   a. cartels   b. accruals   c. commodities   d. liquidations

1. ____a____

2. "I need to borrow some money, Mom; you can hold my bicycle as _____ until I pay you back," pleaded Ben.
   a. cartel   b. recompense   c. liquidation   d. collateral

   2. _____ d

3. Colleen thinks that the safest _____ for investment is soybeans.
   a. accrual   b. security   c. collateral   d. commodity

   3. _____ d

4. Julian was given the school financial records in order to _____ the senior class expenditures.
   a. audit   b. accrue   c. recompense   d. liquidate

   4. _____ a

5. Mr. Hai did not want to use his life-insurance policy as _____ for the loan.
   a. recompense   b. security   c. liquidation   d. conglomerate

   5. _____ b

6. In order to raise cash quickly, Barney had to _____ his collection of 1939 World's Fair memorabilia.
   a. recompense   b. secure   c. audit   d. liquidate

   6. _____ d

7. Marti was just given a _____ job with a local sales company; soon she will be able to afford a new car.
   a. liquidated   b. conglomerate   c. lucrative   d. collateral

   7. _____ c

8. Sam was amazed that his _____ dividends amounted to well over a hundred dollars.
   a. secure   b. liquidated   c. accrued   d. audited

   8. _____ c

9. Mrs. Marsh sold her small sweater company to a large _____ that specialized in the manufacture of clothing, shoes, and building materials.
   a. collateral   b. commodity   c. conglomerate   d. audit

   9. _____ c

10. Because the family could not afford to pay him, Chase was invited to dinner as _____ for his gardening services.
    a. accrual   b. recompense   c. collateral   d. security

    10. _____ b

EXERCISE 4 USING DIFFERENT FORMS OF WORDS

Decide which form of the vocabulary word in parentheses best completes the sentence. The form given may be correct. Write your answer on the answer line.

1. Phoebe rejoiced when she finally accomplished the _____ of all her debts. (liquidate)

   1. _____ liquidation

2. The bank executives devoted several months to preparing for the scheduled _____ by federal examiners. (audit)

   2. _____ audit

3. Besides the textbook, students must read several _____ works. (collateral)

   3. _____ collateral

4. A well-trained financial adviser, Dolores suggested several _____ that seemed appropriate for the investor. (security)

   4. _____ securities

5. Because of a poor harvest, cereal companies in Europe have arranged to purchase several tons of our grain _____. (commodity)

   5. _____ commodities

6. At the age of eighty-five, Aunt Molly says that she looks forward to the wisdom that _____ with age. (accrue)

   6. _____ accrues

7. English may be described as a _____ language. (conglomerate)

   7. _____ conglomerate

8. The international _____ appeared to be more interested in making money than in serving the public. (cartel)

   8. _____ cartel

9. The insurance company offered Tod several thousand dollars in _____ for his back injury. (recompense)

   9. _____ recompense

10. Carlene claims to work for _____, not for glory or satisfaction. (lucrative)

    10. _____ lucre

READING COMPREHENSION

Each numbered sentence in the following passage contains an italicized vocabulary word or related form. After you read the passage, you will complete an exercise.

THE COMMODITY EXCHANGE

(1) The lively marketplace where contracts for *commodities* such as wheat, corn, cotton, wool, tin, lead, and rubber are bought and sold is called a commodity exchange. Through auctions, the world's raw materials pass smoothly from those who produce them to those who use them. Commodity exchanges ensure that producers receive appropriate prices for their materials and that these prices fluctuate as little as possible.

The roots of today's commodity exchanges can be traced to the markets of ancient Greece and Rome and medieval Europe. Historically, farmers brought their produce to fairs in order to trade it for other goods. At these weekly or monthly markets, merchants often drew up contracts and promised to deliver a particular commodity at an agreed-upon future time.

(2) Futures trading is still one of the most *lucrative* aspects of today's commodity exchange. Although some commodities are traded directly in cash, most trading is done on the basis of futures contracts. For example, in March a farmer might agree to sell wheat for four dollars a bushel and to deliver it in September. (3) When the wheat is delivered in September, the current selling price is three dollars a bushel; a profit of one dollar a bushel *accrues* to the farmer. If, however, the selling price of wheat in September is five dollars a bushel, the farmer does not receive the full market price.
(4) In either case, a contract agreed upon in March will be *liquidated* in September. However, the seller may gain protection from fluctuation in the market by buying an opposite futures contract.

Another historical practice that survives today is adherence to a set of trading rules. In the sixteenth century, the availability of new sources of raw materials in widely scattered parts of the world led to a demand for more complex marketing arrangements and for a wider range of facilities to assist buyers and sellers. English merchants established the first regulatory code, called the Law Merchant. (5) This formal code still regulates trade and provides guidelines for appropriate *recompense* in the event of broken agreements.

(6) Today a commodity exchange is a *conglomerate* of firms and individual traders. While a commodity exchange itself does not buy, sell, or price goods, it approves membership, gives it members the physical space in which to trade, and supplies important information about the commodities market. It is the responsibility of committee members to choose whom to admit to the trading floor of their commodity exchange, to formulate trading policy, and to enforce their association's rules.
(7) For example, if an *audit* revealed one member's improper handling of financial obligations, the committee members could penalize the person, suspend membership, or expel the member from the association.

(8) Because of the rigid regulations governing trade practice and admittance to commodity exchanges, there is very little possibility of a *cartel*, or monopoly, of traders dominating the raw materials market. (9) Fortunately, a *collateral* result of commodity exchanges' self-regulation has been an outstanding reputation for fairness and responsibility.

(10) There is no *security* in commodities trading. Unpredictable factors such as bad weather that affects crops, a drop in the demand for a certain product, or the invention of a synthetic make this a risky business. However, the commodity exchange continues to be a vital part of our free enterprise system.

READING COMPREHENSION EXERCISE

Each of the following statements corresponds to a numbered sentence in the passage. Each statement contains a blank and is followed by four answer choices. Decide which choice fits best in the blank. The word or phrase that you choose must express roughly the same meaning as the italicized word in the passage. Write the letter of your choice on the answer line.

1. The marketplace where contracts for _____ are bought and sold is called a commodity exchange.
   - **a.** commercial services
   - **b.** articles of trade
   - **c.** industrial waste
   - **d.** stocks and bonds

1. _____**b**_____

2. Futures trading is still one of the most _____ aspects of today's commodity exchange.

    a. exacting   **b.** ancient   **c.** incomprehensible   **d.** profitable

2. _____d_____

3. The farmer may _____ a profit in September.

    a. count on   **b.** sacrifice   **c.** gain   **d.** invest

3. _____c_____

4. In either case, a contract agreed upon in March will be _____ in September.

    a. doubled   **b.** decreased   **c.** lost   **d.** paid off

4. _____d_____

5. The formal code provides guidelines for appropriate _____ in the event of broken agreements.

    a. amends   **b.** prosecution   **c.** proof   **d.** confirmation

5. _____a_____

6. Today a commodity exchange is a _____ of firms and individual traders.

    a. committee   **b.** cluster   **c.** structure   **d.** community

6. _____b_____

7. A(n) _____ might reveal a member's improper handling of financial obligations.

    a. examination of accounts   **c.** hasty generalization

    b. special inquiry   **d.** unusual certification

7. _____a_____

8. There is little possibility of a _____ of traders dominating the raw materials market.

    a. delegation   **b.** division   **c.** combination   **d.** representative group

8. _____c_____

9. The _____ result of commodity exchanges' self-regulation has been an outstanding reputation for fairness.

    a. prime   **b.** accompanying   **c.** single   **d.** favorite

9. _____b_____

10. There is no _____ in commodities trading.

    a. profit   **b.** loss   **c.** sense   **d.** safety

10. _____d_____

PRACTICE WITH ANALOGIES

See page 79 for some strategies to use with analogies.

Directions   On the answer line, write the letter of the phrase that best completes the analogy.

1. INJURY : RECOMPENSE :: (A) accident : lawsuit
    (B) revenge : forgiveness   (C) damage : amends
    (D) heal : suffering   (E) promotion : salary

1. _____C_____

2. AUDIT : RECORDS :: (A) edit : paper   (B) audition : role
    (C) test : study   (D) finish : race   (E) erase : tapes

2. _____A_____

3. ACCRUE : INTEREST :: (A) count : money   (B) create : boredom
    (C) produce : multiply   (D) spend : deficit   (E) gather : support

3. _____E_____

4. LUCRATIVE : PROFITABLE :: (A) significant : enviable
    (B) amusing : despicable   (C) disloyal : dependable
    (D) lovely : detestable   (E) prominent : notable

4. _____E_____

5. COMPANY : CONGLOMERATE :: (A) picture : collage   (B) puzzle : piece
    (C) farm : factory   (D) employee : employer   (E) guest : party

5. _____A_____

6. COLLATERAL : LOAN :: (A) savings : withdrawal   (B) property : pledge
    (C) promise : guarantee   (D) financial : funds   (E) own : borrow

6. _____B_____

The **Bonus activity** for Lessons 21–25 is on page T32.

Ｈow many of the following expressions about thought and judgment are familiar to you?

> A penny for your thoughts
> To have second thoughts
> Think the matter through
> Sit in judgment
> Reserve judgment

The large number of idioms in our language for these mental abilities emphasizes the value we place on them. The capacities to reason, to form opinions by distinguishing and evaluating, and to make sound decisions are vital in all areas of your life. Whether you reflect on past actions, plan future endeavors, or logically solve a problem, you are exercising your ability to think and make judgments. The words in this lesson will help you to understand the powerful nature of the intellect.

WORD LIST
abstruse
acumen
ascertain
cerebral
faculty
relative
ruminate
surmise
tenet
theoretical

DEFINITIONS

After you have studied the definitions and example for each vocabulary word, write the word on the line to the right.

1. **abstruse** (ăb-stroos′, əb-stroos′) *adjective*   Difficult to understand. (From the Latin word *abstrudere*, meaning "to hide")

   Related Words   **abstrusely** *adverb*; **abstruseness** *noun*
   Example   Eliot could not understand the *abstruse* explanation of the human body's immune system that he found in a medical journal.

   1. _____

2. **acumen** (ə-kyoo′mən) *noun*   Quickness and accuracy of judgment; keen insight; shrewdness. (From the Latin word *acuere,* meaning "to sharpen")

   Example   Donna Karan's business *acumen* has enabled her to build a multi-million dollar fashion empire.

   2. _____

3. **ascertain** (ăs′ər-tān′) *trans. verb*   To discover through examination or experimentation; determine.

   Related Word   **ascertainable** *adjective*
   Example   The detectives *ascertained* the facts of the case by interviewing the witness.

   3. _____

4. **cerebral** (sə-rē′brəl, sĕr′ə-brəl) *adjective*   a. Characterized by thought and reason rather than emotion or action.   b. Appealing to or marked by the workings of the intellect; intellectually refined.   c. Of or pertaining to the brain or cerebrum: *cerebral cortex.*

   Related Word   **cerebrally** *adverb*
   Example   Jonathan prefers *cerebral* pursuits, such as crossword puzzles, to athletics.

   4. _____

5. **faculty** (făk′əl-tē) *noun* **a.** Any of the powers or capacities possessed by the human mind. **b.** A special aptitude or skill. **c.** A group of teachers as distinguished from their students. (From the Latin word *facere,* meaning "to do")

> **Example**   Carmen's *faculty* of hearing was impaired for a short time following the explosion.

5. _____

6. **relative** (rĕl′ə-tĭv) *adjective* **a.** Having pertinence or relevance; connected; related. **b.** Considered in comparison to or in relationship with something else. **c.** Dependent upon or interconnected with something else for intelligibility or significance; not absolute or independent.

> **Related Word**   **relatively** *adverb*
> **Example**   At the international conference, participants discussed matters *relative* to quality education.

6. _____

7. **ruminate** (roo′mə-nāt′) *intrans. verb* **a.** To meditate at length; ponder; muse. **b.** To chew cud. (From the Latin word *ruminare,* meaning "to chew cud")

> **Related Words** **rumination** *noun;* **ruminatively** *adverb*
> **Example**   Mr. Ramos often sits in his rocking chair and *ruminates* on the exciting events of his life.

7. _____

8. **surmise** (sər-mīz′) *trans. verb* To come to a conclusion about something without sufficient evidence. *intrans. verb* To make a guess or conjecture. *noun* An idea or opinion based upon insufficiently conclusive evidence: *a matter of surmise.* (From the Latin *super-,* meaning "over," and *mittere,* meaning "to put")

> **Example**   Napoleon *surmised* that the French army could conquer Russia, but he did not account for the harsh weather conditions his troops would encounter.

8. _____

9. **tenet** (tĕn′ĭt) *noun* An opinion, doctrine, or principle held as being true by a person or group. (From the Latin word *tenere,* meaning "to hold")

> **Example**   Freedom of speech is one of the *tenets* of democracy.

9. _____

10. **theoretical** (thē′ə-rĕt′ĭ-kəl) *adjective* **a.** Of, pertaining to, or based on conclusions reached through logical reasoning. **b.** Restricted to theory; lacking verification or practical application; hypothetical. **c.** Given to theorizing; speculative. (From the Greek word *thēorein,* meaning "to look at")

> **Related Words** **theoretically** *adverb;* **theorize** *verb;* **theory** *noun*
> **Example**   Anita asked a *theoretical* question about what Henri Matisse was trying to accomplish with his cut-paper compositions.

10. _____

EXERCISE 1 COMPLETING DEFINITIONS

On the answer line, write the word from the vocabulary list that best completes
each definition.

1. Something that is difficult to understand is _____.

2. Something that is characterized by reason rather than emotion is _____.

3. Any principle or opinion held to be true by a person or group is called a(n) _____.

4. When you meditate at length about something, you _____.

5. To conclude without sufficient evidence is to _____.

6. To discover or determine through examination or experimentation is to _____.

7. Something that has pertinence or relevance to the matter at hand is _____.

8. If an idea is based on conclusions reached through logical reasoning, it is _____.

9. Quickness and accuracy of judgment is called _____.

10. Any of the powers or capacities of the human mind is called a(n) _____.

1. ___abstruse___
2. ___cerebral___
3. ___tenet___
4. ___ruminate___
5. ___surmise___
6. ___ascertain___
7. ___relative___
8. ___theoretical___
9. ___acumen___
10. ___faculty___

EXERCISE 2 USING WORDS CORRECTLY

Each of the following questions contains an italicized vocabulary word. Choose the
correct answer to the question, and write *Yes* or *No* on the answer line.

1. Is a *tenet* someone who rents rather than owns a home or store?

2. Is *acumen* the inability to make sound judgments?

3. Would a student who has trouble with simple arithmetic find calculus *abstruse*?

4. Would a doctor perform tests to *ascertain* the cause of a patient's symptoms?

5. Is jumping rope a *cerebral* activity?

6. If someone considers the *relative* merits of two cars, is he or she comparing them?

7. If you *ruminate* on your future, do you predict what will happen to you?

8. If astronomers cannot prove what they believe about black holes in space, are their
findings *theoretical*?

9. If you *surmise* that something is true, do you prove it conclusively?

10. Does the human *faculty* of reasoning distinguish us from other species?

1. ___No___
2. ___No___
3. ___Yes___
4. ___Yes___
5. ___No___
6. ___Yes___
7. ___No___
8. ___Yes___
9. ___No___
10. ___Yes___

EXERCISE 3 IDENTIFYING SYNONYMS AND ANTONYMS

Decide which word or phrase has the meaning that is the same as (a synonym) or
opposite to (an antonym) that of the capitalized vocabulary word. Write the letter of
your choice on the answer line.

1. SURMISE (synonym):
   a. find   **b.** restrict   **c.** guess   **d.** elevate

2. CEREBRAL (antonym):
   a. ingenious   **b.** secretive   **c.** vast   **d.** physical

1. ___c___
2. ___d___

3. ABSTRUSE (synonym):
   a. difficult   b. easy   c. purified   d. silent

4. RELATIVE (antonym):
   a. irrelevant   b. constructive c. careless   d. dependable

5. FACULTY (synonym):
   a. aptitude   b. desire   c. tendency   d. deviation

6. TENET (synonym):
   a. stamina   b. topic   c. aim   d. principle

7. ACUMEN (synonym):
   a. postponement   b. advantage   c. shrewdness   d. admiration

8. RUMINATE (antonym):
   a. spend extravagantly   c. decide impulsively
   b. partially execute   d. overturn completely

9. THEORETICAL (synonym):
   a. untimely   b. forgotten   c. proven   d. hypothetical

10. ASCERTAIN (synonym):
    a. extinguish   b. determine   c. ignore   d. ruin

3. _____ a _____
4. _____ a _____
5. _____ a _____
6. _____ d _____
7. _____ c _____
8. _____ c _____
9. _____ d _____
10. _____ b _____

EXERCISE 4 USING DIFFERENT FORMS OF WORDS

Decide which form of the vocabulary word in parentheses best completes the sentence. The form given may be correct. Write your answer on the answer line.

1. The second question on the examination was _____ easy. (*relative*)

2. Time travel is _____ impossible. (*theoretical*)

3. "Based on the figures you have given me, your projected losses for the year are not _____," the accountant told his client. (*ascertain*)

4. The _____ of the chemistry problem did not puzzle Garth. (*abstruse*)

5. Eleanor Franklin's art has been characterized as _____. (*cerebral*)

6. Leonard questioned the _____ of his friend who had recommended the stock of the failing company. (*acumen*)

7. A great deal of _____ on this problem will undoubtedly yield a solution. (*ruminate*)

8. I arrived at my philosophical _____ through study and introspection. (*tenet*)

9. _____ that Elizabeth would not attend, Alice did not invite her to the party. (*surmise*)

10. Warren has the _____ for always saying just the right thing. (*faculty*)

1. _____ relatively _____
2. _____ theoretically _____
3. _____ ascertainable _____
4. _____ abstruseness _____
5. _____ cerebral _____
6. _____ acumen _____
7. _____ rumination _____
8. _____ tenets _____
9. _____ Surmising _____
10. _____ faculty _____

READING COMPREHENSION

Each numbered sentence in the following passage contains an italicized vocabulary word or related form. After you read the passage, you will completely an exercise.

DR. ALBERT EINSTEIN

Few twentieth-century figures have inspired the great body of anecdote and legend that Albert Einstein has. The epitome of genius, the German-born physicist made contributions to science that remain unequaled.

Albert Einstein was born in Ulm, Germany, in 1879. (1) He apparently showed no early signs of genius, although he was a *cerebral* child. (2) His *faculty* for curiosity about the way things work became evident when he was quite young. At the age of five, when his father showed him a pocket compass, he was fascinated with the mysterious behavior of the needle. (3) He wished that he could *ascertain* the principles by which the compass operated. Much later, Einstein said that this incident led him to believe that "something deeply hidden had to be behind things."

In 1884 the Einstein family moved to Munich, Germany, where Albert began his schooling. (4) He was not a particularly good student and disliked the formal instruction that interfered with his *ruminations* about physical reality. According to Einstein himself, his real education occurred at home, where his uncle introduced him to algebra, geometry, and natural science. (5) He showed *acumen* in mathematics and science, experiencing pleasure in solving equations on his own and in teaching himself calculus and physics.

After his college graduation from the Polytechnic Academy in Zurich, Switzerland, where he majored in math and physics, Einstein was uncertain about what he wanted to do. He taught high school science for a short time and then, unable to find a position at a university, took a job as a patent examiner in Berne, Switzerland. It was here that he began a series of papers that revolutionized the science of physics and elevated the name of Albert Einstein to world eminence.

(6) Published in 1905, his papers on relativity, the emission and absorption of light, inertia, and the electrodynamics of moving bodies presented *abstruse* theories about the nature of time, space, mass, motion, and gravity. (7) Previously, scientific *tenets* had held that these elements were absolute. (8) Einstein, on the other hand, proved that they cannot be absolute because they are measured *relative* to the observer. (9) His *theoretical* research led to the development of the photoelectric cell, which made sound motion pictures and television possible. Einstein's work also contributed, years later, to the harnessing of atomic energy and to the creation of the laser. He won the Nobel Prize in 1921 for his work in theoretical physics.

During the political turbulence in Germany, Einstein was deprived of his German citizenship and property by the Hitler regime. He immigrated to the United States, where he became a citizen in 1940. Settling in Princeton, New Jersey, he worked as a research physicist and professor at the Institute for Advanced Study. Though an ardent pacifist, he did not want the German menace to continue. He wrote a letter to Franklin Delano Roosevelt in which he urged the President to initiate the United States' development of the atomic bomb in advance of Germany's work in the same field.

For the last twenty years of his life, Albert Einstein continued to work on his unified-field and general relativity theories. He came to realize that the growth of physics depended on theories far removed from observation and experience. (10) He also knew that the consequences of a *surmise* must be tested thoroughly. According to Einstein, the laws of science must be free creations of the human mind, guided by considerations of philosophy and mathematics. Albert Einstein died in 1955, having done much to prove the harmony and ultimate "knowability" of nature.

READING COMPREHENSION EXERCISE

Each of the following statements corresponds to a numbered sentence in the passage. Each statement contains a blank and is followed by four answer choices. Decide which choice best fits in the blank. The word or phrase that you choose must express roughly the same meaning as the italicized word in the passage. Write the letter of your choice on the answer line.

1. Albert Einstein was a(n) _____ child.
   a. energetic   **b.** friendly   **c.** daring   **d.** intellectual

1. ____d____

2. His _____ curiosity became evident when he was quite young.
   a. mental capacity for
   c. bad habit of
   b. lack of
   d. appearance of

2. _____ **a**

3. He wanted to _____ the principles by which the compass worked.
   a. contradict   b. determine   c. control   d. ignore

3. _____ **b**

4. He felt that formal studies interfered with his _____ about physical reality.
   a. intrigue   b. musings   c. declarations   d. sentiments

4. _____ **b**

5. Einstein showed _____ in mathematics and science.
   a. keen insight   b. little talent   c. good taste   d. diminished interest

5. _____ **a**

6. His theories about the nature of time, space, and gravity are _____.
   a. satisfying
   c. difficult to understand
   b. astonishing
   d. easy to interpret

6. _____ **c**

7. Scientific _____ had previously held that these elements were absolute.
   a. applications   b. principles   c. impressions   d. references

7. _____ **b**

8. Einstein proved that the elements had to be measured _____ the observer.
   a. carefully by
   c. without reference to
   b. constantly by
   d. in relation to

8. _____ **d**

9. Einstein's research, based on _____, led to the development of the photoelectric cell.
   a. studies of moving bodies   c. conclusions reached through logical reasoning
   b. studies of gravity   d. the latest speculations

9. _____ **c**

10. He believed that the consequences of a(n) _____ must be thoroughly tested.
    a. idea based on inconclusive evidence   c. scientific law
    b. theory based on previous discoveries   d. respectable enterprise

10. _____ **a**

WRITING ASSIGNMENT

Suppose that you are a camp counselor who supervises a group of young children. Recently an incident occurred in which one camper, rather than using his or her own judgment, followed the lead of another. Although nothing serious resulted, you still must write up the incident for the camp's files. Using at least five of the vocabulary words from this lesson, write a brief explanation of the incident, stressing why young children need to learn the meaning of thinking for themselves. Underline each vocabulary word that you use.

VOCABULARY ENRICHMENT

You may have been surprised to discover that the word *ruminate* derives from the Latin word meaning "to chew cud." In Latin the word *rumen* means "stomach," especially the stomach of cattle and sheep in which undigested food is stored until the animals are ready to chew and digest it. Because cattle and sheep appear to be thoughtful and subdued as they chew their cud, the Latin word *ruminare* began to be used as a metaphor for meditating about something. Eventually, the word itself came to mean "ponder" or "muse" when applied to people.

Activity   Many other English words have a connection with animals. Look up the definitions and origins of the following words in a dictionary. Then write a brief explanation of the connection between the meaning and the etymology.

1. bovine   2. bucolic   3. cavalcade   4. porcine   5. aquiline

Throughout the ages people have praised honesty as one of the greatest virtues. Easy to pledge but difficult to live up to, honesty sometimes eludes people even when they have the best intentions. Yet most people strive to be honest as a way of life.

Dishonesty is another matter. Some actions, such as those that are intended to trick, to cheat, or to deceive, are deliberately dishonest; and extreme forms of dishonesty are punishable by law. However, dishonest people are not always recognized or known, for theirs is a sneaky business that can succeed only until it is discovered.

The words in this lesson will introduce you to types of honesty, ranging from bluntness to righteousness, and types of dishonesty, ranging from hypocrisy to treachery.

WORD LIST

apocryphal
bona fide
candor
cant
charlatan
chicanery
feign
insidious
rectitude
veritable

DEFINITIONS

After you have studied the definitions and example for each vocabulary word, write the word on the line to the right.

1. **apocryphal** (ə-pŏk′rə-fəl) *adjective*   Of doubtful authorship or authenticity. (From the Greek *apo-*, meaning "away," and *kryptein*, meaning "to hide")

   Related Word   apocryphally *adverb*
   Example   Inconsistencies in the handwriting caused some experts to dismiss the document as *apocryphal*.

   1. _____

2. **bona fide** (bō′nə fīd′, bō′nə fī′dē) *adjective*   **a.** Done or made in good faith; sincere.   **b.** Authentic; genuine. (From the Latin phrase *bona fide*, meaning "in good faith")

   Example   To prove that his offer was *bona fide*, the contractor offered an unconditional, money-back guarantee.

   2. _____

3. **candor** (kăn′dər) *noun*   Frankness of expression; straightforwardness. (From the Latin word *candere*, meaning "to shine")

   Related Word   candid *adjective*
   Example   Maxine's extreme *candor* about her emotions often hurt her friends' feelings.

   3. _____

4. **cant** (kănt) *noun*   **a.** Insincerely pious language.   **b.** The use of trite, conventional, and unexamined statements and ideas.   *intrans. verb*   To speak tediously; moralize. (From the Latin word *cantere*, meaning "to sing")

   Example   I am tired of my neighbor's *cant* about how morally she and her family always act.

   4. _____

5. **charlatan** (shär′lə-tən) *noun*   A person who pretends to possess skill or knowledge; quack.

   Related Word   charlatanism *noun*
   Example   A professor of physics for ten years, the *charlatan* was finally discovered to have no college education whatsoever.

   5. _____

6. **chicanery** (shǐ-kā′nə-rē, chǐ-kā′nə-rē) *noun*   **a.** Deception by trickery.   **b.** A trick. (From the Old French word *chicaner,* meaning "to quibble")

   Example   Because of the street vendor's *chicanery,* I bought a defective watch that I could not return.

   6. _____

7. **feign** (fān) *trans. verb*   **a.** To give a false appearance of.   **b.** To represent falsely; pretend to. (From the Latin word *fingere,* meaning "to make by shaping")

   Related Word   feigned *adjective*
   Example   Although Frank tried to *feign* an interest in his host's slide show, he gave himself away when he started to snore.

   7. _____

8. **insidious** (ĭn-sĭd′ē-əs) *adjective*   **a.** Working or spreading harmfully in a subtle or stealthy manner.   **b.** Intended to entrap; treacherous.   **c.** Alluring but harmful. (From the Latin word *insidiae,* meaning "ambush")

   Related Words   insidiously *adverb;* insidiousness *noun*
   Example   The disease was *insidious;* it could be present for years before being detected, and in time it could spread rapidly.

   8. _____

   USAGE NOTE: Be careful to distinguish between *insidious* and *invidious,* which means "offensive" or "containing a slight."

9. **rectitude** (rĕk′tĭ-tōōd, rĕk′tĭ-tyōōd′) *noun*   Moral uprightness; righteousness. (From the Latin word *rectus,* meaning "right")

   Example   Because of her reputation for *rectitude,* Felicia was invited to speak at the judicial convention.

   9. _____

10. **veritable** (vĕr′ĭ-tə-bəl) *adjective*   Unquestionable; true. (From the Latin word *veritas,* meaning "truth")

    Related Word   veritably *adverb*
    Example   The old man was a *veritable* pauper, having little more than the clothes he wore.

    10. _____

EXERCISE 1 COMPLETING DEFINITIONS

On the answer line, write the word from the vocabulary list that best completes each definition.

1. Something done or made in good faith is _____.

2. Something unquestionable and true is _____.

3. Deception by trickery is _____.

4. To give a false appearance of something is to _____ it.

5. Something of doubtful authorship or authenticity is _____.

6. Moral uprightness is _____.

7. Something that works or spreads harmfully in a subtle or stealthy manner is _____.

8. A person who pretends to possess skill or knowledge is a(n) _____.

9. Frankness of expression is _____.

10. Insincerely pious language is _____.

1. _____ bona fide
2. _____ veritable
3. _____ chicanery
4. _____ feign
5. _____ apocryphal
6. _____ rectitude
7. _____ insidious
8. _____ charlatan
9. _____ candor
10. _____ cant

EXERCISE 2 USING WORDS CORRECTLY

Decide whether the italicized vocabulary word has been used correctly in the sentence. On the answer line, write *Correct* for correct use and *Incorrect* for incorrect use.

1. In Nathaniel Hawthorne's *The Scarlet Letter*, the Reverend Arthur Dimmesdale pretends to be a holy man and *cants* to his congregation while hiding his own great sin.

2. The renowned scientist was given a prize for her work in biology and called a great *charlatan*.

3. The candidate's *rectitude* was the main cause of his losing the election.

4. The mayor's reputation was nearly ruined by *insidious* gossip.

5. Because of Jules's extraordinary *candor*, we were never able to learn anything about his family.

6. Ellen *feigned* calm as she approached the podium, but she actually felt extremely nervous.

7. "We will discuss the contract," the players' negotiator told the club management, "when we feel that you have made a *bona fide* offer."

8. The agent concocted an *apocryphal* past for the movie star to make him appear more mysterious.

9. Sue Ann is a *veritable* genius, with an IQ of 180.

10. The firefighter was commended for her quick thinking and all-around *chicanery* during the emergency.

1. _____ Correct
2. _____ Incorrect
3. _____ Incorrect
4. _____ Correct
5. _____ Incorrect
6. _____ Correct
7. _____ Correct
8. _____ Correct
9. _____ Correct
10. _____ Incorrect

EXERCISE 3 IDENTIFYING SYNONYMS AND ANTONYMS

Decide which word or phrase has the meaning that is the same as (a synonym) or opposite to (an antonym) that of the capitalized vocabulary word. Write the letter of your choice on the answer line.

1. CHARLATAN (synonym):
   a. prophet   **b.** impostor   **c.** thief   **d.** dupe

2. CHICANERY (synonym):
   a. trickery   **b.** falsehood   **c.** honesty   **d.** loyalty

3. RECTITUDE (antonym):
   a. faithfulness   **b.** faithlessness   **c.** morality   **d.** immorality

4. FEIGN (synonym):
   a. tell the truth   **b.** suffer   **c.** fool   **d.** pretend

5. CANT (synonym):
   a. inability   **b.** truth   **c.** insincerity   **d.** prediction

6. VERITABLE (antonym):
   a. true   **b.** false   **c.** imagined   **d.** unstable

7. INSIDIOUS (synonym):
   a. treacherous   **b.** honest   **c.** wealthy   **d.** sincere

8. APOCRYPHAL (antonym):
   a. counterfeit   **b.** biblical   **c.** authentic   **d.** honest

9. CANDOR (synonym):
   a. trust   **b.** straightforwardness   **c.** injury   **d.** mockery

10. BONA FIDE (antonym):
    a. unsophisticated   **b.** genuine   **c.** insincere   **d.** well made

1. _____ b
2. _____ a
3. _____ d
4. _____ d
5. _____ c
6. _____ b
7. _____ a
8. _____ c
9. _____ b
10. _____ c

EXERCISE 4 USING DIFFERENT FORMS OF WORDS

Decide which form of the vocabulary word in parentheses best completes the sentence. The form given may be correct. Write your answer on the answer line.

1. Tired of the official's _____, her assistant exposed her insincerity. *(cant)*

2. After years of successful _____, the impostor was caught and brought to trial for impersonating an investment broker. *(charlatan)*

3. Vladimir's _____ credentials had gotten him a job at the hospital. *(feign)*

4. The thief worked _____, entering houses without making a sound. *(insidious)*

5. Politicians are not generally known for giving _____ answers to difficult questions. *(candor)*

6. We could tell that the silver spoon was a _____ antique by the stamp on the back of the handle. *(bona fide)*

7. Sally's honesty and _____ were beyond question. *(rectitude)*

8. The confidence man had tricked several people out of their savings; for his _____ he had to make restitution to his victims and serve time in jail. *(chicanery)*

9. By the end of the marathon, Fumiko was _____ exhausted. *(veritable)*

10. Many a story that is told in good faith as the actual experience of a friend or relative proves to be _____. *(apocryphal)*

1. _____ cant
2. _____ charlatanism
3. _____ feigned
4. _____ insidiously
5. _____ candid
6. _____ bona fide
7. _____ rectitude
8. _____ chicanery
9. _____ veritably
10. _____ apocryphal

READING COMPREHENSION

Each numbered sentence in the following passage contains an italicized vocabulary word or related form. After you read the passage, you will complete an exercise.

ELEANOR OF AQUITAINE

Probably the most interesting and influential European woman of the twelfth century, Eleanor of Aquitaine was queen of both France and England. Born in France, she was first the Duchess of Aquitaine, a large and powerful principality; soon, through marriage, she became Queen of France.

Queen Eleanor and her husband King Louis VII did not have a happy marriage. (1) First, Louis accused Eleanor of meddling in political affairs, and later Louis became jealous of his wife and questioned her *rectitude.* When their marriage was dissolved, Eleanor quickly married her former husband's most powerful rival, Henry, Duke of Normandy. (2) Medieval law allowed Eleanor to retain her control of Aquitaine after the divorce because she had a *bona fide* claim to it by birth, and this important principality came under Henry's control. Henry also had a claim to the English throne, which he gained two years after his marriage to Eleanor. He became Henry II, and Eleanor was now Queen of England.

(3) Henry and Eleanor's marriage was clearly a political match, and over the years the couple no longer bothered even to *feign* love for each other. Furthermore, Henry had no desire to share any of his great power with his wife or their sons, and this deeply disturbed her. Finally, Henry was not a loyal husband. (4) So angry was Eleanor that some historians have suggested that she was responsible for the assassination of one of Henry's confidantes, but this story is *apocryphal.* (5) Eleanor had no tolerance for pity, *cant,* or moralizing, and when she

did seek revenge, she was both brave and direct about it. She revolted against Henry, joined by their sons and other discontented nobility. (6) Henry hardly appreciated the *candor* of this action: he put down the revolt, captured Eleanor, and held her prisoner until his death.

The next King of England was Henry and Eleanor's son, Richard the Lion-Hearted. When he assumed the throne, he ordered his mother's release, and Eleanor's decisive role in political affairs resumed. Because Richard was away fighting in the Crusades during most of his ten-year reign, it was Eleanor who administered the realm. (7) When Henry and Eleanor's younger son, John, tried *insidiously* to overthrow his brother, Eleanor intervened to make sure that this did not occur. A few years later, when Richard died, it was again Eleanor's actions that influenced history. (8) She helped to make certain that her son John, the true heir to the crown, and not her grandson Arthur, whom she considered a *charlatan,* became King of England. Later, Eleanor also helped John to gain his only victories abroad.

Although Eleanor's influence was great, historians have often viewed her critically. (9) Some have accused her of mere *chicanery,* others of outright treachery. Still others have emphasized her marriages and divorce over her political achievements. Yet few have overlooked her important role as a patron of the arts and especially of literature. (10) It was during her reign that the court of Poitiers became a center of poetry and a *veritable* model of courtly life.

Each of the following statements corresponds to a numbered sentence in the passage. Each statement contains a blank and is followed by four answer choices. Decide which choice fits best in the blank. The word or phrase that you choose must express roughly the same meaning as the italicized word in the passage. Write the letter of your choice on the answer line.

1. Louis questioned Eleanor's _____.
   a. ability to govern
   b. choice of husbands
   c. moral uprightness
   d. sincerity

   1. _____ c

2. By birth Eleanor had a(n) _____ claim to Aquitaine.
   a. false   b. authentic   c. conditional   d. medieval

   2. _____ b

3. Henry and Eleanor eventually no longer bothered even to _____ love.
   a. talk about
   b. pretend
   c. argue about their
   d. try to regain their

   3. _____ b

4. The story of Eleanor's responsibility for an assassination is _____.
   a. of little importance
   b. of great political importance
   c. of uncertain origin
   d. of doubtful authenticity

   4. _____ d

5. Eleanor had no tolerance for _____.
   a. self-justification   b. self-esteem   c. hypocrisy   d. arguments

   5. _____ c

6. Henry did not appreciate the _____ of Eleanor's action.
   a. deviousness
   b. straightforwardness
   c. political nature
   d. personal threat

   6. _____ b

7. John tried _____ to overthrow his brother.
   a. treacherously   b. openly   c. repeatedly   d. wholeheartedly

   7. _____ a

8. Eleanor considered her grandson Arthur to be a _____.
   a. threat to the throne
   b. nuisance
   c. pretender
   d. claimant to the throne

   8. _____ c

9. Some historians have accused Eleanor of _____.
   a. deception by trickery
   b. patronizing the arts
   c. favoring her older son
   d. marrying for political reasons

   9. _____ a

10. During Eleanor's reign Poitiers became a(n) _____ model of courtly life.
    a. questionable   b. unquestionable   c. perfect   d. admired

    10. _____ b

WRITING ASSIGNMENT

Imagine that you have recently been a member of a jury deciding on the guilt or innocence of a quack doctor. Although the accused had a spotless medical record and had treated many needy patients without charge, he had been found to be a hospital technician without any medical degrees. One of his patients sued him for misrepresenting his credentials. Write a letter to a friend in which you discuss the case and your reactions to it. Use at least five of the vocabulary words from this lesson and underline them.

The **Test** for Lessons 25, 26, and 27 is on page T33.

READING SKILLS

THE PREFIXES *INTER-*, *INTRA-*, AND *INTRO-*

When added to a Latin root, the prefix *inter-*, *intra-*, or *intro-* forms a new word with a different meaning. (A **root** is the part of a word that contains its basic meaning. A root can be a complete word.) Each of these prefixes has one common meaning, as shown below.

Prefix Meaning	Root Word	Word	Word Definition
inter-: between; among	*rumpere*, "to break"	interrupt	to break in upon
intra-: within	*vena*, "vein"	intravenous	within a vein or veins
intro-: in; inward	*vertere*, "to turn"	introvert	one whose thoughts are directed inward

To determine the meaning of words with one of the three prefixes, use the following procedure. Remember that the more prefixes and roots you know, the more often you will be able to analyze unfamiliar words.

PROCEDURE

1. *Substitute the prefix and root definitions for the prefix and root.*

2. *Think of a possible definition of the entire word.*

3. *Use the context to help you develop the possible definition.*

4. *Check your definition of the word in the dictionary.*

EXERCISE USING THE PREFIXES *INTER-*, *INTRA -*, AND *INTRO-*

Each sentence in this exercise contains an italicized word beginning with one of the three prefixes in this lesson. The root word and its meaning are given in parentheses after the sentence. *Step 1:* Taking the context into consideration, write your own definition of the word. *Step 2:* Write the dictionary definition of the word. Choose the definition that fits the way in which the word is used in the sentence. *Step 3:* Write a sentence of your own in which you use the word correctly.

1. Buenavista High School has an active program of *intramural* sports. (Root word: *murus*, "wall")

   Your Definition ___Within walls_____

   Dictionary Definition ___Carried on within the bounds of an institution, especially a school___

   Sentence ___We hold an intramural competition to see who will represent the school at the state finals.___

2. After much *introspection* she made the decision. (Root word: *specere*, "to look")

   Your Definition ___Self-examination_____

   Dictionary Definition ___Contemplation of one's own thoughts, feelings, and sensations___

   Sentence ___He wrote the book after a long period of solitude and introspection.___

3. The disorder on the field was brought to an end by the *intervention* of the tournament officials. (Root word: *venire*, "to come")

Your Definition **Coming between**

Dictionary Definition **The coming in or between so as to hinder or modify**

Sentence **Only the intervention of the court saved the old building from destruction.**

4. During the *interregnum*, England was governed without a king. (Root word: *regnum*, "reign")

Your Definition **The period between the reign of one ruler and that of another**

Dictionary Definition **The interval between the reigns of successive rulers**

Sentence **There was an interregnum between the death of the old king and his son's coronation.**

5. During the long performance, Anne often *interjected* a much-needed note of humor. (Root word: *jacer*, "to throw")

Your Definition **Threw in**

Dictionary Definition **To insert between other elements; interpose**

Sentence **The judge told the witness not to interject hearsay evidence into her factual account.**

6. The applause was *interspersed* with cries of delight. (Root word: *spargere*, "to scatter")

Your Definition **Scattered**

Dictionary Definition **To distribute among other things at intervals**

Sentence **In the bouquet a few irises were interspersed among the yellow tulips.**

7. The mayors discussed housing problems at the *interurban* conference. (Root word: *urbs*, "city")

Your Definition **Among cities**

Dictionary Definition **Pertaining to or connecting urban areas**

Sentence **By taking the new interurban highway, you can save time.**

8. A mouse can crawl through the smallest *interstice*. (Root word: *sistere*, "to stand")

Your Definition **A small space or opening**

Dictionary Definition **A space, especially a small or narrow one, between things**

Sentence **The climbers would have fallen if the rope had not caught in the rocky interstice.**

9. Science fiction movies often show *intragalactic* travel.

Your Definition **Within a galaxy**

Dictionary Definition **Occurring or situated within the space of a galaxy**

Sentence **In a few centuries, intragalactic travel may be as commonplace as jet travel is today.**

10. Pocahontas *interceded* to save the life of John Smith. (Root word: *cedere*, "to go")

Your Definition **Pleaded for another**

Dictionary Dictionary **To plead on another's behalf; to act as mediator**

Sentence **The prisoner asked the governor to intercede on his behalf.**

Can something helpful also be harmful? Too much of something helpful might cause unintentional harm. A parent's love for a child, for example, is a wonderful thing. Unwittingly, however, some parents may become overprotective. A parent who is fearful of a child being injured may deprive the child of normal childhood explorations. A parent who insists on helping too much with homework may develop a child who lacks self-sufficiency and who might be unable to meet the challenges of life.

Similarly, something that we think of as negative may serve some positive purposes. Bacteria cause disease, but some also aid digestion. Bees sting us, but they also carry pollen that is essential to flowers.

The words in this lesson center around the concepts of help and harm. They are used in everyday life, as well as in fields such as medicine, psychology, and economics.

WORD LIST

adulterate
bane
boon
exorcise
inimical
panacea
pernicious
salutary
toxic
vitiate

DEFINITIONS

After you have studied the definitions and example for each vocabulary word, write the word on the line to the right.

1. **adulterate** (ə-dŭl′tə-rāt′) *trans. verb*   To make impure or inferior by adding extraneous, unusual, or improper ingredients. (From the Latin word *adulterare*, meaning "to pollute")

   Related Word adulteration *noun*
   Example   When Fred added water to the medicine, he *adulterated* it.

   1. _____

2. **bane** (bān) *noun*   A cause of death, destruction, or ruin. (From the Old English word *bana*, meaning "destroyer")

   Related Word baneful *adjective*
   Example   The great plagues of the 1300s were the *bane* of European life at that time.

   2. _____

3. **boon** (bo͞on) *noun*   Something beneficial that is bestowed; blessing. (From the Old Norse *bon*, meaning "prayer")

   Example   Lifting the trade embargo turned out to be a *boon* to the economy of the small manufacturing town.

   3. _____

4. **exorcise** (ĕk′sôr-sīz′, ĕk′sər-sīz′) *trans. verb*   **a.** To expel (an evil spirit).   **b.** To free from evil spirits. (From the Greek *ex-*, meaning "out," and *horkos*, meaning "oath")

   Related Word exorcism *noun*
   Example   At the end of the tale, the good fairy *exorcised* all the evil influences, permitting the townspeople to live happy lives once again.

   4. _____

5. **inimical** (ĭn-ĭm′ĭ-kəl) *adjective*   **a.** Injurious or harmful in effect.   **b.** Unfriendly; hostile. (From the Latin *in-*, meaning "not," and *amicus*, meaning "friend")

   Example   Eating an unbalanced diet and skipping meals are *inimical* to good health.

5. _____
USAGE NOTE: Do not confuse *inimical* with *inimitable*, meaning "impossible to imitate."

6. **panacea** (păn′ə-sē′ə) *noun*   A remedy for all diseases, evils, or difficulties; cure-all. (From the Greek *pan-*, meaning "all," and *akos*, meaning "cure")

   Example   Throughout recent history people have searched for *panaceas* for such problems as overpopulation, the shrinking of the ozone layer, and nuclear war.

6. _____

7. **pernicious** (pər-nĭsh′əs) *adjective*   **a.** Tending to cause death or serious injury; deadly.   **b.** Causing great harm; destructive; ruinous. (From the Latin *per-*, meaning "intensely," and *nex*, meaning "violent death")

   Related Words   **perniciously** *adverb;* **perniciousness** *noun*
   Example   Carbon monoxide is a *pernicious* gas that is fatal even in small concentrations.

7. _____

8. **salutary** (săl′yə-tĕr′ē) *adjective*   **a.** Designed to effect an improvement; remedial.   **b.** Favorable to health. (From the Latin word *salus*, meaning "health")

   Related Word   **salutariness** *noun*
   Example   The new government program has had a *salutary* effect: it has increased both the number of jobs and the number of new businesses in the depressed economy.

8. _____

9. **toxic** (tŏk′sĭk) *adjective*   **a.** Poisonous.   **b.** Harmful, destructive, or deadly. (From the Greek word *toxikon*, meaning "poison for arrows")

   Related Words   **toxicity** *noun;* **toxin** *noun*
   Example   Primitive warriors often coated the heads of arrows with *toxic* substances to make them more destructive.

9. _____

10. **vitiate** (vĭsh′ē-āt′) *trans. verb*   **a.** To impair the value or quality of.   **b.** To corrupt morally; debase.   **c.** To make ineffective; invalidate. (From the Latin word *vitium*, meaning "fault")

    Related Word   **vitiation** *noun*
    Example   The pharmacist *vitiated* the medicine by adding too much water to the solution.

10. _____

EXERCISE 1 MATCHING WORDS AND DEFINITIONS

Match the definition in Column B with the word in Column A. Write the letter of the
correct definition on the answer line.

Column A

1. boon
2. inimical
3. pernicious
4. bane
5. toxic
6. salutary
7. panacea
8. adulterate
9. exorcise
10. vitiate

Column B

a. a cause of death, destruction, or ruin

b. designed to effect an improvement; remedial

c. a remedy for all diseases, evils, or difficulties

d. injurious; unfriendly

e. something beneficial that is bestowed; blessing

f. poisonous; harmful

g. to expel an evil spirit

h. to make impure or inferior by adding extraneous,
   unusual, or improper ingredients

i. to impair the value or quality of

j. tending to cause death or serious injury; deadly

1. _____e_____
2. _____d_____
3. _____j_____
4. _____a_____
5. _____f_____
6. _____b_____
7. _____c_____
8. _____h_____
9. _____g_____
10. _____i_____

EXERCISE 2 USING WORDS CORRECTLY

Each of the following questions contains an italicized vocabulary word. Choose the
correct answer to the question, and write *Yes* or *No* on the answer line.

1. Is a *bane* a source of good?

2. If something is *pernicious*, is it hospitable?

3. Is a *panacea* a cure-all?

4. If something is *salutary*, is it favorable to health?

5. If you *vitiate* an argument, do you strengthen it?

6. Is something *toxic* poisonous?

7. If something is *inimical*, is it injurious?

8. If you *exorcise* something, do you use it frequently?

9. If you *adulterate* something, do you make it more mature?

10. Is a *boon* a variety of deadly snake?

1. _____No_____
2. _____No_____
3. _____Yes_____
4. _____Yes_____
5. _____No_____
6. _____Yes_____
7. _____Yes_____
8. _____No_____
9. _____No_____
10. _____No_____

EXERCISE 3 IDENTIFYING SYNONYMS AND ANTONYMS

Decide which word or phrase has the meaning that is the same as (a synonym) or
opposite to (an antonym) that of the capitalized vocabulary word. Write the letter of
your choice on the answer line.

1. BANE (synonym):
   a. remedy   b. cause of harm   c. medicine   d. blessing

2. ADULTERATE (antonym):
   a. make pure   b. improve   c. destroy   d. make impure

1. _____b_____
2. _____a_____

3. PERNICIOUS (synonym):
   a. difficult   b. helpful   c. precious   d. deadly

3. _____d_____

4. PANACEA (synonym):
   a. cure-all   b. medicine   c. disease   d. symptom

4. _____a_____

5. BOON (antonym):
   a. bonanza   b. gift   c. curse   d. poison

5. _____c_____

6. EXORCISE (synonym):
   a. employ   c. clean out
   b. arouse anger   d. expel an evil spirit

6. _____d_____

7. TOXIC (antonym):
   a. poisonous   b. salutary   c. smelly   d. shocking

7. _____b_____

8. VITIATE (synonym):
   a. impair   b. repair   c. despair   d. compare

8. _____a_____

9. SALUTARY (synonym):
   a. detracting   b. harmful   c. healthful   d. easy

9. _____c_____

10. INIMICAL (synonym):
    a. harmless   b. helpful   c. beneficial   d. hostile

10. _____d_____

EXERCISE 4 USING DIFFERENT FORMS OF WORDS

Decide which form of the vocabulary word in parentheses best completes the sentence. The form given may be correct. Write your answer on the answer line.

1. Adding any sort of compound to the paint will certainly _____ it. (*adulterate*)

1. _____adulterate_____

2. The new pedestrian shopping mall made the downtown area look better, but the change was not a _____ for the area's failing economy. (*panacea*)

2. _____panacea_____

3. The loss of so many jobs at the factory had a _____ effect on the community. (*bane*)

3. _____baneful_____

4. The strange-looking woman claimed to be a well-known expert at _____. (*exorcise*)

4. _____exorcism_____

5. The early, crucial victory had a _____ effect on the team's performance for the rest of the season. (*salutary*)

5. _____salutary_____

6. The _____ of the pesticide DDT to animals and humans was not discovered for many years. (*toxic*)

6. _____toxicity_____

7. By accidentally altering the substance that she was using, the scientist _____ the experiment. (*vitiate*)

7. _____vitiated_____

8. The large charitable gift was a _____ to the library's dwindling resources. (*boon*)

8. _____boon_____

9. Once the FDA discovered its _____, the chemical was banned permanently. (*pernicious*)

9. _____perniciousness_____

10. "Sugar is _____ to healthy teeth," the dentist warns all his patients. (*inimical*)

10. _____inimical_____

READING COMPREHENSION

Each numbered sentence in the following passage contains an italicized vocabulary word or related form. After you read the passage, you will complete an exercise.

NOISE, NOISE EVERYWHERE

While attending a rock concert or shortly after leaving it, some people experience unpleasant sensations in their ears. These range from slight disturbances, such as ringing and tingling, to severe throbbing pains. **(1)** Other people react to less blatant forms of noise; they may feel extremely irritable, as if demons had entered their ears and were waiting to be *exorcised*. **(2)** What both groups of people are experiencing is one of the recently identified *banes* of modern existence: noise pollution. **(3)** A cause of psychological stress and even bodily damage, noise is *inimical* to health.

Noise is everywhere. **(4)** Sirens, jackhammers, heavy trucks, radio and television, lawnmowers, and airplanes are just a few of the sources of this common form of pollution that *vitiates* the quality of our lives. **(5)** One of the *pernicious* aspects of noise pollution is that we often fail to recognize its presence. So accustomed are we to the range of everyday sounds that we don't stop to question their effect on us. **(6)** Also, because noise pollution does not physically alter our environment, as water and air pollution do, we do not consider noise pollution to be as *toxic* as other pollutants.

Noise does, nevertheless, have a very real effect on us. At a high level and with prolonged exposure, noise can cause loss of hearing. Less serious but very troubling effects include loss of sleep, problems with communication, fatigue, and headaches. Bodily responses to noise include the tensing of muscles, altered rates of breathing and circulation, and other symptoms associated with tension.

(7) There is, unfortunately, no *panacea* for the problem of noise pollution because noise is simply a part of day-to-day living. **(8)** Yet many researchers are striving to create a more *salutary* environment. They are studying and improving sound-absorbing and soundproofing materials. Additionally, they are studying the reduction of sound at its source, which often means designing better mufflers or redesigning engines. **(9)** A recent *boon* to factory workers has been legislation forcing the reduction of noise levels and ensuring that employers take steps to protect their workers' hearing.

Despite these recent measures and advances, most noise-reduction methods are so costly that there seem to be more solutions than good ways to implement them. Eventually, public awareness of the problems, increased research, and new designs that reduce noise will all help to curb this pollutant that can so stealthily affect our physical and mental well-being. **(10)** In the meantime, the simplest way to avoid the *adulteration* of your own environment by noise pollution is to insert a good pair of ear plugs.

Each of the following statements corresponds to a numbered sentence in the passage. Each statement contains a blank and is followed by four answer choices. Decide which choice fits best in the blank. The word or phrase that you choose must express roughly the same meaning as the italicized word in the passage. Write the letter of your choice on the answer line.

1. Some people feel as if they have demons in their ears who are waiting to be _____.
   a. examined   b. expelled   c. exhausted   d. excreted

   1. _____b_____

2. Noise pollution is one of the recently identified _____ in modern existence.
   a. causes of ruin   b. causes of joy   c. causes of sorrow   d. causes of war

   2. _____a_____

3. Noise is _____ to health.
   a. necessary   b. crucial   c. opposite   d. harmful

   3. _____d_____

4. Sirens are one of the forms of pollution that _____ the quality of our lives.
   a. improve   b. impair   c. affect   d. determine

   4. _____b_____

5. One of the more _____ aspects of noise pollution is that we often don't even realize it is affecting us.
   a. serious   b. unpleasant   c. destructive   d. instructive

   5. _____c_____

6. We do not consider noise pollution to be as _____ as other pollutants.
   a. uncomfortable   b. unhealthy   c. deadly   d. noticeable

   6. _____c_____

7. There is no _____ for the problem of noise pollution.
   a. cure-all   b. cure at all   c. compensation   d. recommendation

   7. _____a_____

8. Many researchers are striving to create a more _____ environment.
   a. safe   b. noise-free   c. soundproof   d. healthful

   8. _____d_____

9. Legislation controlling noise levels in factories has been a _____.
   a. blessing
   b. relief
   c. source of economic problems
   d. source of labor problems

   9. _____a_____

10. Using ear plugs can help you avoid the _____ of your environment by noise pollution.
    a. interruption   b. corruption   c. limitation   d. invasion

    10. _____b_____

PRACTICE WITH ANALOGIES

Directions   On the answer line, write the vocabulary word or a form of it that completes each analogy.

See page 79 for some strategies to use with analogies.

1. DENSE : PENETRATE :: _____ : understand *(Lesson 26)*

   1. _____abstruse_____

2. CLEANSE : PURIFY :: pollute : _____ *(Lesson 28)*

   2. _____adulterate_____

3. BOON : BLESSING :: _____ : curse *(Lesson 28)*

   3. _____bane_____

4. DONOR : GIVES :: _____ : cheats *(Lesson 27)*

   4. _____charlatan_____

5. HEALTHFUL : WALKING :: _____ : swimming *(Lesson 28)*

   5. _____salutary_____

6. MAGNET : ATTRACTS :: _____ : poisons *(Lesson 28)*

   6. _____toxin_____

In *Through the Looking Glass*, Lewis Carroll's sequel to *Alice's Adventures in Wonderland*, Alice and the Queen of Hearts have a discussion about the impossible. When Alice insists that one cannot believe impossible things, the queen advances the idea that it only takes practice.

Alice and the Queen of Hearts seem to represent pessimistic and optimistic viewpoints about the likelihood of accomplishing something. Had the Wright brothers followed Alice's example, they might have decided that powered flight was impossible and would never have invented the airplane. Achievements and discoveries seem to come from those who, like the Queen of Hearts, believe in potentially favorable results.

The words in this lesson describe different aspects of the possible and the impossible. They may help you to understand that, as the English poet John Heywood said in the 1540s, "Nothing is impossible to a willing heart."

WORD LIST
contingent
eventuality
feasible
implausible
inconceivable
perchance
preposterous
presumably
proclivity
prone

DEFINITIONS

After you have studied the definitions and example for each vocabulary word, write the word on the line to the right.

1. **contingent** (kən-tĭn′jənt) *adjective* **a.** Dependent upon conditions or events not yet established; conditional. **b.** Likely but not certain to occur. **c.** Happening by chance or accident. *noun* A representative group forming part of an assemblage: *the Idaho contingent at the Democratic convention.* (From the Latin *com-*, meaning "together," and *tangere*, meaning "to touch")

   Related Word **contingency** *noun*
   Example The sale of the house is *contingent* on a thorough structural inspection.

   1. _____

2. **eventuality** (ĭ-vĕn′chōō-ăl′ĭ-tē) *noun* A possible event; possibility. (From the Latin word *evenire*, meaning "to happen")

   Related Words **eventual** *adjective*; **eventually** *adverb*
   Example Wendy believes in being prepared for every *eventuality*.

   2. _____

3. **feasible** (fē′zə-bəl) *adjective* **a.** Capable of being accomplished or brought about. **b.** Capable of being utilized or dealt with successfully; suitable; convenient. **c.** Likely; plausible. (From the Latin word *facere*, meaning "to do")

   Related Word **feasibility** *noun*
   Example Napoleon never doubted that conquering Russia was *feasible*.

   3. _____

4. **implausible** (ĭm-plô′zə-bəl) *adjective* Not valid, likely, or acceptable; difficult to believe. (From the Latin *in-*, meaning "not," and *plaudere*, meaning "to applaud")

   Related Words **implausibility** *noun*; **implausibly** *adverb*
   Example Anna Devlin's newest book is an entertaining though *implausible* mystery.

   4. _____
   USAGE NOTE: *Implausible* means "difficult to believe," whereas *inconceivable* means "incapable of being explained."

5. **inconceivable** (ĭn´kən-sē´və-bəl) *adjective* **a.** Incapable of being imagined, comprehended, or fully grasped. **b.** So unlikely or surprising as to have been thought impossible. (From the Latin *in-*, meaning "not," and *concipere*, meaning "to take in")

   Related Words **inconceivability** *noun*; **inconceivably** *adverb*
   Example   At one time space travel seemed *inconceivable*.

5. _____
USAGE NOTE: See *implausible*.

6. **perchance** (pər-chăns´) *adverb* Perhaps; possibly. (From the Anglo-Norman phrase *par chance*, meaning "by chance")

   Example   Columbus thought that if he sailed far enough in the Atlantic Ocean, *perchance* he would reach India.

6. _____

7. **preposterous** (prĭ-pŏs´tər-əs) *adjective* Contrary to nature, reason, or common sense; absurd; senseless. (From the Latin *prae-*, meaning "before," and *posterus*, meaning "coming later")

   Related Words **preposterously** *adverb;* **preposterousness** *noun*
   Example   Months later we found out that Madeline's *preposterous* tale was actually true.

7. _____

8. **presumably** (prĭ-zoo´mə-blē) *adverb* By reasonable assumption; probably; likely. (From the Latin word *praesumere*, meaning "to anticipate")

   Related Words **presumable** *adjective;* **presume** *verb*
   Example   The swallows will *presumably* return to Capistrano at the usual time this year.

8. _____

9. **proclivity** (prō-klĭv´ĭ-tē) *noun* A natural inclination or tendency; predisposition. (From the Latin *pro-*, meaning "forward," and *clivus*, meaning "slope")

   Example   Mozart showed a *proclivity* for music when he was little more than an infant.

9. _____

10. **prone** (prōn) *adjective* **a.** Tending; inclined. **b.** Lying face downward. *adverb* In a prone manner: *lying prone on the floor.* (From the Latin word *pronus*, meaning "leaning forward")

    Related Word **proneness** *noun*
    Example   "Of course Sam remembered you; he is just *prone* to forget names," said Clayton.

10. _____
USAGE NOTE: Do not confuse *prone*, "lying face downward," with *supine*, "lying on the back."

EXERCISE I WRITING CORRECT WORDS

On the answer line, write the word from the vocabulary list that fits each definition.

1. Tending; inclined; lying face downward
2. Dependent upon conditions not yet established; likely
3. Capable of being accomplished; suitable; plausible
4. By reasonable assumption; probably; likely
5. Contrary to nature or common sense; absurd
6. Not valid, likely, or acceptable; difficult to believe
7. A natural inclination or tendency
8. A possible event; possibility
9. Perhaps; possibly
10. Incapable of being imagined or comprehended

1. _____prone_____
2. _____contingent_____
3. _____feasible_____
4. _____presumably_____
5. _____preposterous_____
6. _____implausible_____
7. _____proclivity_____
8. _____eventuality_____
9. _____perchance_____
10. _____Inconceivable_____

EXERCISE 2 USING WORDS CORRECTLY

Decide whether the italicized vocabulary word has been used correctly in the sentence. On the answer line, write *Correct* for correct use and *Incorrect* for incorrect use.

1. Because construction costs of the proposed city office building would be too high, the board declared that plans for the building were *feasible*.
2. Charles Lindbergh found the idea of transatlantic flight so *preposterous* that he successfully made the attempt in his plane *The Spirit of St. Louis*.
3. The Graves family has stored a large supply of food to be prepared for the *eventuality* of a blizzard.
4. Mrs. Lucas believes that electronic gadgets are *prone* to fail just when you need them the most.
5. All suburban commuters *presumably* use public transportation.
6. The infamous nineteenth-century train robber Jesse James had a *proclivity* for crime.
7. Harrison exceeded his sales quota because his customers found his sales presentation totally *implausible*.
8. "If, *perchance*, you are ever in Minneapolis," Aunt Mildred wrote, "do plan to stay with me."
9. The idea of a billion dollars is *inconceivable*.
10. Getting the federal grant for the children's museum is *contingent* on the community's ability to raise at least half of the funds.

1. _____Incorrect_____
2. _____Incorrect_____
3. _____Correct_____
4. _____Correct_____
5. _____Incorrect_____
6. _____Correct_____
7. _____Incorrect_____
8. _____Correct_____
9. _____Correct_____
10. _____Correct_____

EXERCISE 3 CHOOSING THE BEST WORD

Decide which vocabulary word or related form best completes the sentence, and write the letter of your choice on the answer line.

1. Because she is _____ to motion sickness, Margaret always rides in the front seat of a car.
   a. feasible   **b.** prone   **c.** presumable   **d.** contingent

1. _____b_____

2. A throat culture will indicate whether streptococcal bacteria, _____, are present in a sore throat.
   a. inconceivably **b.** implausibly **c.** preposterously **d.** perchance

2. _____d_____

3. Haven High School's prospects of winning the state swimming championship were _____ on its ability to defeat Cottonwood High in the regional meet.
   a. prone **b.** feasible **c.** implausible **d.** contingent

3. _____d_____

4. We laughed at his _____ claim that the oil stain could be removed from his shirt by rubbing the spot with frozen clams.
   a. feasible **b.** preposterous **c.** contingent **d.** eventual

4. _____b_____

5. A(n) _____ for panicking in emergencies would be undesirable in a paramedic.
   a. proclivity **b.** eventuality **c.** implausibility **d.** contingency

5. _____a_____

6. Abraham Lincoln believed that saving the Union was not only _____ but imperative.
   a. feasible **b.** preposterous **c.** inconceivable **d.** implausible

6. _____a_____

7. The mathematical concept of infinity is _____ to most people.
   a. presumable **b.** contingent **c.** prone **d.** inconceivable

7. _____d_____

8. The hikers are prepared for every _____ that they may encounter on their climb.
   a. feasibility **b.** eventuality **c.** proclivity **d.** preposterousness

8. _____b_____

9. A package sent by overnight mail will _____ arrive the following day.
   a. eventually **b.** inconceivably **c.** presumably **d.** implausibly

9. _____c_____

10. As the ancient Greeks gained scientific knowledge, their myths about natural phenomena seemed to them to be more and more _____.
    a. implausible **b.** feasible **c.** presumable **d.** prone

10. _____a_____

EXERCISE 4 USING DIFFERENT FORMS OF WORDS

Decide which form of the vocabulary word in parentheses best completes the sentence. The form given may be correct. Write your answer on the answer line.

1. Congress, in an attempt to plan for _____ such as natural disasters, has allocated money for emergency supplies. (*contingent*)

1. **contingencies**

2. Unable to reach his wife at her office, Jefferson _____ that she was on her way home. (*presumably*)

2. **presumed**

3. Because there is a _____ in post-operative patients to develop pneumonia, they are usually encouraged to get out of bed as soon as possible. (*proclivity*)

3. **proclivity**

4. The mare's _____ to jumping ditches made her an unsafe mount for small children. (*prone*)

4. **proneness**

5. A legislative committee has been appointed to study the _____ of restricting offshore drilling. (*feasible*)

5. **feasibility**

6. Environmentalists claim that if we are to save our natural resources, we will _____ have to find cleaner forms of energy. (*eventuality*)

6. **eventually**

7. The _____ of the defendant's alibi prompted the prosecuting attorney to question him further. (*implausible*)

7. **implausibility**

8. Unable to find her keys in her purse, Corinne checked to see whether, _____, she had locked them in her car. (*perchance*)

8. **perchance**

9. Polonium 212 is so radioactive that its half-life is _____ short. (*inconceivable*)

9. **inconceivably**

10. Frank's sisters think that he studied for his exams until it was _____ late. (*preposterous*)

10. **preposterously**

READING COMPREHENSION

Each numbered sentence in the following passage contains an italicized vocabulary word. After you read the passage, you will complete an exercise.

THE LOST CONTINENT OF ATLANTIS

The mystery of the continent of Atlantis, a legendary utopian civilization, has aroused the popular imagination for centuries. (1) Reputable geologists and archaeologists, as well as treasure hunters with a *proclivity* for fantasy, have devoted themselves to advancing theories about its location, destruction, and disappearance.

(2) Thus far, Atlantis has never been absolutely identified, causing many scholars to dismiss the story of the lost continent as a *preposterous* myth. (3) At the same time, however, others claim that the former existence of Atlantis is in no way *inconceivable*.

The story of Atlantis was first told by Plato in 355 B.C. in two philosophical dialogues entitled the *Timaeus* and the *Critias*. (4) *Presumably,* Plato got his information from ancient Egyptian oral accounts of the advanced civilization that inhabited the continent. According to Plato's narrative, Atlantis had been a powerful and wealthy nation. Governed according to the standards of Poseidon, the sea god, Atlantis had an ideal political system. The nation was made up of ten equal kingdoms, each administered by one of Poseidon's sons. (5) As time went on, the Atlanteans, once peaceful farmers and fishers, grew increasingly *prone* to aggressive behavior and set out to conquer the lands of the

Mediterranean. As a punishment for the attempted tyranny, the gods sent violent earthquakes and floods against Atlantis, sinking the continent in a single day and night.

(6) Although many investigations have been *contingent* upon Plato's accounts, Plato was not a historian. He was a philosopher who often invented symbolic events to illustrate a point. (7) Scholars argue that, *perchance,* he wanted only to show how a noble race living under a perfect government could fall into moral decline and be punished. This inter-

pretation is supported by the fact that, aside from Plato's dialogues, there is no other source of information on Atlantis in Greek literature or in other ancient literature.

(8) Nevertheless, an expedition off the coast of Greece in 1966 may have uncovered evidence that will ultimately prove that Plato's account of Atlantis was not as *implausible* as some people believe. A Greek seismologist, Angelo Galanopoulos, and an American oceanographer, James W. Mayor, used sonar to map the bottom of the Aegean Sea. They found evidence of a major community that had been destroyed by a volcanic explosion. In 1967 archaeologists began the long process of unearthing the buried island of Thera. Perfectly preserved by layers of volcanic ash, Thera appears to have been part of an advanced culture. Excavation thus far has uncovered well-preserved houses, public buildings, frescoes, and pottery that were produced by a sophisticated people.

(9) Although no definite connection with Atlantis has yet been established, many details of Thera's location, culture, and destruction make such identification *feasible* in time. (10) In fact, archaeologists find it possible to believe in the *eventuality* of Thera's disclosing the secrets of the fabled lost continent.

Each of the following statements corresponds to a numbered sentence in the passage. Each statement contains a blank and is followed by four answer choices. Decide which choice fits best in the blank. The word or phrase that you choose must express roughly the same meaning as the italicized word in the passage. Write the letter of your choice on the answer line.

1. Treasure hunters with a(n) _____ for fantasy have devoted themselves to advancing theories about Atlantis.
   a. habit   b. outline   c. motive   d. inclination

1. _____ d

2. Many scholars have dismissed the story of a lost continent as a(n) _____ myth.
   a. ancient   b. absurd   c. conventional   d. masterful

2. _____ b

3. Others claim that the former existence of Atlantis is in no way _____.
   a. true   b. supported   c. impossible   d. possible

3. _____ c

4. Plato _____ got his information from ancient Egyptian oral accounts.
   a. probably
   b. according to legend
   c. frequently
   d. realistically

4. _____ a

5. The Atlanteans grew increasingly _____ aggressive behavior.
   a. resentful of   b. opposed to   c. inclined to   d. afraid of

5. _____ c

6. Many investigations have been _____ Plato's accounts.
   a. dependent upon
   b. unrelated to
   c. confirmed by
   d. contradicted by

6. _____ a

7. Scholars argue that Plato _____ wanted only to show how a noble race could fall into moral decline.
   a. obviously   b. perhaps   c. without doubt   d. nevertheless

7. _____ b

8. Evidence uncovered by a 1966 expedition may prove that Plato's account of Atlantis was not _____.
   a. correct   b. accurate   c. historic   d. unlikely

8. _____ d

9. Many details of Thera's location, culture, and destruction make such identification _____ in time.
   a. doubtful   b. inconsistent   c. possible   d. inevitable

9. _____ c

10. Archaeologists find it possible to believe in the _____ of Thera's disclosing the secrets of the fabled lost continent.
    a. possibility   b. importance   c. success   d. implication

10. _____ a

Suppose that instead of getting a summer job, you decide to open your own business, such as a baby-sitting service or an errand service. In order to obtain a license for your business, you will need to submit a complete plan, indicating that you have considered all related possibilities and consequences. Using five of the words from this lesson and underlining each one, write a business plan that you will submit to the licensing bureau.

LESSON 30 CHANGE

People react strongly to change. Some individuals resist change, finding any alteration in their daily schedule inconvenient or disruptive. A detour, a new food, or a different job can be uncomfortable for the person who wants to maintain order and security. On the other hand, others welcome change as an opportunity for growth. These people seek variety, finding a move to a new city or the introduction of a new idea to be stimulating.

Regardless of how you view transformation and innovation, both are difficult to avoid in today's ever-changing technological world. The words in this lesson will help you to express positive and negative reactions to change.

WORD LIST

evolve
immutable
inveterate
malleable
metamorphosis
modulate
protean
sporadic
transmute
volatile

DEFINITIONS

After you have studied the definitions and example for each vocabulary word, write the word on the line to the right.

1. **evolve** (ĭ-vŏlv′) *trans. verb* **a.** To develop or achieve gradually. **b.** To work out; devise. **c.** To develop by evolutionary processes from a primitive to a more highly organized form. *intrans. verb* To undergo change or development; emerge. (From the Latin *ex-*, meaning "out," and *volvere*, meaning "to roll")

   Related Word **evolvement** *noun*
   Example In the 1970s Michael Graves *evolved* a new style of architecture called postmodern.

   1. _____

2. **immutable** (ĭ-myoo′tə-bəl) *adjective* Not subject or susceptible to change. (From the Latin *in-*, meaning "not," and *mutare*, meaning "to change")

   Related Words **immutability** *noun;* **immutably** *adverb*
   Example A metal cylinder at the Bureau of Weights and Measures constitutes an *immutable* standard of the weight of one kilogram.

   2. _____

3. **inveterate** (ĭn-vĕt′ər-ĭt) *adjective* **a.** Firmly established by having existed for a long time; long-standing; deep-rooted. **b.** Fixed in habit, custom, or practice; confirmed. (From the Latin *in-*, meaning "into," and *vetus*, meaning "old")

   Related Word **inveterately** *adverb*
   Example Like many people Betty has an *inveterate* resistance to change.

   3. _____

4. **malleable** (măl′ē-ə-bəl) *adjective* **a.** Capable of being altered or influenced; tractable. **b.** Capable of being shaped, as by hammering: *malleable metal.* (From the Latin word *malleus*, meaning "hammer")

   Related Word **malleability** *noun*
   Example The violin teacher will not accept students over the age of ten; she believes in the *malleable* character of youth.

   4. _____

5. **metamorphosis** (mĕt′ə-môr′fə-sĭs) *noun*   **a.** A marked change in appearance, character, or function.   **b.** A transformation, as by magic.   **c.** In biology, change in the structure and habits of an animal during growth: *the metamorphosis of a caterpillar.* (From the Greek words *meta*, meaning "change," and *morphē*, meaning "form")

Related Words   **metamorphic** *adjective;*   **metamorphose** *verb*
Example   The gradual *metamorphosis* of the old building was recorded in a series of photographs.

5. _____

USAGE NOTE: The plural of *metamorphosis* is *metamorphoses*.

6. **modulate** (mŏj′ə-lāt′) *trans. verb*   **a.** To regulate, adjust, or adapt to a certain proportion; temper; soften.   **b.** To change or vary the pitch, intensity, or tone of: *modulate the voice.* (From the Latin word *modus*, meaning "measure")

Related Word   **modulation** *noun*
Example   In the second performance, the actor *modulated* the broad humor of the opening-night performance.

6. _____

7. **protean** (prō′tē-ən, prō-tē′ən) *adjective*   Readily taking on a different shape, form, or character; variable. (From the name of the Greek god Proteus, who could change his shape at will)

Example   The *protean* actor presented ten skits, each time representing a different character.

7. _____

8. **sporadic** (spə-răd′ĭk, spô-răd′ĭk) *adjective*   **a.** Occurring at irregular intervals; having no pattern or order.   **b.** Appearing singly or at widely scattered localities, as a plant.   **c.** Not widespread; isolated: *sporadic cases of measles.* (From the Greek word *sporas*, meaning "scattered")

Related Word   **sporadically** *adverb*
Example   Only *sporadic*, half-hearted applause marked the end of the play.

8. _____

9. **transmute** (trănz-myōōt′) *trans. verb*   To change from one form, nature, or state to another; transform; convert. (From the Latin *trans-*, meaning "over," and *mutare*, meaning "to change")

Related Words   **transmutable** *adjective;*   **transmutation** *noun*
Example   At the paper mill we watched workers *transmute* raw materials into finished paper products.

9. _____

10. **volatile** (vŏl′ə-tl, vŏl′ə-tīl′) *adjective*   **a.** Changeable; inconstant.   **b.** Changing rapidly from one mood or interest to another; fickle.   **c.** Tending to erupt into violent action; explosive.   **d.** Evaporating readily at normal temperatures and pressures. (From the Latin *volare*, meaning "to fly")

Related Word   **volatility** *noun*
Example   Natalie's moods tended to be so *volatile* that many people found her unreliable and untrustworthy.

10. _____

EXERCISE 1 WRITING CORRECT WORDS

On the answer line, write the word from the vocabulary list that fits each definition.

1. Readily taking on a different shape, form, or character

2. To develop or achieve gradually; devise

3. A marked change in appearance, character, or function

4. Not subject or susceptible to change

5. To regulate, adjust, or adapt to a certain proportion; soften

6. Changeable; fickle; explosive

7. Capable of being altered or influenced

8. Occurring at irregular intervals; having no pattern or order

9. Firmly established by having existed for a long time; fixed in habit, custom, or practice

10. To change from one form, nature, or state to another

1. _____ protean _____
2. _____ evolve _____
3. _____ metamorphosis _____
4. _____ immutable _____
5. _____ modulate _____
6. _____ volatile _____
7. _____ malleable _____
8. _____ sporadic _____
9. _____ inveterate _____
10. _____ transmute _____

EXERCISE 2 USING WORDS CORRECTLY

Decide whether the italicized vocabulary word has been used correctly in the sentence. On the answer line, write *Correct* for correct use and *Incorrect* for incorrect use.

1. Marsha delivered her *sporadic* comment in a loud and self-confident fashion.

2. Mr. Berkin preferred not to get *evolved* in other people's difficulties.

3. Spring follows winter in an *immutable* process.

4. Patrick proved how *volatile* he was by continuing his saxophone lessons for fifteen years.

5. The *metamorphosis* of the empty field into a well-groomed park was accomplished quickly.

6. Alchemists attempted to *transmute* lead into gold.

7. Sally is a *malleable* traveling companion; she is willing to go anywhere we suggest.

8. "You'll enjoy this author's novels more if you read them in *inveterate* order," recommended Gene.

9. The special body-building diet called for twenty ounces of *protean* a day.

10. The gardener *modulated* the intensity of the water so that he would not drown the recently planted seedlings.

1. _____ Incorrect _____
2. _____ Incorrect _____
3. _____ Correct _____
4. _____ Incorrect _____
5. _____ Correct _____
6. _____ Correct _____
7. _____ Correct _____
8. _____ Incorrect _____
9. _____ Incorrect _____
10. _____ Correct _____

EXERCISE 3 IDENTIFYING SYNONYMS AND ANTONYMS

Decide which word has the meaning that is the same as (a synonym) or opposite to (an antonym) that of the capitalized vocabulary word. Write the letter of your choice on the answer line.

1. SPORADIC (antonym):
   a. playful   b. nimble   c. continuous   d. faultless

1. _____ c _____

2. MODULATE (synonym):
   a. postpone   b. conform   c. adjust   d. appeal

3. EVOLVE (antonym):
   a. regress   b. consume   c. disgrace   d. revere

4. TRANSMUTE (synonym):
   a. advise   b. scorn   c. infer   d. convert

5. IMMUTABLE (antonym):
   a. changeable   b. beneficial   c. accurate   d. unsightly

6. PROTEAN (synonym):
   a. authoritative   b. variable   c. gloomy   d. superior

7. VOLATILE (antonym):
   a. intentional   b. alert   c. stable   d. fluent

8. MALLEABLE (synonym):
   a. ordinary   b. attentive   c. clandestine   d. tractable

9. INVETERATE (antonym):
   a. dormant   b. new   c. prudent   d. entrancing

10. METAMORPHOSIS (synonym):
    a. transformation   b. tolerance   c. hindrance   d. omen

2. _____ c _____
3. _____ a _____
4. _____ d _____
5. _____ a _____
6. _____ b _____
7. _____ c _____
8. _____ d _____
9. _____ b _____
10. _____ a _____

EXERCISE 4 USING DIFFERENT FORMS OF WORDS

Decide which form of the vocabulary word in parentheses best completes the sentence. The form given may be correct. Write your answer on the answer line.

1. The _____ of copper and tin make them good metals on which to practice jewelry-making techniques. (malleable)

2. _____ characteristics were already apparent; the tadpole had lost its tail and was beginning to grow legs. (metamorphosis)

3. Because of the _____ of readers' preferences, the publishing business has traditionally been considered risky. (volatile)

4. Under the guidance of David Burpee, many new varieties of garden plants, vegetables, and fruits _____. (evolve)

5. The burglar alarm went off _____ throughout the evening. (sporadic)

6. An amoeba is a _____ organism. (protean)

7. Gloria believes that by studying astronomy she will ultimately understand the _____ of the laws of the universe. (immutable)

8. The _____ of water power into electric power can be witnessed at Hoover Dam. (transmute)

9. Stuart is one of the most _____ stubborn people I have ever met. (inveterate)

10. In the first aria on the old recording, Maria Callas's voice _____ were very subtle. (modulate)

1. _____ malleability _____
2. _____ Metamorphic _____
3. _____ volatility _____
4. _____ evolved _____
5. _____ sporadically _____
6. _____ protean _____
7. _____ immutability _____
8. _____ transmutation _____
9. _____ inveterately _____
10. _____ modulations _____

READING COMPREHENSION

Each numbered sentence in the following passage contains an italicized vocabulary word or related form. After you read the passage, you will complete an exercise.

THE GREAT BARRIER REEF

(1) Stretching for 1260 miles along Australia's eastern coast is an enormous range of limestone hills, a *volatile* environment that supports an infinite variety of marine life. Despite its name, the Great Barrier Reef is not an unbroken wall. Instead, it is a complex maze of innumerable coral reefs, cays, lagoons, rocky islands, underwater caverns, and shallow pools. (2) The area has been an *inveterate* source of curiosity for scientists and tourists interested in over fifteen hundred species of fish and other forms of life. Perhaps even a greater fascination exists with the nature of the reef itself, however. The Great Barrier Reef is the largest structure on the planet built entirely by living organisms.

(3) According to geologists and oceanographers, the reef probably began to *evolve* 60 million years ago during the Ice Age. (4) Evidently, the key to the reef's size and complexity lies in the various *transmutations* effected by geological phenomena. Scientists theorize that during the Ice Age the Continental Shelf was broken by a series of terraces. When faults cut across the terraces, a varied underwater landscape of hills, valleys, ravines, and basins was created. (5) *Modulations* in the sea level left coral exposed to the attack of waves. When these segments broke, they filled the valleys and basins. New coral grew until it reached the surface, where it toppled again into deeper water. In this way the reef came to cover its present 100,000 square miles.

(6) Today the *immutable* process of growth and destruction continues. (7) *Sporadic* storms that occur between November and February attack the underwater reefs, tearing up coral and piling up rubble. The broken fragments serve as the basis for new growth. As long as the water is warm and well-oxygenated, the reef remains a living, self-repairing entity.

Perhaps the most astonishing fact about the Great Barrier Reef is that it is built by animals only one-half inch long. Coral polyps have fleshy bodies at the larva stage. These tiny animals drift along until they settle on a suitably hard surface, develop tentacles, and attach themselves firmly. (8) As the larvae mature into adult polyps, they divide and redivide into elaborate *protean* colonies. During the maturation process, each polyp also secretes an external cuplike skeleton of limestone, which cements it to its base.

Coral polyps leave gaps as they build their colonies. (9) The activity of plants and other animals takes the reef to the last stage of its construction—the *metamorphosis* into reef rock. A fine sediment is created by clams and sponges that bore into the coral seeking protection. Other animals swallow the sand and reduce it to an even finer sediment. Still other plants and animals contribute their skeletons when they die. Algae act as plant mortar to hold the sediment in place and fill the gaps. (10) Constantly wet and under increasing pressure from new corals growing above, all of this *malleable* matter gradually hardens into creamy brown limestone. The irregular surface of the reef thus consists of a relatively thin veneer of living coral resting on the fossilized limestone skeletons of countless earlier generations.

The Great Barrier Reef is a contrast of delicate beauty and massive strength. The upper level resembles a garden with the blossomlike appearance of the densely clustered, fragile living coral. At fifty feet the coral is more sparse but also more spectacular. Branching antlers, plates, fans, and hemispherical masses with convoluted surfaces resembling the human brain range in size from a few inches to many feet. The deeper levels consist of coral debris and the solid rock forged by generations into the massive limestone edifice that supports this fascinating marine environment.

Each of the following statements corresponds to a numbered sentence in the passage. Each statement contains a blank and is followed by four answer choices. Decide which choice fits best in the blank. The word or phrase that you choose must express roughly the same meaning as the italicized word in the passage. Write the letter of your choice on the answer line.

1. The Great Barrier Reef is a(n) _____ environment that supports an infinite variety of marine life.
   a. majestic   b. dangerous   c. changeable   d. unyielding

   1. _____ c

2. The area has been a(n) _____ source of curiosity for scientists and tourists.
   a. long-standing   b. elusive   c. legendary   d. vigorous

   2. _____ a

3. The reef probably began to _____ 60 million years ago.
   a. sink   c. develop gradually
   b. break down   d. become intricate

   3. _____ c

4. The key to the reef's size and complexity lies in the _____ effected by geological phenomena.
   a. changes in temperature   c. changes in tides
   b. changes in nature   d. changes in plant life

   4. _____ b

5. _____ in the sea level left coral exposed to the attack of waves.
   a. Elevations   b. Openings   c. Variations   d. Deficiencies

   5. _____ c

6. The _____ process of growth and destruction continues today.
   a. unchanging   b. lengthy   c. indispensable   d. fruitful

   6. _____ a

7. _____ storms attack the underwater reefs.
   a. Violent   b. Brief   c. Mild   d. Occasional

   7. _____ d

8. The larvae divide into elaborate _____ colonies.
   a. continuous   c. multicolored
   b. constantly changing   d. beneficial

   8. _____ b

9. The last stage of reef construction is its _____ into reef rock.
   a. unparalleled drop   c. swift passage
   b. adjacent movement   d. marked change of character

   9. _____ d

10. By nature _____, the matter gradually hardens into limestone.
    a. capable of being shaped   c. capable of changing color
    b. capable of being measured   d. capable of absorbing moisture

   10. _____ a

WRITING ASSIGNMENT

The British writer Arnold Bennett once said, "Any change, even a change for the better, is always accompanied by drawbacks and discomforts." Using specific examples from your experience, write an essay in which you agree or disagree with the quotation. Be sure to use at least five of the vocabulary words from this lesson in your essay and underline each one of them.

The **Bonus activity** for Lessons 26–30 is on page T35. The **Test** for Lessons 28, 29, and 30 is on page T36.

READING SKILLS

THE PREFIXES *ANTE-* AND *POST-*

Many English words are made up of the prefix *ante-* or *post-* and an English or Latin root or root word. The words *antecedent* and *postscript* are two examples. Like all prefixes, *ante-* and *post-* change the meaning of the roots to which they are attached.

Prefix Meaning	Root Word	Word	Word Definition
ante-, "before"	*cedere*, "to go"	antecedent	going before; preceding
post-, "after"	*scribere*, "to write"	postscript	a message at the end of a letter

It is important to distinguish *ante-* words from those with the prefix *anti-*, which means "opposite" or "against."

You can determine the meaning of unfamiliar words that begin with *ante-* or *post-* by adding the prefix meaning to the meaning of the root or root word. Remember that context clues may also help you to arrive at a possible definition. Be sure to verify the meaning by looking the word up in the dictionary.

EXERCISE USING THE PREFIXES *ANTE-* AND *POST-*

Each sentence in this exercise contains an italicized word beginning with *ante-* or *post-*. When appropriate, the root word and its meaning are given in parentheses after the sentence. *Step 1:* Taking the context into consideration, write your own definition of the word. *Step 2:* Write the dictionary definition of the word. Choose the definition that fits the way in which the word is used in the sentence. *Step 3:* Write a sentence of your own in which you use the word correctly.

1. Stephanie did *postgraduate* work in business administration.

   Your Definition ___ After graduation _____

   Dictionary Definition ___ Pertaining to advanced study after graduation from high school or college ___

   Sentence ___ A career in law requires three years of postgraduate work. ___

2. The patients waited in the *antechamber* until the nurse summoned them.

   Your Definition ___ Waiting room outside an office _____

   Dictionary Definition ___ A smaller room serving as an entryway into a larger room ___

   Sentence ___ Lobbyists thronged the antechamber outside the state senate. ___

3. The patient's *postoperative* condition was said to be excellent.

   Your Definition ___ After an operation _____

   Dictionary Definition ___ Happening or done after surgery _____

   Sentence ___ Postoperative instructions included having the patient cough at regular intervals. ___

4. At the historical museum, you can see *antebellum* fashions. (Root word: *bellum,* "war")

Your Definition ___Before a war___

Dictionary Definition ___Belonging to the period prior to the Civil War___

Sentence ___The Georgia historian will give a talk on antebellum life in the South.___

5. At the service the organist played a work by Handel as the *postlude.*

Your Definition ___Musical work played afterward___

Dictionary Definition ___An organ work played at the end of a church service___

Sentence ___Because of the sudden illness of the organist, no postlude was played that day.___

6. A *postprandial* toast to the bridal couple was made by the bride's uncle. (Root word: *prandium,* "late breakfast")

Your Definition ___After a wedding breakfast___

Dictionary Definition ___Following a meal, especially dinner___

Sentence ___The postprandial entertainment consisted of reggae music.___

7. That town ordinance is so old that it must be *antediluvian!* (Root word: *diluvium,* "flood")

Your Definition ___Occurring before a flood___

Dictionary Definition ___Occurring before the flood written about in the Bible___

Sentence ___Aunt Jane sighed and said that her clothes were positively antediluvian.___

8. During the *postglacial* period, temperatures slowly began to rise.

Your Definition ___After the glacier(s)___

Dictionary Definition ___Pertaining to the time following a period characterized by glaciers___

Sentence ___During the postglacial period, some of the largest boulders split into sections.___

9. The Middle Ages *antedated* the Renaissance.

Your Definition ___Came before___

Dictionary Definition ___Preceded in time___

Sentence ___My group's agreement to play at the wedding antedated the other invitation.___

10. Because the baby was premature, she received special *postnatal* care.

Your Definition ___After the birth___

Dictionary Definition ___Of or occurring during the period immediately after birth___

Sentence ___On his third postnatal day, the baby had his picture taken.___

11. In the word "anonymous," the stress falls on the *antepenult,* which is the syllable "non." (Root word: *paenultima,* "next to last")

Your Definition ___Syllable preceding the next to the last syllable of a word___

Dictionary Definition ___The third syllable from the end in a word___

Sentence ___In the word "posterity," the stress also falls on the antepenult.___

CONTENTS

USING BONUS ACTIVITIES AND TESTS

For your convenience, the lesson **Tests** and **Bonus** activities that accompany *Vocabulary for Achievement*, Fifth Course, are available as reproducible masters in this section. Answers are printed in color on the front of each reproducible master for ease in locating.

TESTS

There are ten multiple-choice tests, each covering three consecutive lessons. This format ensures that students can demonstrate proficiency with a wider set of vocabulary words than is found in a single lesson.

Test formats resemble those of the lesson exercises. Each test is divided into two parts of fifteen items each, allowing for the testing of all words in the three lessons. Part A focuses on recognizing and recalling definitions, while Part B emphasizes placing words within the context or discriminating among a choice of antonyms.

BONUSES

Seven Bonus activities, each covering four or five consecutive lessons, offer students further opportunities for reinforcement and enrichment. These activities consist of crossword puzzles, word searches, sentence completions, scrambled words, and other word-game formats. Depending on classroom needs, use these activities as added practice, as reviews of already-mastered words, or as extra-credit assignments.

VERBAL APTITUDE TESTS

Each of the four-page tests reinforces material taught in the skill features and helps prepare students for taking college-entrance examinations. Each test covers antonyms, sentence completions, word analogies, and reading comprehension.

In order to conform to the customary fall and early-spring scheduling of college-entrance testing, Test 1 appears after Lesson 10; Test 2 appears after Lesson 20.

Many of the words from this grade level are used in the Verbal Aptitude Tests; these words are marked for your reference with a colored asterisk on the **Complete Word List** on page xv in this Teacher's Edition.

Vocabulary
FOR ACHIEVEMENT
FIFTH COURSE

Student Record

Class Period _____

	Lesson 1 Exercises	Lesson 2 Exercises	Lesson 3 Exercises	Test: Lessons 1, 2, 3	Skill Lesson	Lesson 4 Exercises	Bonus: Lessons 1–4	Lesson 5 Exercises	Lesson 6 Exercises	Test: Lessons 4, 5, 6	Skill Lesson	Lesson 7 Exercises	Lesson 8 Exercises	Bonus: Lessons 5–8	Lesson 9 Exercises	Test: Lessons 7, 8, 9	Skill Lesson	Lesson 10 Exercises	Verbal Aptitude Test 1	Lesson 11 Exercises	Lesson 12 Exercises	Bonus: Lessons 9–12	Test: Lessons 10, 11, 12	Skill Lesson	Lesson 13 Exercises	Lesson 14 Exercises	Lesson 15 Exercises	Test: Lessons 13, 14, 15	Skill Lesson
1.																													
2.																													
3.																													
4.																													
5.																													
6.																													
7.																													
8.																													
9.																													
10.																													
11.																													
12.																													
13.																													
14.																													
15.																													
16.																													
17.																													
18.																													
19.																													
20.																													
21.																													
22.																													
23.																													
24.																													
25.																													
26.																													
27.																													
28.																													
29.																													
30.																													
31.																													
32.																													
33.																													
34.																													
35.																													

	Lesson 16 Exercises	Bonus: Lessons 13–16	Lesson 17 Exercises	Lesson 18 Exercises	Test: Lessons 16, 17, 18	Skill Lesson	Lesson 19 Exercises	Lesson 20 Exercises	Bonus: Lessons 17–20	Verbal Aptitude Test 2	Lesson 21 Exercises	Test: Lessons 19, 20, 21	Skill Lesson	Lesson 22 Exercises	Lesson 23 Exercises	Lesson 24 Exercises	Test: Lessons 22, 23, 24	Skill Lesson	Lesson 25 Exercises	Bonus: Lessons 21–25	Lesson 26 Exercises	Lesson 27 Exercises	Test: Lessons 25, 26, 27	Skill Lesson	Lesson 28 Exercises	Lesson 29 Exercises	Lesson 30 Exercises	Bonus: Lessons 26–30	Test: Lessons 28, 29, 30	Skill Lesson
1.																														
2.																														
3.																														
4.																														
5.																														
6.																														
7.																														
8.																														
9.																														
10.																														
11.																														
12.																														
13.																														
14.																														
15.																														
16.																														
17.																														
18.																														
19.																														
20.																														
21.																														
22.																														
23.																														
24.																														
25.																														
26.																														
27.																														
28.																														
29.																														
30.																														
31.																														
32.																														
33.																														
34.																														
35.																														

TEST LESSONS 1, 2, AND 3

(pages 1–18)

PART A CHOOSING THE BEST DEFINITION

On the answer line, write the letter of the best definition of the italicized word.

1. The water becomes turbulent where the two rivers *converge.*
   a. separate b. join c. descend d. increase in velocity

   1. ___b___

2. The personnel manager frowned as he read the *solecism* "I have graduated high school in 1982" on the applicant's résumé.
   a. ungrammatical construction c. exaggeration
   b. incorrect fact d. illegible sentence

   2. ___a___

3. Hannah superstitiously muttered an *incantation* to ward off bad luck.
   a. warning b. rhyme c. request d. magic charm

   3. ___d___

4. The *diphthong* in the word *join* combines the sounds of long *o* and *e*.
   a. silent letter c. consonant
   b. predominant sound d. sound formed from vowels

   4. ___d___

5. When Jill arrived Angela *terminated* her telephone conversation.
   a. interrupted b. reduced c. started d. concluded

   5. ___d___

6. Evidently kidney damage is one possible *sequel* to untreated diabetes.
   a. forerunner b. side effect c. consequence d. reason

   6. ___c___

7. Carrie was amused by the *vagaries* of young children's imaginations.
   a. preciseness b. uncertainty c. odd fancies d. silliness

   7. ___c___

8. "Debug" and "byte" are *neologisms* of the computer industry.
   a. newly made-up words c. slang expressions
   b. humorous terminology d. technical terms

   8. ___a___

9. My desire for a vacation is *subordinate* to my need for a car.
   a. inferior b. unrelated c. more important d. equal

   9. ___a___

10. The rotation of doctors caused a lack of *continuity* in patient care.
    a. uninterrupted flow c. quality
    b. interest d. excessive costs

    10. ___a___

11. The Baums *initiated* their son's musical training with a trip to the symphony.
    a. insisted on b. began c. increased d. paid for

    11. ___b___

12. Martial arts expert Bruce Lee was given the *appellation* "the Dragon."
    a. award b. mascot c. title d. symbol

    12. ___c___

13. The Jamaican *patois* has a lilting, musical quality.
    a. lifestyle b. anthem c. accent d. regional dialect

    13. ___d___

14. The knight wore his lady's handkerchief as an *amulet.*
    a. decoration b. charm c. memento d. bandage

    14. ___b___

15. Dr. Hoopes attributed her discovery of a new vaccine to *serendipity.*
    a. inspiration b. study c. determination d. luck

    15. ___d___

TEST LESSONS 1, 2, AND 3

(pages 1–18)

PART A CHOOSING THE BEST DEFINITION

On the answer line, write the letter of the best definition of the italicized word.

1. The water becomes turbulent where the two rivers *converge*.
   a. separate   **b.** join   **c.** descend   **d.** increase in velocity

   1. _____

2. The personnel manager frowned as he read the *solecism* "I have graduated high school in 1982" on the applicant's résumé.
   a. ungrammatical construction   **c.** exaggeration
   b. incorrect fact   **d.** illegible sentence

   2. _____

3. Hannah superstitiously muttered an *incantation* to ward off bad luck.
   a. warning   **b.** rhyme   **c.** request   **d.** magic charm

   3. _____

4. The *diphthong* in the word *join* combines the sounds of long *o* and *e*.
   a. silent letter   **c.** consonant
   b. predominant sound   **d.** sound formed from vowels

   4. _____

5. When Jill arrived Angela *terminated* her telephone conversation.
   a. interrupted   **b.** reduced   **c.** started   **d.** concluded

   5. _____

6. Evidently kidney damage is one possible *sequel* to untreated diabetes.
   a. forerunner   **b.** side effect   **c.** consequence   **d.** reason

   6. _____

7. Carrie was amused by the *vagaries* of young children's imaginations.
   a. preciseness   **b.** uncertainty   **c.** odd fancies   **d.** silliness

   7. _____

8. "Debug" and "byte" are *neologisms* of the computer industry.
   a. newly made-up words   **c.** slang expressions
   b. humorous terminology   **d.** technical terms

   8. _____

9. My desire for a vacation is *subordinate* to my need for a car.
   a. inferior   **b.** unrelated   **c.** more important   **d.** equal

   9. _____

10. The rotation of doctors caused a lack of *continuity* in patient care.
    a. uninterrupted flow   **c.** quality
    b. interest   **d.** excessive costs

    10. _____

11. The Baums *initiated* their son's musical training with a trip to the symphony.
    a. insisted on   **b.** began   **c.** increased   **d.** paid for

    11. _____

12. Martial arts expert Bruce Lee was given the *appellation* "the Dragon."
    a. award   **b.** mascot   **c.** title   **d.** symbol

    12. _____

13. The Jamaican *patois* has a lilting, musical quality.
    a. lifestyle   **b.** anthem   **c.** accent   **d.** regional dialect

    13. _____

14. The knight wore his lady's handkerchief as an *amulet*.
    a. decoration   **b.** charm   **c.** memento   **d.** bandage

    14. _____

15. Dr. Hoopes attributed her discovery of a new vaccine to *serendipity*.
    a. inspiration   **b.** study   **c.** determination   **d.** luck

    15. _____

TEST LESSONS 1, 2, AND 3

PART B CHOOSING THE BEST WORD

On the answer line, write the letter of the word that best completes the sentence.

16. Desipte a lack of political experience, Flynn was propelled into a _____ position in his party's leadership.
    a. pivotal   **b.** providential   **c.** subordinate   **d.** tangential

    16. _____ **a**

17. The airport store, patronized by international customers, hires only _____ employees.
    a. polyglot   **b.** capricious   **c.** subordinate   **d.** propitious

    17. _____ **a**

18. _____ is the belief that we cannot alter the course of our lives.
    a. Serendipity   **b.** Incantation   **c.** Fatalism   **d.** Neologism

    18. _____ **c**

19. To Cassandra, the duchess's gaudy jewelry was _____.
    a. subordinate   **b.** providential   **c.** propitious   **d.** vulgar

    19. _____ **d**

20. In formal _____ an ambassador is addressed as "Your Excellency."
    a. linguistics   **b.** parlance   **c.** patois   **d.** eponym

    20. _____ **b**

21. Although Terry's major in college is _____, he is also interested in the related fields of speech and drama.
    a. solecisms   **b.** eponyms   **c.** diphthongs   **d.** linguistics

    21. _____ **d**

22. An unshakable calm is the _____ of Susan's approach to life.
    a. appellation   **b.** amulet   **c.** crux   **d.** incantation

    22. _____ **c**

23. Lavell always consults *The Old Farmer's Almanac* to determine the most _____ time to begin the spring planting.
    a. tangential   **b.** capricious   **c.** fatalistic   **d.** propitious

    23. _____ **d**

24. The pioneers' discovery of a mountain spring was _____ because their water supply was very low.
    a. providential   **b.** tangential   **c.** pivotal   **d.** capricious

    24. _____ **a**

25. Pennsylvania's _____, William Penn, was a devout Quaker.
    a. appellation   **b.** eponym   **c.** quirk   **d.** solecism

    25. _____ **b**

26. A woman of _____ taste, Mrs. Stone frequently redecorates.
    a. providential   **b.** propitious   **c.** capricious   **d.** tangential

    26. _____ **c**

27. Soap operas seem to emphasize the _____ of other people's lives.
    a. vicissitudes   **b.** solecisms   **c.** patois   **d.** sequels

    27. _____ **a**

28. The cruise ship provided the _____ in luxuries—five restaurants, a movie theater, a shopping arcade, and a health spa.
    a. tangent   **b.** propitiousness   **c.** ultimate   **d.** vagaries

    28. _____ **c**

29. One of Justine's most endearing _____ is her expression of enthusiasm by clapping her hands.
    a. appellations   **b.** quirks   **c.** vagaries   **d.** terminations

    29. _____ **b**

30. "Let's deal with the major problem, not _____ issues," said Mark.
    a. capricious   **b.** pivotal   **c.** ultimate   **d.** tangential

    30. _____ **d**

TEST LESSONS 1, 2, AND 3

PART B CHOOSING THE BEST WORD

On the answer line, write the letter of the word that best completes the sentence.

16. Desipte a lack of political experience, Flynn was propelled into a _____ position in his party's leadership.
    a. pivotal   **b.** providential   **c.** subordinate   **d.** tangential

    16. _____

17. The airport store, patronized by international customers, hires only _____ employees.
    a. polyglot   **b.** capricious   **c.** subordinate   **d.** propitious

    17. _____

18. _____ is the belief that we cannot alter the course of our lives.
    a. Serendipity   **b.** Incantation   **c.** Fatalism   **d.** Neologism

    18. _____

19. To Cassandra, the duchess's gaudy jewelry was _____.
    a. subordinate   **b.** providential   **c.** propitious   **d.** vulgar

    19. _____

20. In formal _____ an ambassador is addressed as "Your Excellency."
    a. linguistics   **b.** parlance   **c.** patois   **d.** eponym

    20. _____

21. Although Terry's major in college is _____, he is also interested in the related fields of speech and drama.
    a. solecisms   **b.** eponyms   **c.** diphthongs   **d.** linguistics

    21. _____

22. An unshakable calm is the _____ of Susan's approach to life.
    a. appellation   **b.** amulet   **c.** crux   **d.** incantation

    22. _____

23. Lavell always consults *The Old Farmer's Almanac* to determine the most _____ time to begin the spring planting.
    a. tangential   **b.** capricious   **c.** fatalistic   **d.** propitious

    23. _____

24. The pioneers' discovery of a mountain spring was _____ because their water supply was very low.
    a. providential   **b.** tangential   **c.** pivotal   **d.** capricious

    24. _____

25. Pennsylvania's _____, William Penn, was a devout Quaker.
    a. appellation   **b.** eponym   **c.** quirk   **d.** solecism

    25. _____

26. A woman of _____ taste, Mrs. Stone frequently redecorates.
    a. providential   **b.** propitious   **c.** capricious   **d.** tangential

    26. _____

27. Soap operas seem to emphasize the _____ of other people's lives.
    a. vicissitudes   **b.** solecisms   **c.** patois   **d.** sequels

    27. _____

28. The cruise ship provided the _____ in luxuries—five restaurants, a movie theater, a shopping arcade, and a health spa.
    a. tangent   **b.** propitiousness   **c.** ultimate   **d.** vagaries

    28. _____

29. One of Justine's most endearing _____ is her expression of enthusiasm by clapping her hands.
    a. appellations   **b.** quirks   **c.** vagaries   **d.** terminations

    29. _____

30. "Let's deal with the major problem, not _____ issues," said Mark.
    a. capricious   **b.** pivotal   **c.** ultimate   **d.** tangential

    30. _____

BONUS LESSONS 1–4

(pages 1–18, 21–26)

Use the clues to complete the crossword puzzle.

```
          ¹C                    ²E
³A D V E R S I T Y        ⁴F    X
          U              I     P
          C       ⁵R E P L I C A
⁶I N I T I A T E         K     A
          A         ⁷S O L E C I S M
     ⁸S  ⁹L U ¹⁰C K      E     N
     U     R   ¹¹I   ¹²S E
     P  ¹³E P O N Y M  ¹⁴E N D
     P     S   P  ¹⁵D  R
¹⁶F O L L O W S L  I   E
 O   E         I   P   N
 R             C   H   D
 T      ¹⁷V U L G A R T I
 U             T   H   P
 N        ¹⁸N E O L O G I S M
¹⁹V A G A R Y      N   T
 I             G   Y
 F
```

Across

3. A *plight* is a condition or situation of _____.

5. A reproduction of a work of art

6. To begin

7. "Between you and I" is an example of a(n) _____.

9. An *amulet* is thought to bring _____ when worn.

13. A person for whom something is named

14. Synonym for *terminate*

16. A *sequel* is something that _____.

17. From a Latin word meaning "common people"

18. A newly made-up word, phrase, or expression

19. A wild notion or odd fancy

Down

1. Synonym for *pivotal*

2. An *inexplicable* event cannot be _____.

4. Synonym for *capricious*

8. Antonym for *rigid*

10. In Latin *crux* means " _____."

11. To involve incriminatingly

12. The ability to make valuable discoveries by chance

15. A speech sound that consists of two vowels

16. Synonym for *providential*

BONUS LESSONS 1–4

(pages 1–18, 21–26)

Use the clues to complete the crossword puzzle.

Across

3. A *plight* is a condition or situation of _____.

5. A reproduction of a work of art

6. To begin

7. "Between you and I" is an example of a(n) _____.

9. An *amulet* is thought to bring _____ when worn.

13. A person for whom something is named

14. Synonym for *terminate*

16. A *sequel* is something that _____.

17. From a Latin word meaning "common people"

18. A newly made-up word, phrase, or expression

19. A wild notion or odd fancy

Down

1. Synonym for *pivotal*

2. An *inexplicable* event cannot be _____.

4. Synonym for *capricious*

8. Antonym for *rigid*

10. In Latin *crux* means " _____."

11. To involve incriminatingly

12. The ability to make valuable discoveries by chance

15. A speech sound that consists of two vowels

16. Synonym for *providential*

TEST LESSONS 4, 5, AND 6

(pages 21–38)

PART A COMPLETING THE DEFINITION

On the answer line, write the letter of the word or phrase that correctly completes each sentence.

1. When two nations reach an *accord*, they _____.
   a. come to an agreement   c. discuss an issue
   b. reach a stalemate   d. write regulations

   1. _____ a _____

2. When you *explicate* a poem, you _____ it.
   a. memorize   b. explain   c. retain   d. discredit

   2. _____ b _____

3. A father who *rebukes* his son for insolence _____ him.
   a. threatens   b. praises   c. reprimands   d. ignores

   3. _____ c _____

4. Young children generally have *supple* joints that are _____.
   a. stiff   b. uncoordinated   c. small   d. limber

   4. _____ d _____

5. A person convicted of *complicity* in a crime is found to be _____.
   a. involved in wrongdoing   c. pretending ignorance
   b. innocent   d. wrongly accused

   5. _____ a _____

6. A person who *deprecates* his or her own work _____ its merit.
   a. praises   b. overestimates   c. believes in   d. belittles

   6. _____ d _____

7. A *vitriolic* verbal attack is _____.
   a. mild   b. humorous   c. harsh   d. unnecessary

   7. _____ c _____

8. When you choose something of your own *volition*, you select it _____.
   a. honestly   b. accidentally   c. voluntarily   d. unnecessarily

   8. _____ c _____

9. In order to *propitiate* a friend, you would attempt to _____ him or her.
   a. escape from   b. argue with   c. persuade   d. soothe

   9. _____ d _____

10. A *tractable* dog is one that is easily _____.
    a. excited   b. tricked   c. managed   d. angered

    10. _____ c _____

11. A *replica* of a valuable piece of jewelry is _____.
    a. impressive   b. a reproduction   c. worthless   d. an original

    11. _____ b _____

12. A group that is *ostracized* is made to feel _____.
    a. excluded   b. welcome   c. afraid   d. guilty

    12. _____ a _____

13. An *accommodating* host attempts to be _____.
    a. obliging   b. friendly   c. generous   d. wise

    13. _____ a _____

14. *Aspersions* regarding a person's integrity are _____.
    a. damaging statements   c. unkind remarks
    b. high praise   d. true evaluations

    14. _____ a _____

15. When military troops are *deployed*, they are _____.
    a. sent home   c. furloughed
    b. in combat   d. stationed systematically

    15. _____ d _____

TEST LESSONS 4, 5, AND 6

(pages 21–38)

PART A COMPLETING THE DEFINITION

On the answer line, write the letter of the word or phrase that correctly completes each sentence.

1. When two nations reach an *accord*, they _____.
   a. come to an agreement   c. discuss an issue
   b. reach a stalemate   d. write regulations

   1. _____

2. When you *explicate* a poem, you _____ it.
   a. memorize   b. explain   c. retain   d. discredit

   2. _____

3. A father who *rebukes* his son for insolence _____ him.
   a. threatens   b. praises   c. reprimands   d. ignores

   3. _____

4. Young children generally have *supple* joints that are _____.
   a. stiff   b. uncoordinated   c. small   d. limber

   4. _____

5. A person convicted of *complicity* in a crime is found to be _____.
   a. involved in wrongdoing   c. pretending ignorance
   b. innocent   d. wrongly accused

   5. _____

6. A person who *deprecates* his or her own work _____ its merit.
   a. praises   b. overestimates   c. believes in   d. belittles

   6. _____

7. A *vitriolic* verbal attack is _____.
   a. mild   b. humorous   c. harsh   d. unnecessary

   7. _____

8. When you choose something of your own *volition*, you select it _____.
   a. honestly   b. accidentally   c. voluntarily   d. unnecessarily

   8. _____

9. In order to *propitiate* a friend, you would attempt to _____ him or her.
   a. escape from   b. argue with   c. persuade   d. soothe

   9. _____

10. A *tractable* dog is one that is easily _____.
    a. excited   b. tricked   c. managed   d. angered

    10. _____

11. A *replica* of a valuable piece of jewelry is _____.
    a. impressive   b. a reproduction   c. worthless   d. an original

    11. _____

12. A group that is *ostracized* is made to feel _____.
    a. excluded   b. welcome   c. afraid   d. guilty

    12. _____

13. An *accommodating* host attempts to be _____.
    a. obliging   b. friendly   c. generous   d. wise

    13. _____

14. *Aspersions* regarding a person's integrity are _____.
    a. damaging statements   c. unkind remarks
    b. high praise   d. true evaluations

    14. _____

15. When military troops are *deployed*, they are _____.
    a. sent home   c. furloughed
    b. in combat   d. stationed systematically

    15. _____

TEST LESSONS 4, 5, AND 6

PART B CHOOSING THE BEST WORD

On the answer line, write the letter of the word that best expresses the meaning of the italicized word or phrase.

16. The *spirit of good will* between Carl and Jack dissipated when they competed for the same position on the soccer team.
    a. complicity **b.** willfulness **c.** compliance **d.** camaraderie

16. _____ d

17. The colonists would not *consent passively to* unfair taxes.
    a. deride **b.** spurn **c.** deploy **d.** acquiesce to

17. _____ d

18. The ambassador's placement of blame for the incident was *clearly implied*.
    a. implicit **b.** adamant **c.** inexplicable **d.** execrable

18. _____ a

19. The documentary was about the *adverse situation* of homeless people.
    a. ostracism **b.** plight **c.** aspersion **d.** vituperation

19. _____ b

20. Police were unable to *involve* the dark-haired woman in the robbery.
    a. implicate **b.** replicate **c.** deprecate **d.** accommodate

20. _____ a

21. Terry's mother remained *inflexible* in her decision that he could not try out for the skydiving team.
    a. tractable **b.** scurrilous **c.** adamant **d.** implicit

21. _____ c

22. Grandfather firmly believes that hard work discourages *unreasonable stubbornness* in children.
    a. volition **b.** vituperation **c.** willfulness **d.** camaraderie

22. _____ c

23. The runner *disdainfully refused* help at the finish line.
    a. propitiated **b.** spurned **c.** acquiesced to **d.** derided

23. _____ b

24. Falstaff, a Shakespearean character, is somewhat *foul mouthed*.
    a. scurrilous **b.** inexplicable **c.** implicit **d.** vitriolic

24. _____ a

25. *The process of yielding to* environmental regulations required the company to add filters to the factory's smokestack.
    a. Camaraderie with **c.** Willfulness toward
    b. Vituperation toward **d.** Compliance with

25. _____ d

26. Although Wally *scoffs at* Jenny's drawings, he is secretly envious of her artistic talent.
    a. spurns **b.** implicates **c.** rebukes **d.** derides

26. _____ d

27. The novelist described the *detestable* living conditions in prisons.
    a. scurrilous **b.** inexplicable **c.** adamant **d.** execrable

27. _____ d

28. *Sustained, bitter condemnation* will not earn a person friends.
    a. Vituperation **c.** Willfulness
    b. Acquiescence **d.** Compliance

28. _____ a

29. Wanda could not *duplicate* the famous chef's casserole.
    a. explicate **b.** accommodate **c.** propitiate **d.** replicate

29. _____ d

30. Much of brain physiology is *incapable of being explained*.
    a. implicit **b.** inexplicable **c.** tractable **d.** scurrilous

30. _____ b

TEST LESSONS 4, 5, AND 6

PART B CHOOSING THE BEST WORD

On the answer line, write the letter of the word that best expresses the meaning of the italicized word or phrase.

16. The *spirit of good will* between Carl and Jack dissipated when they competed for the same position on the soccer team.
    a. complicity   **b.** willfulness   **c.** compliance   **d.** camaraderie

16. _____

17. The colonists would not *consent passively to* unfair taxes.
    a. deride   **b.** spurn   **c.** deploy   **d.** acquiesce to

17. _____

18. The ambassador's placement of blame for the incident was *clearly implied*.
    a. implicit   **b.** adamant   **c.** inexplicable   **d.** execrable

18. _____

19. The documentary was about the *adverse situation* of homeless people.
    a. ostracism   **b.** plight   **c.** aspersion   **d.** vituperation

19. _____

20. Police were unable to *involve* the dark-haired woman in the robbery.
    a. implicate   **b.** replicate   **c.** deprecate   **d.** accommodate

20. _____

21. Terry's mother remained *inflexible* in her decision that he could not try out for the skydiving team.
    a. tractable   **b.** scurrilous   **c.** adamant   **d.** implicit

21. _____

22. Grandfather firmly believes that hard work discourages *unreasonable stubbornness* in children.
    a. volition   **b.** vituperation   **c.** willfulness   **d.** camaraderie

22. _____

23. The runner *disdainfully refused* help at the finish line.
    a. propitiated   **b.** spurned   **c.** acquiesced to   **d.** derided

23. _____

24. Falstaff, a Shakespearean character, is somewhat *foul mouthed*.
    a. scurrilous   **b.** inexplicable   **c.** implicit   **d.** vitriolic

24. _____

25. *The process of yielding to* environmental regulations required the company to add filters to the factory's smokestack.
    a. Camaraderie with   **c.** Willfulness toward
    b. Vituperation toward   **d.** Compliance with

25. _____

26. Although Wally *scoffs at* Jenny's drawings, he is secretly envious of her artistic talent.
    a. spurns   **b.** implicates   **c.** rebukes   **d.** derides

26. _____

27. The novelist described the *detestable* living conditions in prisons.
    a. scurrilous   **b.** inexplicable   **c.** adamant   **d.** execrable

27. _____

28. *Sustained, bitter condemnation* will not earn a person friends.
    a. Vituperation   **c.** Willfulness
    b. Acquiescence   **d.** Compliance

28. _____

29. Wanda could not *duplicate* the famous chef's casserole.
    a. explicate   **b.** accommodate   **c.** propitiate   **d.** replicate

29. _____

30. Much of brain physiology is *incapable of being explained*.
    a. implicit   **b.** inexplicable   **c.** tractable   **d.** scurrilous

30. _____

BONUS LESSONS 5–8

(pages 27–32, 41–53)

Use the following clues to identify the words, and write the words on the lines to the right. Then circle each word in the word-search box below. The words may overlap and may read in any direction.

1. To banish or exclude from a group   (9 letters)

2. Synonym for *accord*   (7 letters)

3. Awkward or clumsy   (5 letters)

4. To *spurn* is to _____ disdainfully.   (6 letters)

5. Synonym for *circumspect*   (7 letters)

6. Supremely accomplished or skilled   (10 letters)

7. An innate inclination   (10 letters)

8. Attended by favorable circumstances   (10 letters)

9. Antonym for *properly qualified*   (11 letters)

10. A *spectrum* is a broad _____ of related qualities or ideas.   (5 letters)

11. To *acquiesce* is to consent without _____.   (7 letters)

12. Synonym for *vituperation*   (5 letters)

13. A spirit of loyalty, trust, and good will among friends   (11 letters)

14. *Execrable* food would be _____.   (8 letters)

15. Synonym for *despicable*   (4 letters)

1. **ostracize**
2. **harmony**
3. **inept**
4. **reject**
5. **prudent**
6. **consummate**
7. **propensity**
8. **auspicious**
9. **incompetent**
10. **range**
11. **protest**
12. **blame**
13. **camaraderie**
14. **inferior**
15. **vile**

```
O T E R T I N F E R P E T C O S C A R
S R J C T C E J E R O I R E F N I O T
E Z I C A R T S O F V S E O L V T I O
O E L O C E O P I N S T T E O R A H N
S A V L I N E P T I N P C I R Z F A C
T C O E A N Z R I E R D E R I D E U I
J U L T S P R O T E S T P E O G T R Y
S I I I M R O E F A U V S D N Z M A N
A T T A U S P I C I O U S A E S B C O
C Y I U D M S H C O M P R R T L O N M
A N O S O A U T N A M A D A A U I S R
U O N C O N S U M M A T E M L Z M V A
S C N M E T N E D U R P E A R A B O H
P I M A R P R U N C A M A C A D A N T
```

Challenge

Locate and circle the five additional vocabulary words in the word-search box.

acuity
adamant
deride
specter
volition

BONUS LESSONS 5–8

(pages 27–32, 41–53)

Use the following clues to identify the words, and write the words on the lines to the right. Then circle each word in the word-search box below. The words may overlap and may read in any direction.

1. To banish or exclude from a group   (9 letters)

2. Synonym for *accord*   (7 letters)

3. Awkward or clumsy   (5 letters)

4. To *spurn* is to _____ disdainfully.   (6 letters)

5. Synonym for *circumspect*   (7 letters)

6. Supremely accomplished or skilled   (10 letters)

7. An innate inclination   (10 letters)

8. Attended by favorable circumstances   (10 letters)

9. Antonym for *properly qualified*   (11 letters)

10. A *spectrum* is a broad _____ of related qualities or ideas.   (5 letters)

11. To *acquiesce* is to consent without _____.   (7 letters)

12. Synonym for *vituperation*   (5 letters)

13. A spirit of loyalty, trust, and good will among friends   (11 letters)

14. *Execrable* food would be _____.   (8 letters)

15. Synonym for *despicable*   (4 letters)

1. _____

2. _____

3. _____

4. _____

5. _____

6. _____

7. _____

8. _____

9. _____

10. _____

11. _____

12. _____

13. _____

14. _____

15. _____

```
O T E R T I N F E R P E T C O S C A R
S R J C T C E J E R O I R E F N I O T
E Z I C A R T S O F V S E O L V T I O
O E L O C E O P I N S T T E O R A H N
S A V L I N E P T I N P C I R Z F A C
T C O E A N Z R I E R D E R I D E U I
J U L T S P R O T E S T P E O G T R Y
S I I I M R O E F A U V S D N Z M A N
A T T A U S P I C I O U S A E S B C O
C Y I U D M S H C O M P R R T L O N M
A N O S O A U T N A M A D A A U I S R
U O N C O N S U M M A T E M L Z M V A
S C N M E T N E D U R P E A R A B O H
P I M A R P R U N C A M A C A D A N T
```

Challenge

Locate and circle the five additional vocabulary words in the word-search box.

TEST LESSONS 7, 8, AND 9

(pages 41–58)

PART A MATCHING WORDS AND DEFINITIONS

Match the definition of Column B with the word in Column A. Write the letter of the correct definition on the answer line.

Column A

1. specious
2. enjoin
3. specter
4. endowment
5. blandishment
6. spectrum
7. injunction
8. introspective
9. cajole
10. auspicious
11. perspicuity
12. propensity
13. exigent
14. auspices
15. beseech

Column B

a. to coax gently and persistently

b. attended by favorable circumstances

c. a broad sequence or range of related ideas, qualities, or activities

d. the act of coaxing by flattery

e. an apparition; a threatening possibility

f. a natural gift or quality; funds donated as a source of income for an institution or individual

g. an innate inclination; tendency

h. the quality of being clearly expressed and easily understood; the ability to perceive keenly

i. requiring immediate attention; demanding a great deal

j. to address an earnest or urgent request to

k. given to self-examination

l. having the appearance of truth but actually false

m. a command, directive, or order

n. protection or support; a portent or omen

o. to direct with authority; prohibit or forbid

1. ____l____
2. ____o____
3. ____e____
4. ____f____
5. ____d____
6. ____c____
7. ____m____
8. ____k____
9. ____a____
10. ____b____
11. ____h____
12. ____g____
13. ____l____
14. ____n____
15. ____j____

TEST LESSONS 7, 8, AND 9

(pages 41–58)

PART A MATCHING WORDS AND DEFINITIONS

Match the definition of Column B with the word in Column A. Write the letter of the correct definition on the answer line.

Column A

1. specious
2. enjoin
3. specter
4. endowment
5. blandishment
6. spectrum
7. injunction
8. introspective
9. cajole
10. auspicious
11. perspicuity
12. propensity
13. exigent
14. auspices
15. beseech

Column B

a. to coax gently and persistently

b. attended by favorable circumstances

c. a broad sequence or range of related ideas, qualities, or activities

d. the act of coaxing by flattery

e. an apparition; a threatening possibility

f. a natural gift or quality; funds donated as a source of income for an institution or individual

g. an innate inclination; tendency

h. the quality of being clearly expressed and easily understood; the ability to perceive keenly

i. requiring immediate attention; demanding a great deal

j. to address an earnest or urgent request to

k. given to self-examination

l. having the appearance of truth but actually false

m. a command, directive, or order

n. protection or support; a portent or omen

o. to direct with authority; prohibit or forbid

1. _____
2. _____
3. _____
4. _____
5. _____
6. _____
7. _____
8. _____
9. _____
10. _____
11. _____
12. _____
13. _____
14. _____
15. _____

TEST LESSONS 7, 8, AND 9

PART B IDENTIFYING ANTONYMS

On the answer line, write the letter of the word or phrase that has the meaning that is opposite to that of the capitalized word.

16. CIRCUMSPECT:
    a. noisy   b. careless   c. outgoing   d. linear

16. _____ b _____

17. MENDICANT:
    a. philanthropist   b. liar   c. tax collector   d. aristocrat

17. _____ a _____

18. FACILE:
    a. luxuriant   b. serious   c. singular   d. laborious

18. _____ d _____

19. INEPT:
    a. smooth   b. competent   c. correct   d. clever

19. _____ b _____

20. DESPICABLE:
    a. pleasant   b. sanitary   c. noble   d. popular

20. _____ c _____

21. ELICIT:
    a. plead   b. arrest   c. demand   d. withdraw

21. _____ d _____

22. CUNNING:
    a. deceptive   b. guileless   c. absurd   d. darling

22. _____ b _____

23. QUERY:
    a. request   b. response   c. regret   d. announcement

23. _____ b _____

24. PROSPECTIVE:
    a. unlikely   b. unintended   c. unplanned   d. undesirable

24. _____ a _____

25. IMPREIOUS:
    a. meek   b. commanding   c. dangerous   d. haughty

25. _____ a _____

26. INCOMPETENT:
    a. untrained   b. attractive   c. valuable   d. capable

26. _____ d _____

27. DEFT:
    a. with acute hearing   c. intelligent
    b. awkward   d. slow-witted

27. _____ b _____

28. CONSUMMATE:
    a. terse   b. deficient   c. unreasonable   d. delicious

28. _____ b _____

29. PROFICIENT:
    a. skilled   b. abundant   c. maladroit   d. insufficient

29. _____ c _____

30. ACUITY:
    a. dullness   b. falsehood   c. correction   d. sharpness

30. _____ a _____

TEST LESSONS 7, 8, AND 9

PART B IDENTIFYING ANTONYMS

On the answer line, write the letter of the word or phrase that has the meaning that is opposite to that of the capitalized word.

16. CIRCUMSPECT:
    a. noisy **b.** careless **c.** outgoing **d.** linear

16. _____

17. MENDICANT:
    a. philanthropist **b.** liar **c.** tax collector **d.** aristocrat

17. _____

18. FACILE:
    a. luxuriant **b.** serious **c.** singular **d.** laborious

18. _____

19. INEPT:
    a. smooth **b.** competent **c.** correct **d.** clever

19. _____

20. DESPICABLE:
    a. pleasant **b.** sanitary **c.** noble **d.** popular

20. _____

21. ELICIT:
    a. plead **b.** arrest **c.** demand **d.** withdraw

21. _____

22. CUNNING:
    a. deceptive **b.** guileless **c.** absurd **d.** darling

22. _____

23. QUERY:
    a. request **b.** response **c.** regret **d.** announcement

23. _____

24. PROSPECTIVE:
    a. unlikely **b.** unintended **c.** unplanned **d.** undesirable

24. _____

25. IMPREIOUS:
    a. meek **b.** commanding **c.** dangerous **d.** haughty

25. _____

26. INCOMPETENT:
    a. untrained **b.** attractive **c.** valuable **d.** capable

26. _____

27. DEFT:
    a. with acute hearing **c.** intelligent
    b. awkward **d.** slow-witted

27. _____

28. CONSUMMATE:
    a. terse **b.** deficient **c.** unreasonable **d.** delicious

28. _____

29. PROFICIENT:
    a. skilled **b.** abundant **c.** maladroit **d.** insufficient

29. _____

30. ACUITY:
    a. dullness **b.** falsehood **c.** correction **d.** sharpness

30. _____

VERBAL APTITUDE TEST I

For each question in this section, choose the best answer and blacken the corresponding space on the answer sheet.

PART A ANTONYMS

Each question below consists of a word in capital letters, followed by five lettered words or phrases. Choose the word or phrase that is most nearly <u>opposite</u> in meaning to the word in capital letters. Since some of the questions require you to distinguish fine shades of meaning, consider all the choices before deciding which is best.

EXAMPLE:

GOOD :   (A) sour   (B) bad   (C) red
(D) hot   (E) ugly

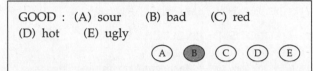

1. CONTEMPT: (A) resignation   (B) restraint
   (C) frivolity   (D) admiration   (E) tolerance

2. REBUKE: (A) solicit   (B) entrust
   (C) commend   (D) wheedle   (E) concede

3. FABRICATE: (A) replicate   (B) confess
   (C) raze   (D) deprive   (E) refrain

4. INTEGRITY: (A) notoriety   (B) deception
   (C) irony   (D) discontinuity   (E) dismay

5. RAMPANT: (A) substantive   (B) execrable
   (C) decrepit   (D) constrained   (E) lenient

6. FETID: (A) mournful   (B) blithe   (C) savory
   (D) rigorous   (E) askew

7. IMPERIOUS: (A) submissive   (B) refined
   (C) oligarchic   (D) liberal   (E) savage

8. ERSTWHILE: (A) prospective   (B) virtuous
   (C) concomitant   (D) supreme
   (E) deferential

9. PLAUDIT: (A) remedy   (B) solecism
   (C) reprieve   (D) prohibition   (E) invective

10. INTRANSIGENT: (A) complaisant   (B) manic
    (C) transcendent   (D) lusty   (E) vehement

PART B SENTENCE COMPLETIONS

Each sentence below has one or two blanks, each blank indicating that something has been omitted. Beneath the sentence are five lettered words or sets of words. Choose the word or set of words that <u>best</u> fits the meaning of the sentence as a whole.

EXAMPLE:

Although its publicity has been - - - - , the film itself is intelligent, well-acted, handsomely produced, and altogether - - - - .
(A) tasteless .. respectable
(B) extensive .. moderate
(C) sophisticated .. amateur
(D) risqué .. crude   (E) perfect .. spectacular

(A) (B) (C) (D) (E)

11. The new research facility, charged with scrutinizing the effects of brain hormones on memory, is a(n) - - - - of the National Institutes of Health.
    (A) reckoning   (B) auxiliary
    (C) accomplice   (D) imperative
    (E) retort

12. Although the leaders of the Allies all publicly - - - - Woodrow Wilson's Fourteen Points, many privately expressed their - - - - them.
    (A) ridiculed .. misgivings about
    (B) endorsed .. approbation of
    (C) sanctioned .. reservations about
    (D) denounced .. distress over
    (E) conceded to .. resignation to

13. Samuel Yellin, whose handmade wrought-iron designs - - - - many of the grandest buildings in the United States, was an early twentieth-century - - - - of mass production.
    (A) embellish .. adversary
    (B) elicit .. initiator
    (C) incise .. proponent
    (D) occupy .. enemy
    (E) nullify .. agent

14. A coalition of environmental groups - - - - lawmakers to impose stringent penalties for the illegal dumping of toxic waste materials.
    (A) enjoined   (B) assessed   (C) extricated
    (D) convened   (E) rebuffed

15. Because she has tact, intelligence, and shrewdness, the new ambassador possesses all the qualities of the - - - - diplomat.
    (A) officious   (B) warranted
    (C) quintessential   (D) indolent
    (E) spurious

16. Although some sociologists maintain that the actions of many criminal offenders are determined by environmental factors, other researchers argue that these offenders act on their own - - - - .
    (A) malice   (B) recognizance   (C) complicity
    (D) volition   (E) ignorance

17. - - - - their failure to rescue the old market from rapacious developers, members of the conservation society are working energetically to preserve other landmarks.
    (A) Demoralized by
    (B) Adamant about
    (C) Aggravated by
    (D) Consoled by
    (E) Undaunted by

18. Although both candidates had a - - - - understanding of the issues, Ms. Henrie ultimately won the debate because of the - - - - with which she argued her position.
    (A) negligible .. reticence
    (B) biased .. expertise
    (C) comprehensive .. articulateness
    (D) superfluous .. loquacity
    (E) vehement .. vagueness

19. Marcus Aurelius, Roman emperor and philosopher, is said to have been rather - - - - , but scholars maintain that ancient Romans were not generally - - - - to such reflectiveness.
    (A) intellectual .. adverse
    (B) recondite .. amendable
    (C) insubordinate .. inclined
    (D) genteel .. inspired
    (E) introspective .. prone

20. The thief gained entrance to the exclusive jewelry exhibit by - - - - a police officer's badge and thoroughly - - - - the guard at the door.
    (A) brandishing .. intimidating
    (B) rendering .. vanquishing
    (C) impugning .. mystifying
    (D) offering .. mollifying
    (E) purloining .. provoking

PART C ANALOGIES

Each question below consists of a related pair of words or phrases, followed by five lettered pairs of words or phrases. Select the lettered pair that best expresses a relationship similar to that expressed in the original pair.

EXAMPLE:

YAWN : BOREDOM ::   (A) dream : sleep
(B) anger : madness   (C) smile : amusement
(D) face : expression   (E) impatience : rebellion

(A) (B) (C) (D) (E)

21. PROVIDE : FURNISH ::
    (A) cultivate : reap   (B) accept : eliminate
    (C) choose : select   (D) converge : diverge
    (E) exonerate : implicate

22. PATRIOTISM : JINGOISM ::
    (A) abhorrence : dislike
    (B) diplomacy : Machiavellianism
    (C) jubilation : melancholy
    (D) nourishment : sustenance
    (E) parsimony : lavishness

23. VALEDICTORY : COMMENCEMENT ::
    (A) election : inauguration
    (B) conviviality : festivity
    (C) arraignment : incarceration
    (D) symphony : concerto
    (E) eulogy : funeral

24. CULPABLE : RIGHTEOUS ::
    (A) concise : obscure
    (B) conventional : prevailing
    (C) ponderous : inert
    (D) incessant : sporadic
    (E) dolorous : mournful

25. CRUCIBLE : MELT ::
    (A) awl : perforate   (B) bellows : compress
    (C) scissors : suture   (D) socket : bolt
    (E) dolly : excavate

26. THESPIAN : HISTRIONIC ::
    (A) terpsichorean : graceful
    (B) eccentric : deviant
    (C) entrepreneur : capricious
    (D) connoisseur : sanctimonious
    (E) diva : corpulent

27. BURNISH : PATINA ::
(A) rust : oxidation
(B) revoke : privilege
(C) coalesce : aggregate
(D) debilitate : health
(E) desiccate : coruscation

28. CONDESCEND : DEIGN ::
(A) propitiate : regenerate
(B) obliterate : expunge
(C) espouse : foment
(D) parody : flout
(E) inure : scourge

29. PIQUE : ENRAGE ::
(A) exculpate : stigmatize
(B) wane : dilate
(C) assuage : pacify
(D) admire : esteem
(E) devour : nibble

30. ITINERANT : PERMANENT ::
(A) mercurial : restive
(B) avaricious : prodigal
(C) tractable : docile
(D) cogent : relevant
(E) salubrious : benign

PART D READING COMPREHENSION

Each passage below is followed by questions based on its content. Answer all questions following a passage on the basis of what is <u>stated</u> or <u>implied</u> in that passage.

In pursuing a strategy of planned obsolescence, marketers have three choices: they can make the product obsolete in materials, function, or style.

Planned material obsolescence is the strategy of deliberately changing a product's materials and components to those that are subject to breakage, wear, and corrosion, causing the product to wear out more quickly. It sometimes is charged that manufacturers deliberately design products to deteriorate quickly. For example, when drapery manufacturers started using a higher percentage of rayon in their fabrics, they were accused of doing so because rayon blends cannot survive as many cleanings. The manufacturers, however, pointed out that rayon reduces the price of fabric and also increases its holding power. . . . Although inferior materials sometimes are used to achieve a trade-off in product benefits, they are also used simply to reduce production costs. But when materials offer few, if any, compensating benefits in performance characteristics and when the price of the product is not reduced, then the strategy of planned material obsolescence is subject to attack.

Planned functional obsolescence is the policy of staggering or withholding the introduction of new products in order to encourage replacements of existing products. For example, American Telephone & Telegraph has been accused of withholding new telephone technology, and a widespread rumor has persisted for years that automobile manufacturers have withheld carburetors that could increase a car's mileage. This is highly unlikely, of course. Manufacturers may not put all the latest technology and potential features into a product because of the costs of making current products and production capacities obsolete. . . . Like anyone else, marketing managers must adopt new technology at an opportune time—when it is practical and worthwhile to do so. The trick is to identify that time before competitors do.

Planned style obsolescence is the strategy of changing consumers' concepts of what an acceptable product looks like, thus creating dissatisfaction with existing products. The manufacturers of clothing, automobiles, furniture, and appliances use this strategy extensively. Planned style obsolescence is associated particularly with women's clothing, for each new season introduces styles, colors, fabrics, and accessories that threaten to make entire wardrobes obsolete.

Questions abound concerning style obsolescence. Do industry leaders get together and decide to produce a new style in order to make current inventories obsolete? Or does a new style reflect the decisions of a single leading designer, who, as a competitive strategy, offers something new that will become fashionable? Are style changes thrust on consumers, or do consumers demand the changes? Do people buy products like clothing and furnishings simply to serve a function, or must such products also give consumers an opportunity to express themselves?

There are arguments on both sides of such questions. Some propose that new styles catch on and become fashionable only because style is intrinsic to a product's ability to satisfy consumers. . . . Yet there is no doubt that fewer and less frequent style changes would have a positive effect on marketers' ability to conserve demand for their products.

31. Which of the following titles best represents the content of the passage?
(A) The Causes of Material Obsolescence
(B) How Planned Obsolescence Benefits Consumers
(C) The Controversy of Planned Style Obsolescence
(D) Types of Planned Obsolescence
(E) Why Products Deteriorate

32. Which of the following is not suggested as a reason for pursuing a strategy of planned obsolescence?
  (A) A desire to make materials less durable so that they must be replaced more frequently
  (B) A desire to appeal to the vagaries of consumer taste for new colors and styles
  (C) A desire to make the latest technology available immediately to consumers
  (D) A propensity to reduce the costs of manufacturing a product
  (E) An inclination to influence consumers to replace old products with new ones

33. All of the following statements can be inferred from the passage except
  (A) keen evaluation of market trends and careful appraisal of competitors are pivotal to decisions about introducing new products.
  (B) charges that manufacturers use shoddy materials to promote obsolescence are always invalid.
  (C) constant changes in acceptable styles hamper a marketer's ability to maintain demand for a product.
  (D) some consumers suspect complicity on the part of fashion designers who regularly alter styles.
  (E) consumers initially were reluctant to use draperies made of rayon.

34. Which of the following products might the author have offered as an example of planned functional obsolescence?
  (A) The Edsel automobile
  (B) The miniskirt
  (C) Software compatible with only recently introduced computer systems
  (D) Disposable diapers
  (E) Cordless telephones

During World War II, while the U.S. Army Air Force was trying to bomb Pacific islands belonging to Japan, the pilots inadvertently made a discovery that was to prove of immense importance to the science of meteorology. Many of the planes encountered winds blowing from West to East; winds so strong that they retarded the flight of the craft heading West. . . .

Their discovery of these fierce winds at heights of about 10 km (6 mi) led meteorologists to investigate the winds, now known as the jet stream. Jet streams are usually concentrated in the middle latitudes and form part of the westerlies. There are several jet streams that meander across the Earth in a girdling band. One of the primary ones is the polar-front jet stream, which is found in the middle latitudes along the polar front where polar and tropical air meet. . . . The other major jet stream, which dominates in Asia especially, is the sub-tropical jet stream, between about 20° and 30° latitudes.

During the war, Japanese scientists devised a plan that utilized the jet stream. . . . In 1944, they released 10,000 balloons carrying incendiary bombs, hoping that the baloons would be carried to their targets [on the U.S. mainland] by the jet stream. . . . Fortunately only about 10% of the balloons survived the meanderings of the jet stream, and the ones that lasted the course did little damage when they finally did make it to the ground. With wartime censorship in force, no U.S. newspapers carried the story. The Japanese heard nothing about the bombing, thought it was a failure, and did not follow up with any others.

35. The author's main purpose in the passage is to
  (A) give examples of wartime strategies.
  (B) explain the influence of the jet stream on aerodynamics.
  (C) describe the movements of the jet stream.
  (D) praise the efforts of Air Force pilots who discovered the jet stream.
  (E) give an overview of the discovery of the jet stream.

36. Which of the following conclusions cannot be inferred from the passage?
  I The need to protect national security limited the news media's access to information during the war.
  II Japanese meteorologists were not as up-to-date as their American counterparts.
  III The discovery of the jet stream was serendipitous.
  IV The jet stream causes certain weather patterns to develop.
  V Jets flying east to west make better time than those making up an equivalent trip in the opposite directions.
  (A) I, II, and II
  (B) II, III, and IV
  (C) III, IV, and V
  (D) II, IV, and V
  (E) I, III, and V

If you finish before time is called, check your work on this test.

VERBAL APTITUDE TEST I

Answer Sheet

Use a No. 2 pencil for completing this answer sheet. Make sure that your marks are dark and completely fill the space. Erase any errors or stray marks. If a test has fewer than 50 questions, leave the extra answer spaces blank.

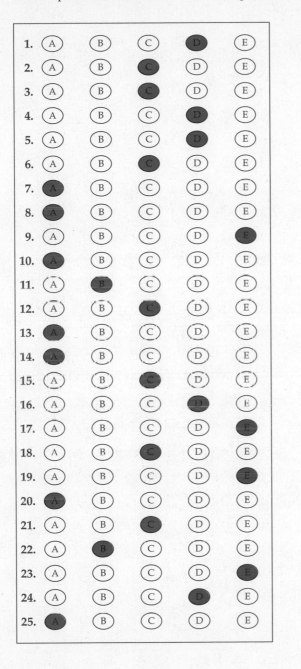

Answer Sheet

Use a No. 2 pencil for completing this answer sheet. Make sure that your marks are dark and completely fill the space. Erase any errors or stray marks. If a test has fewer than 50 questions, leave the extra answer spaces blank.

1.	A	B	C	D	E		26.	A	B	C	D	E
2.	A	B	C	D	E		27.	A	B	C	D	E
3.	A	B	C	D	E		28.	A	B	C	D	E
4.	A	B	C	D	E		29.	A	B	C	D	E
5.	A	B	C	D	E		30.	A	B	C	D	E
6.	A	B	C	D	E		31.	A	B	C	D	E
7.	A	B	C	D	E		32.	A	B	C	D	E
8.	A	B	C	D	E		33.	A	B	C	D	E
9.	A	B	C	D	E		34.	A	B	C	D	E
10.	A	B	C	D	E		35.	A	B	C	D	E
11.	A	B	C	D	E		36.	A	B	C	D	E
12.	A	B	C	D	E		37.	A	B	C	D	E
13.	A	B	C	D	E		38.	A	B	C	D	E
14.	A	B	C	D	E		39.	A	B	C	D	E
15.	A	B	C	D	E		40.	A	B	C	D	E
16.	A	B	C	D	E		41.	A	B	C	D	E
17.	A	B	C	D	E		42.	A	B	C	D	E
18.	A	B	C	D	E		43.	A	B	C	D	E
19.	A	B	C	D	E		44.	A	B	C	D	E
20.	A	B	C	D	E		45.	A	B	C	D	E
21.	A	B	C	D	E		46.	A	B	C	D	E
22.	A	B	C	D	E		47.	A	B	C	D	E
23.	A	B	C	D	E		48.	A	B	C	D	E
24.	A	B	C	D	E		49.	A	B	C	D	E
25.	A	B	C	D	E		50.	A	B	C	D	E

NAME ______________________________ DATE ______________

BONUS LESSONS 9–12

(pages 53–58, 61–78)

Use the clues to complete the crossword puzzle.

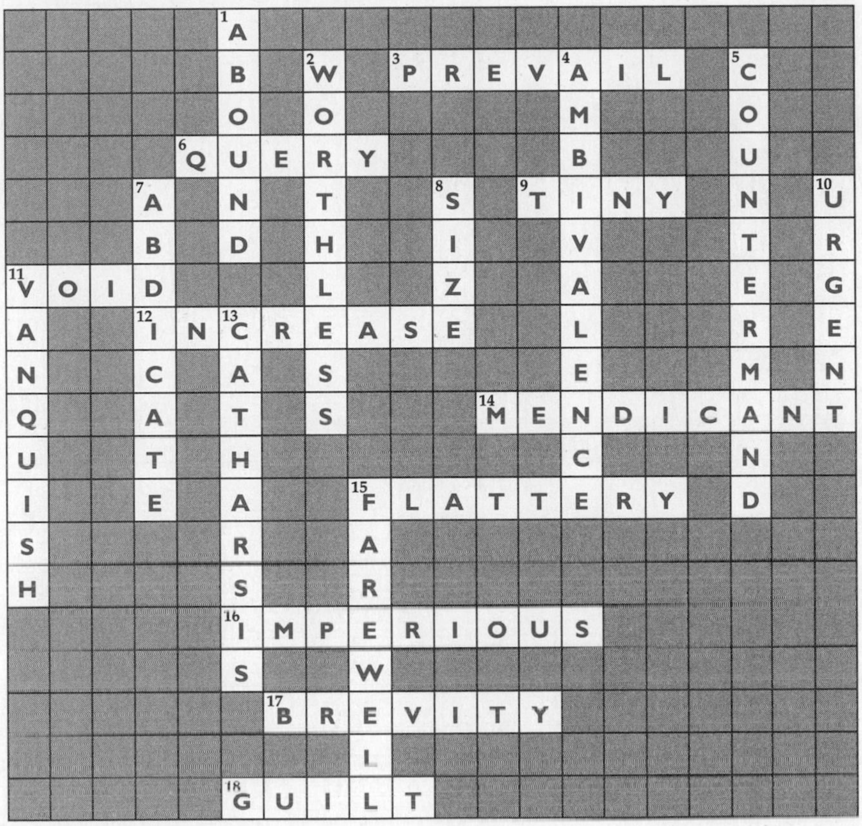

3 PREVAIL
6 QUERY
9 TINY
11 VOID
12 INCREASE
14 MENDICANT
15 FLATTERY
16 IMPERIOUS
17 BREVITY
18 GUILT
1 ABOUND
2 WORTHLESS
4 AMBIVALENCE
5 COUNTERMAND
7 ABDICATE
8 SIZE
10 URGENT
11 VANQUISH
13 CATHARSIS
15 FAREWELL

Across

3. To be greater in strength or influence
6. Antonym for answer
9. An *infinitesimal* amount is immeasurably ______.
11. To *rescind* is to make ______.
12. Synonym for *augment*
14. Another word for a beggar
15. A *blandishment* involves coaxing by ______.
16. Arrogantly domineering
17. Concise expression
18. To *absolve* is to pronounce clear of ______.

Down

1. To be great in number or amount
2. Synonym for the adjective *invalid*
4. The simultaneous existence of conflicting feelings about a person, object, or idea
5. To cancel or reverse
7. To relinquish high office
8. *Amplitude* refers to ______.
10. Synonym for *exigent*
11. To overcome or subdue
13. From a Greek word meaning "pure"
15. A *valedictory* is a(n) ______ address.

BONUS LESSONS 9–12

(pages 53–58, 61–78)

Use the clues to complete the crossword puzzle.

Across

3. To be greater in strength or influence

6. Antonym for answer

9. An *infinitesimal* amount is immeasurably _____.

11. To *rescind* is to make _____.

12. Synonym for *augment*

14. Another word for a beggar

15. A *blandishment* involves coaxing by _____.

16. Arrogantly domineering

17. Concise expression

18. To *absolve* is to pronounce clear of _____.

Down

1. To be great in number or amount

2. Synonym for the adjective *invalid*

4. The simultaneous existence of conflicting feelings about a person, object, or idea

5. To cancel or reverse

7. To relinquish high office

8. *Amplitude* refers to _____.

10. Synonym for *exigent*

11. To overcome or subdue

13. From a Greek word meaning "pure"

15. A *valedictory* is a(n) _____ address.

TEST LESSONS 10, 11, AND 12

(pages 61–78)

PART A CHOOSING THE BEST DEFINITION

On the answer line, write the letter of the best definition of the italicized word.

1. The outgoing president of the drama club will deliver a *valedictory*.
   a. award   b. poem   c. farewell address   d. budget report

   1. ___c___

2. The airline may *abnegate* its responsibility for overbooking flights.
   a. renounce   b. increase   c. reduce   d. give away

   2. ___a___

3. Which amendment to the Constitution *rescinded* prohibition?
   a. endorsed   b. made void   c. made effective d. avoided

   3. ___b___

4. Our photography teacher gives us assignments that are *commensurate* with our abilities.
   a. dignify   b. undermine   c. correspond to   d. account for

   4. ___c___

5. Emily's outfit was chosen with only a *modicum* of good taste.
   a. shade   b. wide stroke   c. splash   d. small amount

   5. ___d___

6. The defendant *evinced* great anxiety as he awaited the verdict.
   a. overcame   b. pretended   c. disguised   d. exhibited

   6. ___d___

7. Homeowners can *recoup* closing costs by refinancing when mortgage rates drop.
   a. acquire   b. repay   c. make up for   d. exceed

   7. ___c___

8. The governments set *quotas* on the purchase of some commodities.
   a. requirements   c. regulations
   b. maximum amounts   d. restrictions

   8. ___b___

9. Galileo refused to *recant* his theory about the solar system.
   a. retract   b. explain   c. disprove   d. publish

   9. ___a___

10. Many seniors feel *ambivalence* about graduation.
    a. anxiety   c. mild regret
    b. conflicting emotions   d. excitement

    10. ___b___

11. Bill's smattering of French was of no *avail* to him when he traveled abroad.
    a. interest   b. significance   c. distraction   d. use

    11. ___d___

12. A small night light did much to *vanquish* Paul's fear of the dark.
    a. diminish   b. mock   c. overcome   d. extend

    12. ___c___

13. The student council declared all improperly marked ballots *invalid*.
    a. not in effect b. incorrect   c. legal   d. unofficial

    13. ___a___

14. The Cahills hope to *augment* the size of their farm.
    a. improve   b. protect   c. confine   d. increase

    14. ___d___

15. Gisella's scholarship partially *absolved* her parents from the responsibility to pay her college tuition.
    a. prevented   b. released   c. excluded   d. discouraged

    15. ___b___

TEST LESSONS 10, 11, AND 12

(pages 61–78)

PART A CHOOSING THE BEST DEFINITION

On the answer line, write the letter of the best definition of the italicized word.

1. The outgoing president of the drama club will deliver a *valedictory*.
   a. award   b. poem   c. farewell address   d. budget report

   1. _____

2. The airline may *abnegate* its responsibility for overbooking flights.
   a. renounce   b. increase   c. reduce   d. give away

   2. _____

3. Which amendment to the Constitution *rescinded* prohibition?
   a. endorsed   b. made void   c. made effective   d. avoided

   3. _____

4. Our photography teacher gives us assignments that are *commensurate* with our abilities.
   a. dignify   b. undermine   c. correspond to   d. account for

   4. _____

5. Emily's outfit was chosen with only a *modicum* of good taste.
   a. shade   b. wide stroke   c. splash   d. small amount

   5. _____

6. The defendant *evinced* great anxiety as he awaited the verdict.
   a. overcame   b. pretended   c. disguised   d. exhibited

   6. _____

7. Homeowners can *recoup* closing costs by refinancing when mortgage rates drop.
   a. acquire   b. repay   c. make up for   d. exceed

   7. _____

8. The governments set *quotas* on the purchase of some commodities.
   a. requirements   c. regulations
   b. maximum amounts   d. restrictions

   8. _____

9. Galileo refused to *recant* his theory about the solar system.
   a. retract   b. explain   c. disprove   d. publish

   9. _____

10. Many seniors feel *ambivalence* about graduation.
    a. anxiety   c. mild regret
    b. conflicting emotions   d. excitement

    10. _____

11. Bill's smattering of French was of no *avail* to him when he traveled abroad.
    a. interest   b. significance   c. distraction   d. use

    11. _____

12. A small night light did much to *vanquish* Paul's fear of the dark.
    a. diminish   b. mock   c. overcome   d. extend

    12. _____

13. The student council declared all improperly marked ballots *invalid*.
    a. not in effect   b. incorrect   c. legal   d. unofficial

    13. _____

14. The Cahills hope to *augment* the size of their farm.
    a. improve   b. protect   c. confine   d. increase

    14. _____

15. Gisella's scholarship partially *absolved* her parents from the responsibility to pay her college tuition.
    a. prevented   b. released   c. excluded   d. discouraged

    15. _____

TEST LESSONS 10, 11, AND 12

PART B CHOOSING THE BEST WORD

On the answer line, write the letter of the word that best expresses the meaning of the italicized word or phrase.

16. The ancient Greeks considered watching the performance of a tragedy to be a *purging of emotions.*
    a. abdication   **b.** countermand   **c.** renunciation   **d.** catharsis

16. _____ d

17. The Duke of Windsor *formally relinquished* the British throne.
    a. abdicated   **b.** waived   **c.** rescinded   **d.** recanted

17. _____ a

18. The employee whose sales are the most *impressively extensive* will win a trip to Hawaii.
    a. invaluable   **c.** commensurate
    b. infinitesimal   **d.** prodigious

18. _____ d

19. The written *appraisal* mentioned all aspects of Lee's audition.
    a. quota   **b.** valedictory   **c.** renunciation   **d.** evaluation

19. _____ d

20. Old farming methods *are the most common* in developing countries.
    a. prevail   **b.** diminish   **c.** augment   **d.** evince

20. _____ a

21. The new detector can pick up *incalculably small* amounts of radioactivity.
    a. prodigious   **b.** infinitesimal   **c.** invaluable   **d.** invalid

21. _____ b

22. When the patient's fever rose, the surgeon *reversed* her decision to operate.
    a. abnegated   **b.** waived   **c.** abdicated   **d.** countermanded

22. _____ d

23. The university *dispensed with* Spencer's freshman history requirement.
    a. rescinded   **b.** recouped   **c.** waived   **d.** countermanded

23. _____ c

24. A liter is *practically equal* to thirty-four ounces.
    a. cathartic   **b.** commensurate   **c.** equivalent   **d.** invaluable

24. _____ c

25. Siddhartha, following his *act of giving up* his wealth and social position, became a beggar.
    a. catharsis from   **c.** ambivalence toward
    b. renunciation of   **d.** abdication from

25. _____ b

26. Each drop of pond water *teems* with minute forms of life.
    a. avails   **b.** prevails   **c.** augments   **d.** abounds

26. _____ d

27. Modifying the *magnitude* of a sound wave changes its loudness.
    a. amplitude   **b.** modicum   **c.** ambivalence   **d.** brevity

27. _____ a

28. The lecturer's unenthusiastic delivery *detracted from* his message.
    a. vanquished   **b.** abnegated   **c.** diminished   **d.** absolved

28. _____ c

29. A knowledge of survival techniques is *of inestimable worth* to anyone planning to hike in the mountains.
    a. invaluable   **b.** equivalent   **c.** invalid   **d.** prodigious

29. _____ a

30. The agency produces commercials marked by humor and *terseness.*
    a. catharsis   **b.** amplitude   **c.** ambivalence   **d.** brevity

30. _____ d

TEST LESSONS 10, 11, AND 12

PART B CHOOSING THE BEST WORD

On the answer line, write the letter of the word that best expresses the meaning of the italicized word or phrase.

16. The ancient Greeks considered watching the performance of a tragedy to be a *purging of emotions.*
    a. abdication   **b.** countermand   **c.** renunciation   **d.** catharsis

16. _____

17. The Duke of Windsor *formally relinquished* the British throne.
    a. abdicated   **b.** waived   **c.** rescinded   **d.** recanted

17. _____

18. The employee whose sales are the most *impressively extensive* will win a trip to Hawaii.
    a. invaluable   **c.** commensurate
    b. infinitesimal   **d.** prodigious

18. _____

19. The written *appraisal* mentioned all aspects of Lee's audition.
    a. quota   **b.** valedictory   **c.** renunciation   **d.** evaluation

19. _____

20. Old farming methods *are the most common* in developing countries.
    a. prevail   **b.** diminish   **c.** augment   **d.** evince

20. _____

21. The new detector can pick up *incalculably small* amounts of radioactivity.
    a. prodigious   **b.** infinitesimal   **c.** invaluable   **d.** invalid

21. _____

22. When the patient's fever rose, the surgeon *reversed* her decision to operate.
    a. abnegated   **b.** waived   **c.** abdicated   **d.** countermanded

22. _____

23. The university *dispensed with* Spencer's freshman history requirement.
    a. rescinded   **b.** recouped   **c.** waived   **d.** countermanded

23. _____

24. A liter is *practically equal* to thirty-four ounces.
    a. cathartic   **b.** commensurate   **c.** equivalent   **d.** invaluable

24. _____

25. Siddhartha, following his *act of giving up* his wealth and social position, became a beggar.
    a. catharsis from   **c.** ambivalence toward
    b. renunciation of   **d.** abdication from

25. _____

26. Each drop of pond water *teems* with minute forms of life.
    a. avails   **b.** prevails   **c.** augments   **d.** abounds

26. _____

27. Modifying the *magnitude* of a sound wave changes its loudness.
    a. amplitude   **b.** modicum   **c.** ambivalence   **d.** brevity

27. _____

28. The lecturer's unenthusiastic delivery *detracted from* his message.
    a. vanquished   **b.** abnegated   **c.** diminished   **d.** absolved

28. _____

29. A knowledge of survival techniques is *of inestimable worth* to anyone planning to hike in the mountains.
    a. invaluable   **b.** equivalent   **c.** invalid   **d.** prodigious

29. _____

30. The agency produces commercials marked by humor and *terseness.*
    a. catharsis   **b.** amplitude   **c.** ambivalence   **d.** brevity

30. _____

TEST LESSONS 13, 14, AND 15

(pages 81–98)

PART A COMPLETING THE DEFINITION

On the answer line, write the letter of the definition that correctly completes each sentence.

1. An *egregious* mistake is _____ .
   a. apparently accidental   c. excusable
   b. humorous   d. outrageously bad

1. _____d_____

2. A *Machiavellian* ruler is one who governs with _____ .
   a. mercy   b. greed   c. deceit   d. ignorance

2. _____c_____

3. One who *adheres* to a particular plan of action _____ it.
   a. promotes   b. holds fast to   c. abhors   d. justifies

3. _____b_____

4. An *altercation* is also known as a _____ .
   a. postponement   b. scarcity   c. quarrel   d. contradiction

4. _____c_____

5. One who suffers an *affront* experiences a(n) _____ .
   a. lavish display   c. awkward situation
   b. intentional insult   d. social error

5. _____b_____

6. A group that is *segregated* from others has been _____ .
   a. separated   b. protected   c. disrupted   d. entrapped

6. _____a_____

7. A musical *ensemble* _____ .
   a. impedes harmony   c. demands attention
   b. requires publicity   d. performs together

7. _____d_____

8. A person who *dissimulates* _____ .
   a. hides true feelings   c. merits praise
   b. meets requirements   d. captivates others

8. _____a_____

9. An *inherent* ability is _____ .
   a. a natural characteristic   c. a learned skill
   b. an inherited talent   d. not readily seen

9. _____a_____

10. One who demands *retribution* seeks _____ .
    a. an audience   b. a refuge   c. forgiveness   d. repayment

10. _____d_____

11. An *aggregate* work force is the _____ of employees.
    a. total   b. absence   c. allowance   d. remuneration

11. _____a_____

12. *Gregarious* people are _____ .
    a. aggressive   b. deceitful   c. sociable   d. glum

12. _____c_____

13. *Bellicose* behavior is _____ .
    a. melancholy   b. warlike   c. tolerant   d. fearful

13. _____b_____

14. A *semblance* of calm is the _____ tranquility.
    a. appearance of   c. desire for
    b. reputation for   d. preservation of

14. _____a_____

15. A *contentious* person is _____ .
    a. pessimistic   b. extravagant   c. fearful   d. quarrelsome

15. _____d_____

TEST LESSONS 13, 14, AND 15

(pages 81–98)

PART A COMPLETING THE DEFINITION

On the answer line, write the letter of the definition that correctly completes each sentence.

1. An *egregious* mistake is _____.
   - **a.** apparently accidental
   - **b.** humorous
   - **c.** excusable
   - **d.** outrageously bad

   1. _____

2. A *Machiavellian* ruler is one who governs with _____.
   - **a.** mercy
   - **b.** greed
   - **c.** deceit
   - **d.** ignorance

   2. _____

3. One who *adheres* to a particular plan of action _____ it.
   - **a.** promotes
   - **b.** holds fast to
   - **c.** abhors
   - **d.** justifies

   3. _____

4. An *altercation* is also known as a _____.
   - **a.** postponement
   - **b.** scarcity
   - **c.** quarrel
   - **d.** contradiction

   4. _____

5. One who suffers an *affront* experiences a(n) _____.
   - **a.** lavish display
   - **b.** intentional insult
   - **c.** awkward situation
   - **d.** social error

   5. _____

6. A group that is *segregated* from others has been _____.
   - **a.** separated
   - **b.** protected
   - **c.** disrupted
   - **d.** entrapped

   6. _____

7. A musical *ensemble* _____.
   - **a.** impedes harmony
   - **b.** requires publicity
   - **c.** demands attention
   - **d.** performs together

   7. _____

8. A person who *dissimulates* _____.
   - **a.** hides true feelings
   - **b.** meets requirements
   - **c.** merits praise
   - **d.** captivates others

   8. _____

9. An *inherent* ability is _____.
   - **a.** a natural characteristic
   - **b.** an inherited talent
   - **c.** a learned skill
   - **d.** not readily seen

   9. _____

10. One who demands *retribution* seeks _____.
    - **a.** an audience
    - **b.** a refuge
    - **c.** forgiveness
    - **d.** repayment

    10. _____

11. An *aggregate* work force is the _____ of employees.
    - **a.** total
    - **b.** absence
    - **c.** allowance
    - **d.** remuneration

    11. _____

12. *Gregarious* people are _____.
    - **a.** aggressive
    - **b.** deceitful
    - **c.** sociable
    - **d.** glum

    12. _____

13. *Bellicose* behavior is _____.
    - **a.** melancholy
    - **b.** warlike
    - **c.** tolerant
    - **d.** fearful

    13. _____

14. A *semblance* of calm is the _____ tranquility.
    - **a.** appearance of
    - **b.** reputation for
    - **c.** desire for
    - **d.** preservation of

    14. _____

15. A *contentious* person is _____.
    - **a.** pessimistic
    - **b.** extravagant
    - **c.** fearful
    - **d.** quarrelsome

    15. _____

TEST LESSONS 13, 14, AND 15

PART B CHOOSING THE BEST WORD

On the answer line, write the letter of the word that best completes the sentence.

16. The selection of music is left to the _____ of the director.
    a. discretion   b. semblance   c. affront   d. protocol

16. _____ a

17. The ancient _____ between the countries was displayed at the museum.
    a. ensemble   b. covenant   c. breach   d. dissimulation

17. _____ b

18. The lack of trust between the heads of state made the chances for _____ highly unlikely.
    a. protocol   b. entente   c. affront   d. altercation

18. _____ b

19. The diplomats and their _____ are invited to a formal reception.
    a. attachés   b. antagonists   c. altercations   d. consulates

19. _____ a

20. In diplomatic circles, an error of _____ could lead to international misunderstanding.
    a. schism   b. retribution   c. protocol   d. facsimile

20. _____ c

21. While many employees were satisfied with the _____, others sought changes in wages and benefits.
    a. entente   b. dissension   c. consulate   d. status quo

21. _____ d

22. Hester's husband serves as her _____ in Hawthorne's *Scarlet Letter*.
    a. adherent   b. aggregate   c. antagonist   d. dissimulator

22. _____ c

23. In the fairy tale, Puss in Boots acts as a(n) _____ to the king for his poor, young master.
    a. emissary   b. ensemble   c. adherent   d. dissenter

23. _____ a

24. Although the famous battle between the Hatfields and the McCoys occurred in 1882, the _____ between the families still exists.
    a. altercation   b. covenant   c. protocol   d. schism

24. _____ d

25. Copies of trade agreements are filed at the French _____ in New York.
    a. consulate   b. emissary   c. antagonist   d. retribution

25. _____ a

26. Susan felt no _____ when Thelma was promoted to head cashier.
    a. egregiousness   b. discretion   c. rancor   d. segregation

26. _____ c

27. Thelma feared that her promotion would cause a(n) _____ in her relationships with the other employees.
    a. breach   b. facsimile   c. arbitration   d. entente

27. _____ a

28. An atmosphere of _____ made the office an unpleasant place to work.
    a. gregariousness   b. dissension   c. facsimile   d. protocol

28. _____ b

29. Unless it can be solved by the parties involved, the labor dispute will go to _____.
    a. segregation   b. dissimulation   c. discretion   d. arbitration

29. _____ d

30. The _____ of the Rodin sculpture almost fooled the museum director.
    a. ensemble   b. aggregate   c. facsimile   d. consulate

30. _____ c

TEST LESSONS 13, 14, AND 15

PART B CHOOSING THE BEST WORD

On the answer line, write the letter of the word that best completes the sentence.

16. The selection of music is left to the _____ of the director.
    a. discretion   **b.** semblance   **c.** affront   **d.** protocol

    16. _____

17. The ancient _____ between the countries was displayed at the museum.
    a. ensemble   **b.** covenant   **c.** breach   **d.** dissimulation

    17. _____

18. The lack of trust between the heads of state made the chances for _____ highly unlikely.
    a. protocol   **b.** entente   **c.** affront   **d.** altercation

    18. _____

19. The diplomats and their _____ are invited to a formal reception.
    a. attachés   **b.** antagonists   **c.** altercations   **d.** consulates

    19. _____

20. In diplomatic circles, an error of _____ could lead to international misunderstanding.
    a. schism   **b.** retribution   **c.** protocol   **d.** facsimile

    20. _____

21. While many employees were satisfied with the _____, others sought changes in wages and benefits.
    a. entente   **b.** dissension   **c.** consulate   **d.** status quo

    21. _____

22. Hester's husband serves as her _____ in Hawthorne's *Scarlet Letter*.
    a. adherent   **b.** aggregate   **c.** antagonist   **d.** dissimulator

    22. _____

23. In the fairy tale, Puss in Boots acts as a(n) _____ to the king for his poor, young master.
    a. emissary   **b.** ensemble   **c.** adherent   **d.** dissenter

    23. _____

24. Although the famous battle between the Hatfields and the McCoys occurred in 1882, the _____ between the families still exists.
    a. altercation   **b.** covenant   **c.** protocol   **d.** schism

    24. _____

25. Copies of trade agreements are filed at the French _____ in New York.
    a. consulate   **b.** emissary   **c.** antagonist   **d.** retribution

    25. _____

26. Susan felt no _____ when Thelma was promoted to head cashier.
    a. egregiousness   **b.** discretion   **c.** rancor   **d.** segregation

    26. _____

27. Thelma feared that her promotion would cause a(n) _____ in her relationships with the other employees.
    a. breach   **b.** facsimile   **c.** arbitration   **d.** entente

    27. _____

28. An atmosphere of _____ made the office an unpleasant place to work.
    a. gregariousness   **b.** dissension   **c.** facsimile   **d.** protocol

    28. _____

29. Unless it can be solved by the parties involved, the labor dispute will go to _____.
    a. segregation   **b.** dissimulation   **c.** discretion   **d.** arbitration

    29. _____

30. The _____ of the Rodin sculpture almost fooled the museum director.
    a. ensemble   **b.** aggregate   **c.** facsimile   **d.** consulate

    30. _____

BONUS LESSONS 13–16

(pages 81–98, 101–106)

Use the clues to spell out the words on the answer blanks. Then identify the mystery person at the bottom of the page by writing the numbered letters on the lines with the corresponding numbers.

1. The single effect of a(n) _____ is achieved by combining complementary parts.

   1. E N S E M B L E
                1

2. Disputing parties may sign a(n) _____ of peace.

   2. C O V E N A N T
           15   6

3. Synonym for *estrangement*

   3. B R E A C H
              9

4. A *gregarious* person is _____.

   4. S O C I A B L E
           14

5. An adversary

   5. A N T A G O N I S T
        2   12

6. Warlike

   6. B E L L I C O S E
           7

7. To command

   7. A D J U R E
             10

8. Authority, power, or control

   8. J U R I S D I C T I O N
       13

9. A photocopy

   9. F A C S I M I L E
              5

10. A plant infested with insects should be _____ from other plants.

    10. S E G R E G A T E D
        16

11. Synonym for *discretion*

    11. P R U D E N C E
          3

12. Given or demanded in repayment

    12. R E T R I B U T I O N
              8

13. A difference of opinion

    13. D I S S E N S I O N
        17

14. A *semblance* of something is a(n) _____ appearance.

    14. T O K E N
          11

15. Faithfulness and loyalty

    15. F I D E L I T Y
             4

M A R T I N   L U T H E R   K I N G   J R
1 2 3 4 5 6   7 8 4 9 10 3   11 5 6 12 , 13 3 .'

C I V I L   R I G H T S   L E A D E R
14 5 15 5 7   3 5 12 9 4 16   7 10 2 17 10 3

BONUS LESSONS 13–16

(pages 81–98, 101–106)

Use the clues to spell out the words on the answer blanks. Then identify the mystery person at the bottom of the page by writing the numbered letters on the lines with the corresponding numbers.

1. The single effect of a(n) _____ is achieved by combining complementary parts.

1. __ __ __ __ __ __ __ __
          1

2. Disputing parties may sign a(n) _____ of peace.

2. __ __ __ __ __ __ __ __
     15   6

3. Synonym for *estrangement*

3. __ __ __ __ __ __ __
            9

4. A *gregarious* person is _____.

4. __ __ __ __ __ __ __
     14

5. An adversary

5. __ __ __ __ __ __ __ __ __ __
  2   12

6. Warlike

6. __ __ __ __ __ __ __ __ __
    7

7. To command

7. __ __ __ __ __ __
         10

8. Authority, power, or control

8. __ __ __ __ __ __ __ __ __ __ __
  13

9. A photocopy

9. __ __ __ __ __ __ __ __
         5

10. A plant infested with insects should be _____ from other plants.

10. __ __ __ __ __ __ __ __ __
  16

11. Synonym for *discretion*

11. __ __ __ __ __ __ __ __
    3

12. Given or demanded in repayment

12. __ __ __ __ __ __ __ __ __
        8

13. A difference of opinion

13. __ __ __ __ __ __ __ __ __
  17

14. A *semblance* of something is a(n) _____ appearance.

14. __ __ __ __ __
    11

15. Faithfulness and loyalty

15. __ __ __ __ __ __ __
      4

__ __ __ __ __ __   __ __ __ __ __ __   __ __ __ __ , __ __ ,
1 2 3 4 5 6   7 8 4 9 10 3   11 5 6 12   13 3

__ __ __ __ __   __ __ __ __ __ __   __ __ __ __ __ __
14 5 15 5 7   3 5 12 9 4 16   7 10 2 17 10 3

TEST LESSONS 16, 17, AND 18

(pages 101–118)

PART A CHOOSING THE BEST DEFINITION

On the answer line, write the letter of the best definition of the italicized word.

1. The Parthenon is the *epitome* of classical architecture.
   a. perfect example   c. best preservation
   b. worst imitation   d. oldest surviving structure

   1. _____ a

2. Maxine's most faithful *confidante* has always been her mother.
   a. trusted person   b. companion   c. advocate   d. flatterer

   2. _____ a

3. The trainer *inferred* from the dog's listlessness that it was ill.
   a. deduced   b. disregarded   c. revealed   d. disputed

   3. _____ a

4. The Spanish Armada was once the *peerless* ruler of the seas.
   a. authorized   b. unmatched   c. mighty   d. lawless

   4. _____ b

5. The woman and her *fiancé* planned a large party.
   a. future bridegroom   c. immediate family member
   b. grateful parent   d. partner

   5. _____ a

6. All contestants are required to sign *affidavits*.
   a. complaints   c. promissory notes
   b. endorsements   d. declarations under oath

   6. _____ d

7. The judge warned the witness against *perjuring* himself.
   a. incriminating   c. giving false evidence
   b. harming   d. purposefully elevating

   7. _____ c

8. Construction of the hotel cannot *proceed* until financing is secured.
   a. go forward   c. be completed
   b. be guaranteed   d. be decided

   8. _____ a

9. Liza looked to the ceiling as if to *conjure* the answer from above.
   a. portray readily   b. produce by magic   c. pinpoint   d. extricate

   9. _____ b

10. Many literary scholars view Shakespeare's play *King Lear* as the *quintessence* of tragic drama.
    a. finest example   b. worst   c. solitary survivor   d. precursor

    10. _____ a

11. High interest rates adversely *affected* economic recovery.
    a. exhausted   b. stimulated   c. restricted   d. influenced

    11. _____ d

12. The police were unable to pursue the suspect after he left their *jurisdiction*.
    a. community   c. territory of authority
    b. premises   d. field of vision

    12. _____ c

13. Time has not *eclipsed* Babe Ruth's fame as one of baseball's greats.
    a. augmented   b. explained   c. obscured   d. verified

    13. _____ c

14. King Philip II of Spain did not *avenge* the execution of Mary, Queen of Scots, by the British.
    a. condone   b. take revenge for   c. require   d. acknowledge

    14. _____ b

15. In Shakespeare's tragedy, Prince Hamlet *adjures* the ghost he sees to divulge its identity.
    a. prohibits   b. expects   c. commands   d. coaxes

    15. _____ c

TEST LESSONS 16, 17, AND 18

(pages 101–118)

PART A CHOOSING THE BEST DEFINITION

On the answer line, write the letter of the best definition of the italicized word.

1. The Parthenon is the *epitome* of classical architecture.
   a. perfect example
   b. worst imitation
   c. best preservation
   d. oldest surviving structure

   1. _____

2. Maxine's most faithful *confidante* has always been her mother.
   a. trusted person **b.** companion **c.** advocate **d.** flatterer

   2. _____

3. The trainer *inferred* from the dog's listlessness that it was ill.
   a. deduced **b.** disregarded **c.** revealed **d.** disputed

   3. _____

4. The Spanish Armada was once the *peerless* ruler of the seas.
   a. authorized **b.** unmatched **c.** mighty **d.** lawless

   4. _____

5. The woman and her *fiancé* planned a large party.
   a. future bridegroom
   b. grateful parent
   c. immediate family member
   d. partner

   5. _____

6. All contestants are required to sign *affidavits*.
   a. complaints
   b. endorsements
   c. promissory notes
   d. declarations under oath

   6. _____

7. The judge warned the witness against *perjuring* himself.
   a. incriminating
   b. harming
   c. giving false evidence
   d. purposefully elevating

   7. _____

8. Construction of the hotel cannot *proceed* until financing is secured.
   a. go forward
   b. be guaranteed
   c. be completed
   d. be decided

   8. _____

9. Liza looked to the ceiling as if to *conjure* the answer from above.
   a. portray readily **b.** produce by magic **c.** pinpoint **d.** extricate

   9. _____

10. Many literary scholars view Shakespeare's play *King Lear* as the *quintessence* of tragic drama.
    a. finest example **b.** worst **c.** solitary survivor **d.** precursor

    10. _____

11. High interest rates adversely *affected* economic recovery.
    a. exhausted **b.** stimulated **c.** restricted **d.** influenced

    11. _____

12. The police were unable to pursue the suspect after he left their *jurisdiction*.
    a. community
    b. premises
    c. territory of authority
    d. field of vision

    12. _____

13. Time has not *eclipsed* Babe Ruth's fame as one of baseball's greats.
    a. augmented **b.** explained **c.** obscured **d.** verified

    13. _____

14. King Philip II of Spain did not *avenge* the execution of Mary, Queen of Scots, by the British.
    a. condone **b.** take revenge for **c.** require **d.** acknowledge

    14. _____

15. In Shakespeare's tragedy, Prince Hamlet *adjures* the ghost he sees to divulge its identity.
    a. prohibits **b.** expects **c.** commands **d.** coaxes

    15. _____

TEST LESSONS 16, 17, AND 18

PART B IDENTIFYING ANTONYMS

On the answer line, write the letter of the word or phrase that has the meaning that is opposite to that of the capitalized word.

16. SUBLIME:
   a. old-fashioned   b. ridiculous   c. conscious   d. inexpensive

16. _____ b

17. ZENITH:
   a. quasar   b. rejection   c. summit   d. nadir

17. _____ d

18. IMPECCABLE:
   a. well-to-do   b. defective   c. generous   d. efficient

18. _____ b

19. OPTIMUM:
   a. invisible   b. peculiar   c. detrimental   d. convenient

19. _____ c

20. INIMITABLE:
   a. systematic   b. clever   c. violent   d. commonplace

20. _____ d

21. PRECEDE:
   a. benefit   b. follow   c. dominate   d. desist

21. _____ b

22. IMPLY:
   a. state explicitly   b. lose track of   c. determine   d. submerge

22. _____ a

23. UNINTERESTED:
   a. preoccupied   b. devastated   c. obligated   d. registered

23. _____ a

24. REVENGE:
   a. selfishness   b. acceptance   c. forgiveness   d. sensibility

24. _____ c

25. DISINTERESTED:
   a. educated   b. pecuniary   c. biased   d. attentive

25. _____ c

26. FEALTY:
   a. disloyalty   b. ownership   c. generosity   d. wisdom

26. _____ a

27. INFIDEL:
   a. mentor   b. liar   c. mascot   d. believer

27. _____ d

28. EFFECT:
   a. aim   b. cause   c. influence   d. change

28. _____ b

29. FIDELITY:
   a. clarity   b. unfaithfulness   c. safety   d. foolishness

29. _____ b

30. CULMINATE:
   a. expel   b. climax   c. commence   d. terminate

30. _____ c

TEST LESSONS 16, 17, AND 18

PART B IDENTIFYING ANTONYMS

On the answer line, write the letter of the word or phrase that has the meaning that is opposite to that of the capitalized word.

16. SUBLIME:
   a. old-fashioned   b. ridiculous   c. conscious   d. inexpensive

   16. _____

17. ZENITH:
   a. quasar   b. rejection   c. summit   d. nadir

   17. _____

18. IMPECCABLE:
   a. well-to-do   b. defective   c. generous   d. efficient

   18. _____

19. OPTIMUM:
   a. invisible   b. peculiar   c. detrimental   d. convenient

   19. _____

20. INIMITABLE:
   a. systematic   b. clever   c. violent   d. commonplace

   20. _____

21. PRECEDE:
   a. benefit   b. follow   c. dominate   d. desist

   21. _____

22. IMPLY:
   a. state explicitly   b. lose track of   c. determine   d. submerge

   22. _____

23. UNINTERESTED:
   a. preoccupied   b. devastated   c. obligated   d. registered

   23. _____

24. REVENGE:
   a. selfishness   b. acceptance   c. forgiveness   d. sensibility

   24. _____

25. DISINTERESTED:
   a. educated   b. pecuniary   c. biased   d. attentive

   25. _____

26. FEALTY:
   a. disloyalty   b. ownership   c. generosity   d. wisdom

   26. _____

27. INFIDEL:
   a. mentor   b. liar   c. mascot   d. believer

   27. _____

28. EFFECT:
   a. aim   b. cause   c. influence   d. change

   28. _____

29. FIDELITY:
   a. clarity   b. unfaithfulness   c. safety   d. foolishness

   29. _____

30. CULMINATE:
   a. expel   b. climax   c. commence   d. terminate

   30. _____

BONUS LESSONS 17–20

(pages 107–118, 121–132)

Unscramble the letters of each italicized word, and write the word on the answer line to the right.

1. In order to judge cases fairly, magistrates must be knowledgeable and *steeieinsddtr*.

2. A peerless jewel has no *lueaq*.

3. An animal that receives a surrogate mother gets a *ttsbseuiut* parent.

4. By taking a *ruouiicsct* route home, Janine was able to pass the motorcycle shop.

5. The zenith of a career is its *hetihgs* point.

6. The reporters would be *iigknrhs* their duty if they failed to cover this newsworthy event.

7. Many *uraoioscqtnds* were successful in their search for territory and wealth in the New World.

8. Despite the threat of rain, we *eeeorddpc* on our hike.

9. The play was an excellent showcase for the actor's *mnbeliiiat* style.

10. To Lionel, the steaming radiator of the car *eaedgprs* trouble.

11. On the basis of several trials, the research scientist *rfeniedr* that the new antibiotic was effective.

12. Health-conscious people lead *tsbaeiuoms* lives.

13. In the movie the detective seeks to *eaegnv* the loss of his job.

14. The *snoviae* of her responsibilities cost Ellen her promotion.

15. Their *suetq* for religious freedom led the Pilgrims to New England in 1620.

16. An optimum effort represents one's *etbs*.

17. The younger children *reeeddpc* the older ones to the cafeteria.

18. Garrison is known for his stylish and *iccblmpeae* attire.

19. One of the *qseierpstui* of working at the boutique was an employee discount on clothing.

20. Nell kept her dream of becoming a travel writer in *ynaeaecb* until she had graduated from college.

1. **disinterested**

2. **equal**

3. **substitute**

4. **circuitous**

5. **highest**

6. **shirking**

7. **conquistadors**

8. **proceeded**

9. **inimitable**

10. **presaged**

11. **inferred**

12. **abstemious**

13. **avenge**

14. **evasion**

15. **quest**

16. **best**

17. **preceded**

18. **impeccable**

19. **perquisites**

20. **abeyance**

BONUS LESSONS 17–20

(pages 107–118, 121–132)

Unscramble the letters of each italicized word, and write the word on the answer line to the right.

1. In order to judge cases fairly, magistrates must be knowledgeable and *steeieinsddtr*.

   1. _____

2. A peerless jewel has no *lueaq*.

   2. _____

3. An animal that receives a surrogate mother gets a *ttsbseuiut* parent.

   3. _____

4. By taking a *ruouiicsct* route home, Janine was able to pass the motorcycle shop.

   4. _____

5. The zenith of a career is its *hetihgs* point.

   5. _____

6. The reporters would be *iigknrhs* their duty if they failed to cover this newsworthy event.

   6. _____

7. Many *uraoioscqtnds* were successful in their search for territory and wealth in the New World.

   7. _____

8. Despite the threat of rain, we *eeeorddpc* on our hike.

   8. _____

9. The play was an excellent showcase for the actor's *mnbeliiiat* style.

   9. _____

10. To Lionel, the steaming radiator of the car *eaedgprs* trouble.

   10. _____

11. On the basis of several trials, the research scientist *rfeniedr* that the new antibiotic was effective.

   11. _____

12. Health-conscious people lead *tsbaeiuoms* lives.

   12. _____

13. In the movie the detective seeks to *eaegnv* the loss of his job.

   13. _____

14. The *snoviae* of her responsibilities cost Ellen her promotion.

   14. _____

15. Their *suetq* for religious freedom led the Pilgrims to New England in 1620.

   15. _____

16. An optimum effort represents one's *etbs*.

   16. _____

17. The younger children *reeeddpc* the older ones to the cafeteria.

   17. _____

18. Garrison is known for his stylish and *iccblmpeae* attire.

   18. _____

19. One of the *qseierpstui* of working at the boutique was an employee discount on clothing.

   19. _____

20. Nell kept her dream of becoming a travel writer in *ynaeaecb* until she had graduated from college.

   20. _____

VERBAL APTITUDE TEST 2

For each question in this section, choose the best answer and blacken the corresponding space on the answer sheet.

PART A ANTONYMS

Each question below consists of a word in capital letters, followed by five lettered words or phrases. Choose the word or phrase that is most nearly <u>opposite</u> in meaning to the word in capital letters. Since some of the questions require you to distinguish fine shades of meaning, consider all the choices before deciding which is best.

EXAMPLE:

GOOD : (A) sour   (B) bad   (C) red
(D) hot   (E) ugly

(A) (B) (C) (D) (E)

1. IRRITANT: (A) eventuality   (B) emollient
   (C) whim   (D) quorum   (E) regent

2. SEGREGATE: (A) enslave   (B) expel
   (C) delegate   (D) procure   (E) integrate

3. INGRATIATE: (A) spurn   (B) inhibit
   (C) taunt   (D) alleviate   (E) equivocate

4. VERBOSE: (A) petty   (B) composed
   (C) succinct   (D) grim   (E) vacant

5. AUTHENTICATE: (A) countermand
   (B) eradicate   (C) pervade   (D) refute
   (E) abnegate

6. ABSTEMIOUS: (A) dogmatic   (B) ostensible
   (C) somber   (D) nurtured   (E) intemperate

7. INCONGRUOUS: (A) consonant
   (B) inquisitive   (C) contentious
   (D) collaborative   (E) immutable

8. AMENABLE: (A) reactionary   (B) persuasive
   (C) circuitous   (D) recalcitrant   (E) vicarious

9. EGREGIOUS: (A) gregarious   (B) sterling
   (C) posthumous   (D) solitary   (E) copious

10. PERIPATETIC: (A) apocryphal   (B) symmetrical
    (C) stagnant   (D) indigent   (E) pitiable

PART B SENTENCE COMPLETIONS

Each sentence below has one or two blanks, each blank indicating that something has been omitted. Below the sentence are five lettered words or sets of words. Choose the word or set of words that <u>best</u> fits the meaning of the sentence as a whole.

EXAMPLE:

Although its publicity has been - - - - , the film itself is intelligent, well-acted, handsomely produced, and altogether - - - - .
(A) tasteless .. respectable
(B) extensive .. moderate
(C) sophisticated .. amateur
(D) risqué .. crude   (E) perfect .. spectacular

(A) (B) (C) (D) (E)

11. Notwithstanding the frozen, snow-patched ground, hearty crocuses are punctual - - - - of spring.
    (A) harbingers   (B) zephyrs
    (C) covenants   (D) allusions
    (E) prodigies

12. The - - - - for Louis Braille's system of writing for the blind was a French army officer's experiments with an embossed code that allowed soldiers to communicate silently in darkness.
    (A) rival   (B) necessity
    (C) premeditation   (D) intricacies
    (E) prototype

13. Manuscript illuminators, who invested - - - - subjects with new spiritual and intellectual force, were the single most - - - - factor in the growth and dissemination of medieval art.
    (A) tangible .. sensible
    (B) standard .. potent
    (C) passive .. oblique
    (D) superficial .. ethereal
    (E) inelegant .. zealous

14. The late fourteenth century was a - - - - time when war, plague, and doubt - - - - to undermine the medieval consensus on the nature of human beings and society.
    (A) cataclysmic .. allied
    (B) rational .. contrived
    (C) mutinous .. recoiled
    (D) baneful .. diminished
    (E) remote .. surrendered

15. Dangerous and expensive, with life spans short enough to be lost at the blink of an eye, fireworks are so - - - - that for more than six hundred years, people have rocketed these glittering particles into the sky to inaugurate, to celebrate, and to - - - - .
    (A) glorious .. exhibit
    (B) contradictory .. distinguish
    (C) cathartic .. announce
    (D) compelling .. commemorate
    (E) dramatic .. emulate

16. By the end of the nineteenth century, American agriculture had been transformed from the self-sufficient, - - - - farm of the past to a more specialized and commercialized business enterprise.
    (A) peculiar   (B) deprecated
    (C) diversified   (D) industrial
    (E) accessible

17. People tend to - - - - the theory of relativity a kind of reverential awe, believing that Einstein's principles of space and time are so - - - - that only the most advanced scientists can comprehend them.
    (A) lend .. infinitesimal
    (B) accord .. complex
    (C) associate with .. uniform
    (D) deny .. authoritative
    (E) anticipate .. explicit

18. The formality and respect for academic rules characteristic of Neoclassicism scarcely concealed the upsurge of romantic feeling that was already beginning to - - - - art of the eighteenth century.
    (A) diffuse   (B) disfigure   (C) convulse
    (D) ratify   (E) infuse

19. The original presidential inauguration was a dignified, almost - - - - occasion that was no doubt a reaction to the - - - - ceremonies forced on colonial subjects of King George III.
    (A) reprehensible .. prodigious
    (B) austere .. elaborate
    (C) ostentatious .. gratifying
    (D) paltry .. notorious
    (E) customary .. gratuitous

20. Realizing that photographic and scientific studies of wild plants, moths, and birds would never reach the wide audience she hoped to - - - - , Gene Stratton-Porter turned to fiction as a vehicle for advocating the preservation of nature.
    (A) affect   (B) discipline   (C) disconcert
    (D) invoke   (E) berate

PART C ANALOGIES

Each question below consists of a related pair of words or phrases, followed by five lettered pairs of words or phrases. Select the lettered pair that best expresses a relationship similar to that expressed in the original pair.

EXAMPLE:

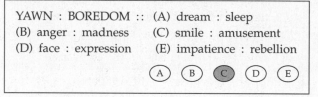

YAWN : BOREDOM :: (A) dream : sleep
(B) anger : madness   (C) smile : amusement
(D) face : expression   (E) impatience : rebellion
(A) (B) (C) (D) (E)

21. HULL : SHIP ::
    (A) rifle : breech   (B) cone : funnel
    (C) trademark : product   (D) wheel : spoke
    (E) fuselage : airplane

22. DIVULGE : REVEAL ::
    (A) blemish : purify   (B) divest : invest
    (C) renounce : recant   (D) stablilize : fluctuate
    (E) defend : malign

23. NEGLIGENCE : BLUNDER ::
    (A) treason : execution
    (B) congestion : crowding
    (C) malady : cure
    (D) starvation : atrophy
    (E) population : census

24. DOLPHIN : MARINE ::
    (A) cloud : celestial   (B) opossum : arboreal
    (C) fathom : nautical   (D) virus : aerial
    (E) reptile : terrestrial

25. VAPID : PIQUANT ::
    (A) sagacious : inane   (B) baroque : simple
    (C) ardent : fervid   (D) terse : curt
    (E) feeble : virile

26. PLUMB : DEPTH ::
    (A) caliper : amplitude
    (B) megaphone : sound
    (C) compass : bearing
    (D) level : surface
    (E) transit : corner

27. FORGO : ESCHEW ::
    (A) foil : thwart   (B) annul : ameliorate
    (C) indemnify : remunerate
    (D) motivate : goad   (E) immure : exempt

28. PATENTLY : EVIDENTLY ::
    (A) currently : temporarily
    (B) willingly : willfully
    (C) viably : feasibly
    (D) exactly : variably
    (E) almost : always

29. ARBITRATOR : DISINTERESTED ::
    (A) confederate : cunning
    (B) optimist : sanguine
    (C) maestro : ineffable
    (D) gentlemen : puissant
    (E) writer : illustrious

30. NEFARIOUS : VIRTUOUS ::
    (A) equivocal : enigmatic
    (B) affluent : indigent
    (C) earnest : modest
    (D) adroit : maladroit
    (E) grievous : salutary

PART D READING COMPREHENSION

Each passage below is followed by questions based on its content. Answer all questions following a passage on the basis of what is <u>stated</u> or <u>implied</u> in that passage.

For exactly two and a quarter centuries after the suppression of the Shimabara revolt in 1638, there was no significant political change or any warfare in Japan— only occasional riots by villagers or townsmen or perhaps a political assassination. This was probably the longest period of complete peace and political stability that any sizable body of people has every enjoyed. And yet it was a time not of stagnation but of very dynamic economic and cultural growth. After centuries of warfare and disunity, peace alone proved a strong stimulus to change,

as did also the thorough centralization of controls that the Tokugawa had instituted.

The impact of peace and political unity was felt perhaps most strongly by the samurai class itself. To rule a land at peace, the Tokugawa needed educated administrators more than rough soldiers. The writing brush replaced the sword as the chief implement of the samurai, as they rapidly evolved from a body of fighting men into an urbanized class of well educated bureaucrats and petty government functionaries. Numerous enough to have furnished the mass armies of a country in constant civil war, they provided in time of peace a superabundance of would-be administrators, which proved a needlessly heavy burden on government finances.

The samurai remained organized for the most part into military units and made a fetish of their two swords, but warfare had become a matter of theory, not practice. Schools were founded in the various domains to teach the military arts, but gunnery and the use of firearms, which had proved the decisive military techniques, were largely ignored in favor of the medieval military disciplines of swordsmanship and archery, which were favored for their character-building qualities as much as for their military value. From this grew the emphasis on other character-building martial arts, such as the wrestling-fighting technique of *judo* and its modern variant *karate*.

The samurai value system, which had been a natural outgrowth of a feudal warrior society, gradually became transformed into a self-conscious philosophy. The feudal ethical principles of unquestioning loyalty to one's lord, fierce defense of one's own status and honor, and strict fulfillment of all obligations became codified as *Bushidō*, the "Way of the Warrior." Social realities, however, were moving away from the feudal conditions that had created this value system, as is illustrated by the prohibition in 1663 of suicide by retainers in order to "follow their lord in death."

31. According to the passage, which of the following statements about seventeenth- and eighteenth-century Japan is most accurate?
    (A) The samurai value system changed as society changed.
    (B) *Judō* and *karate* were used to avenge attacks on one's status and honor.
    (C) The period between 1638 and 1863 represented years of little change of any kind in Japan.
    (D) Localized riots and political assassinations necessitated centralized government control.
    (E) Defensive strategies and warfare training were modernized.

32. When the author states that "The writing brush replaced the sword as the chief implement of the samurai," he or she probably means that
(A) the samurai sought to redress wrongs through the written word.
(B) the sumarai were so busy writing that they forgot about fighting.
(C) efficient bureaucratic techniques influenced the tools of war.
(D) the focus shifted from military to governmental control.
(E) swordsmanship became a lost art among the samurai.

33. Which of the following statements best characterize the "Way of the Warrior"?
   I Unquestioning fealty to one's lord
   II The prohibition against suicide by retainers
   III An emphasis on character-building skills
   IV The defense of one's reputation
   V The strict attitude toward honoring one's duties and responsibilities
   (A) II, III, and IV   (B) I, III, IV, and V
   (C) I, II, and V   (D) I, II, III, and IV
   (E) III, IV, and V

Gravity is the main agent in getting an interstellar cloud to condense into a star, but there is a complication. Most nebulae have too much energy to contract; the atoms, molecules, and dust particles have enough kinetic energy to resist the pull of gravity, and so the clouds do not contract. Only if a cloud can lose its excess energy, by radiating it away, for example, will gravity be successful in bringing on a collapse.

Once a nebula has started to contract under its own gravity, as will happen if it becomes cool and dense enough, then it is past the main hurdle, and further contraction will automatically follow. The object will continue to get smaller, and the internal pressures will build up. Eventually the pressures become large enough to balance gravity, and the contraction will tend to stop. Meanwhile, energy exchanges are taking place that very much affect our star-to-be or *protostar*.

It takes energy to lift an object against the force of gravity. The energy used to do the lifting goes into the potential energy of the object. This potential energy is due to the force of gravity, and it is customary to call it *gravitational energy* to distinguish it from other types of potential energy. If the body is released and falls under gravity, the gravitational energy is released and changed to kinetic energy.

It is exactly the same in nebula. When a nebula contracts, the different parts of it are falling under the force of gravity, and the nebula is changing gravitational energy into kinetic energy. This kinetic energy of the contracting cloud is changed into heat energy and radiation as the atoms and molecules collide with each other. As a result, a contracting cloud will automatically become hot as it grows smaller. This is why stars are hot: Their contraction from very large interstellar clouds to much smaller stars releases great amounts of gravitational energy, and part of the released energy goes into heating the material.

34. According to the passage, not all nebulae collapse and form stars because
(A) some nebulae are too cool and dense.
(B) some nebulae have too little pressure to balance gravity.
(C) some nebulae have so much kinetic energy that they resist gravity.
(D) some nebulae suffer from a dearth of dust particles.
(E) contraction stops too early in some nebulae, thereby not creating enough of an energy exchange.

35. It can be inferred from the passage that an interstellar cloud is composed of
(A) a nebulae surrounded by protostars.
(B) atoms, molecules, and dust particles
(C) potential energy, gravitational energy, and kinetic energy.
(D) a conglomerate of small stars that are rapidly expanding.
(E) a modicum of matter mixed with ice crystals.

36. Which of the following statements about star development are accurate?
   I As a contracting cloud grows smaller, its internal temperature diminishes.
   II Most nebulae have enough kinetic energy to counteract the pull of gravity.
   III Once contraction of nebula has begun, it will continue indefinitely.
   IV A cloud's radiant energy allows it to collapse.
   V Stars are smaller than the interstellar clouds from which they were formed.
   (A) I and III   (B) I, II, and V
   (C) III and IV   (D) II and V
   (E) II, IV, and V

If you finish before time is called, check your work on this test.

VERBAL APTITUDE TEST 2

Answer Sheet

Use a No. 2 pencil for completing this answer sheet. Make sure that your marks are dark and completely fill the space. Erase any errors or stray marks. If a test has fewer than 50 questions, leave the extra answer spaces blank.

1.	A	**B**	C	D	E
2.	A	B	C	D	**E**
3.	**A**	B	C	D	E
4.	A	B	**C**	D	E
5.	A	B	C	**D**	E
6.	A	B	C	D	**E**
7.	**A**	B	C	D	E
8.	A	B	C	**D**	E
9.	A	**B**	C	D	E
10.	A	B	**C**	D	E
11.	**A**	B	C	D	E
12.	A	B	C	D	**E**
13.	A	**B**	C	D	E
14.	**A**	B	C	D	E
15.	A	B	C	**D**	E
16.	A	B	**C**	D	E
17.	A	**B**	C	D	E
18.	A	B	C	D	**E**
19.	A	**B**	C	D	E
20.	**A**	B	C	D	E
21.	A	B	C	D	**E**
22.	A	B	**C**	D	E
23.	A	B	C	**D**	E
24.	A	**B**	C	D	E
25.	A	B	C	D	**E**

26.	**A**	B	C	D	E
27.	A	B	C	**D**	E
28.	A	B	**C**	D	E
29.	A	**B**	C	D	E
30.	A	B	C	D	**E**
31.	**A**	B	C	D	E
32.	A	B	C	**D**	E
33.	A	**B**	C	D	E
34.	A	B	**C**	D	E
35.	A	**B**	C	D	E
36.	A	B	C	D	**E**
37.	A	B	C	D	E
38.	A	B	C	D	E
39.	A	B	C	D	E
40.	A	B	C	D	E
41.	A	B	C	D	E
42.	A	B	C	D	E
43.	A	B	C	D	E
44.	A	B	C	D	E
45.	A	B	C	D	E
46.	A	B	C	D	E
47.	A	B	C	D	E
48.	A	B	C	D	E
49.	A	B	C	D	E
50.	A	B	C	D	E

Answer Sheet

Use a No. 2 pencil for completing this answer sheet. Make sure that your marks are dark and completely fill the space. Erase any errors or stray marks. If a test has fewer than 50 questions, leave the extra answer spaces blank.

1.	Ⓐ	Ⓑ	Ⓒ	Ⓓ	Ⓔ	26.	Ⓐ	Ⓑ	Ⓒ	Ⓓ	Ⓔ
2.	Ⓐ	Ⓑ	Ⓒ	Ⓓ	Ⓔ	27.	Ⓐ	Ⓑ	Ⓒ	Ⓓ	Ⓔ
3.	Ⓐ	Ⓑ	Ⓒ	Ⓓ	Ⓔ	28.	Ⓐ	Ⓑ	Ⓒ	Ⓓ	Ⓔ
4.	Ⓐ	Ⓑ	Ⓒ	Ⓓ	Ⓔ	29.	Ⓐ	Ⓑ	Ⓒ	Ⓓ	Ⓔ
5.	Ⓐ	Ⓑ	Ⓒ	Ⓓ	Ⓔ	30.	Ⓐ	Ⓑ	Ⓒ	Ⓓ	Ⓔ
6.	Ⓐ	Ⓑ	Ⓒ	Ⓓ	Ⓔ	31.	Ⓐ	Ⓑ	Ⓒ	Ⓓ	Ⓔ
7.	Ⓐ	Ⓑ	Ⓒ	Ⓓ	Ⓔ	32.	Ⓐ	Ⓑ	Ⓒ	Ⓓ	Ⓔ
8.	Ⓐ	Ⓑ	Ⓒ	Ⓓ	Ⓔ	33.	Ⓐ	Ⓑ	Ⓒ	Ⓓ	Ⓔ
9.	Ⓐ	Ⓑ	Ⓒ	Ⓓ	Ⓔ	34.	Ⓐ	Ⓑ	Ⓒ	Ⓓ	Ⓔ
10.	Ⓐ	Ⓑ	Ⓒ	Ⓓ	Ⓔ	35.	Ⓐ	Ⓑ	Ⓒ	Ⓓ	Ⓔ
11.	Ⓐ	Ⓑ	Ⓒ	Ⓓ	Ⓔ	36.	Ⓐ	Ⓑ	Ⓒ	Ⓓ	Ⓔ
12.	Ⓐ	Ⓑ	Ⓒ	Ⓓ	Ⓔ	37.	Ⓐ	Ⓑ	Ⓒ	Ⓓ	Ⓔ
13.	Ⓐ	Ⓑ	Ⓒ	Ⓓ	Ⓔ	38.	Ⓐ	Ⓑ	Ⓒ	Ⓓ	Ⓔ
14.	Ⓐ	Ⓑ	Ⓒ	Ⓓ	Ⓔ	39.	Ⓐ	Ⓑ	Ⓒ	Ⓓ	Ⓔ
15.	Ⓐ	Ⓑ	Ⓒ	Ⓓ	Ⓔ	40.	Ⓐ	Ⓑ	Ⓒ	Ⓓ	Ⓔ
16.	Ⓐ	Ⓑ	Ⓒ	Ⓓ	Ⓔ	41.	Ⓐ	Ⓑ	Ⓒ	Ⓓ	Ⓔ
17.	Ⓐ	Ⓑ	Ⓒ	Ⓓ	Ⓔ	42.	Ⓐ	Ⓑ	Ⓒ	Ⓓ	Ⓔ
18.	Ⓐ	Ⓑ	Ⓒ	Ⓓ	Ⓔ	43.	Ⓐ	Ⓑ	Ⓒ	Ⓓ	Ⓔ
19.	Ⓐ	Ⓑ	Ⓒ	Ⓓ	Ⓔ	44.	Ⓐ	Ⓑ	Ⓒ	Ⓓ	Ⓔ
20.	Ⓐ	Ⓑ	Ⓒ	Ⓓ	Ⓔ	45.	Ⓐ	Ⓑ	Ⓒ	Ⓓ	Ⓔ
21.	Ⓐ	Ⓑ	Ⓒ	Ⓓ	Ⓔ	46.	Ⓐ	Ⓑ	Ⓒ	Ⓓ	Ⓔ
22.	Ⓐ	Ⓑ	Ⓒ	Ⓓ	Ⓔ	47.	Ⓐ	Ⓑ	Ⓒ	Ⓓ	Ⓔ
23.	Ⓐ	Ⓑ	Ⓒ	Ⓓ	Ⓔ	48.	Ⓐ	Ⓑ	Ⓒ	Ⓓ	Ⓔ
24.	Ⓐ	Ⓑ	Ⓒ	Ⓓ	Ⓔ	49.	Ⓐ	Ⓑ	Ⓒ	Ⓓ	Ⓔ
25.	Ⓐ	Ⓑ	Ⓒ	Ⓓ	Ⓔ	50.	Ⓐ	Ⓑ	Ⓒ	Ⓓ	Ⓔ

TEST LESSONS 19, 20, AND 21

(pages 121–138)

PART A MATCHING WORDS AND DEFINITIONS

Match the definition in Column B with the word in Column A. Write the letter of the correct definiton on the answer line.

Column A

1. acquisition
2. cirumvent
3. platitude
4. sagacity
5. evasion
6. emulate
7. requisite
8. abstemious
9. sham
10. surrogate
11. shirk
12. banal
13. presage
14. malinger
15. simulation

Column B

a. the act of escaping or avoiding by cleverness or deceit

b. the act or process of gaining possession

c. to pretend illness or injury in order to avoid duty

d. to strive to equal or excel, expecially through imitation

e. to avoid by passing around; get the better of by artful maneuvering

f. to indicate or warn in advance; foretell or predict

g. to negelct, put off, or avoid discharging a responsibility

h. keenness of perception; wisdom

i. sparing; moderate; temperate

j. the taking on of the appearance, form, or sound of something else; imitation

k. someone or something that takes the place of another; substitute

l. something false or empty that is supposed to be genuine

m. required; essential

n. a trite remark or statement

o. lacking freshness or originality; trite

1. ___b___
2. ___e___
3. ___n___
4. ___h___
5. ___a___
6. ___d___
7. ___m___
8. ___i___
9. ___l___
10. ___k___
11. ___g___
12. ___o___
13. ___f___
14. ___c___
15. ___j___

PART B CHOOSING THE BEST WORD

On the answer line, write the letter of the word that best expresses the meaning of the italicized word or phrase.

16. The wily raccoon *escaped from* the inexperienced hunter.
    a. eschewed   b. eluded   c. emulated   d. abrogated

16. ___b___

17. Maria amused her parents with her *musical interpretation* of Beethoven's Fifth Symphony played on the kazoo.
    a. rendition   b. sagacity   c. acquisition   d. recapitulation

17. ___a___

TEST LESSONS 19, 20, AND 21

(pages 121–138)

PART A MATCHING WORDS AND DEFINITIONS

Match the definition in Column B with the word in Column A. Write the letter of the correct definiton on the answer line.

Column A

1. acquisition
2. cirumvent
3. platitude
4. sagacity
5. evasion
6. emulate
7. requisite
8. abstemious
9. sham
10. surrogate
11. shirk
12. banal
13. presage
14. malinger
15. simulation

Column B

a. the act of escaping or avoiding by cleverness or deceit

b. the act or process of gaining possession

c. to pretend illness or injury in order to avoid duty

d. to strive to equal or excel, especially through imitation

e. to avoid by passing around; get the better of by artful maneuvering

f. to indicate or warn in advance; foretell or predict

g. to negelct, put off, or avoid discharging a responsibility

h. keenness of perception; wisdom

i. sparing; moderate; temperate

j. the taking on of the appearance, form, or sound of something else; imitation

k. someone or something that takes the place of another; substitute

l. something false or empty that is supposed to be genuine

m. required; essential

n. a trite remark or statement

o. lacking freshness or originality; trite

1. _____
2. _____
3. _____
4. _____
5. _____
6. _____
7. _____
8. _____
9. _____
10. _____
11. _____
12. _____
13. _____
14. _____
15. _____

PART B CHOOSING THE BEST WORD

On the answer line, write the letter of the word that best expresses the meaning of the italicized word or phrase.

16. The wily raccoon *escaped from* the inexperienced hunter.
    a. eschewed   **b.** eluded   **c.** emulated   **d.** abrogated

16. _____

17. Maria amused her parents with her *musical interpretation* of Beethoven's Fifth Symphony played on the kazoo.
    a. rendition   **b.** sagacity   **c.** acquisition   **d.** recapitulation

17. _____

TEST LESSONS 19, 20, AND 21

PART B CHOOSING THE BEST WORD (CONTINUED)

18. The privilege of sending their official business mail free of charge is a *benefit* of senators.
   a. sham   **b.** prototype   **c.** perquisite   **d.** abeyance

18. _____ c

19. In calling Alan a "perennial child," Betty was making an *indirect* comparison between Alan and Peter Pan.
   a. oblique   **b.** redundant   **c.** surrogate   **d.** elusive

19. _____ a

20. Aristotle regarded the plays of Sophocles as the *model* for dramatic tragedy.
   a. perquisite   **b.** surrogate   **c.** prototype   **d.** simulation

20. _____ c

21. Exorbitant prices for seafood prompted the owner of the restaurant to *cancel* his contract with local suppliers.
   a. presage   **b.** emulate   **c.** abrogate   **d.** eschew

21. _____ c

22. Competitve athletes *habitually avoid* excessive amounts of highly caloric foods.
   a. recapitulate   **b.** circumvent   **c.** eschew   **d.** abrogate

22. _____ c

23. A mynah bird generates words and phrases through *copying*, not through linguistics processes.
   a. sagacity   **b.** circumvention   **c.** abeyance   **d.** mimicry

23. _____ d

24. According to legend, Sir Galahad was the only knight worthy of completing the *search* for the Holy Grail.
   a. conquistador   **b.** quest   **c.** evasion   **d.** prototype

24. _____ b

25. The runner held her hopes for an Olympic medal in *suspension* until her injury healed.
   a. rendition   **b.** emulation   **c.** acquisition   **d.** abeyance

25. _____ d

26. The students asked their teacher to *repeat concisely* the topics to be covered on the midterm exam.
   a. simulate   **b.** abrogate   **c.** mimic   **d.** recapitulate

26. _____ d

27. Moctezuma mistook the *Spanish conqueror* Cortés for Quetzalcoatl, the powerful god of Aztec mythology.
   a. conquistador   **b.** surrogate   **c.** prototype   **d.** sham

27. _____ a

28. Paula apologized for her discourtesy in a *roundabout* fashion.
   a. circuitious   **b.** redundant   **c.** sagacious   **d.** banal

28. _____ a

29. The editor eliminated several chapters from Jamal's book becasue they were *repetitious*.
   a. oblique   **b.** redundant   **c.** abstemious   **d.** banal

29. _____ b

30. Annie's habit of dismantling her toys is proof of her *curious* nature.
   a. redundant   **b.** abstemious   **c.** inquisitive   **d.** surrogate

30. _____ c

TEST LESSONS 19, 20, AND 21

PART B CHOOSING THE BEST WORD (CONTINUED)

18. The privilege of sending their official business mail free of charge is a *benefit* of senators.
    a. sham   **b.** prototype   **c.** perquisite   **d.** abeyance

    18. _____

19. In calling Alan a "perennial child," Betty was making an *indirect* comparison between Alan and Peter Pan.
    a. oblique   **b.** redundant   **c.** surrogate   **d.** elusive

    19. _____

20. Aristotle regarded the plays of Sophocles as the *model* for dramatic tragedy.
    a. perquisite   **b.** surrogate   **c.** prototype   **d.** simulation

    20. _____

21. Exorbitant prices for seafood prompted the owner of the restaurant to *cancel* his contract with local suppliers.
    a. presage   **b.** emulate   **c.** abrogate   **d.** eschew

    21. _____

22. Competitve athletes *habitually avoid* excessive amounts of highly caloric foods.
    a. recapitulate   **b.** circumvent   **c.** eschew   **d.** abrogate

    22. _____

23. A mynah bird generates words and phrases through *copying*, not through linguistics processes.
    a. sagacity   **b.** circumvention   **c.** abeyance   **d.** mimicry

    23. _____

24. According to legend, Sir Galahad was the only knight worthy of completing the *search* for the Holy Grail.
    a. conquistador   **b.** quest   **c.** evasion   **d.** prototype

    24. _____

25. The runner held her hopes for an Olympic medal in *suspension* until her injury healed.
    a. rendition   **b.** emulation   **c.** acquisition   **d.** abeyance

    25. _____

26. The students asked their teacher to *repeat concisely* the topics to be covered on the midterm exam.
    a. simulate   **b.** abrogate   **c.** mimic   **d.** recapitulate

    26. _____

27. Moctezuma mistook the *Spanish conqueror* Cortés for Quetzalcoatl, the powerful god of Aztec mythology.
    a. conquistador   **b.** surrogate   **c.** prototype   **d.** sham

    27. _____

28. Paula apologized for her discourtesy in a *roundabout* fashion.
    a. circuitious   **b.** redundant   **c.** sagacious   **d.** banal

    28. _____

29. The editor eliminated several chapters from Jamal's book becasue they were *repetitious*.
    a. oblique   **b.** redundant   **c.** abstemious   **d.** banal

    29. _____

30. Annie's habit of dismantling her toys is proof of her *curious* nature.
    a. redundant   **b.** abstemious   **c.** inquisitive   **d.** surrogate

    30. _____

TEST LESSONS 22, 23, AND 24

(pages 141–158)

PART A COMPLETING THE DEFINITION

On the answer line, write the letter of the definition that correctly completes each sentence.

1. *Deciduous* trees _____.
   a. lose their leaves
   b. grow in acrid climates
   c. have needles
   d. bear fruit

   1. _____**a**_____

2. A *feckless* action is _____.
   a. shrewd
   b. irresponsible
   c. temporary
   d. productive

   2. _____**b**_____

3. When a seed *germinates*, it _____.
   a. dries up and dies
   b. puts nitrogen into the soil
   c. begins to grow
   d. loses its color

   3. _____**c**_____

4. An *onerous* assignment is one that is _____.
   a. challenging
   b. solitary
   c. unparalleled
   d. troublesome

   4. _____**d**_____

5. If it is *incumbent* upon you to accomplish a task, the task is _____.
   a. stable
   b. obligatory
   c. unnecessary
   d. advantageous

   5. _____**b**_____

6. Scientists who study the *fauna* of a particular region study _____.
   a. minerals
   b. volcanoes
   c. weather
   d. animals

   6. _____**d**_____

7. A *sonata* is a musical piece composed _____.
   a. by several musicians
   b. for several instruments
   c. at different times
   d. of different movements

   7. _____**d**_____

8. A *horticultural* society encourages _____.
   a. plant cultivation
   b. socializing
   c. charitable activities
   d. community service

   8. _____**a**_____

9. *Dissonance* among the members of a group causes _____.
   a. vigor
   b. reconciliation
   c. conflict
   d. waste

   9. _____**c**_____

10. If you are guilty of *negligence*, you have _____.
    a. failed to act
    b. not obeyed
    c. not commended others
    d. not managed money properly

    10. _____**a**_____

11. In music terminology, an *octave* is a(n) _____.
    a. interval of eight tones
    b. example of sophisticated technique
    c. full measure
    d. syncopated rhythm

    11. _____**a**_____

12. A *sylvan* landscape is characterized by _____.
    a. rivers
    b. forests
    c. mountains
    d. rugged terrain

    12. _____**b**_____

13. The *libretto* of an opera is the _____ of the work.
    a. composer
    b. text
    c. criticism
    d. cast

    13. _____**b**_____

14. To be *remiss* is to be _____ duty.
    a. skillful in performing
    b. dedicated to
    c. engaged in
    d. lax in attending to

    14. _____**d**_____

15. An *aria* is a(n) _____.
    a. live performance
    b. operatic solo
    c. poem
    d. hymn

    15. _____**b**_____

TEST LESSONS 22, 23, AND 24

(pages 141–158)

PART A COMPLETING THE DEFINITION

On the answer line, write the letter of the definition that correctly completes each sentence.

1. *Deciduous* trees _____.
   a. lose their leaves
   b. grow in acrid climates
   c. have needles
   d. bear fruit

   1. _____

2. A *feckless* action is _____.
   a. shrewd b. irresponsible c. temporary d. productive

   2. _____

3. When a seed *germinates*, it _____.
   a. dries up and dies
   b. puts nitrogen into the soil
   c. begins to grow
   d. loses its color

   3. _____

4. An *onerous* assignment is one that is _____.
   a. challenging b. solitary c. unparalleled d. troublesome

   4. _____

5. If it is *incumbent* upon you to accomplish a task, the task is _____.
   a. stable b. obligatory c. unnecessary d. advantageous

   5. _____

6. Scientists who study the *fauna* of a particular region study _____.
   a. minerals b. volcanoes c. weather d. animals

   6. _____

7. A *sonata* is a musical piece composed _____.
   a. by several musicians
   b. for several instruments
   c. at different times
   d. of different movements

   7. _____

8. A *horticultural* society encourages _____.
   a. plant cultivation
   b. socializing
   c. charitable activities
   d. community service

   8. _____

9. *Dissonance* among the members of a group causes _____.
   a. vigor b. reconciliation c. conflict d. waste

   9. _____

10. If you are guilty of *negligence*, you have _____.
    a. failed to act
    b. not obeyed
    c. not commended others
    d. not managed money properly

    10. _____

11. In music terminology, an *octave* is a(n) _____.
    a. interval of eight tones
    b. example of sophisticated technique
    c. full measure
    d. syncopated rhythm

    11. _____

12. A *sylvan* landscape is characterized by _____.
    a. rivers b. forests c. mountains d. rugged terrain

    12. _____

13. The *libretto* of an opera is the _____ of the work.
    a. composer b. text c. criticism d. cast

    13. _____

14. To be *remiss* is to be _____ duty.
    a. skillful in performing
    b. dedicated to
    c. engaged in
    d. lax in attending to

    14. _____

15. An *aria* is a(n) _____.
    a. live performance b. operatic solo c. poem d. hymn

    15. _____

TEST LESSONS 22, 23, AND 24

PART B CHOOSING THE BEST WORD

On the answer line, write the letter of the word that best completes the sentence.

16. Before examining the layers of the rock, the geologist had to scrape thick _____ from its surface.
    a. fauna   b. germination   c. motif   d. lichen

    16. _____d_____

17. An insurance investigator will determine the _____ of each driver involved in the accident.
    a. liability   b. default   c. motif   d. commitment

    17. _____a_____

18. The climactic scene in the movie was signaled by a(n) _____ in the accompanying musical score.
    a. germination   b. libretto   c. crescendo   d. octave

    18. _____c_____

19. Following her first play, critics hailed Kay's _____ talent.
    a. deciduous   b. feckless   c. dissonant   d. burgeoning

    19. _____d_____

20. Ben is _____ for the success or failure of the project.
    a. incumbent   b. accountable   c. negligent   d. onerous

    20. _____b_____

21. The koala bear is a(n) _____ creature that eats eucalyptus leaves.
    a. verdant   b. arboreal   c. feckless   d. horticultural

    21. _____b_____

22. The laws in some states make the wearing of seat belts _____.
    a. mandatory   b. burgeoning   c. staccato   d. defaulting

    22. _____a_____

23. The _____ tap of high heels signaled Ms. Sanchez's return to the room.
    a. dissonant   b. remiss   c. staccato   d. verdant

    23. _____c_____

24. The song was about a(n) _____ meadow in the springtime.
    a. a cappella   b. onerous   c. verdant   d. deciduous

    24. _____c_____

25. Ms. Drummey is known for her _____ to excellence in teaching.
    a. commitment   b. crescendo   c. liability   d. negligence

    25. _____a_____

26. The overpowering _____ of Vachel Lindsay's poem "The Congo" causes one to chant the poem rather than read it.
    a. staccato   b. motif   c. libretto   d. cadence

    26. _____d_____

27. Charles was fascinated by the variety of _____ growing on the island.
    a. burgeoning   b. flora   c. motifs   d. cadences

    27. _____b_____

28. Because the organ wasn't working, the choir practiced _____.
    a. fecklessly   b. negligently   c. onerously   d. a cappella

    28. _____d_____

29. In signing the contract with the credit union, Mr. Crosby pledged that he would not _____ his payments.
    a. be liable for b. burgeon   c. default on   d. commit to

    29. _____c_____

30. Anthony's report focuses on the _____ of light and darkness throughout Conrad's *Secret Sharer*.
    a. accountability b. motif   c. libretto   d. octave

    30. _____b_____

TEST LESSONS 22, 23, AND 24

PART B CHOOSING THE BEST WORD

On the answer line, write the letter of the word that best completes the sentence.

16. Before examining the layers of the rock, the geologist had to scrape thick _____ from its surface.
    a. fauna   **b.** germination   **c.** motif   **d.** lichen

16. _____

17. An insurance investigator will determine the _____ of each driver involved in the accident.
    a. liability   **b.** default   **c.** motif   **d.** commitment

17. _____

18. The climactic scene in the movie was signaled by a(n) _____ in the accompanying musical score.
    a. germination   **b.** libretto   **c.** crescendo   **d.** octave

18. _____

19. Following her first play, critics hailed Kay's _____ talent.
    a. deciduous   **b.** feckless   **c.** dissonant   **d.** burgeoning

19. _____

20. Ben is _____ for the success or failure of the project.
    a. incumbent   **b.** accountable   **c.** negligent   **d.** onerous

20. _____

21. The koala bear is a(n) _____ creature that eats eucalyptus leaves.
    a. verdant   **b.** arboreal   **c.** feckless   **d.** horticultural

21. _____

22. The laws in some states make the wearing of seat belts _____.
    a. mandatory   **b.** burgeoning   **c.** staccato   **d.** defaulting

22. _____

23. The _____ tap of high heels signaled Ms. Sanchez's return to the room.
    a. dissonant   **b.** remiss   **c.** staccato   **d.** verdant

23. _____

24. The song was about a(n) _____ meadow in the springtime.
    a. a cappella   **b.** onerous   **c.** verdant   **d.** deciduous

24. _____

25. Ms. Drummey is known for her _____ to excellence in teaching.
    a. commitment   **b.** crescendo   **c.** liability   **d.** negligence

25. _____

26. The overpowering _____ of Vachel Lindsay's poem "The Congo" causes one to chant the poem rather than read it.
    a. staccato   **b.** motif   **c.** libretto   **d.** cadence

26. _____

27. Charles was fascinated by the variety of _____ growing on the island.
    a. burgeoning   **b.** flora   **c.** motifs   **d.** cadences

27. _____

28. Because the organ wasn't working, the choir practiced _____.
    a. fecklessly   **b.** negligently   **c.** onerously   **d.** a cappella

28. _____

29. In signing the contract with the credit union, Mr. Crosby pledged that he would not _____ his payments.
    a. be liable for   **b.** burgeon   **c.** default on   **d.** commit to

29. _____

30. Anthony's report focuses on the _____ of light and darkness throughout Conrad's *Secret Sharer*.
    a. accountability   **b.** motif   **c.** libretto   **d.** octave

30. _____

BONUS LESSONS 21–25

(pages 133–138, 141–158, 161–166)

Use the clues to complete the crossword puzzle.

							¹R	²E	D	U	N	D	A	N	T	
								Q								
		³L						U								
		⁴A	C	C	O	⁵M	P	A	N	I	M	E	N	T		
⁶E	X				A	L						⁷O	
I		⁸D			N	L		⁹M			¹⁰F	N	
¹¹G	R	E	E	N	D		¹²L	I	Q	U	I	D	A	T	E
H		C		A		M			L	E	R	
T		¹³I	M	I	T	A	T	I	O	N	S	O	
	D	O		C			E	U	
¹⁴A	C	C	R	U	E		¹⁵T	R	E	E	S	S	
U		O		Y		Y	
D		U	¹⁶C	
I		¹⁷S	T	A	C	C	A	T	O	
T		R	
		¹⁸W	E	A	L	T	H	
	L	
¹⁹C	R	E	S	C	E	N	D	O	
S	
²⁰S	Y	L	V	A	N	

Across

1. Wordy

4. *A cappella* singing is without musical _____.

11. *Verdant* refers to the color _____.

12. From a Latin word meaning "to melt"

13. Synonym for *simulation*

14. What interest on a savings account will do

15. *Arboreal* refers to _____.

17. Cut short crisply

18. In a *lucrative* business, you can accumulate _____.

19. A gradual increase in the volume of sound

20. From a Latin word meaning "forest"

Down

2. To *emulate* is to try to _____.

3. Synonym for *remiss*

5. Antonym for *optional*

6. An *octave* is a musical interval of _____ full tones.

7. From a Latin word meaning "burden"

8. _____ trees lose their leaves.

9. A close resemblance

10. A *sham* is something _____ that is supposed to be genuine.

14. To examine financial accounts

16. Synonym for *feckless*

BONUS LESSONS 21–25

(pages 133–138, 141–158, 161–166)

Use the clues to complete the crossword puzzle.

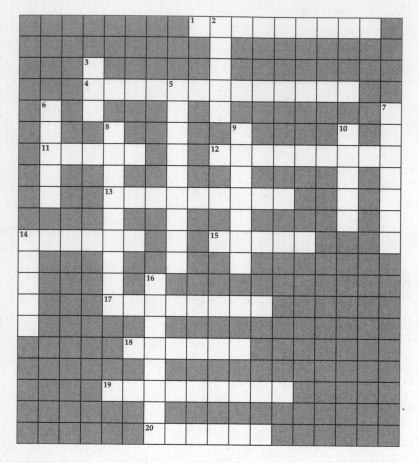

Across

1. Wordy
4. *A cappella* singing is without musical _____.
11. *Verdant* refers to the color _____.
12. From a Latin word meaning "to melt"
13. Synonym for *simulation*
14. What interest on a savings account will do
15. *Arboreal* refers to _____.
17. Cut short crisply
18. In a *lucrative* business, you can accumulate _____.
19. A gradual increase in the volume of sound
20. From a Latin word meaning "forest"

Down

2. To *emulate* is to try to _____.
3. Synonym for *remiss*
5. Antonym for *optional*
6. An *octave* is a musical interval of _____ full tones.
7. From a Latin word meaning "burden"
8. _____ trees lose their leaves.
9. A close resemblance
10. A *sham* is something _____ that is supposed to be genuine.
14. To examine financial accounts
16. Synonym for *feckless*

TEST LESSONS 25, 26, AND 27

(pages 161–178)

PART A CHOOSING THE BEST DEFINITION

On the answer line, write the letter of the best definition of the italicized word.

1. Max enjoys *cerebral* games such as chess and bridge.
   a. boisterous   b. earnest   c. monetary   d. intellectual

   1. _____d_____

2. A company representative will *audit* the financial records of our franchise.
   a. examine   b. duplicate   c. confiscate   d. convert

   2. _____a_____

3. The private detective offered his law school diploma as proof that he was not a *charlatan*.
   a. foreigner   b. accountant   c. quack   d. interloper

   3. _____c_____

4. Astronomers use spectrography to *ascertain* the composition of stars.
   a. misinterpret   b. control   c. determine   d. illustrate

   4. _____c_____

5. The Jensens used their car as *collateral* for a home improvement loan.
   a. payment   c. property pledged as security
   b. a substitute   d. proof of having applied

   5. _____c_____

6. Jonathan Swift despised the *cant* of the English aristocracy.
   a. helplessness   c. feeble complaints
   b. ignorance   d. insincerely pious language

   6. _____d_____

7. Mitch *ruminates* frequently about his future.
   a. philosophizes   b. ponders   c. predicts   d. brags

   7. _____b_____

8. The only *commodity* that Wanda will invest in is gold.
   a. article of trade   c. object of adornment
   b. extravagance   d. foreign coin

   8. _____a_____

9. State-wide reform ended *chicanery* that was once involved in awarding government contracts.
   a. humility   b. deception   c. idleness   d. foolishness

   9. _____b_____

10. The mechanic *surmised* that the problem was the transmission.
    a. prescribed   b. verified   c. rejoiced   d. guessed

    10. _____d_____

11. The company that Margo works for will *liquidate* its assets.
    a. convert to cash   b. buy back   c. sell at a loss   d. stockpile

    11. _____a_____

12. A sage grouse will *feign* an injury to protect her nest from predators.
    a. pretend   b. imagine   c. incur   d. inflict

    12. _____a_____

13. Free enterprise is a basic *tenet* of capitalism.
    a. mistake   b. benefit   c. principle   d. side effect

    13. _____c_____

14. It is unlikely that the automobile producers of the world will form a *cartel* to regulate car prices.
    a. open forum   c. democratic society
    b. labor union   d. group formed to control distribution of goods

    14. _____d_____

15. Doctors warn against the *insidious* effects of prolonged exposure to the sun.
    a. immediate   b. harmful   c. positive   d. attractive

    15. _____b_____

TEST LESSONS 25, 26, AND 27

(pages 161–178)

PART A CHOOSING THE BEST DEFINITION

On the answer line, write the letter of the best definition of the italicized word.

1. Max enjoys *cerebral* games such as chess and bridge.
   a. boisterous   b. earnest   c. monetary   d. intellectual

   1. _____

2. A company representative will *audit* the financial records of our franchise.
   a. examine   b. duplicate   c. confiscate   d. convert

   2. _____

3. The private detective offered his law school diploma as proof that he was not a *charlatan*.
   a. foreigner   b. accountant   c. quack   d. interloper

   3. _____

4. Astronomers use spectrography to *ascertain* the composition of stars.
   a. misinterpret   b. control   c. determine   d. illustrate

   4. _____

5. The Jensens used their car as *collateral* for a home improvement loan.
   a. payment   c. property pledged as security
   b. a substitute   d. proof of having applied

   5. _____

6. Jonathan Swift despised the *cant* of the English aristocracy.
   a. helplessness   c. feeble complaints
   b. ignorance   d. insincerely pious language

   6. _____

7. Mitch *ruminates* frequently about his future.
   a. philosophizes   b. ponders   c. predicts   d. brags

   7. _____

8. The only *commodity* that Wanda will invest in is gold.
   a. article of trade   c. object of adornment
   b. extravagance   d. foreign coin

   8. _____

9. State-wide reform ended *chicanery* that was once involved in awarding government contracts.
   a. humility   b. deception   c. idleness   d. foolishness

   9. _____

10. The mechanic *surmised* that the problem was the transmission.
    a. prescribed   b. verified   c. rejoiced   d. guessed

    10. _____

11. The company that Margo works for will *liquidate* its assets.
    a. convert to cash   b. buy back   c. sell at a loss   d. stockpile

    11. _____

12. A sage grouse will *feign* an injury to protect her nest from predators.
    a. pretend   b. imagine   c. incur   d. inflict

    12. _____

13. Free enterprise is a basic *tenet* of capitalism.
    a. mistake   b. benefit   c. principle   d. side effect

    13. _____

14. It is unlikely that the automobile producers of the world will form a *cartel* to regulate car prices.
    a. open forum   c. democratic society
    b. labor union   d. group formed to control distribution of goods

    14. _____

15. Doctors warn against the *insidious* effects of prolonged exposure to the sun.
    a. immediate   b. harmful   c. positive   d. attractive

    15. _____

TEST LESSONS 25, 26, AND 27

PART B IDENTIFYING ANTONYMS

On the answer line, write the letter of the word that has the meaning that is opposite to that of the capitalized word.

16. SECURITY:
   a. expansiveness   b. vulnerability   c. ignorance   d. solitude

17. RELATIVE:
   a. absolute   b. miscellaneous   c. friend   d. complete

18. CANDOR:
   a. laziness   b. deceit   c. morality   d. transparency

19. ACCRUE:
   a. review   b. deny   c. entrap   d. decrease

20. THEORETICAL:
   a. beneficial   b. multiple   c. actual   d. incomprehensible

21. BONA FIDE:
   a. counterfeit   b. disloyal   c. hostile   d. solemn

22. LUCRATIVE:
   a. righteous   b. serious   c. unprofitable   d. free

23. ABSTRUSE:
   a. lucid   b. insensitive   c. modest   d. pliable

24. RECTITUDE:
   a. narrowness   c. conformity
   b. endurance   d. unscrupulousness

25. CONGLOMERATE:
   a. liquefy   b. clarify   c. accumulate   d. disband

26. ACUMEN:
   a. obtuseness   b. rigidity   c. adherence   d. corruption

27. VERITABLE:
   a. dubious   b. outstanding   c. radical   d. unintentional

28. RECOMPENSE:
   a. initiate   b. salute   c. resign   d. deprive

29. FACULTY:
   a. hesitancy   b. incompetence   c. curriculum   d. inclination

30. APOCRYPHAL:
   a. secular   b. misinformed   c. genuine   d. significant

16. _____ b
17. _____ a
18. _____ b
19. _____ d
20. _____ c
21. _____ a
22. _____ c
23. _____ a
24. _____ d
25. _____ d
26. _____ a
27. _____ a
28. _____ d
29. _____ b
30. _____ c

TEST LESSONS 25, 26, AND 27

PART B IDENTIFYING ANTONYMS

On the answer line, write the letter of the word that has the meaning that is opposite to that of the capitalized word.

16. SECURITY:
    a. expansiveness   **b.** vulnerability   **c.** ignorance   **d.** solitude

16. _____

17. RELATIVE:
    a. absolute   **b.** miscellaneous   **c.** friend   **d.** complete

17. _____

18. CANDOR:
    a. laziness   **b.** deceit   **c.** morality   **d.** transparency

18. _____

19. ACCRUE:
    a. review   **b.** deny   **c.** entrap   **d.** decrease

19. _____

20. THEORETICAL:
    a. beneficial   **b.** multiple   **c.** actual   **d.** incomprehensible

20. _____

21. BONA FIDE:
    a. counterfeit   **b.** disloyal   **c.** hostile   **d.** solemn

21. _____

22. LUCRATIVE:
    a. righteous   **b.** serious   **c.** unprofitable   **d.** free

22. _____

23. ABSTRUSE:
    a. lucid   **b.** insensitive   **c.** modest   **d.** pliable

23. _____

24. RECTITUDE:
    a. narrowness   **c.** conformity
    b. endurance   **d.** unscrupulousness

24. _____

25. CONGLOMERATE:
    a. liquefy   **b.** clarify   **c.** accumulate   **d.** disband

25. _____

26. ACUMEN:
    a. obtuseness   **b.** rigidity   **c.** adherence   **d.** corruption

26. _____

27. VERITABLE:
    a. dubious   **b.** outstanding   **c.** radical   **d.** unintentional

27. _____

28. RECOMPENSE:
    a. initiate   **b.** salute   **c.** resign   **d.** deprive

28. _____

29. FACULTY:
    a. hesitancy   **b.** incompetence   **c.** curriculum   **d.** inclination

29. _____

30. APOCRYPHAL:
    a. secular   **b.** misinformed   **c.** genuine   **d.** significant

30. _____

BONUS LESSONS 26–30

(pages 167–178, 181–198)

Choose a vocabulary word from the box to complete each of the following sentences.
You may need to change the form of some of the words to fit correctly in the sentence.
Use each word only once, and write your answer on the answer line to the right.

acumen	charlatan	panacea	salutary
adulterate	feasible	preposterous	sporadic
apocryphal	inconceivable	prone	tenet
ascertain	malleable	rectitude	toxic
bona fide	metamorphosis	ruminate	volatile

1. The principal _____ what had happened by talking with the participants.

2. Dr. Blesse was exposed as a(n) _____ by a reporter who checked Blesse's alleged academic credentials.

3. Sleep may be a(n) _____ for many ills.

4. "Walk carefully down those icy steps," begged Alex. "You are _____ to having accidents."

5. Ned realized that the controversial issue was too _____ to examine calmly and logically.

6. The Shaeffers were amazed to discover that their painting was a(n) _____ American primitive.

7. Freedom of religion is one of the basic _____ of democracy.

8. Louise _____ her grandmother's recipe for marinara sauce by adding dried, rather than fresh, herbs.

9. The suspect's alibi was so _____ that neither detective bothered to investigate it.

10. Through time-lapse photography, the _____ of the butterfly can be observed.

11. Handwriting experts proved that the historical document was _____.

12. Sara's _____ in the stock market has made her a wealthy investor.

13. _____ wastes must be handled and disposed of with special safety procedures.

14. Automobiles would have seemed _____ to people of fifteenth-century Europe.

15. Dan's understanding of the new software was marred by his _____ attempts at using it.

1. __ascertained__

2. __charlatan__

3. __panacea__

4. __prone__

5. __volatile__

6. __bona fide__

7. __tenets__

8. __adulterated__

9. __preposterous__

10. __metamorphosis__

11. __apocryphal__

12. __acumen__

13. __Toxic__

14. __inconceivable__

15. __sporadic__

BONUS LESSONS 26–30

(pages 167–178, 181–198)

Choose a vocabulary word from the box to complete each of the following sentences.
You may need to change the form of some of the words to fit correctly in the sentence.
Use each word only once, and write your answer on the answer line to the right.

acumen	charlatan	panacea	salutary
adulterate	feasible	preposterous	sporadic
apocryphal	inconceivable	prone	tenet
ascertain	malleable	rectitude	toxic
bona fide	metamorphosis	ruminate	volatile

1. The principal _____ what had happened by talking with the participants.

    1. _____

2. Dr. Blesse was exposed as a(n) _____ by a reporter who checked Blesse's alleged academic credentials.

    2. _____

3. Sleep may be a(n) _____ for many ills.

    3. _____

4. "Walk carefully down those icy steps," begged Alex. "You are _____ to having accidents."

    4. _____

5. Ned realized that the controversial issue was too _____ to examine calmly and logically.

    5. _____

6. The Shaeffers were amazed to discover that their painting was a(n) _____ American primitive.

    6. _____

7. Freedom of religion is one of the basic _____ of democracy.

    7. _____

8. Louise _____ her grandmother's recipe for marinara sauce by adding dried, rather than fresh, herbs.

    8. _____

9. The suspect's alibi was so _____ that neither detective bothered to investigate it.

    9. _____

10. Through time-lapse photography, the _____ of the butterfly can be observed.

    10. _____

11. Handwriting experts proved that the historical document was _____.

    11. _____

12. Sara's _____ in the stock market has made her a wealthy investor.

    12. _____

13. _____ wastes must be handled and disposed of with special safety procedures.

    13. _____

14. Automobiles would have seemed _____ to people of fifteenth-century Europe.

    14. _____

15. Dan's understanding of the new software was marred by his _____ attempts at using it.

    15. _____

T35

TEST LESSONS 28, 29, AND 30

(pages 181–198)

PART A MATCHING WORDS AND DEFINITIONS

Match the definition in Column B with the word in Column A. Write the letter of the correct definition on the answer line.

Column A

1. modulate
2. presumable
3. exorcise
4. protean
5. proclivity
6. adulterate
7. transmute
8. perchance
9. inimical
10. immutable
11. inconceivable
12. salutary
13. inveterate
14. eventuality
15. pernicious

Column B

a. perhaps; possibly

b. designed to effect an improvement; favorable to health

c. to expel an evil spirit

d. tending to cause death or serious injury; deadly; destructive

e. to make impure or inferior by adding extraneous or improper ingredients

f. to regulate or adjust to a certain proportion

g. long-standing; deep-rooted

h. a possible event or outcome

i. by reasonable assumption; likely

j. not subject to or susceptible to change

k. readily taking on a different shape, form, or character; variable

l. a natural inclination or tendency

m. to change from one form, nature, or state to another; convert

n. injurious or harmful in effect; unfriendly

o. incapable of being imagined, comprehended, or fully grasped

1. _____ f
2. _____ i
3. _____ c
4. _____ k
5. _____ l
6. _____ e
7. _____ m
8. _____ a
9. _____ n
10. _____ j
11. _____ o
12. _____ b
13. _____ g
14. _____ h
15. _____ d

PART B CHOOSING THE BEST WORD

On the answer line, write the letter of the word that best expresses the meaning of the italicized word or phrase.

16. The athlete's autobiography describes her *gradual change* from a recreational skater to an Olympic champion.
    a. proclivity
    b. adulteration
    c. metamorphosis
    d. immutability

16. _____ c

TEST LESSONS 28, 29, AND 30

(pages 181–198)

PART A MATCHING WORDS AND DEFINITIONS

Match the definition in Column B with the word in Column A. Write the letter of the correct definition on the answer line.

Column A

1. modulate
2. presumable
3. exorcise
4. protean
5. proclivity
6. adulterate
7. transmute
8. perchance
9. inimical
10. immutable
11. inconceivable
12. salutary
13. inveterate
14. eventuality
15. pernicious

Column B

a. perhaps; possibly

b. designed to effect an improvement; favorable to health

c. to expel an evil spirit

d. tending to cause death or serious injury; deadly; destructive

e. to make impure or inferior by adding extraneous or improper ingredients

f. to regulate or adjust to a certain proportion

g. long-standing; deep-rooted

h. a possible event or outcome

i. by reasonable assumption; likely

j. not subject to or susceptible to change

k. readily taking on a different shape, form, or character; variable

l. a natural inclination or tendency

m. to change from one form, nature, or state to another; convert

n. injurious or harmful in effect; unfriendly

o. incapable of being imagined, comprehended, or fully grasped

1. _____
2. _____
3. _____
4. _____
5. _____
6. _____
7. _____
8. _____
9. _____
10. _____
11. _____
12. _____
13. _____
14. _____
15. _____

PART B CHOOSING THE BEST WORD

On the answer line, write the letter of the word that best expresses the meaning of the italicized word or phrase.

16. The athlete's autobiography describes her *gradual change* from a recreational skater to an Olympic champion.
   a. proclivity
   b. adulteration
   c. metamorphosis
   d. immutability

16. _____

TEST LESSONS 28, 29, AND 30

PART B CHOOSING THE BEST WORD (CONTINUED)

17. The commencement speaker stressed that ignorance is the *cause of ruin* of progress.
    a. implausibility **b.** boon **c.** panacea **d.** bane

17. _____ d _____

18. Physicists are still debating whether using nuclear power to propel spacecraft is *capable of being accomplished*.
    a. malleable **b.** preposterous **c.** inimical **d.** feasible

18. _____ d _____

19. Mr. Ribero's pizza stand *developed gradually* into a multimillion-dollar of chain stores.
    a. vitiated **b.** adulterated **c.** evolved **d.** modulated

19. _____ c _____

20. The discovery of penicillin was a great *blessing* to medical science.
    a. proclivity **b.** boon **c.** eventuality **d.** panacea

20. _____ b _____

21. The success of any experiment is *dependent* upon the proper use of chemicals and equipment.
    a. contingent **b.** inimical **c.** immutable **d.** salutary

21. _____ a _____

22. Pewter is a particularly *capable of being shaped* metal that was once used to produce kitchen utensils and tableware.
    a. malleable **b.** inveterate **c.** toxic **d.** volatile

22. _____ a _____

23. "Snake oil" salesmen in the Old West sold bottles of liniment as a *cure-all* to their unsuspecting customers.
    a. bane **b.** contingent **c.** exorcism **d.** panacea

23. _____ d _____

24. Many great inventions were at one time judged to be *absurd* ideas.
    a. volatile **b.** malleable **c.** preposterous **d.** pernicious

24. _____ c _____

25. To become successful as a writer requires much more than *irregular* attempts at writing and publishing.
    a. sporadic **b.** protean **c.** feasible **d.** salutary

25. _____ a _____

26. Bee stings can have a *poisonous* effect on some people.
    a. inconceivable **b.** toxic **c.** sporadic **d.** adulterated

26. _____ b _____

27. It is not *difficult to believe* that people will one day colonize the moon.
    a. immutable **b.** implausible **c.** salutary **d.** contingent

27. _____ b _____

28. Our basketball coach is known for his *explosive* temper.
    a. volatile **b.** sporadic **c.** immutable **d.** preposterous

28. _____ a _____

29. By forgetting to erase the equations on the chalkboard, the teacher *impaired the value of* the test.
    a. evolved **b.** transmuted **c.** vitiated **d.** exorcised

29. _____ c _____

30. Mrs. Gable is *inclined* to drink warm milk just before bedtime.
    a. inveterate **b.** inimical **c.** prone **d.** salutary

30. _____ c _____

TEST LESSONS 28, 29, AND 30

PART B CHOOSING THE BEST WORD (CONTINUED)

17. The commencement speaker stressed that ignorance is the *cause of ruin* of progress.
    a. implausibility   **b.** boon   **c.** panacea   **d.** bane

    17. _____

18. Physicists are still debating whether using nuclear power to propel spacecraft is *capable of being accomplished*.
    a. malleable   **b.** preposterous   **c.** inimical   **d.** feasible

    18. _____

19. Mr. Ribero's pizza stand *developed gradually* into a multimillion-dollar of chain stores.
    a. vitiated   **b.** adulterated   **c.** evolved   **d.** modulated

    19. _____

20. The discovery of penicillin was a great *blessing* to medical science.
    a. proclivity   **b.** boon   **c.** eventuality   **d.** panacea

    20. _____

21. The success of any experiment is *dependent* upon the proper use of chemicals and equipment.
    a. contingent   **b.** inimical   **c.** immutable   **d.** salutary

    21. _____

22. Pewter is a particularly *capable of being shaped* metal that was once used to produce kitchen utensils and tableware.
    a. malleable   **b.** inveterate   **c.** toxic   **d.** volatile

    22. _____

23. "Snake oil" salesmen in the Old West sold bottles of liniment as a *cure-all* to their unsuspecting customers.
    a. bane   **b.** contingent   **c.** exorcism   **d.** panacea

    23. _____

24. Many great inventions were at one time judged to be *absurd* ideas.
    a. volatile   **b.** malleable   **c.** preposterous   **d.** pernicious

    24. _____

25. To become successful as a writer requires much more than *irregular* attempts at writing and publishing.
    a. sporadic   **b.** protean   **c.** feasible   **d.** salutary

    25. _____

26. Bee stings can have a *poisonous* effect on some people.
    a. inconceivable   **b.** toxic   **c.** sporadic   **d.** adulterated

    26. _____

27. It is not *difficult to believe* that people will one day colonize the moon.
    a. immutable   **b.** implausible   **c.** salutary   **d.** contingent

    27. _____

28. Our basketball coach is known for his *explosive* temper.
    a. volatile   **b.** sporadic   **c.** immutable   **d.** preposterous

    28. _____

29. By forgetting to erase the equations on the chalkboard, the teacher *impaired the value of* the test.
    a. evolved   **b.** transmuted   **c.** vitiated   **d.** exorcised

    29. _____

30. Mrs. Gable is *inclined* to drink warm milk just before bedtime.
    a. inveterate   **b.** inimical   **c.** prone   **d.** salutary

    30. _____